Lecture Notes in Computer Science   **11491**

Commenced Publication in 1973
Founding and Former Series Editors:
Gerhard Goos, Juris Hartmanis, and Jan van Leeuwen

More information about this series at http://www.springer.com/series/7409

Bengisu Tulu · Soussan Djamasbi ·
Gondy Leroy (Eds.)

Extending the Boundaries of Design Science Theory and Practice

14th International Conference on Design Science Research
in Information Systems and Technology, DESRIST 2019
Worcester, MA, USA, June 4–6, 2019
Proceedings

 Springer

Editors
Bengisu Tulu 🆔
Foisie Business School
Worcester Polytechnic Institute
Worcester, MA, USA

Soussan Djamasbi 🆔
Foisie Business School
Worcester Polytechnic Institute
Worcester, MA, USA

Gondy Leroy 🆔
Eller College of Management
University of Arizona
Tucson, AZ, USA

ISSN 0302-9743   ISSN 1611-3349   (electronic)
Lecture Notes in Computer Science
ISBN 978-3-030-19503-8   ISBN 978-3-030-19504-5   (eBook)
https://doi.org/10.1007/978-3-030-19504-5

LNCS Sublibrary: SL3 – Information Systems and Applications, incl. Internet/Web, and HCI

This Springer imprint is published by the registered company Springer Nature Switzerland AG
The registered company address is: Gewerbestrasse 11, 6330 Cham, Switzerland

Preface

The goal of the design science research paradigm is to extend the boundaries of human and organizational capabilities and bridge the confines of humans and machines by designing new and innovative artifacts. In design science, a broad definition of artifact is accepted and it is indicated to mean constructs, models, methods, processes, or systems. Scholars from different backgrounds, such as information systems, computer science, operations research, cognitive science and informatics, are actively engaged in generating novel solutions to interesting design problems. The problems originate in a variety of different domains, ranging from business problems, medical and biomedical problems, to education and a wide variety of applications that touch our lives. The need for design science research to develop smart, effective and efficient solutions addressing business and societal challenges and providing new opportunities continues to grow.

The International Conference on Design Science Research in Information Systems and Technology (DESRIST) serves as a major annual forum for the presentation of innovative ideas, approaches, developments and research projects. It aims to facilitate the exchange of ideas between researchers and industry professionals around the world. This volume contains papers that were presented at the 14th event in the series – which was held June 4–6, 2019, at Worcester, Massachusetts, USA. The 2019 DESRIST continued the tradition of previous conferences that were held in Chennai, Claremont, Pasadena, Atlanta, Philadelphia, St. Gallen, Milwaukee, Las Vegas, Helsinki, Miami, Dublin, St. John, and Karlsruhe by providing a major forum for presenting innovative ideas, approaches, developments, and research projects. The theme for the 2019 DESRIST was "Extending the Boundaries of Design Science Theory and Practice."

This volume contains 20 full research papers that were selected from the 54 full research paper submissions received, with an acceptance rate of 37%. All accepted full papers were presented by authors during oral presentation sessions. An additional 30 research-in-progress submissions received were made available digitally to attendees and were presented in rapid-fire short presentation format followed by a poster session at the conference.

We would like to thank all the authors for their submissions to the 2019 DESRIST. Additionally, we would like to acknowledge the crucial role of all Program Committee members, including associate editors and reviewers, in making this conference a success and we thank them for their invaluable service. We also extend our thanks to members of the Organizing Committee and the volunteers for their hard work and help. Finally, we thank Worcester Polytechnic Institute for providing access to their facilities and all our sponsors for their support.

The papers in these proceedings provide valuable insights into design science research and practice and as such they motivate new possibilities for future design science research. We hope you enjoy reading the papers as much as we did.

May 2019

Bengisu Tulu
Soussan Djamasbi
Gondy Leroy

Organization

General Chairs

Samir Chatterjee	Claremont Graduate University, USA
Kaushik Dutta	University of South Florida, USA
R. P. Sundarraj	Indian Institute of Technology Madras, India

Program Chairs

Bengisu Tulu	Worcester Polytechnic Institute, USA
Soussan Djamasbi	Worcester Polytechnic Institute, USA
Gondy Leroy	University of Arizona, USA

Associate Editors

Kaveh Abhari	San Diego State University, USA
Tamara Babaian	Bentley University, USA
Victor Benjamin	Arizona State University, USA
Richard Burkhard	San Jose State University, USA
Michael S. Dohan	Lakehead University, Canada
Dennis Fehrenbacher	Monash University, Australia
Heiko Gewald	Neu-Ulm University of Applied Sciences, Germany
Alicia Iriberri	California State University, Fresno, USA
Chih-Hao Ku	Lawrence Technological University, USA
Oliver Posegga	University of Bamberg, Germany
René Riedl	University of Applied Sciences Upper Austria, Austria
Bonnie Rohde	Albright College, USA
Jim Ryan	Auburn University at Montgomery, USA
Romilla Syed	University of Massachusetts, Boston, USA
Chi Zhang	Kennesaw State University, USA

Local Arrangements Chair

Brent French	Worcester Polytechnic Institute, USA

Doctoral Consortium Chairs

Monica Tremblay	Mason School of Business William and Mary, USA
Benjamin Schooley	University of South Carolina, USA
Sue Feldman	University of Alabama at Birmingham, USA

Website

Ke Wu   Worcester Polytechnic Institute, USA

Reviewers

Moayad Alshawmar
Jisun An
Brent Auernheimer
Carina Benz
Alfred Benedikt Brendel
Philipp Brune
Chris Chagnon
Chih-Ling Chen
Mohammadreza Ebrahimi
Evren Eryilmaz
Bernie Farkas
Jasper Feine
Thomas Fischer
Andrea Fronzetti Colladon
Kaushik Ghosh
David Goldberg
Roland Graef
Yang Gu
Meng Han
Timothy Hardie
Maximilian Haug
Alan Hevner
Johann Holm
Konstantin Hopf
Fabian Hunke
Roland Hübscher
Aimee Jacobs
Prateek Jain
Shan Jiang

Jongheon Kim
Mark Kim
Falco Klemm
Jacqueline Klug
Manasvi Kumar
Jens Lachenmaier
Damien Lambert
Carol Lee
Ingyu Lee
Lei Li
Weifeng Li
Zhigang Li
Shuai Luo
Dawn McKell
Haadi Mombini
Stefan Morana
Matthew Mullarkey
Josephine Namayanja
Dana Naous
Dietmar Nedbal
Hoang D. Nguyen
Javad Norouzinia
Brian O'Flaherty
Christoph Peters
Brad Prince
Richard Pucci
Swati Ramani
Tim Rietz
David Rueckel

Sagar Samtani
Maximilian Schreieck
Vivek Singh
Kane Smith
Daniel Szopinski
Anthony Tang
Xin Tian
Roman Tilly
Heikki Topi
Karthikeyan Umapathy
Maureen Van Devender
Conny Walchshofer
Neha Warikoo
Manuel Wiesche
Paul Witman
Jheng-Long Wu
Shikui Wu
Jennifer Xu
Lucky Xue
Jingshan Yang
Doane Ye
Shuo Yu
Nohel Zaman
Min Zhang
Qiunan Zhang
Jack Zheng
Haonan Zhong
Matthäus Zylka

Contents

Design Science Research Theory and Methodology

Inducing Creativity in Design Science Research

Richard Baskerville[1,2], Mala Kaul[3], Jan Pries-Heje[4(✉)],
and Veda Storey[1]

[1] Georgia State University, Atlanta, USA
baskerville@acm.org, vstorey@bellsouth.net
[2] Curtin Business School, Perth, WA, Australia
[3] University of Nevada, Reno, USA
mkaul@unr.edu
[4] Roskilde University, Roskilde, Denmark
janph@ruc.dk

Abstract. The importance of creativity is widely acknowledged in design science research, yet there is a lack of understanding of *how* this creativity is manifested throughout the design science lifecycle. This research examines the effects of the boundaries that are placed on creativity by the particular design science research method used throughout the design cycles and iterations. The progressive and methodical nature of design science research imposes structure comprising rational and creative, boundaries on the problem-solving process. These boundaries determine *when* and *where* to iterate to a specific previous stage. A set of iteration indicators, derived from the literature on creativity and bounded rationality, provide the design researcher with guidance on how to recognize that the time for iteration is nigh. These indicators are evaluated using a case study for the design of creative, pervasive games.

Keywords: Creativity · Design science research · Rigor ·
Bounded rationality · Bounded creativity · Designing · Theorizing ·
Site-storming · Iteration indicators

1 Introduction

Design Science Research strives for both scientific rigor and practical relevance. Scientific rigor implies careful attention to a design science method, which is a key aspect of the science of design [1]. The most prominent design science methods incorporate cycles or iterations within their stages, with a widely held assumption that deciding *when* and *where* such iteration should be decided is intuitive: reasonably obvious and simple. At most, the decision is anchored to the "nature of the research venue" [2, p. 56]. Research into imposing boundaries on creativity by design science research methods triggers interest in this issue. But how do we preserve the creativity that is so key to invention and innovation, while maintaining scientific rigor?

There is a widespread assumption that imposing method and rigor in designing generally diminishes the creativity and innovation of the designs produced, thereby reducing their relevance [3–5]. Because these assumptions overlook the iterative and progressive way that rationality and creativity unfold under the rigor of design science

© Springer Nature Switzerland AG 2019
B. Tulu et al. (Eds.): DESRIST 2019, LNCS 11491, pp. 3–17, 2019.
https://doi.org/10.1007/978-3-030-19504-5_1

research, they incorrectly assume creativity and scientific rigor cannot co-exist. The need to obtain a better understanding of the role creativity plays leads to the question:

How does creativity affect the activities of theorizing and designing in design science research?

The objective of this research is to explain the distinct nature of creativity in design science research and explicate its most obvious characteristics. Although creativity is generally associated with the researcher's intuitiveness, we propose that a design science research method progressively narrows the boundaries on both design rationality and design creativity. When these boundaries become so narrow that the creative aspects are left tedious and uninteresting, the design search must retreat to a previous stage to reopen the boundaries. Iteration is then partly a consequence of bounded creativity in design science research.

2   Theoretical Background

Creativity is a companion to rigor and utility. It is important to incorporate creativity into the research process so that the analytical processes supporting rigor and practicality do not impede the novelty of the solutions. But what of the possibility that creativity impedes the rigor or practicality? Creativity is necessary for designs to be robust, practical, useful and effective. But to preserve rigor, the creative processes must interact with design knowledge and satisfy evaluations that identify the validity and reliability of the results. Creativity must also be incorporated within the bounds or the structure of design theories, frameworks, and methodologies.

2.1   Bounded Rationality and Bounded Creativity

Bounded rationality recognizes that individuals and organizations are limited by constraints, such as knowledge of a problem, inability to fully conceptualize complex systems, and resources [12]. Decisions must be both satisfactory and sufficient; not necessarily optimal. Decisions only satisfice; they satisfy the aspirations represented by a problem [13, p. 30]. But design differs from decisions. Decision theory focuses on a choice among alternatives; design focuses on "the discovery and elaboration of alternatives" [12, p. 172]. The search aspect of design involves a series of incremental and progressive decisions, each of which sets a direction. Designers evaluate and compare possible design directions. From bounded rationality theory, it is not possible to consider all design directions and choose the optimal. Rather, each progressive decision narrows the boundaries placed on future decisions. It is a selective search through a "maze of possibilities" [13, p. 54]. Each decision selects a satisfactory solution. The search then proceeds to the next dimension, and so on. In design science, bounded creativity (the amalgamation of Simon's bounded rationality in design and bounded creativity in engineering) means that humans are limited in their ability to make perfectly creative designs. The design discovery process is a search through a limited range of progressively creative designs, so designs are satisfactorily creative rather than optimal.

2.2   Creativity

How is bounded creativity akin to or different from any other notion of creativity? The topic of creativity has had a rich history in many fields. Creativity is a cognitive process that operates at the level of the individual[1] in the generation of ideas, and at the process level in the generation of creative artifacts [7]. Both aspects of creativity are inter-twined, and difficult to discern for design science research, because the outcomes are driven by the knowledge and creativity of the designer(s). Although the presence of creativity is well recognized, its process is largely taken for granted. At the core of the creative design process are iterations.

There are two schools of thought regarding creativity. *Thinking outside the box* exemplifies randomness and advocates the generation of many ideas, so that some good ones will appear [8]. *Thinking inside the box* is restrained by pragmatics, and similar to *structured ideation* [9, 10]. Creativity research also distinguishes *divergent* from *convergent thinking*. *Divergent thinking* is associated with fluency, flexibility, origi-nality, elaboration, and transformational abilities [11]. Convergent thinking is generally associated with deductive generation of a single, concrete, accurate, and effective solution [12]. Divergent and convergent thinking may both be present in creative episodes, whether outside- or inside-the-box, but neither is analogous to bounded creativity. Thinking within a frame of reference actually enhances the creation of new ideas [13, 14]. That is, individuals are *more* creative when given operating limits [15]. This explains why creativity must increase as design decisions progress. Moreover, ideas or solutions must be effective [16]. Bounded creativity specifically addresses the operating limits of effectiveness in creativity.

3   Bounded Creativity in Design Science Research

A distinguishing attribute of science is its dependence on a scientific method. This means that design science research must also be characterized by its methodical approach to design, making the methodological approach one of the most distinctive operating limits in design science research. There are a variety of well-known methods. E.g. Nunamaker et al. [17] framed a multi-methodological approach that centers system development within theory building, experimentation and observation. Walls et al. [18] propose using a design method and a meta-design. Design science frameworks add further scientific structure to the design process (e.g., [2, 19]). For our purpose of illustrating how methods progressively create boundaries on rationality and creativity, we use a generalized model that contains the most common process steps. Figure 1 illustrates these steps, which, like most design science methods, are fully iterative.

---

[1] Although the terms creativity and innovation are often used as synonyms, creativity is usually attributed to individuals or groups, whereas innovation is attributed to organizations. Wang, C.-J., *Does leader-member exchange enhance performance in the hospitality industry? The mediating roles of task motivation and creativity.* International Journal of Contemporary Hospitality Management, 2016. **28**(5): pp. 969-987.

The general process involves steps that flow downward (large arrows). Any step can stop the downward progress and iterate back to previous steps instead (small arrows).

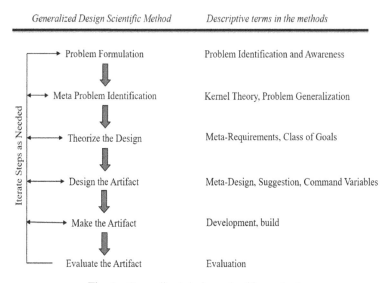

Fig. 1. Generalized design scientific method

In addition to narrowing the progressive rationality and creativity boundaries on any unstructured design process, a design science method adds further structure and further boundaries to the design process. We are accustomed to considering such boundaries from the more functional perspective of satisfying requirements and achieving practical utility. Each step of the design process limits the range of possible design components or assemblies that can be invoked in the solution artifact from this point forward.

An important consideration is when to stop and when to continue iterating. From the perspective of bounded rationality, progress in a step can break down if there are no available design decisions that satisfice the design aspirations. In this situation, the functional requirements and practical utility have been made impossible by previous design decisions. The breakdown is an indication to iterate to a previous stage.

Bounded creativity exists to some extent in any design setting. Why is design science research any different? Because design science research aspires to the rigor of a scientific method. While such a methodical approach improves the reliability and the validity of the knowledge resulting from the design process, the methodical process introduces structural boundaries on the progression of the design decisions.

3.1 How Problem Formulation Develops Subsequent Creativity Boundaries and Iteration Indicators

Problem formulation can be creative in the sense that the available evidence about the problem is characterized by uncertainty. At this step, this uncertainty arises from evidence that is incomplete or inadequately understood [20]. Identifying a starting point in the problem may not be easy because sometimes it is difficult to identify the exact problem or its boundaries [21]. Such incomplete diagnostic evidence makes a completely deductive problem diagnostic process difficult at best. An abductive, creative leap may be required to move from this incomplete evidence to a diagnosis. As a design decision, the creativity boundaries can be wide at this step. In other words, the leap can be quite a big one.

Identifying the problem narrows the creativity boundaries moving forward. Note that each design decision within the current stage develops conditions that bound creativity at the next step. This thread helps in understanding how the creativity boundaries narrow from this design decision. The medical concept of misdiagnosis is an appropriate analogy; in business it aligns with fads and fashions [22]. Misdiagnosing a problem narrows the boundaries for the identification of the meta-problem, i.e., the class of problems to which the problem-at-hand relates. For example, if there has been an increase in the number of intrusions into the system, we might focus on evidence that our users are being careless. If instead we might focus on the evidence that the access control system is inadequate. Depending on how this evidence is interpreted, the design creativity boundaries at the next step (meta-problem) will narrow. If the users are careless, the meta-problem (at issue for the next step) will be bound to other human and social kinds of problems. If, instead, the access control system is diagnosed as inadequate, the meta-problem will be bound to software, hardware and technical systems kinds of problems. In the former, creativity will become bound to ideas about human resources. In the latter, creativity will become bound to ideas about technologies.

3.2 How Meta-problem Identification Develops Subsequent Creativity Boundaries and Iteration Indicators

This research deals with creativity. We are not identifying a new class of problems, but, rather, addressing a new class of solutions. In a design science research problem, creativity is involved in classifying a problem that has been formulated in the previous step. This task is complicated because "there are more variables … than can be represented in a finite model" [23, p. 79]. Because the boundaries are still quite broad at this stage (there are myriad problem sources), the limits of the designer's knowledge about similar kinds of problems, or limitations of the designers' domain knowledge may impose a rational boundary. If the designer has experience with similar problems, an inductive classification might follow, with a tinge of creativity in inventing a new class of problems. If the designer is familiar with classifications that cover the identified problems, a deductive classification might follow. However, if neither is the case, we need a creative leap to abductively classify the problem within some range that is within the designer's field of knowledge. For example, if the problem is diagnosed as an issue of access control technology, and the designer's expertise is anchored to intrusion detection systems, there may be a creative leap to classify the technology problem as belonging to the class of intrusion detection problems.

Classifying the problem as one kind or another means it will have shared characteristics with other problems of its kind. The shared characteristics should encompass the aspirations the design will seek to satisfy. These characteristics, and their implied aspirations, will narrow the creativity boundaries for the step that follows: design theorizing. The design decision to classify the problem among a category of similar problems predefines the aspirations that will become the main constructs in the design theory. For example, if our security intrusion problem is identified as user carelessness, then creativity becomes bound to solutions for human and social problems. But do we classify the problem at hand as a cognitive problem or an affective problem? Are the users ignorant or indifferent? Do they not know or not care? If it is a cognitive problem, the aspirations might include changes in user behavior and new user experiences that change their knowledge and understanding. For an affective problem, aspirations might include aspiration changes in user behavior and new user attitudes that change their motivation. Deciding which class of problems is at hand is a design decision that will narrow the boundaries on the creativity that can be exercised in the next step, design theorizing.

3.3   How Design Theorizing Develops Subsequent Creativity Boundaries and Iteration Indicators

Theorizing is itself a creative act. For Weick [25], imagination is essential for sense-making. Theorizing is improved through disciplined imagination, a bounded form of creativity in which creativity is bound to a consistent process. The 'discipline' in theorizing comes from the consistent application of selection criteria to 'trial and error' thinking and the 'imagination' comes from "deliberate diversity introduced into the problem statements, thought trials, and selection criteria that comprise that thinking" (p. 516). Within the design science process, Weick's notion of a consistent process of disciplined imagination invokes a series of thought experiments. These experiments take the designer from the defined class of problems to the class of solutions and to the potential instance of an ultimate solution. Unlike some other forms of theorizing, design theorizing operates between an abstract and instance domain [26, 27]. For design theorizing, creativity can support the induction and abduction necessary for theory building [28], its inventiveness [29] and its "intuitive, blind, wasteful, serendipitous, creative quality" [25, p. 519].

Settling on a design theory further narrows the creativity boundaries for the next step, artifact design. It sets up the conceptual framework under which, and the vocabulary with which, the designers will make the main design decisions for the solution artifact. The framework will provide the kinds of components, features, functions, interfaces, protocols, etc. Because these are the meta-requirements for the ultimate artifact, the design theory determines the language and the grammar of the final artifact design. The boundaries constitute the criteria, such as principles, practice rules, or procedures that must be met by the artifact design [30].

For example, if we have decided that user carelessness is caused by indifference, perhaps protection motivation theory [31] would offer good grounds as a kernel for the design. Consistent with this theory, we might decide that a training program could provide the solution. The goal of this training program would involve motivating users to protect themselves from the losses. Based on this theory, the features would include building their appraisals of severe noxiousness the loss, their expectation of its likely occurrence, and their belief that the prescribed coping response is effective. These are the major constructs of the kernel theory. The design theory would involve translating this language and these concepts into an artifact (e.g., an educational program). Such a design theory now narrows the boundaries of creativity to a range that includes the use of training to build protection motivation in employees.

Creativity problems may arise at this step if the designer is unable to satisfactorily generate a design theory that addresses all the aspirations present in the given class of problems using the constructs implied by the shared characteristics in the class given in the previous step. A creative theory may be missing from those that satisfice the aspirations. For example, the possible theories may all seem commonplace and unsatisfying from a creative standpoint: the usual approach to problems of this sort. Where no interesting design theories are at hand, it might be assumed that the problem has been misclassified into the wrong kind of problem. Then the design process retreats to iterate the meta-problem identification stage in search of a less usual set of constructs and aspirations on which to begin the design.

3.4   How Artifact Design Develops Subsequent Creativity Boundaries and Iteration Indicators

Creativity in the design step becomes more narrowly focused on the specification of the ultimate artifact. It is crucial in the design of an artifact. The creative challenge is the production of both novel and useful ideas [32]. The design decisions at this step must be increasingly creative to fit the solution, the problem, and the design theory to one another. The step further invokes creativity and abduction because the focus is growing more practical. The designed solution must work to solve the practical problem. Still the design decisions must be made in a climate where the theory has narrowed the boundaries for consideration, even though there are myriad variables [23], yet uncertain evidence about the practical setting This uncertain evidence has not only involved incomplete or misunderstood information about the problem as formulated earlier, but also the difficulty in differentiating between the design alternatives at this step in designing [20]. Aspects of alternative designs can inhabit each other. Creativity is important in this step to ensure that the design fits within the theory's boundaries, operates within the practical criteria of the problem setting, and incorporates those aspects of the alternative designs necessary to solve the problem, all under the uncertainty of evidence about the problem and its solutions. The designer must be particularly creative because the design theory is anchored to constructs shared among similar problems. Not only must the designed artifact fit the theory, the practical criteria and the setting, but it should be distinctive. It should be different – somehow better than previous designs that regard similar problems. It should be inventive, novel, and interesting.

The design decisions taken in this step impose narrower creativity boundaries on the next step, artifact making or building. The specifications for the artifact will necessarily limit any further design decisions to relatively low-level, details. Such issues often arise from imprecision or provisionality in the design and ambiguity in the communication of the design between designers and builders [33]. Where these issues exist, the builders have some latitude to interpret the design specification. But their ability to develop any major design decisions is quite bounded.

3.5   How Making Artifacts Develops Subsequent Creativity Boundaries and Iteration Indicators

Creativity in the 'make' step is further narrowed by the design specifications. But it would be naïve to assume that there are no further design decisions left for the make/build activity. As previously mentioned, there is uncertainty in the communication of the design, and imprecision and provisionality in the design itself. There may also be errors that arise from the design or the theory behind the design. The components or assemblies applied to the design may operate differently from that expected by the designer. Considerable creativity can be required to make the artifact work, both practically and as intended by the designer, yet without departing in essential ways from the design as developed in the previous step.

The design decisions in this step complete the imposition of the narrowest boundaries on the next step, evaluation. The typical evaluation step compares the characteristics of the artifact with the specifications in the design. While there is still a limited range of creativity in evaluation, the characteristics of the artifact are most often unchangeable physically or logically (at least in terms of the evaluation). The results of the evaluation may be used formatively or summatively [34], but these results must pertain to the artifact as produced. Creativity is bounded by the immutability of the artifact during the evaluation step.

3.6   How Artifact Evaluation Develops Iteration Indicators

Boundaries on creativity in the artifact evaluation step are further narrowed by the presence of a constructed artifact. Although evaluators may creatively tinker with an artifact, evaluation is usually focused on examinations and experiments with the artifact designed. Still, there is room for creativity in the environment into which the artifact is positioned for evaluation. There is also creativity needed for choosing the parameters under which the evaluation takes place. While evaluations sometimes aim to break the artifact, such as with extreme or out-of-specification conditions, creativity is sometimes needed to make the artifact work successfully in normal operating conditions. An example is creative experimentation with an artifact in search for a situation in which the artifact satisfies all the aspirations in its design.

4   Indicators for Iteration in Design Science Research

Based on the analysis of bounded creativity, we can now compile a set of indicators that prescribe when iteration is appropriate. These are summarized in Table 1. Although some design science research methods suggest that iteration can retreat to any previous step, we suggest that such retreats be incremental. Iterative retreats step back only one stage at a time. For example, if during the make/build step, it is not possible to make the artifact operate, the process should iterate back to the design step. This would allow the designer to search for another satisfactory design within the existing design theory. If the designer cannot, then we can assume the design theory is faulty and retreat iteratively back to the design theorizing step.

Table 1. Indicators for iteration

Iterate from	Iterate to	Bounded creativity
Meta problem identification	Problem formulation	No problem class can be created: the problem has been misdiagnosed
Problem formulation	Meta-problem identification	The designer cannot find any similar problems and cannot classify the problem
Design theorizing	Meta-problem identification	The designer is unable to satisfactorily generate a design theory that addresses all the aspirations present in the meta-problem using its constructs
Artifact design	Design theorizing	The designer cannot translate the given design theory into a set of design specifications that deliver a promising, practical artifact design. The design theory is leading to designs that are unimaginative, mundane, and imitative
Making artifacts	Artifact design	The builders cannot invent a way to make the artifact operate as designed
Evaluation	Making artifacts	The evaluators cannot invent a situation in which the artifact satisfies the aspirations of its design

The use of bounded creativity indicators for determining when to iterate also makes creativity a specific companion to the scientific aspect of design science research.

5   Unfolding Iteration in the Case of "Craggy Cliffs"

To evaluate the iteration indicators, a case study is appropriate [34]. The indicators are evaluated within the context of a research project involving the design, development and evaluation of a novel location-based educational game. The design problem in the Craggy Cliffs Case (anonymized) was rooted in the failure of a creative project that was tasked to develop the location-based game. The project comprised a series of unstructured, yet creative, design experiments. However, initial work on the project was unsuccessful in yielding a novel and innovative game. This failure created the conundrum of whether the failure of the creative project resulted from the lack of grounding in a structured methodology or, whether the use of a structured scientific approach such as design science research would stem creativity in the design process and in the design outcome. The meta-problem within this case study was: how to incorporate the rigorous aspects of science (such as methodical approach, reliability, and repeatability) to a creative task without diminishing the creativity in a design setting.

5.1   Problem Description

After the initial failure of the creative design project, the Craggy Cliffs Case used a design science research approach to solve the problem of designing a creative location-based solution for engaging and educating youth visiting a national park. This project underwent three further design iterations to yield: (2) a novel artifact instantiated in the form of a site-specific location-based educational game; (3) a general method for creatively developing site-specific location-based games; and (4) an explanatory design theory for the design of creative location-based games [35, 36].

5.2   Iterations 1 and 2: Design Cycle

The Craggy Cliffs Nature Center was having trouble attracting young people to engage in outdoor nature appreciation and was interested in using smart mobile phone technology to engage young visitors. With this objective, the project proceeded. The first iteration proceeded without using a design science research methodology. The physical site was explored, and the topography, cliffs, and specific and interesting trees in the forest were identified. "We explored the affordances" of the site, states the main designer. Then several iterations followed where prototypes were built and tried at the site. For example, GPS technology was relatively new at the time. Therefore, the designers built a prototype of a mobile phone using GPS which displayed a map with a dot pointing to one's location. This prototype was tested, and two problems identified. First, the mobile coverage was not very good at the Craggy Cliffs site. Hence, what worked in the laboratory did not work at the site. Second, using a mobile phone with a map led the young people to look more at the phone than the nature around them. Third, the Craggy Cliffs Center wanted to increase engagement through a multi-player game, which required a network that could not be established in the forest and around the cliffs.

Thus, fulfilling the main purpose of appreciating nature through a site-specific multi-player game failed at first. In a second iteration the boundary posed by the bad mobile phone and GPS connection led to the creative exploration of different design decisions within the boundaries of the technology given at the site. Here we see an indication that evaluators could not invent a satisfying situation, and an iteration from *Evaluation* back to *Making Artifacts* ensued (see Table 1). The final decision was made to not give everyone a mobile phone, but rather, provide each team with one. A further iteration of creatively addressing the problem of having the game-players spend too much time looking at the phone led to a decision not to use the screen of the mobile phone but just play the sound of a narrative that a group of game-players could gather around and listen to together. Here we see an iteration from *Making Artifacts* back to *Artifact Design* (see Table 1).

During the iterations mentioned above, it became clear that the design process was a series of unstructured experiments using prototyping but lacked any well-defined methodology. The key objective of the site-specific game was to engage the visitors with the location. However, there were, at the time, few methods to incorporate the special characteristics of the physical site into the development of the game. Thus, in the iterations 1 and 2 the design work was focused more on the use of the technology than the game environment with the design activities having many unknown/unclear requirements. Therefore, a more structured approach was needed.

5.3   Iteration 3: Meta-level Design

The problem that initiated the design of a general method for site-specific game design was a realization that no specific method existed for developing site-specific games. Furthermore, there was a need for a more structured way of working. Here we find indications that, first, that the builders could not invent a way to make the artifact operate. Then that the design was too unimaginative. There was a stepwise series of iterations from *Making Artifacts* back to *Design Theorizing*; thence to *Problem Formulation* (see Table 1): To develop this general method, the designers drew on several kernel theories. These included: theories of pervasive game design, theories of site-specific computer games, theories of performance in play and games, embodied design, concepts of space, time, and players, other concepts such as rules, game artifacts, and game culture, as well as game affordances.

The method that was developed was named "site-storming" (reference left out to preserve author anonymity), which combined the idea of brainstorming for site-specific ideas, and was developed in several iterations. At first it was just a structured approach; "we need to analyze the site first before we have a creative phase coming up with ideas for how to use the site and so on." In the second iteration of the development of the site-storming method, it was found that different creative outcomes were elicited when designers worked independently than when they brainstormed in groups. Therefore, the method came to include an individual brainstorming phase followed by a group-oriented phase. A third iteration tried the idea of using cards. This was inspired by cards published by the design company IDEO [37]. Thus, the design artifact was of mission-based gaming style game-cards including mission cards, game cards, prop-cards and site cards. The iterations continued. When to continue iterating and when to stop was determined by either the rational boundaries or the creative boundaries in the situation. Gradually and progressively more severe design boundaries become imposed on the designer and the iterations were planned an enacted accordingly. Each design decision involved selecting a satisfactory solution to one of the aspirations in the design problem. e.g. deciding what type of cards were needed in the site-storming method.

5.4   Iteration 4: Meta-level Design

Learning from the previous iterations helped develop a meta-level explanatory design theory. Here we find indications that the designers could not imagine similar problems within the design theory. There was an iteration from *Problem Formulation* back to *Meta Problem Identification* (see Table 1): Developing a generic approach was intended to provide the grounding for finding ways to induce creativity within the structured design process described above, so better ideas could be generated in the time spent iterating. This approach helped to define a balance between structure and creativity where the structure enabled creativity, rather than inhibiting it. Observations and learning from prior iterations, consideration of design science research, theories of game performance, and performance requirements of site-specific games were all abstracted into an explanatory design theory. From this, the game from prior iterations was redesigned and evaluated, and twenty-six additional games designed. The redesigned games were evaluated by student participants and potential users for design pervasiveness and performance pervasiveness. The general requirements and solution components are shown in Fig. 2.

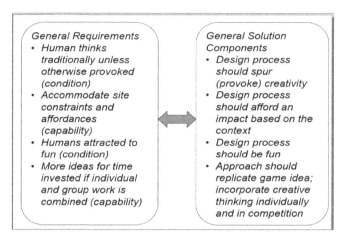

Fig. 2. Requirements and solution components

Figure 2 is presented as an explanatory design theory [38]. The abstraction of a design theory expressed as general requirements and general solution components required several iterations. The notation chosen determined some boundaries, e.g. one must express requirements as either conditions or capabilities in accordance with an ISO standard for requirements.

6   Discussion and Conclusion

This research has proposed bounded creativity as a mechanism for achieving novelty in design science research. Bounded creativity, in conjunction with bounded rationality, provides iteration indicators to achieve creative outcomes. As demonstrated in the case, the design science research process is iterative and incremental providing opportunities for feedback, improvement, and refinement. Design science research methodologies involve cycles and iterations. It is a common assumption that the decision to iterate is somehow obvious and simple, but this assumption overlooks two difficult problems. First, how does a design researcher know when it is an appropriate time to iterate and which previous stage is an appropriate choice? Second, when is the design science process sufficiently complete so further iteration is unnecessary? We posit that the problem of *when and where* to iterate is scoped by the rational and creativity boundaries imposed by the progressive and methodical nature of design science research.

There are extremely significant implications for the role and application of creativity within design science research. First, the structure and rigor of this research approach induces the need for creativity despite given constraints. This challenges the designer to draw on skills, curiosity, observation, and imagination to combine experience, style, other domains, patterns, or other creativity generating mechanisms, to find a new and innovative solution to a given problem. Second, bounded creativity iterations will drive outcomes that are more robust and reliable, by weaning out creative ideas that may be unable to stand the test of evaluation, through the progression of ever narrowing bounds of rationality and creativity.

Although the importance of creativity within information systems has been widely acknowledged, we lack an understanding of the effects of the boundaries placed on creativity by design science research. The structure of scientific rigor marshals the principled search for an artifact that demonstrates utility. However, this progressively narrows the boundaries of both rationality and creativity as the research process proceeds. Identifying when the narrowing of the boundaries has brought the rational or creative search to failure, will indicate that the current stage of the design search should be terminated. Then, iteration to a specific previous stage is suggested.

This research provides a perspective of bounded creativity in design science research, demonstrating how boundaries are placed on creativity at different stages of iteration. Bounded creativity scopes or narrows the range of options through the methodological lifecycle, often forcing the designer to retreat and rework a design. The forward iterations are much narrower in scope than earlier stages, with the designers' decision significant in determining the extent and bounds of the creative space and creative processes. Bounded creativity can help achieve a "creative enough" outcome. Furthermore, the notion of bounded creativity works at any level of outcome ranging from instantiates artifacts, to mid-level methods, to abstract level theoretical outcomes. This work contributes to design science research by analyzing and defining the role of bounded creativity in both theorizing and artifact development. Certainly, the pursuit of design science research meta-requirements and resulting design principles demands rigorous methods, but the implementation of an instantiation of the design principles is still replete with creative possibilities. It is often a process of creativity, or more precisely, of bounded creativity. Future research should examine how bounded creativity, as analyzed in this paper, can be applied within other contexts; for example, creating a health app for individuals with a specific disease condition.

References

1. Baskerville, R.L., Kaul, M., Storey, V.C.: Genres of inquiry in design-science research: justification and evaluation of knowledge production. MIS Q. **39**(3), 541–564 (2015)
2. Peffers, K., et al.: A design science research methodology for information systems research. J. Manage. Inf. Syst. **24**(3), 45–77 (2007)
3. Brooks, F.P.: The Design of Design: Essays from a Computer Scientist. Addison-Wesley, Upper Saddle River (2010)
4. Iivari, J.: A paradigmatic analysis of information systems as a design science. Scand. J. Inf. Syst. **19**(2), 5 (2007)

5. Gacenga, F., et al.: A proposal and evaluation of a design method in design science research. Electron. J. Bus. Res. Methods **10**(2), 89–100 (2012)
6. Wang, C.-J.: Does leader-member exchange enhance performance in the hospitality industry? the mediating roles of task motivation and creativity. Int. J. Contemp. Hospitality Manage. **28**(5), 969–987 (2016)
7. Greene, S.L.: Characteristics of applications that support creativity. Commun. ACM **45**(10), 100–104 (2002)
8. Hamel, G.: Innovation's New Math in Fortune, Time Inc, pp. 130–132 (2001)
9. Goldenberg, J., Efroni, S.: Using cellular automata modeling of the emergence of innovations. Technol. Forecast. Soc. Change **68**(3), 293–308 (2001)
10. Goldenberg, J., Mazursky, D., Solomon, S.: Toward identifying the inventive templates of new products: a channeled ideation approach. J. Market. Res. **36**(2), 200–210 (1999)
11. Guilford, J.: Transformotion abilities or functions. J. Creative Behav. **17**(2), 75–83 (1983)
12. Guilford, J.P.: Creativity: yesterday, today and tomorrow. J. Creative Behav. **1**(1), 3–14 (1967)
13. Hoegl, M., Gibbert, M., Mazursky, D.: Financial constraints in innovation projects: when is less more? Res. Policy **37**(8), 1382–1391 (2008)
14. Ward, T.B.: Cognition, creativity, and entrepreneurship. J. Bus. Ventur. **19**(2), 173–188 (2004)
15. Finke, R.A., Ward, T.B., Smith, S.M.: Creative Cognition: Theory, Research, and Applications (1992)
16. Runco, M.A.: Commentary: divergent thinking is not synonymous with creativity. Psychol. Aesthetics, Creativity Arts **2**(2), 93–96 (2008)
17. Nunamaker, J.F., Chen, M., Purdin, T.D.: Systems development in information systems research. J. Manage. Inf. Syst. **7**(3), 89–106 (1990)
18. Walls, J.G., Widmeyer, G.R., El Sawy, O.A.: Building an information system design theory for vigilant EIS. Inf. Syst. Res. **3**(1), 36–59 (1992)
19. Vaishnavi, V.K., Kuechler, W.: Design Science Research Methods and Patterns: Innovating Information and Communication Technology. CRC Press, Boca Raton (2015)
20. Lipshitz, R., Strauss, O.: Coping with uncertainty: a naturalistic decision-making analysis. Organ. Behav. Hum. Decis. Process. **69**(2), 149–163 (1997)
21. Clegg, G.L.: The Design of Design. Cambridge University Press, Cambridge (1969)
22. Armenakis, A.A., Harris, S.G.: Reflections: our journey in organizational change research and practice. J. Change Manage. **9**(2), 127–142 (2009)
23. Schön, D.: The Reflective Practitioner: How Practitioners Think in Action. Basic Books, New York (1984)
24. Secord, P.: Determinism, free will and self-intervention: a psychological perspective. New Ideas Psychol. **2**, 25–33 (1983)
25. Weick, K.E.: Theory construction as disciplined imagination. Acad. Manage. Rev. **14**(4), 516–531 (1989)
26. Kuechler, W., Vaishnavi, V.: A framework for theory development in design science research: multiple perspectives. J. Assoc. Inf. syst. **13**(6), 395 (2012)
27. Sein, M.K., et al.: Action design research. MIS Q. **35**(2), 37–56 (2011)
28. Gregor, S.: Building theory in the sciences of the artificial. In: Proceedings of the 4th International Conference on Design Science Research in Information Systems and Technology, pp. 1–10. ACM, Philadelphia (2009)
29. Gregor, S., Hevner, A.R.: The front end of innovation: perspectives on creativity, knowledge and design. In: Donnellan, B., Helfert, M., Kenneally, J., VanderMeer, D., Rothenberger, M., Winter, R. (eds.) DESRIST 2015. LNCS, vol. 9073, pp. 249–263. Springer, Cham (2015). https://doi.org/10.1007/978-3-319-18714-3_16

30. Markus, M.L., Majchrzak, A., Gasser, L.: A design theory for systems that support emergent knowledge processes. MIS Q., 179–212 (2002)
31. Rogers, R.W.: A protection motivation theory of fear appeals and attitude change. J. Psychol. **91**(1), 93–114 (1975)
32. George, J.M., Zhou, J.: Dual tuning in a supportive context: joint contributions of positive mood, negative mood, and supervisory behaviors to employee creativity. Acad. Manage. J. **50**(3), 605–622 (2007)
33. Eckert, C.: The communication bottleneck in knitwear design: analysis and computing solutions. Comput. Support. Coop. Work (CSCW) **10**(1), 29–74 (2001)
34. Venable, J., Pries-Heje, J., Baskerville, R.: FEDS: a framework for evaluation in design science research. Eur. J. Inf. Syst. **25**(1), 77–89 (2016)
35. Pries-Heje, J., Baskerville, R.: The design theory nexus. MIS Q., 731–755 (2008)
36. Gregor, S., Hevner, A.R.: Positioning and presenting design science research for maximum impact. MIS Q. **37**(2), 337–355 (2013)
37. IDEO: IDEO Method Cards: 51 Ways to Inspire Design. William Stout (2003)
38. Baskerville, R., Pries-Heje, J.: Explanatory design theory. Bus. Inf. Syst. Eng. **2**(5), 271–282 (2010)

Conceptualization of the Problem Space in Design Science Research

Alexander Maedche[1], Shirley Gregor[2], Stefan Morana[1(✉)],
and Jasper Feine[1]

[1] Institute of Information Systems and Marketing (IISM),
Karlsruhe Institute of Technology (KIT), Karlsruhe, Germany
{alexander.maedche, stefan.morana,
jasper.feine}@kit.edu
[2] Australian National University, Canberra, Australia
shirley.gregor@anu.edu.au

Abstract. Design science research (DSR) aims to deliver innovative solutions for real-world problems. DSR produces Information Systems (IS) artifacts and design knowledge describing means-end relationships between problem and solution spaces. A key success factor of any DSR research endeavor is an appropriate understanding and description of the underlying problem space. However, existing DSR literature lacks a solid conceptualization of the problem space in DSR. This paper addresses this gap and suggests a conceptualization of the problem space in DSR that builds on the four key concepts of stakeholders, needs, goals, and requirements. We showcase the application of our conceptualization in two published DSR projects. Our work contributes methodologically to the field of DSR as it helps DSR scholars to explore and describe the problem space in terms of a set of key concepts and their relationships.

Keywords: Problem space · Design science research · Requirements ·
Needs · Goals · Stakeholders

1 Introduction

The Design Science Research (DSR) paradigm is increasingly adopted in the Information Systems (IS) community and beyond in order to develop innovative solutions for real-world problems [1]. Much work providing methodological guidance for conducting DSR projects has been suggested in the past decade, with research suggesting frameworks or processes to conduct DSR projects [2, 3], addressing the evaluation of DSR projects [4, 5], the formulation of design principles [6, 7], and the formulation of design theories [1, 8, 9]. These seminal articles assist scholars in engaging successfully with the DSR paradigm.

Generally speaking, any DSR project should produce design knowledge describing a means-end relationship between the problem and the solution space. However, the current body of knowledge on the methodological aspects of DSR lacks a detailed conceptualization of what is termed the problem space of a DSR project. In their comprehensive literature review on the current state of DSR in IS, Deng and Ji [10]

© Springer Nature Switzerland AG 2019
B. Tulu et al. (Eds.): DESRIST 2019, LNCS 11491, pp. 18–31, 2019.
https://doi.org/10.1007/978-3-030-19504-5_2

identify some shortcomings in the current methodological fundaments of conducting DSR. These authors suggest some opportunities for future research on the DSR approach, including amongst others the need for a dedicated process model and description of the problem identification step [10]. Purao [11] discusses the underlying ontology of DSR and how the understanding of a problem is interconnected with the design of the artifact. During the research process and by building the artifact, the understanding of the process is re-interpreted by the researcher while at the same time the design of the artifact is informed by the researcher's interpretation of the problem [11]. Although the relationship between problem and the resulting artifact and its importance is identified by many scholars [1, 11–14], there is no common agreement or conceptualization of key concepts and their interrelationships for describing the problem space of DSR projects.

An everyday illustration shows how we use different terms to distinguish different aspects of a problem space. Consider a case where a house is subject to flooding during storms. Flooding is the **problem** and avoidance of flooding is a **need** of the homeowner (the **stakeholder**). A design team articulates a **goal or multiple goals** in cooperation with the stakeholders in order to solve this problem by constructing an artifact whose **purpose** is to meet the need. Different artifacts with different purposes could be constructed depending on how the problem is framed. Creative thinking or ideation could assist the design team in identifying alternative courses of action, leading to different artifacts. For example, the problem could be framed as either "the base of the house being too low" or "earth build up on one side of the house is too high". These different framings would lead to different artifacts, one whose purpose is to raise the house and the other whose purpose is to provide drainage along one side of the house. Each of these different artifacts would also have different **requirements**, e.g. (1) height to which the house should be raised and (2) depth and slope of drains. It can be seen that distinguishing the different components in this problem space with different terms allows for the complexities of problem space definition, particularly where problem definition may co-evolve with different ideas for solutions. Defining requirements precisely should not be done until a particular approach to solving the problem has been decided upon. Settling on one solution and defining requirements for this solution too early on can limit creativity. A further problem is that of level-of-analysis. The construction of a DSR artifact to address a specific need can occur within a larger project where an overall problem can be defined in quite general terms. The word **"goal"** usually refers to the higher level problem space, congruent with usage in strategic and project management and in research activities. For the house flooding problem, the overall goal would be to stop flooding in the specified context. The measurable project **objectives** (e.g., no flooding in 100 years) and the solution **requirements** (e.g. cost should be below $x) could be inherited by different solutions approached. The **purpose** of the individual artifacts constructed to address the project goals could vary depending on which approach to a solution is adopted. Further, the individual artifact constructed in DSR should have some level of generality, and not be tied to a particular project. That is, the knowledge represented in the artifact should allow similar purposes to be achieved by similar artifacts even after the particular research project ends. The usage of the term "purpose" here is congruent with that in Gregor and Jones [9].

This paper provide more clarity to existing problem space terminology by suggesting a comprehensive conceptualization and showcasing the application of the conceptualization in selected example DSR projects. We address the following research question:

What are the key concepts in the formulation of the problem space in Design Science Research and how are these concepts related?

The paper contributes methodologically to the field of DSR as it helps DSR scholars to explore and describe the problem space in terms of a set of key concepts and their inter-relationships. It addresses the difficulties shown by Van de Ven [15] that face researchers in problem formulation, as discussed below, and thus should improve research practice. The remainder of the paper proceeds as follows. First we present related work on the formulation of a problem and the problem space. Next, we discuss existing conceptualizations and definitions for the problem space and outline our conceptualization for the DSR problem space.

2 Existing Work

2.1 The Broader Literature

Discussion of how problems are specified and addressed is widespread across many fields including the conduct of science in general, creativity, innovation, and design disciplines. The relevant literature is very large and we can touch on only a relatively small subset here, while identifying some key implications for DSR.

Early work on creativity in science noted the importance of problem formalization. For example Getzels [16] cites the following quote by Einstein [17]: *"The formulation of a problem is often more essential than its solution, which may be merely a matter of mathematical or experimental skill. To raise new questions, new possibilities, to regard old questions from a new angle, requires creative imagination and marks real advance in science."*

Van de Ven [15] presents a model of engaged scholarship in which he says problem formulation is often the first and most important task. He describes a process of problem formulation as consisting of four activities: *"(1) recognizing and situating a problem; (2) gathering information to ground the problem and its setting; (3) diagnosing the information to ascertain the characteristics or symptoms of the problem and (4) deciding what actions or questions to pursue to resolve the research problem"* [15, p. 72]. He further points out that these activities are inter-related: working out what the puzzle really is, and what the answer should look like, often happens in parallel with discovering the answer itself. Further, a key challenge in situating a problem is deciding what persons or **stakeholder** groups will be served by the research: that is, whose perceived **needs** are to be met. The stakeholder perspectives addressed will influence the focus, level and scope of a project. Van de Ven notes four common difficulties in formulating a problem space: (1) Showing what stakeholder groups are served; 2) Solving the "wrong problem" with the "right method"; (3) Ensuring there is a real problem or need rather than a "pseudo-problem" that lacks grounding in reality;

(4) Delineating the problem space so that finding solutions will lead to creative theorizing. These difficulties are revisited in the discussion section where we reflect on the contributions of the paper.

Methods used in what is termed "design thinking" also stress the importance of problem formulation. Designers can explore a stated problem and its context and, rather than accept the problem as given, may restructure or re-interpret the problem to suggest alternate routes to a solution [18]. Cross [19] expresses views congruent with those of Van de Ven [15] and says that *"Designers tend to use solution conjectures as the means of developing their understanding of the problem"*. He found support for this view in protocol studies of designers, especially the more expert designers.

Herbert Simon's work, which has had a strong influence on DSR, talks less about the complexities of problem formulation, and has a more algorithmic approach to the relationship between problem space and solution space. He gives examples of linear programming where, once a problem is specified, along with its **constraints (requirements)**, a solution can be found using optimization methods [20, p. 117].

To sum up this account of work on problem formulation in design from the wider literature, we note that problem formulation is not always a simple matter and may co-evolve with solution development. Important ideas associated with problem formulation are stakeholder identification, the perceived needs of stakeholders, requirements for a solution, and the direction of research that addresses the problem.

2.2 Problem Formulation in DSR Methodologies and Design Theory

Seminal work on DSR [e.g. 1–3, 13, 21–23] recognizes the proper understanding and formulation of an addressed problem as the focal starting point of a DSR project. The need for a clear understanding and description of the problem is also acknowledged in three of the most common DSR and Action Design Research (ADR) methodologies [2, 3, 21].

In the first process step of their general design research cycle, Kuechler and Vaisnhavi [2] include "awareness of problem". In this starting phase of the DSR project, the problem needs to be sufficiently specified. Within this problem specification, the overall goal of the research project is defined and comprises *"typically the development of a technological solution to all or an aspect of the problem. The problem and potential solution are set out, at least in functional terms, in the awareness of problem phase"* [2, p. 406].

Similarly, Peffers et al. [3] include a starting phase to set the scope and goal of the DSR project in in their process model. In contrast to the "awareness of problem" process step by Kuechler and Vaisnhavi [2], Peffers et al. break the beginning of a DSR project into two phases, "Identify Problem & Motivate" and "Define Objectives of a Solution". The first phase "Identify Problem & Motivate" serves to *"define the specific research problem and justify the value of the solution"* [3, p. 52] and the researchers also note that it may be useful to fully conceptualize the problem and its complexity. Building on this specification, the second phase "Define Objectives of a Solution" infers the qualitative and/or quantitative objectives of the solution [3].

In ADR, the proper specification of the problem is also recognized. Sein et al. [21] emphasize problem formulation with two principles in their ADR method, namely "Principle 1: Practice-Inspired Research" and "Principle 2: Theory-Ingrained Artifact". The first principle stresses the importance of addressing a real-world or field problem in the ADR project and Sein et al. argue that the *"trigger for the first stage is a problem perceived in practice or anticipated by researchers"* [21, p. 4].

Table 1 summarizes the three DSR and ADR methodologies and their perception of the importance of the proper problem formulation.

Table 1. The "problem" in DSR and ADR methodologies

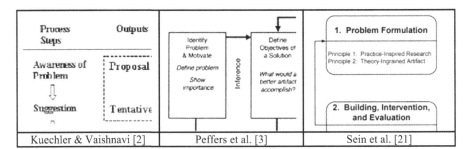

The analytical framework proposed by Thuan et al. [24] distinguishes the phases of construction, formulation and answer. In the construction phase they introduce the two dimensions: (1) motivation and (2) problem statement. Within the dimension problem statement they further distinguish (i) research challenges, (ii) research gaps, (iii) research problems, (iv) requirements, and (v) research opportunities. In their comprehensive literature review, they show that 36.5% of the DSR publications identify research challenges, followed by research gaps (25%) and research problems (16.3%). An interesting finding is that only 12.5% of the publications use requirements to frame the problem statement of their research.

vom Brocke and Lippe [21] apply a project management approach to DSR and argue that professional project management can support the execution of DSR projects. In particular, these authors suggest that the problem-solving nature of DSR can benefit from insights from the project scope management literature. In their paper they make suggestions as to how to define the scope of a DSR project and how to manage changes in scope [21].

From a design theory point of view, Walls et al. [22] initially introduced the term meta-requirements as part of their seminal work in information systems design theory. They argue that a design theory has as a primary component "a **set of meta-require-ments** which describe **the class of goals** to which the theory applies" [22]. However, they also state that "problem identification" precedes the commencement of design [22]. A meta-requirement is defined as a requirement that represents a class of systems and not just one instance of a system. However, there is no clear definition of what exactly makes up a class of systems. In the subsequent work on design theory by Gregor and Jones [9] the terminology of Walls et al. [22] is adopted and "**purpose and**

scope" is considered to be a core component of a design theory. Specifically, "purpose and scope" is described as a set of meta-requirements or goals that specify the type of artifact to which the theory applies and in conjunction also defines the scope, or boundaries, of the theory. However, reflection by the first author on the Gregor and Jones paper indicates that further work is needed on teasing out differences amongst the terms used.

DSR appears to be distinctive in its adoption of the terms *requirements* and *meta-requirements* in connection with problem identification as part of a research process, and this situation is perhaps because of the background that a number of researchers have in software engineering. However, it is important to keep in mind that DSR is not the same as software engineering or systems development, although these activities may also require considerable creativity as well as a depth of professional knowledge [see 1]. Zobel [25] in writing for novice computer scientists points out how software development needs to be differentiated from research. The problem investigated in research needs to provide challenge and the possibility of unexpected discovery in order to lead to interesting research. Specifying requirements as a step in software engineering methodologies has a different flavor as there can be an expectation that requirements, once set, are not expected to change, as could be the case in a research discovery project [as shown by 15, 19].

Gregor and Hevner [1] discuss contributions to knowledge in DSR and provide a taxonomy that has two dimensions: application domain maturity and solution maturity. These dimensions have parallels in the idea of problem space maturity versus solution space maturity. However, the labelling of the axes in the DSR contribution framework allows for the idea that with projects that have very novel outcomes, "opportunities" rather than "problems" might be recognized, as with these inventions the need or opportunity for something new (a problem) is not necessarily well recognized when the research begins.

In part the discussion above concerns steps in a DSR process rather than the conceptualization of a problem space in a structural (ontological) sense. Nevertheless, some recognition of the research process in which the conceptualization occurs is needed because of the linkage between process and structural elements of knowledge such as problem identification. What the above discussion has shown is that there is some difference in emphasis on descriptions of how problems are formulated in more creative problem-solving endeavors, where problem and solution are seen to co-evolve, and more algorithmic or software engineering influenced approaches where a problem and requirements are defined and then a search for a solution in a solution space occurs.

In sum, a detailed conceptualization of the problem scope and how it is interconnected with other important aspects of DSR projects is missing in the current DSR body of knowledge. This shortcoming exists despite the fact that the importance of problem finding and formulation has long been recognized in the literature on creativity [e.g. 16, 26] and in other disciplines [e.g. 27].

3 Conceptualization

This section introduces our problem space conceptualization in the form of key concepts and relationships amongst them.

3.1 Illustration of Key Concepts

Terminology relevant to problem formulation varies across and within a number of the disciplinary areas in which DSR researchers work: e.g. academic research, software engineering, systems development and project management. There is particular difficulty with the terms goals, purpose, objectives and requirements, as these terms have similar meanings in everyday usage. Here, we distinguish them on the basis of their definition in the areas most relevant to DSR. Historically DSR has been influenced by the work of Martin Heidegger, which is well-founded in philosophy [see 9]. In his essay on the "The Question of Technology" [28, pp. 311–341] Heidegger employs terminology from Aristotle in discussing the four "causes" of an artifact. The cause that is of primary interest here is the *causa finalis* (cause or purpose), the "end" that the artifact is designed to achieve. In using the example of a silver chalice he says that its end is to serve in a sacrificial rite and that it must have the "aspect" of "chaliceness". Knowing that the chalice is to serve as a sacrificial vessel in a religious rite means that the chalice in advance is "circumscribed", in that "bounds" are given to the thing.

If we are to translate this terminology to the domain of design science research and also software engineering, we could say that the "**need**" (also called the "problem situation") is that something is needed as a sacrificial vessel. The "**goal**" of the artifact constructed is to serve this need and solve this problem. In this case someone has decided that the goal will be fulfilled by constructing a silver chalice as the resulting artifact. Note that other artifacts could achieve the same end e.g. a golden chalice or a silver cup. Even at this point there is indeterminacy in how the need or problem is addressed and a range of solutions could meet the need. Further, there are "**requirements**" that must be considered in achievement of the goal: for example, the chalice should be beautiful to suit the atmosphere of a religious ceremony. Other "aspects of chaliceness" place other demands on design: the chalice needs to be able to hold liquid, be of an appropriate size and so on. Finally, in a religious ceremony there may be different participants who should be considered as independent "**stakeholders**". Different stakeholders may have different needs and different set of requirements may be derived to address different solutions for the need/problem.

We propose the four concepts "needs", "goals", "requirements", and "stakeholders" as fundamental for the conceptualization of the problem space in DSR, taking the level of analysis as the construction of one artifact. We have avoided the use of the prefix "meta-" in connection with any of the concepts. It is taken as understood that in DSR an aim is that knowledge developed about a solution to a problem in one project should be generalizable to some extent; that is, a solution should apply to other instances of the same class of problems. We make this assumption explicit in our discussion of the "purpose" of an artifact below. Note that the level of generality will depend on how components of the problem space are defined in a specific research project.

Table 2. Concepts in the DSR problem space

Concept	Definition
Needs	The "need" is the essence of the problem and indicates what is wanted or desired. The term "need" could be used almost interchangeably with the term "problem": i.e. a need to resolve a difficulty or deal with a threat, or a need for a new product or service, is seen as the "problem". However the term "need" has broader connations in that "need" includes the idea of allowing for opportunities that may not have been realized yet as "problems". From a psychological point of view a need is a feature that arouses an organism to action toward a goal, giving purpose and direction to behavior, e.g. a need for religious ritual and hence the need for a chalice-like object. However, with DSR a need may also be expressed for a non-human actor, e.g. a need in a system for a natural language interpreter. Needs are perceived by stakeholders and needs of different stakeholders may conflict with one another
	From a software engineering point of view an emphasis is set on so-called information needs, defined as "… insights necessary to manage objectives, goals, risks, and problems" [29]
Goals	As introduced above, the concepts purpose, goals, and objectives relate to each other and are sometimes used interchangeable. However, they differ in their meaning and level of abstraction. First of all, a purpose (aim, causa finalis) is an "intended outcome" [29] that will allow a recognized need to be satisfied. An artifact developed during DSR allows an outcome to be achieved and a need to be met or a problem to be solved – that is its purposes, as embedded in it by designers. Differing user needs may need to be reconciled in arriving at a purpose for an artifact. The purpose is also the reason for which something is done or created or for which something exists
	Goals represent desired results or a desired state of affairs. They describe intentions of stakeholders. Goals may conflict with one another. Finally, objectives are more specific than goals. For example project management emphasizes that objectives should be measurable [29]. One may refer to them as "… predetermined results towards which effort is directed. Objectives may be defined in terms of outputs, outcomes and/or benefits" [30]
	We consider goals as the key conceptual entity that should be explicitly articulated as part of a problem space conceptualization
Requirements	Software engineering has established a common and stable understanding of what a requirement is. According to the IEEE standard [29] it can be defined as following: 1. a condition or capability needed by a user to solve a problem or achieve an objective 2. a condition or capability that must be met or possessed by a system, system component, product, or service to satisfy an agreement, standard, specification, or other formally imposed documents 3. a documented representation of a condition or capability as in (1) or (2) 4. a condition or capability that must be met or possessed by a system, product, service, result, or component to satisfy a contract, standard, specification, or other formally imposed document
	Requirements include the quantified and documented needs and goals of stakeholders

(continued)

Table 2. (*continued*)

Concept	Definition
Stakeholder	A stakeholder is a "… person or organization (e.g., customer, sponsor, performing organization, or the public) that is actively involved in a DSR project, or whose interests may be positively or negatively affected by execution or completion of the DSR project. A stakeholder may also exert influence over the DSR project and its deliverables [29]. Stakeholders have "… a (direct or indirect) influence on a system's requirements. Indirect influence also includes situations where a person or organization is impacted by the system [31]

For example, requirements could be broadly conceived (e.g. be beautiful, as with Heidegger's chalice), or be more specific (e.g. provide metrics of user trustworthiness, as in the Arazy et al. [32] paper showcased below).

Table 2 below provides short definitions for each concept. Our proposed definitions are mainly based on previous work in software and requirements engineering, although we enrich the definitions with important definition ideas from other disciplines.

3.2   Conceptual Model

As introduced above with Heidegger's example the different concepts are related to each other. We first emphasize the relationship between needs, goals, and requirements as fundamental for the problem space. In general there are 1:n relationships between the different concepts, thus, one need can inform several goals, and one goal can be achieved by many requirements.

Furthermore, different stakeholders contextualize and influence all three interconnected concepts. As mentioned above, different stakeholders may also contribute to conflicting needs, goals, or requirements in the problem space. The role of the design team is to clarify and focus the problem space. In order to do this successfully the stakeholders should be identified and involved. Figure 1 depicts the conceptual model.

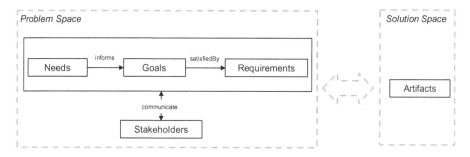

Fig. 1. Conceptual model

Our core conceptual model follows a minimalistic approach. As introduced in Table 2 there are several related concepts that could be added to the conceptual model, e.g. the purpose or objectives. Furthermore, one may also refine the introduced concepts, e.g. different types of typical stakeholders may be explicitly introduced. We consider the introduced concepts as a least common denominator that should be introduced as part of a problem space description. Further details may be introduced depending on the specific DSR project context.

4   Showcase

We showcase the proposed conceptual model with two exemplary DSR papers published in the Journal of the Association of Information Systems (JAIS). The first paper by Arazy et al. [32] is about social recommender systems that utilize data regarding users' social relationships in filtering relevant information to their users. It follows a theory-driven design methodology to realize social recommender systems with the aim of improving prediction accuracy. Table 3 summarizes the key results of instantiating our conceptual model within the context of this showcase paper.

Table 3. First showcase

Problem space element	Extracted from paper Arazy et al. [32]
Stakeholders	The paper does not explicitly mention stakeholders. However, information about stakeholders can be extracted from the paper. Basically, two different stakeholders are mentioned • Providers of recommender systems • Users
Needs	The paper does not explicitly articulate specific needs
Goals	The paper explicitly articulates one general design goal: Associate a recipient with the sources that would provide the most relevant information for making a recommendation. The key target of the work presented in the paper is to increase recipient's "likelihood of accepting a source's advice"
Requirements	The paper articulates seven requirements: • Establish a metric of users' preference similarity • Establish metrics of users' tie strength • Establish metrics of users' trustworthiness • Arrive at a single similarity score, based on all the relationship data • Predict the relevancy of items to users • Make recommendation of the relevant items to users • Protect users' privacy

The second paper we are using to showcase our conceptual model is by Meth et al. [33]. The work presents a DSR project that delivers a so-called requirements mining system that supports requirements engineers in identifying and classifying requirements documented in natural language. Table 4 summarizes the key results.

Table 4. Second showcase

Problem space element	Extract from paper Meth et al. [33]
Stakeholders	The paper does not explicitly mention stakeholders. However, information about stakeholders can be extracted from the figures presented in the paper. Several stakeholders are introduced: • Requirements engineers (primary stakeholder) • Users • Software vendors • Product managers • Software engineers
Needs	The paper does not explicitly articulate specific needs. However, as part of the motivation several issues (problems) are raised, e.g. requirements extraction from natural language is time consuming, error prone, and monotonous
Goals	The paper explicitly articulates goals at the level of decision makers and translates them into design goals. Specifically, it articulates the following generic decision maker goals: • Maximize decision quality • Minimize cognitive effort • Maintain control over decision strategy selection
Requirements	The paper articulates three major requirements for requirements mining systems: • Increase the quality of approved requirements • Decrease the cognitive efforts required to execute and prepare requirement mining • Limit system restrictiveness during requirement mining. The requirements are directly connected to the articulated goals

Both papers explicitly articulate requirements and introduce goals. The first paper articulates one high level goal, but does not interconnect the goal with the specific requirements. The second paper articulates goals at different levels and interlinks them with requirements. However, they do not explicitly document the relevant stakeholders for the published DSR projects. Furthermore, they also do not provide specific information on the relationship between stakeholders and needs, goals, and requirements.

5 Discussion

We showed that there is variation in thinking and terminology used in describing the problem space. Problems formulation occurs in many areas and is considered in science as an important characteristic of engaged scholarship. Independent of the specific scientific area, the co-evolution of problem definition with the envisaging of tentative solutions is recognized and is seen to encourage greater creativity in problem solving. However, the degree of exploitation of the problem space differs, in some areas there is less recognition that stated descriptions of a problem situation should be investigated fully at the beginning of a research project.

We believe that providing a foundational conceptual model for the problem space contributes to organizing and structuring the processes of problem space analysis and description. Our conceptual model follows a minimalist approach. The model could be easily extended with further concepts (e.g. goals could be refined with objectives) and concepts could be described with descriptive properties. Besides that, more specific and typed relationships may be introduced (e.g. a subsumption (is-a) relationship between end-users and stakeholders). A finer granular description of the conceptual model, comes with pros and cons. On the one hand, a finer granular description would further standardize and sharpen the concepts and relationships to be captured as part of a problem space description. On the other hand, a more generic model is easier to understand and more broadly applicable in different fields of interest. In order to establish a least common denominator, we decided to follow a minimalist approach to lay a solid foundation that may be refined in the future.

Van de Ven [15] noted that there common difficulties that researchers encountered in grounding, situating, diagnosing and resolving a research problem. We highlight the contributions offered by our model for problem space formulation by showing how the model addresses each of Van de Ven's difficulties:

(1) What stakeholder groups are served? Needs and problems are "uniquely perceived and framed by different people. Knowing from whose perspective a problem is being addressed and engaging them in problem formulation is necessary to frame the focus, level and scope of a research study" [15, p. 73]. Our model explicitly includes stakeholders as part of the problem space formulation.

(2) Solving the "wrong problem" with the "right method" is unfortunately common. If problem space formulation is rushed "important dimensions of a problem often go unrecognized and opportunities to advance knowledge of the problem are missed" [15, p. 73]. Our model encourages creativity by separating "requirements" from "goals", with the former not specified in detail until the need and goal being addressed are fully investigated.

(3) Is there a real problem or need or is there a "pseudo-problem" that lacks grounding in reality? Encouraging researchers to explicitly state what problem/need they are addressing for which stakeholders lessens the chance that imaginary or trivial problems are addressed.

(4) Will finding solutions to match the problem space lead to creative theorizing? The problem should be formulated in such a way that it has "applicability beyond the situation in which it is observed" [15, p. 74]. As discussed, our position is that all DSR should aim, to a greater or less extent, to develop solutions that apply to a class of problems rather than one specific problem. Further our model has addressed this difficulty by showing in our discussion of the "goal" component of the problem space that the artifacts constructed should be recognized as having a "purpose" that is inscribed in them during the solution phase, which allows them to meet the goal in the current context, but may persist and have wider applicability outside that context.

A limitation of the paper is that only two showcase examples could be included due to space constraints. Evidence from other cases, including cases where stakeholder needs are necessarily more prominent, would be expected to show more explicit recognition of some components of the problem space framework.

6 Summary

We motivated this paper by a perceived lack of a detailed and commonly agreed conceptualization of what is termed the problem space of a DSR project. The conceptual model of the DSR problem space we have developed includes four fundamental concepts: need (problem), goals, requirements and stakeholders. We argue that this conceptualization will assist researchers in overcoming key difficulties that have been recognized in grounding, situating, diagnosing and resolving a research problem.

Future research may apply our proposed conceptual model and validate its applicability in DSR projects. We also believe that providing more specific problem space "templates" for instantiating the introduced concepts and their relationships may help DSR researchers in capturing the problem space. Furthermore, in order to enable reuse and accumulation of design knowledge, it could be very helpful to represent the problem space description in a machine-readable format in order to allow for querying and searching problem repositories.

References

1. Gregor, S., Hevner, A.R.: Positioning and presenting design science research for maximum impact. MIS Q. **37**, 337–355 (2013)
2. Kuechler, W., Vaishnavi, V.: A framework for theory development in design science research: multiple perspectives science research: multiple perspectives. J. Assoc. Inf. Syst. **13**, 395–424 (2012)
3. Peffers, K., Tuunanen, T., Rothenberger, M.A., Chatterjee, S.: A design science research methodology for information systems research. J. Manage. Inf. Syst. **24**, 45–77 (2007)
4. Venable, J., Pries-Heje, J., Baskerville, R.: FEDS: a framework for evaluation in design science research. Eur. J. Inf. Syst. **25**, 77–89 (2016)
5. Sonnenberg, C., vom Brocke, J.: Evaluations in the science of the artificial – reconsidering the build-evaluate pattern in design science research. In: Peffers, K., Rothenberger, M., Kuechler, B. (eds.) DESRIST 2012. LNCS, vol. 7286, pp. 381–397. Springer, Heidelberg (2012). https://doi.org/10.1007/978-3-642-29863-9_28
6. Denyer, D., Tranfield, D., Van Aken, J.E.: Developing design propositions through research synthesis. Organ. Stud. **29**, 393–413 (2008)
7. Chandra, L., Seidel, S., Gregor, S.: Prescriptive knowledge in IS research: conceptualizing design principles in terms of materiality, action, and boundary conditions. In: Proceedings of the Annual Hawaii International Conference on System Sciences, pp. 4039–4048 (2015)
8. Baskerville, R., Pries-Heje, J.: Explanatory design theory. Bus. Inf. Syst. Eng. **2**, 271–282 (2010)
9. Gregor, S., Jones, D.: The anatomy of a design theory. J. Assoc. Inf. Syst. **8**, 312–335 (2007)
10. Deng, Q., Ji, S.: A review of design science research in information systems: concept, process, outcome, and evaluation. Pacific Asia J. Assoc. Inf. Syst. **10**, 1–36 (2018)
11. Purao, S.: Truth or Dare. J. Database Manag. **24**, 51–66 (2013)
12. Peffers, K., Tuunanen, T., Niehaves, B.: Design science research genres: introduction to the special issue on exemplars and criteria for applicable design science research. Eur. J. Inf. Syst. **27**, 129–139 (2018)

13. Baskerville, R., Baiyere, A., Gregor, S., Hevner, A., Rossi, M.: Design science research contributions: finding a balance between artifact and theory. J. Assoc. Inf. Syst. **19**, 358–376 (2018)
14. Winter, R.: Design science research in Europe. Eur. J. Inf. Syst. **17**, 470–475 (2008)
15. Van de Ven, A.H.: Engaged Scholarship: A Guide for Organizational and Social Research. Oxford University Press, Oxford (2007)
16. Getzels, J.W.: Problem finding: a theoretical note. Cogn. Sci. **3**, 167–172 (1979)
17. Einstein, A., Infeld, L.: The Evolution of Physics. Simon & Schuster, New York (1938)
18. Dorst, K.: The core of "design thinking" and its application. Des. Stud. **32**, 521–532 (2011)
19. Cross, N.: Expertise in design: an overview. Des. Stud. **25**, 427–441 (2004)
20. Simon, H.: The Sciences of the Artificial. MIT Press, Cambridge (1998)
21. Sein, M.K., Henfridsson, O., Purao, S., Rossi, M., Lindgren, R.: Action design research. MIS Q. **35**, 1–20 (2011)
22. Walls, J.G., Widmeyer, G.R., El Sawy, O.A.: Building an information system design theory for vigilant EIS. Inf. Syst. Res. **1**, 36–59 (1992)
23. Hevner, A.R., March, S.T., Park, J., Ram, S.: Design science in information systems research. MIS Q. **28**, 75–105 (2004)
24. Thuan, N.H., Drechsler, A., Antunes, P.: Construction of design science research questions. Commun. Assoc. Inf. Syst. **44**(1), 20 (2019)
25. Zobel, J.: Writing for Computer Science, 3rd Edn. (2014)
26. Getzels, J.W.: Problem-finding and the inventiveness of solutions. J. Creat. Behav. **9**, 12–18 (1975)
27. Alvesson, M., Sandberg, J.: Generating research questions through problematization. Acad. Manage. Rev. **36**, 247–271 (2011)
28. Heidegger, M.: Basic Writings. HarperCollins, New York (1993)
29. ISO/IEC/IEEE International Standard: Systems and software engineering – Vocabulary. ISO/IEC/IEEE (2010)
30. Association for Project Management: Glossary. https://www.apm.org.uk/body-of-knowledge/glossary/
31. Glinz, M.: A Glossary of Requirements Engineering Terminology (2017)
32. Arazy, O., Kumar, N., Shapira, B.: A theory-driven design framework for social recommender systems. J. Assoc. Inf. Syst. **11**, 455–490 (2010)
33. Meth, H., Mueller, B., Maedche, A.: Designing a requirement mining system. J. Assoc. Inf. Syst. **16**, 799–837 (2015)

Design Archaeology: Generating Design Knowledge from Real-World Artifact Design

Leona Chandra Kruse[(✉)], Stefan Seidel, and Jan vom Brocke

University of Liechtenstein, Vaduz, Liechtenstein
{leona.chandra,stefan.seidel,jan.vom.brocke}@uni.li

Abstract. When formulating prescriptive design knowledge in design science research (DSR), we usually reflect on our vision of created artifacts, relevant design decisions, and what we have learned throughout the design process. Seldom do we attempt to extract prescriptive knowledge from existing and widely acknowledged artifacts in the manner of *ex-post facto* or *in situ*. But what *can* we learn from decades of designing digital artifacts that have fundamentally revamped work processes across industries, allowed for the emergence of new business models, and even spurred entirely new industries? This essay is inspired by the way archaeologists make sense of the past and represent the resulting knowledge. We propose a novel approach to the analysis of digital artifacts based on the archaeological approaches to context reconstruction and artifact analysis. We explain how a design archaeologist can shift among the perspectives of designers, users, and the generated artifact to make inferences about the artifact (i.e., design artifact), how it has been designed (i.e., design process), the context in which it has been designed (i.e., the design context), and the situations in which it has been used (i.e., the use contexts).

Keywords: Design theorizing · Design knowledge · Design science research · Artifact analysis · Archaeology · Information systems

1 Introduction

Compare the two main characters in the following narrative. Primo and Secondo were the sons of a mighty ruler who was determined to teach those without a profession to make good wine. She expressed her wish to both sons and, at the end of their conversation, it became clear that they must go on separate ways. Pluralism of truths was a principle held dearly in their family.

Primo left for Bourgogne and Bordeaux to observe the best winemakers in action. He would also ask them about the past and how their craft of making wine had evolved. Not seldom did he find himself running out of parchment and ink in a lively discussion. Secondo stayed home and established several vineyards that stretched from coast to hill. He enjoyed experimenting with various techniques and different grape varieties. He never failed to keep a daily record of his progress. Time flew since both enjoyed themselves. The mighty ruler found herself scanning through the work of her sons, overwhelmed with multiple visions of possible brighter futures.

© Springer Nature Switzerland AG 2019
B. Tulu et al. (Eds.): DESRIST 2019, LNCS 11491, pp. 32–45, 2019.
https://doi.org/10.1007/978-3-030-19504-5_3

We notice that Primo and Secondo followed two different approaches to acquire the "how to" knowledge (design knowledge) on making exceptional wine. Secondo made wine and tried to make the best his soil would allow him. Primo tasted the most prestigious wines and got his knowledge from the winemakers. He also tasted old wines and learned about the crafts of the past. While the narrative does not tell us how their design knowledge compared with each other, it shows us that design knowledge can indeed be acquired through first-hand experience as well as second-hand experience.

In this essay, we suggest that design science research (DSR) in information systems (IS) should follow the paths of *both* Primo and Secondo. First, it should actively engage in design and evaluation processes in order to generate design knowledge. Second, it should study the artifacts of our past and present to reconstruct the meaning and consequences of their material properties in the various contexts in which they have been used. This will give the DSR field access to a world full of past and present artifacts—a world full of design knowledge. Instead of only including the design of artifacts in the research processes themselves, we suggest to also observe and learn from the design processes taking place in our economy and society and the resulting artifacts that are often exposed to millions of users. This lens is aimed at deriving design knowledge from "naturally occurring" design and evaluation.

Archaeology is the study of (past) human activity through recovering and analyzing artifacts and other physical remains. In analogy, a *design archaeology* in the realm of IS is *the study of design activity by recovering and analyzing digital artifacts;* this, we contend, can provide important insight into key design decisions that were involved in creating these artifacts.

We argue that such view complements the prevailing practice scripts in the DSR field [1] and can help derive design knowledge. The primary purpose of DSR is to formulate prescriptive knowledge about the design of IS artifacts, such as software systems or development methods. The dominant DSR practice script is one where the researcher is at the same time also the designer who develops and experiments with an artifact. Typical stages involve problem identification, objective definition, artifact design, demonstration, and evaluation, followed by the communication of results [2]. Through this process, the researcher makes contributions at different levels of abstraction, ranging from specific instantiations to more abstract knowledge about artifacts that belong to the same class—typically expressed in terms of design princi-ples [3–5] or design theory [3, 6–8]. An archaeological approach to design science holds a number of promises:

- There is a wide range of problem and solution spaces that can be explored to identify underlying principles. Once the design process has been completed, these are *problem spaces of the past.* The design science researcher is thus challenged to reconstruct the design context to be able to understand salient design decisions.
- Industry practitioners often possess years of experience in designing artifacts and are thus invaluable sources of information about design.
- The identified abstract principles underlying existing designs can also be applied in other contexts, contributing to solving a broader class of problems.

- Observing real-world designs in their past and present contexts allows for cross-sectional as well as longitudinal studies and can provide insights about specific design decisions that may have eventually led to its success or failure.
- Finally, DSR has been described as difficult and effortful to conduct. Studying real-world design may open the community toward those who wish to contribute to the derivation of design knowledge, capitalizing on their interest and experience in other research traditions. This, in turn, can foster the development of knowledge in order to tackle relevant societal problems.

We proceed as follows. The next section discusses the theoretical background in terms of IT/IS artifacts, artifacts-in-use, and design knowledge. We then highlight some relevant insights from the field of archaeology, which we then draw upon to devise our approach to design archaeology in IS research.

2 Artifacts and Design Knowledge

2.1 On the Notion of *Artifact* in IS and DSR

While design can be considered universal, the product is usually context related—which is why semiotics or the interpretation of meaning are indispensable [9]. Consequently, we need to define the notion of *artifact* in the context of IS and DSR. A classic definition in any discussion about this notion is that of Simon [10]:

> "my dictionary defines "artificial" as, "produced by art rather than by nature; not genuine or natural; affected; not pertaining to the essence of the matter" (p. 4).

Recent discussions called for more clarity in defining IS artifacts, in order to reduce confusion between the terms IT artifact and IS artifact [e.g., 11, 12]. Lee et al. [12] redefined the notion of IS artifact as "a system, in which the whole (the IS artifact) is greater than the sum of its parts (the IT artifact, the social artifact and the information artifact), where the constituents are not separate, but interactive, as are any subsystems that form a larger system" (p. 9).

With specific focus on DSR, several scholars have also elaborated on the notion of artifact in a DSR project [5, 13–15]. This essay, however, will follow the categorization proposed by Gregor and Hevner [16] that highlights the different levels of abstraction DSR studies can produce: design theory (abstract level), nascent design theory (intermediate level), and tangible end products, such as a software or process (specific level). Many, if not most of, the tangible end products produced through a DSR endeavor take a digital form. For the rest of the essay, we refer to this category of DSR artifacts as **"digital artifacts"** (i.e., artifacts at the specific level). When referring to the more abstract category of DSR artifacts, we use the term **"design knowledge"** (i.e., artifacts at the intermediate and abstract level).

2.2   On Artifacts and Artifacts-in-Use

The literature in Information Systems, Interaction Design, and Digital Humanities is rich in describing the notion of digital artifacts. Consider the following definition: "By digital artifact we mean existing as well as potential types of physical product that delivers digital contents through its interactive features" [17, p. 154].

What is interesting about this definition is its distinction between digital contents and their carriers. It also implies that digital artifacts possess some characteristics or attributes that distinguish them from their non-digital counterparts. The following attributes have been suggested in Kallinikos et al. [18]: digital artifacts are (1) editable, (2) interactive, (3) open or reprogrammable, and (4) distributed. While physical artifacts have fixed forms that are difficult to change, digital artifacts can be acted upon and modified continuously by a human agent or even another digital artifact (such as a program).

However, artifacts are first and foremost outcomes of design that communicate designers' intentions and fulfill sets of requirements. They become more meaningful when analyzed *in situ*, as artifact-in-use or technology-in-use. If the context cannot be readily observed, it is necessary for the design researcher to reconstruct this context—only then she can understand the meaning of the digital artifact in terms of its physical and digital materialities. The important question is, however, when should we wear the "designer hat" in analyzing an artifact and when to wear the "user hat." It is important to note that some users are also creators of their own applications (e.g., spreadsheets) and information items, a phenomenon dubbed as secondary design [19]. Nevertheless, considering a more designerly point of view can be fruitful.

We can also decompose the notion of digital artifact into its modular layered components [20] or revisit artifact-related concepts we often use interchangeably and clearly identify which is our object of study. Despite the common use of the term IT/IS artifact in relation to design (for instance, in conceptualizing IS artifact [e.g., 12]), Iivari [21, p. 761] argues that "IS artifact is not necessarily an appropriate unit of design" and suggests the concept of "IS application as the design nexus"—consistent with the notion of artifact-in-use. The implications for the overall idea of this essay are summarized in three points:

- Digital artifacts include digital contents and digital applications that can be analytically separated for the purpose of interpretation.
- Digital artifacts can be treated as standalone products or as artifacts-in-use.
- Digital artifacts need to be studied in their context of development and use.

2.3   On Design Knowledge

Design knowledge is "knowledge that can be used to produce designs" [22, p. 9]. In other words, it is the "knowledge about creating other instances of artifacts that belong to the same class" [5, p. 39]. We can also view design knowledge as a manifestation of the theory for design and action, that "says how to do something [...] gives explicit prescriptions (e.g., methods, techniques, principles of form and function) for constructing an artifact" [23, p. 620]. Knowledge is beyond information, as it incorporates agency and purpose [24]. Consequently, deriving design knowledge is a far more complex activity compared to simply gathering information.

Design knowledge in DSR is the result from processes of reflection and abstraction, where the design researcher applies different types of reasoning to identify mental causes (i.e., the designer's vision), active causes (how the artifact produces an outcome), and passive causes (how the artifact offers affordances that are identified and enacted by users) [25].

Resulting from such processes of abstraction and reflection is design knowledge in different forms and at various levels of abstraction. With regards to the form of representing design knowledge, the notion of design theory [3, 6–8] has gained some prominence in the IS field, and various design theories have been proposed such as for IT support for emergent knowledge processes [26], secure information systems design methods [27], green information systems [28], and sensemaking support systems [4], all of which represent classes of digital artifacts—these theories are abstractions that provide prescriptive statements in relation to a set of boundary conditions. Another, more atomic form of design knowledge is that of a design principle, and typically scholars develop sets of design principles in order to say something about the design of a class of digital artifacts [29]. Design principles are prescriptive statements and are a key element of design theory [6].

3 Insights from Archaeological Approaches

3.1 Discourse on Archaeology and Digitization

What has archaeology got to do with IS and digital artifacts? Recent development in archaeology points out several themes that are similar to the contemporary discourse on digital artifacts in the IS field. The widespread digitization of data and infrastructure has led to the rise of digital archaeology, sometimes also referred to as cyber archaeology and virtual archaeology [30]. This phenomenon has been described as follows: "archaeologists are creating multimedia experiences of the past, directly authored by archaeologists collaborating with stakeholders, and these experiences are available to anyone with a connection to the Internet" [31, p. 521].

Recent discussion in digital archaeology has been moving toward how to do archaeology digitally [e.g., 32–34]. Recording archaeological data digitally, for instance, results in increased transparency because stakeholders can view generated data during the excavation and can participate in post-excavation artifacts analysis. Finally, digital media enrich the representation of artifacts. IS researchers in related fields have contributed significantly in this area, appropriating augmented reality in museums and exhibitions [e.g., 35, 36] and developing interpretive archaeology systems [e.g., 37, 38]. We conclude that digital archaeology views digital technologies as artifacts, exploration and analytical tools, as well as representation media and infrastructures.

3.2 On the Interpretation of Meaning

The classical definition of archaeology still rings true today: "Archaeology is the study of human history and prehistory through the excavation of sites and the analysis of artifacts and other physical remains" (Oxford Dictionary). In other words, the interpretation of meaning occupies a central role in all archaeological endeavors [40]. In what follows, we highlight four general features of archaeological approaches that are relevant to the purpose of this essay.

First, archaeology is about *using and investigating meaning of material signs in order to produce knowledge* [39]. Note that producing knowledge is the purpose of any archaeological endeavor. It its simplest form, knowledge is knowing what a sign (e.g., an object, a word, a gesture) means—that is, through semiotic analysis. Semiotics occupy a central role in present-day interpretive archaeological practice [38, 40]. Among the widely adopted approaches is Peirce's sign-interpretant-object triad [39]. This focus on semiotic analysis of material artifacts is consistent with the focus of the IS field on material artifacts, both in terms of physical and digital components [41, 42].

Second, *artifact analysis occupies a fundamental role in archaeological endeavors*: "In order to find an answer to the question 'what is this thing?'—a question posed when curious remains or ruins were found—scientists created a new science: archaeology" [43, p. 41]. Some approaches in IS also study artifacts in situ (e.g., works on technology-in-practice and sociomateriality [44]), proposing that digital technologies get their meaning from their context of use.

Third, archaeological endeavors are aimed towards *reconstruction of the past*. When we interpret objects, we are actually trying to find out how people engaged with those objects in the past [39]. Such reconstruction of contextual factors becomes particularly challenging in the context of emergent information technologies characterized by multilayered architectures providing the basis for the emergence, evolution, and at times disruptive change of digital ecosystems [20]. The context is a different context at potentially every point in time.

Fourth, it is *not only about looking backward, but also about looking forward* at how we use objects today and what meaning they possess in the present that can be projected into the future [39]. This feature is in sync with what Peirce once argued: "Whatever is truly general refers to the indefinite future, for the past contains only a certain collection of such cases that have occurred. The past is actual fact. But a general law cannot be fully realized. It is a potentiality; and its mode of being is esse in futuro" [45, p. 414]. This understanding is key for IS and for the sciences of the artificial in general.

4 Towards an Archaeology of Digital Artifacts

4.1 Four Analytical Dimensions

IS researchers tend to describe the roles of artifacts in organizations from the perspective of sociotechnical systems (STS) [46–48] or Neo-STS [49]. This perspective views organizations as consisting of interdependent and interconnected social systems (knowledgeable human actors and social structures) and technical systems (artifacts connected in a functional and meaningful system). Artifacts are viewed as tools if a study focuses on their instrumental aspects, or as ornaments, if the focus is on their symbolic aspects [50]. On this view, the instrumental perspective requires to attend to the digital artifact in its context of use. Although often downplayed, understanding the aesthetic aspects of artifacts is an integral part of artifact analysis [51, 52]. Integrating these prior works, we adopt four analytical dimensions [51] for design archaeologists:

- **Historical dimension:** When analyzing an artifact we need to consider the context that surrounds its production and conception in the past. This dimension includes organizational context, social context, and other boundary conditions.
- **Instrumental dimension:** This dimension specifies the extent to which the artifact contributes to performance or to promoting goals. Artifacts can be evaluated as to how well they help users accomplish their goals.
- **Aesthetic dimension:** The aesthetics of an artifact refer to the sensory experience (both formal and sensory) when encountering and using it.
- **Symbolic dimension:** The symbolic dimension of an artifact represents the meanings or associations that are elicited when interacting with the artifact. Symbolism is contextual and is based on subjective interpretation made by users.

4.2   Aspects of Design and Usage

In interpreting the meaning of artifacts, archaeologists differentiate among various aspects. The three-step cognitive is a widely recognized approach in archaeological artifact analysis that follows Peircean semiotic. At the level of the artifact analysis (the "physical find analysis" in archaeology, compared to the "excavation site analysis"), it can be described as follows [43, p. 50]:

- Acquisition: perception, description, recording, coding intrinsic information
- Structuration: partition
- Object reconstitution: intrinsic and extrinsic added explanations

Intrinsic knowledge is "information perceived by an archaeologist about an artifact, formalizing a (and not the) representation of this artifact" (p. 43). The resulting knowledge is shaped by the cognitive interaction between the archaeologist and the artifact. Extrinsic information is recorded from the context of the artifact and results from the precision of an excavation. Intrinsic knowledge can be broadly distinguished into the appearance (design) aspects and the usage aspects.

The "appearance aspect" covers size, material, color, texture, and the underlying technology. It captures the materiality of digital artifacts which can be understood as having a certain degree of durability [53], combining physical and digital elements [41]. The usage aspect relates the digital artifact to its context, including the purpose of the artifact. It highlights the need for a perspective of the artifact-in-use.

Certain properties of digital artifacts impact on how users perceive, interpret, and interact with this technology, and thus impact on the social construction of meaning [48]. These are the symbolic expressions of the technology—its communicative possibilities (sic). What specifically the artifact affords its users depends on the context, including the specific action goals pursued in that context.

4.3   Anticipated and Unanticipated Consequences

Designers when conceiving of digital artifacts imbue the artifact with their vision—their idea of how the artifact should solve a problem or class of problems. Digital artifacts are technologies and as such they always have purpose [10, 54].

There is some agreement in IS research that digital artifacts are not deterministic in the sense that they bring about specific results with certainty [55]. Instead, they are seen as deeply embedded in organizational practice. They provide opportunities for change [56], they provide spaces for organizational action, now typically captured through the notion of affordance [48, 55, 57], and they may impact beyond the envisioned effect boundaries [58].

As a consequence, an archaeology of digital artifacts must attend to both the anticipated and unanticipated consequences of IT adoption and use. The relevance of this perspective is highlighted by the understanding that digital artifacts are malleable and are increasingly part of digital ecosystems which are characterized by emergence, change, and combinatorial innovation [20]. It is noteworthy that by "unanticipated" we do not mean "negative." Many of the consequences of Internet based technologies such as in the sphere of social media were unintended, but have indeed spurred the development of entirely new revenue streams and even industries.

While the designer perspective can only provide insight into anticipated consequences, the user perspective may do both. Still, it is always possible that there are differences between designer intentions and what the user sees in an artifact and its use [59], the analysis of which can provide important insight into how artifacts should be designed if the design archaeologist pays attention to those unanticipated uses.

4.4   Specifying the Unit of Analysis

Clearly, the design archaeologist is confronted with a complex situation when reconstructing the design of artifacts in contemporary organizing, calling for a decomposition of this analytical problem. She needs to clearly define the unit and level of her analysis. First, we contend it to be a strength of an archaeological perspective on design to be potentially able to consider different points of view. The design archaeologist thus needs to decide whether she wants to follow the perspective of the creator/designer or the user of the artifact. This consideration also determines whom to collect empirical data from.

Second, basic assumptions about the nature of the artifact need to be clarified—is it viewed as a static product or a dynamic object that changes across use contexts? In any case we can assume a certain durability and relative stability [60] that makes the artifact amenable for analysis. Finally, the design archaeologist may attend to different material aspects of the digital artifact—most notably its content versus its underlying logics such as algorithms or presentation to users. These can be analytically separated for the purpose of interpretation.

5   A Framework for Design Theorizing from Artifacts

Grounded in our understanding of digital artifacts, design knowledge, and insights from archaeology, we now describe a framework for design theorizing from artifacts. An archaeology of digital artifacts must (1) attend to various analytical dimensions (aesthetic, symbolic, historical, instrumental); (2) consider both aspects of appearance and function; (3) explore both intended and unintended consequences; and (4) be clear about the unit and level of analysis, in terms of points of view (designer vs. user), assumptions, and contents. Together, these dimensions allow us to view the artifact in context and reconstruct its meaning—and in turn derive abstract knowledge about the artifact/class of artifacts. Figure 1 summarizes these ideas.

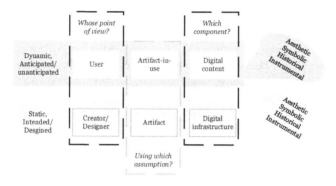

Fig. 1. Towards a design archaeology

We can continue to suggest a set of design principles or guidelines about how to conduct archaeology of digital artifacts:

First, the design archaeologist choses the relevant points of view, assumptions, and components. For instance, she might be interested in how designers and users conceive of an artifact-in-use. From the designer's perspective she may ask what practices the designer envisioned. From a user's perspective she may ask what practices the artifact *actually* allowed for—and why.

Second, the design archaeologist will consider both the appearance of the artifact of interest and its functional aspects. It is necessary to consider simultaneously both dimensions in order to recreate the meaning users assigned to the artifact in context—as well as to consider the designer intentions.

Third, the design archaeologist will consider the digital artifact in focus in terms of instrumental, historical, symbolic, and aesthetic dimensions to construct a holistic understanding that allows her to reconstruct the artifact's meaning in context—including its purpose, performance, and outcomes.

Finally, she will attend to both the intended and unintended consequences and will aim to relate these to the specific design features and underlying design decisions. This approach carries the potential to understand and distinguish "good" design from "bad" design. At the same time, it may reveal unintended positive effects—if the underlying design decisions are understood this can have important implications for the practice of design. At the same time, this approach may help avoid situations where the archaeology of a design artifact only confirms what practitioners already knew.

Next, we illustrate an application of these principles in the analysis of a particular stress management mobile application.

6 Illustrative Example

One of the coauthors of this essay, in a team of researchers, has conducted an analysis of available mobile applications (apps) that help users to cope with stress [61]. They began with both systematic sampling of apps from major application stores and snowball sampling using reference from online articles on digital stress management. After several screenings, they ended up with more than 100 apps for further analysis. They wanted to find out the theoretical basis for each stress management approach that has been operationalized in the apps. It was clear that they were interested in identifying the intention of the designers of each app. Consequently, the analysis concerned only the anticipated consequences. The following is an excerpt of the analysis protocol for a particular anonymized app as a means of illustration.

- **Digital artifact:** An AI counsellor app.
- **Whose point of view:** They took the designer perspective.
- **Using which assumption:** They assumed the app as a static artifact.
- **Which component:** They were mainly concerned with the content of the app.
- **Instrumental dimension:** The AI counsellor can converse naturally with users. Users can share their thoughts, feelings, and experience in an anonymous, neutral setting and receive uplifting responses from their personal AI counsellor. Users can release their anxiety and plan appropriate mitigation mechanisms. The mitigation mechanisms range from simple daily reminders of activities or events that users have claimed to elicit positive emotions to a step-by-step guide to relaxation.
- **Aesthetics dimension:** Clean layout dominated by bluish green tones. The AI counsellor is represented as a friendly-looking penguin that changes its facial expressions and gestures according to the context of the conversation. The space designed for user interaction with the counsellor looks similar to conventional chat windows.
- **Symbolic dimension:** The penguin character has juvenile features (cuteness) that symbolize openness, friendliness, honesty, non-judgmental attitude, and sincerity. It is expected to make users feel safe within their comfort zone and free to voice their inner thoughts. The conventionally designed chat window lets users feel familiar as if they were talking to a best friend. The color scheme has a calming effect.
- **Historical dimension:** The app was developed as an unexpected outcome of a research project that originally aimed to build machine learning models to detect depression, using sensor feeds from the phone.
- **Unanticipated consequence:** Due to high user acceptance, the mobile app has been used to coach both parents and children in bullying issues.

From the excerpt we see that the principles of design archaeology work well for the analysis of a single artifact. The researchers repeated the same procedure for all apps in the sample to make sense of each of them individually. The design archaeology of individual artifacts was then followed by a cross-case analysis, where they tried to discern similarities and differences among the tools and identify their underlying support mechanisms (consult [61] for a further account on the study).

7 Discussion and Conclusion

This essay takes a step towards a design archaeology in Information Systems DSR. Our analysis is based on the differentiation between (1) digital artifacts as deployed, contextual, and observable configurations of physical and digital materialities and (2) design knowledge as (abstract) knowledge about these artifacts and their construction. We further attend to the context-specificity of digital artifacts, both in terms of past contexts and present contexts. We thus suggest that an analysis of digital artifacts with the purpose of generating abstract design knowledge needs to be an analysis across contexts and across time.

Drawing on insights from the field of archaeology, we suggest that a design archaeology of digital artifacts must consider key analytical dimensions in terms of historical, instrumental, symbolic, and aesthetic dimensions; (1) define the level of analysis including different viewpoints such as designer and user; (2) attend to both functional and symbolic properties of the artifact in its context(s) of use; and (3) attend to both anticipated (intended) and unanticipated (unintended) consequences—both negative and positive.

What we discuss in this essay should be seen as a preliminary step toward a more comprehensive design archaeology approach and its application in DSR research and reporting practice. We identify several important directions for future works. First, we aim to come up with a hands-on framework or template of design archaeology for DSR researchers. Second, we imagine that guidance on how to integrate the results of design archaeology into the DSR body of work would be useful in accommodating diversity in DSR-related publications. Third, we deem it important to discuss the whole spectrum of design archaeology, for instance, how to integrate the analysis of individual artifacts and find patterns to make sense of classes of artifacts.

Summing up, we contend that the systematic observation of designed artifacts and their deployment in organizational and inter-organizational contexts can add an important methodological approach to the toolbox of DSR researchers. The exploration of artifact performances and outcomes that transcend the defined boundary conditions in particular—and the study of how these effects are related to specific design features and design decisions—may create important insight and further our knowledge about the design of digital artifacts. Studying real-world designs of the past and present may open the DSR community towards more like-minded colleagues contributing to the derivation of design knowledge, specifically those with an interest and experience in conducting empirical research. This, in turn, may lead to an increase in contributions to the field, and thus can foster knowledge on solving relevant problems of society.

Acknowledgement. This research is funded by the Research Fund of the University of Liechtenstein (Forschungsförderungsfonds der Universität Liechtenstein).

References

1. Goldkuhl, G., Sjöström, J.: Design science in the field: practice design research. In: Chatterjee, S., Dutta, K., Sundarraj, R.P. (eds.) DESRIST 2018. LNCS, vol. 10844, pp. 67–81. Springer, Cham (2018). https://doi.org/10.1007/978-3-319-91800-6_5
2. Peffers, K., Tuunanen, T., Rothenberger, M.A., Chatterjee, S.: A design science research methodology for information systems research. J. Manage. Inf. Syst. **24**, 45–77 (2007)
3. Baskerville, R., Pries-Heje, J.: Explanatory design theory. Bus. Inf. Syst. Eng. **5**, 271–282 (2010)
4. Seidel, S., Chandra Kruse, L., Székely, N., Gau, M., Stieger, D.: Design principles for sensemaking support systems in environmental sustainability transformations. Eur. J. Inf. Syst. **27**, 221–247 (2018)
5. Sein, M.K., Henfridsson, O., Purao, S., Rossi, M., Lindgren, R.: Action design research. MIS Q. **35**, 37–56 (2011)
6. Gregor, S., Jones, D.: The anatomy of a design theory. J. Assoc. Inf. Syst. **8**, 312–335 (2007)
7. Walls, J.G., Widmeyer, G.R., El Sawy, O.A.: Building an information system design theory for vigilant EIS. Inf. Syst. Res. **3**, 36–59 (1992)
8. Walls, J.G., Widmeyer, G.R., El Sawy, O.A.: Assessing information system design theory in perspective: how useful was our 1992 initial rendition? J. Inf. Technol. Theor. Appl. **6**, 43–58 (2004)
9. Latour, B.: A cautious prometheus? A few steps toward a philosophy of design (with special attention to Peter Sloterdijk). In: Proceedings of the 2008 Annual International Conference of the Design History Society, pp. 2–10 (2008)
10. Simon, H.: The Sciences of the Artificial. MIT Press, Cambridge (1996)
11. Alter, S.: The concept of 'IT artifact' has outlived its usefulness and should be retired now. Inf. Syst. J. **25**, 47–60 (2015)
12. Lee, A.S., Thomas, M., Baskerville, R.L.: Going back to basics in design science: from the information technology artifact to the information systems artifact. Inf. Syst. J. **25**, 5–21 (2015)
13. Hevner, A.R., Chatterjee, S.: Design Research in Information Systems. Springer, New York (2010). https://doi.org/10.1007/978-1-4419-5653-8
14. Hevner, A.R., March, S.T., Park, J.: Design science in information systems research. MIS Q. **28**, 75–105 (2004)
15. Iivari, J.: Distinguishing and contrasting two strategies for design science research. Eur. J. Inf. Syst. **24**, 107–115 (2015)
16. Gregor, S., Hevner, A.R.: Positioning and presenting design science research for maximum impact. MIS Q. **37**, 337–355 (2013)
17. Jung, H., Stolterman, E.: Material probe: exploring materiality of digital artifacts. In: Proceedings of the 5th International Conference on Tangible, Embedded, and Embodied Interaction, pp. 153–156. ACM (2011)
18. Kallinikos, J., Aaltonen, A., Marton, A.: The ambivalent ontology of digital artifacts. MIS Q. **37**, 357–370 (2013)
19. Germonprez, M., Hovorka, D., Gal, U.: Secondary design: a case of behavioral design science research. J. Assoc. Inf. Syst. **12**, 662–683 (2011)

20. Yoo, Y., Henfridsson, O., Lyytinen, K.: Research commentary—the new organizing logic of digital innovation: an agenda for information systems research. Inf. Syst. Res. **21**, 724–735 (2010)
21. Iivari, J.: Information system artefact or information system application: that is the question. Inf. Syst. J. **27**, 753–774 (2017)
22. Van Aken, J.E.: Management research based on the paradigm of the design sciences: the quest for field-tested and grounded technological rules. J. Manage. Stud. **41**, 219–246 (2004)
23. Gregor, S.: The nature of theory in information systems. MIS Q. **30**, 611–642 (2006)
24. Friedman, K.: Creating design knowledge: from research into practice. In: Design and Technology Educational Research and Curriculum Development: The Emerging International Research Agenda, p. 31 (2001)
25. Gregor, S., Müller, O., Seidel, S.: Reflection, abstraction, and theorizing in design and development research. In: Proceedings of the 21st European Conference on Information Systems, Utrecht (2013)
26. Markus, M.L., Majchrzak, A., Gasser, L.: A design theory for systems that support emergent knowledge processes. MIS Q. **26**, 179–212 (2002)
27. Siponen, M., Baskerville, R., Heikka, J.: A design theory for secure information systems design methods. J. Assoc. Inf. Syst. **7**, 725–770 (2006)
28. Recker, J.: Toward a design theory for green information systems. In: Proceedings of the 49th Hawaii International Conference on System Sciences, pp. 4474–4483. IEEE (2016)
29. Chandra, L., Seidel, S., Gregor, S.: Prescriptive knowledge in IS research: conceptualizing design principles in terms of materiality, action, and boundary conditions. In: Proceedings of the 48th Hawaii International Conference on System Sciences, pp. 4039–4084. IEEE (2015)
30. Jones, Q.: Virtual-communities, virtual settlements & cyber-archaeology: a theoretical outline. J. Comput. Mediated Commun. **3**, JCMC331 (1997)
31. Morgan, C., Eve, S.: DIY and digital archaeology: what are you doing to participate? World Archaeol. **44**, 521–537 (2012)
32. Daly, P., Evans, T.L.: Digital Archaeology: Bridging Method and Theory. Routledge, New York (2004)
33. Costopoulos, A.: Digital archeology is here (and has been for a while). Frontiers **3**, 1 (2016)
34. Eve, S.: Digital applications and new media. In: Tsipopoulou, M. (ed.) Archaeological practice and management in digital heritage in the new knowledge management: shared spaces and open paths to cultural content. Directorate of the National Archive of Monuments, Athens (2008)
35. Chang, K.-E., Chang, C.-T., Hou, H.-T., Sung, Y.-T., Chao, H.-L., Lee, C.-M.: Development and behavioral pattern analysis of a mobile guide system with augmented reality for painting appreciation instruction in an art museum. Comput. Educ. **71**, 185–197 (2014)
36. Sommerauer, P., Müller, O.: Augmented reality in informal learning environments: a field experiment in a mathematics exhibition. Comput. Educ. **79**, 59–68 (2014)
37. Monod, E., Klein, H., Missikoff, O., Isari, D.: Cultural heritage systems evaluation and design: the virtual heritage center of the city of Rome. In: Proceedings of the 12th Americas Conference on Information systems (2006)
38. Monod, E., Klein, H.K.: From ehertitage to interpretive archaeology systems (IAS): a research framework for evaluating cultural heritage communication in the digital age. In: Proceedings of the 13th European Conference on Information Systems (2005)
39. Bauer, A.A.: Is what you see all you get? Recognizing meaning in archaeology. J. Soc. Archaeol. **2**, 37–52 (2002)
40. Preucel, R.W.: Archaeological Semiotics. Blackwell Publishing, Oxford (2006)

41. Leonardi, P.M.: Materiality, sociomateriality, and socio-technical systems: what do these terms mean? How are they related? Do we need them? In: Leonardi, P.M., Nardi, B.A., Kallinikos, J. (eds.) Materiality and Organizing: Social Interaction in a Technological World, pp. 25–48. Oxford University Press, Oxford (2012)
42. Orlikowski, W.J., Iacono, C.S.: Research commentary: desperately seeking the "IT" in IT research—a call to theorizing the IT artifact. Inf. Syst. Res. **12**, 121–134 (2001)
43. Djindjian, F.: Artefact analysis. In: Proceedings of CAA (2000)
44. Scott, S.V., Orlikowski, W.J.: Entanglement in practice: performing anonymity through social media. MIS Q. **38**, 873–893 (2014)
45. Keane, W.: Semiotics and the social analysis of material things. Lang. Commun. **23**, 409–425 (2003)
46. Robey, D., Anderson, C., Raymond, B.: Information technology, materiality, and organizational change: a professional odyssey. J. Assoc. Inf. Syst. **14**, 379–398 (2013)
47. Sarker, S., Chatterjee, S., Xiao, X.: How "sociotechnical" is our IS research? An assessment and possible ways forward. In: Proceedings of the 34th International Conference on Information Systems (2013)
48. Markus, M.L., Silver, M.S.: A foundation for the study of IT effects: a new look at DeSanctis and Poole's concepts of structural features and spirit. J. Assoc. Inf. Syst. **9**, 609–632 (2008)
49. Winter, S., Berente, N., Howison, J., Butler, B.: Beyond the organizational 'container': conceptualizing 21st century sociotechnical work. Inf. Organ. **24**, 250–269 (2014)
50. Kaghan, W.N., Lounsbury, M.: Artifacts, articulation work and institutional residue. In: Rafaeli, A., Pratt, M.G. (eds.) Artifacts and Organizations: Beyond Mere Symbolism, pp. 279–289. Lawrence Erlbaum Associates Inc., New Jersey (2006)
51. Rafaeli, A., Vilnai-Yavetz, I.: Emotion as a connection of physical artifacts and organizations. Organ. Sci. **15**, 671–686 (2004)
52. Baskerville, R.L., Kaul, M., Storey, V.C.: Aesthetics in design science research. Eur. J. Inf. Syst. **27**, 1–14 (2018)
53. Faulkner, P., Runde, J.: The social, the material, and the ontology of non-material technological objects. Documento de trabajo (2010)
54. Arthur, W.B.: The Nature of Technology: What it is and How it Evolves. Simon and Schuster, New York (2009)
55. Leonardi, P.M.: When flexible routines meet flexible technologies: affordance, constraint, and the imbrication of human and material agencies. MIS Q. **35**, 147–168 (2011)
56. Barley, S.R.: Technology as an occasion for structuring: evidence from observations of CT scanners and the social order of radiology departments. Adm. Sci. Q. **31**(1), 78–108 (1986)
57. Zammuto, R.F., et al.: Information technology and the changing fabric of organization. Organ. Sci. **18**, 749–762 (2007)
58. Watson, R., Seidel, S.: Three strategies for information systems research in the presence of an efficient knowledge market. In: Proceedings of the 39th International Conference on Information Systems (2018)
59. DeSanctis, G.P., Poole, M.S.: Capturing the complexity in advanced technology use: adaptive structuration theory. Organ. Sci. **5**, 121–147 (1994)
60. Faulkner, P., Runde, J.: Technological objects, social positions, and the transformational model of social activity. MIS Q. **37**, 803–818 (2013)
61. Agogo, D., Kruse, L.C.: Open Affect-Responsive Systems (OARS): toward personalized AI to beat back the waves of technostress. In: Association for the Advancement of Artificial Intelligence Spring Symposium Series, Palo Alto (2019)

We Need the Open Artefact: Design Science as a Pathway to Open Science in Information Systems Research

Cathal Doyle[(⊠)]🆔, Markus Luczak-Roesch🆔, and Abhinav Mittal

Victoria University of Wellington, Wellington, New Zealand
cathal.doyle@vuw.ac.nz

Abstract. Design science research (DSR) is facing some significant challenges such as how to make the knowledge and artefacts we create more accessible; exclusion from competitive funding schemes that require open practices; and a potential reproducibility crisis if scholars do not have access to everything needed to repeat past research. To help tackle these challenges we suggest that the community should strongly engage with open science, which has been growing in prominence in other fields in recent years. A review of current DSR literature suggests that researchers have not yet discussed how open science practices can be adopted within the field. Thus, we propose how the concepts of open science, namely open access, open data, open source, and open peer review, can be mapped to a DSR process model. Further, we identify an emerging concept, the open artefact, which provides an opportunity to make artefacts more accessible to practice and scholars. The aim of this paper is to stimulate a discussion amongst researchers about these open science practices in DSR, and whether it is a necessary step forward to keep the pace of the changing academic environment.

Keywords: Design science research · Open science · Open access ·
Open data · Open source · Open peer review · Open artefact ·
DSR process model

1 Introduction

Baskerville [1] states that at its core, design science research (DSR) is *"directed toward understanding and improving the search among potential components in order to construct an artefact that is intended to solve a problem"*. Thus, DSR can be understood as follows. First a relevant problem to practice must be identified [2, 3]. An artefact should then be designed, built, and evaluated for its usefulness at solving the problem [3, 4]. This leads to contributions that should be communicated, resulting in new knowledge for practice, and the knowledge base [5]. However, DSR is facing significant challenges related to limited accessibility of knowledge and artefacts produced: First, the often emphasised goal to be particularly impactful for practice [3] is hardly achievable if knowledge and artefacts are not easily accessible. Second, DSR will soon be precluded from most competitive funding schemes that require open practices to be eligible for funding [6, 7]. Third, the field is in danger of a reproducibility crisis if scholars do not have access to everything needed to repeat past research.

© Springer Nature Switzerland AG 2019
B. Tulu et al. (Eds.): DESRIST 2019, LNCS 11491, pp. 46–60, 2019.
https://doi.org/10.1007/978-3-030-19504-5_4

We therefore suggest that the community should strongly engage with open science (OS), which has been growing in prominence in other fields in recent years. OS refers to making scientific knowledge freely available to the public. The spectrum ranges from simply making published research articles freely available under an open access licence, to requiring researchers to make research data publicly available with their submitted article if it should be considered for publication, to open peer review where both submitted articles (and the related data) as well as expert reviews get persistent identifiers and are publicly accessible for the public to see. To this end, open science provides us with a lens with which we can use to understand researchers approach to the open movement.

This paper aims to stimulate a discussion amongst IS scholars in general and DSR scholars in particular about how open science practices could be adopted within the field, and whether this is a necessary step forward to keep the pace of the changing academic environment. The remainder of the paper is structured as follows: an understanding of open science is presented, creating an OS lens to review current DSR literature. A methodology for gathering this literature is first explained. The lens is then applied to this literature, with an explanation of the findings. This leads to a mapping of OS concepts to a DSR process model, and a new concept, the open artefact, is identified and discussed. A conclusion with some limitations is then presented.

2   Open Science

Traditionally, the scientific process followed by researchers when conducting research consists of identifying a research problem, setting research questions, gathering, analysing and interpreting data, and publishing the results in an academic outlet. This last part of the scientific process, the dissemination of scientific results, has over the centuries developed into a market dominated by a few very large publishers [8, 9]. Scientists follow such protectionist practices because of the pressure to achieve academic merit by publishing the most genuine work first. However, conducting, publishing, and communicating, research has changed drastically with the advent of information technology, and the internet [10, 11] where scientists are no longer restricted by the traditional scientific process [12]. For example, some scientists have adopted more open approaches to their research projects, referred to as open science (OS). Open science is *"the process of making the content and process of producing evidence and claims transparent and accessible to others"* [13]. This is in contrast to how many research projects are currently run, where they often lack openness, with research that is publicly funded not making their results freely available to the general public, and/or data used in the studies not being made accessible either [10, 13]. The former results in the public having to pay twice to gain access to research results, while the latter reduces the verifiability and reproducibility aspect of findings in research. Open science looks to counter these issues by promoting open practices which include: open access; open data; open source; and open peer review [12–15]. More and more tools become available that support different or all stages of the open scientific process including ScienceOpen (open access and scholarly communication and outreach, https://www.scienceopen.com/), Figshare (for research data sharing, https://figshare.com/),

Publons (to reward open peer review, https://publons.com), or the open science framework (OSF, introducing registered reports as an integrated solution covering all stages of the scientific lifecycle, https://osf.io/rr/) [16–20]. In the following sections we review the various concepts of OS.

2.1 Open Access

Open access refers to *"online, peer-reviewed scholarly outputs, which are free to read, with limited or no copyright and licensing restrictions"* [14]. There are two types of OA available: the first is referred to as *"green"* open access, where the article is published in a non-open access journal but has permission to be archived by the researcher to an online repository [21, 22] such as https://arxiv.org/, their own website, or their institutions own repository [23]. This may be available before, or alongside, the publication in the journal, or may have an embargo from the publishers until after the release of the article [21, 22]. The second is referred to as *"gold"* open access, where the article is immediately made available by the publishers in an open access format [14, 22, 23]. Here, the researchers may retain their copyrights, while also licensing their articles with the Creative Commons Attribution license or a similar license [23]. It is suggested that open access can increase the dissemination of a researcher's work, as well as having a bigger impact than paid for articles [21, 24] due to their open availability to the public and researchers [9].

2.2 Open Data

Open data is *"the online publication of the research data gathered during a research project and made available for access and re-use"* [14]. Text, data, and/or meta-data generated during a project can be re-used for other purposes by researchers [24], or used to reproduce, verify, and build on results [25]. The Panton Principles were developed to help with the publishing of open scientific data, and were laid out as follows: 1. When publishing data, make an explicit and robust statement of your wishes; 2. Use a recognised copyright waiver or license that is appropriate for data; 3. If you want your data to be effectively used and added to by others, it should be open as defined by the Open Knowledge/Data Definition - in particular, non-commercial and other restrictive clauses should not be used; 4. Explicit dedication of data underlying published science into the public domain via PDDL (http://opendatacommons.org/licenses/pddl/1-0/) or CCZero (http://creativecommons.org/publicdomain/zero/1.0/) is strongly recommended and ensures compliance with both the Science Commons Protocol for Implementing Open Access Data and the Open Knowledge/Data Definition [25]. While the sharing of data has not been a culture that disciplines have embraced in recent years, there are many advantages that can be gained from doing so, such as accountability, data longevity, efficiency and quality [13]. Further, it is again suggested that by publicly sharing data, citation rates increase [25].

2.3 Open Source

Open source denotes *"software that can be accessed online for free, with a source code license that allows its use, creation of derivatives and distribution"* [14]. From this understanding, there are some key criteria that must be applied: 1. the redistribution of the software must be royalty free; 2. the source code must be released; and 3. any modifications to the source code must be distributed under the same terms as the license of the original software [26]. From a research perspective, this provides an opportunity to make any code developed during a research project freely available for others to reivew, use, or improve upon. There are many open source platforms available for researchers to use, including GitHub and SourceForge. It should also be noted that there is much debate around the terms used to describe open source which is outside of the scope of this project. However, some of these terms include Free Software ("FS"), Open Source Software ("OSS"), Free Open Source Software ("FOSS"), Free Libre Open Source Software ("FLOSS"), Open Code, and nonpro-prietary software - each have their own philosophies and ideologies, and different types of licenses used to distribute the software [27].

2.4 Open Peer Review

There's not yet a precise definition for open peer review as it is an evolving phe-nomena, with many having different views on what it constitutes [15]. Thus there are different aspects to consider. There can be both pre- and post-publication peer review mechanisms. In terms of pre-publication, researchers can share preprints, and receive feedback quickly from a diverse community [13] allowing them to improve on the article before submitting for publication. Post-publication allows for reviewers to make critical commentary on published articles instantly, rather than having to write a commentary and submitting it to a journal [21]. Another aspect is referred to as open identify peer review, which consists of a *"review where authors and reviewers are aware of each other's identities"* [15], where they can communicate with each other about the review, helping to improve the quality of reviews received [13, 15]. This can be taken further, where the actual reviews are also made public alongside the published articles, which can again attract comments from other people.

2.5 An Open Science Lens to Review DSR

While the concept of *"open"* is not new (some date it the Royal Society of London in 1667 to disseminate knowledge), it has grown in importance in more recent times. And it's not just scientists pushing for it, but institutions across the world now require open practices to access their funding opportunities. For example, the European Commission [28] has made it a requirement that any project that receives Horizon 2020 funding must make any peer-reviewed publications openly accessible, while Research Coun-cils UK in the United Kingdom and the National Institutes of Health (NIH) and National Science Foundation (NSF) in the United States, have been putting pressure on researchers to share their data [13, 29]. Thus, with such advancements coming in the way researchers currently conduct and disseminate their research, we use the lens of open science in Fig. 1 to assess DSR literature for its alignment with open science principles and practices. The methodology for collecting the literature for review is explained next.

Fig. 1. Open science lens

3   Methodology

The cornerstone of a good literature review is to apply a conceptual framework that helps to focus it [30]. Bandara et al. [31] offer such a framework, which has been adapted for this literature review. This approach consists of five phases: **1. Selecting the Sources**; **2. Search Strategy**; **3. Coding Schemes**; **4. Article Review**; and **5. Analysis and Write-Up**. Starting with **1. Selecting the Sources:** the researcher(s) must specify the domain of interest for their research, and then identify relevant sources for which articles can be obtained for the literature review. The domain of interest for this research focused on conceptual, methodological, and empirical DSR articles, thus a selection of IS specific sources was sought, which is a scope that has been justified in prior research [31]. The IS specific sources identified are the AIS senior scholars' basket of (eight) journals, and DESRIST, the conference dedicated to DSR studies in IS research.

2. Search Strategy: The next stage involves searching the selected sources. A list of key search terms related to the domain should be identified by the researchers. The key terms identified included "design science", "design science research", and "action design research". Then each source should be searched, identifying articles that contain any of the key search terms in their title, abstract, keywords, or body, creating a pool of articles referred to as iteration 1. For this study Web of Science was used to search each of the basket of eight journals (from 1977–2019), while Springer was used to search DESRIST (from 2010–2018). A total of 184 articles were identified in the basket of eight, and 324 articles in DESRIST (508 in total).

A more detailed review is then required of this initial pool of articles, where the researchers read the title, abstract, body, and keywords to determine if the article is relevant to the domain they want to research, referred to as iteration 2. Such a detailed review was undertaken of the 508 articles. Non-related articles consisted of instances where the researcher(s) biography contained the keywords, or conceptual articles that briefly mention one of the keywords but don't actually talk about the topic (often in the form of the state of IS research). Following this iteration, a final pool of relevant articles is created, which can then be reviewed. This resulted in a total of 155 articles from the basket of eight, and 324 from DESRIST (479 in total). This search strategy was executed by the first researcher, and then a second researcher executed it to ensure reliability. This resulted in iteration 1 having the same results, while iteration 2 had minor discrepancies. For these, the researchers discussed the differences, and came to an agreement on whether the additional articles should be included or not.

3. Coding Schemes: The researcher(s) need to determine what is going to be captured from the articles, which is critical to conduct an effective and efficient literature review [31]. This can consist of predetermined concepts, and/or have the concepts emerge as the researcher is reviewing the articles. This study used the OS lens presented in Fig. 1 to assess the articles. **4. Article Review:** Reviewing the articles through the lens of OS consisted of searching through each article for the concepts of open access, open data, open source, and open peer review (and open science itself), and building a concept matrix. 25 articles from the basket of eight, and 19 from DESRIST (44 in total), contained at least one of these terms. **5. Analysis and Write-Up:** When each article has been reviewed, an understanding of the domain can be presented. This review provides an understanding of OS practices in DSR which is explained next.

4 Paving the Pathway to Open Science in Design Science Research

44 articles were identified as containing at least one of the terms of OS, namely open access, open data, open source, or open peer review (none of the articles contained the term open science). However, from reviewing these articles, it was evident that there was a distinction in the use of the terms. For example, 17 of the articles from the basket of eight mentioned an OS concept, but were not applying it to their DSR process, but instead using them as the focus of their research, i.e. Abbasi et al. [32] discuss open data but from an organisation's perspective. The other 16 articles focused on open source aspects, such as and Germonprez et al. [33] studying corporate engagement with open source communities. A similar trend was observed with the DESRIST articles, where 4 followed the same pattern, such as Hjalmarsson and Rudmark [34] focusing on open data when discussing digital innovation contests, and Malgonde and Hevner [35] studying an open-source software development project. 2 conceptual articles discussed the concept of open access in relation to DSR. The first, Gregor and Hevner [36], state (in the appendix) that *"copyright restrictions on scientific literature that limit open access to the latest journals and conference proceedings without paying access fees"* in relation to the problem for researchers in being able to access knowledge. The second, Samuel-Ojo et al. [37], has one sentence suggesting *"open access can help with citation"* when discussing DESRIST papers that have been cited.

The other 7 articles from the basket of eight referred to the OS concept of open source in relation to their DSR process although did not explicitly state that this was done with OS in mind. For example, two of the articles, Hariharan et al. [38], and Coenen et al. [39], mention that the artefacts that they built were made available on open source platforms. In fact Hariharan et al. [38] go further than just making their artefact available, but also make it so others can replicate the experiments that they implemented, which could also be considered as a form of open peer review. The other five articles stated that they used some form of open source software in the building of their artefacts such as [40]. Similar trends were observed in the 15 DESRIST articles. For example, Kowatsch et al. [41] made their artefact available on an open source platform; and Mustafa et al. [42] used open source components to build their artefact. The concept of open data was also applied in 2 DESRIST articles such as Fedorschak et al. [43] using open data to help design their three artefacts.

Overall, the findings suggest that DSR researchers have not discussed how OS practices could be adopted within the field, and whether this is a necessary step forward to keep the pace of the changing academic environment. Further, no methodological article has discussed how DSR researchers could apply OS practices. And the articles that have applied them do so more implicitly rather than explicitly, i.e. they discuss using open source components to build their artefacts but do not relate this to OS. This provides an excellent opportunity to start this discussion. Thus, the next section discusses how DSR researchers could apply OS practices in their research.

4.1 Mapping Open Science Concepts to DSR Process Models

There are numerous studies in the IS literature that have provided different process models for conducting DSR [4, 44–48]. We focus on three of these: Peffers et al. [4], Kuechler and Vaishnavi [46], and Sein et al. [45], and identify four common steps amongst them: *"Problem Identification"*; *"Design and Build"*; *"Evaluate"*; and *"Contributions"*. This is consistent with Nagle et al. [2], who also identify these four steps as a simplified synthesis of DSR process models. For example, Peffers et al. [4] suggests researchers should start with *"Problem Identification"*, while Kuechler and Vaishnavi [46] have *"Awareness of Problem"*, and Sein et al. [45] have *"Problem Formulation"*. Similarly, Peffers et al. [4] has *"Design and Development"*, Kuechler and Vaishnavi [46] have *"Development"* and Sein et al. [45] have *"Building, Intervention, and Evaluation"*. In terms of evaluation steps, Peffers et al. [4] have *"Evaluation"*, Kuechler and Vaishnavi [46] also have an *"Evaluation"* step, while Sein et al. [45] have evaluation as part of their *"Building, Intervention, and Evaluation"* step. Lastly, Peffers et al. [4] have *"Communication"* as a step, Kuechler and Vaishnavi [46] have *"Conclusion"*, and Sein et al. [45] have *"Formalization of Learning"*.

Presented in Fig. 2 are the concepts of OS mapped to these four process steps. This mapping comes from our understanding of the OS concepts, as well as examples from the DSR literature that we reviewed. We also take a unique approach in terms of our understanding of the OS concepts, where we consider them to offer "input" and "output" opportunities for DSR. For example inputs include using open data to identify a problem; using open source software when developing an artefact; and/or using open peer review for feedback when identifying a problem. Outputs include making different versions of the artefact available on an open source platform; making data used to evaluate the artefact available for others to use; and/or communicating the contributions in an open access publication (these outputs all depend on the permissions researchers have to share such data/knowledge). These are explained in greater detail over the following sections, starting with *"Problem Identification"*.

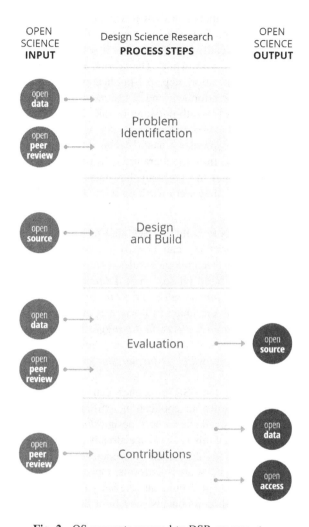

Fig. 2. OS concepts mapped to DSR process steps

Problem Identification: Hevner et al. [49] suggests that DSR should focus on solving real-world problems that practice will benefit from. Peffers et al. [4] defines this step as the *"specific research problem"*. Kuechler and Vaishnavi [46] follow Hevner et al. [49] stating *"a design science research project seeks a solution to a real-world problem of interest to practice"*, while Sein et al. [45] state it as a *"problem perceived in practice or anticipated by researchers"*. Further, while the problem can be identified in practice [46], it can also come from *"end-users, the researchers, existing technologies, and/or review of prior research"* Sein et al. [45]. The problem identification should consist of a problem statement which helps to stimulate the research effort of the researcher(s) and the intended audience [4, 45].

There are two types of OS inputs that DSR researchers can apply when identifying a relevant problem to practice. The first input comes from open data, which DSR researchers can use to help identify a problem worth solving, or to confirm that the problem they are looking at is worthwhile. The second input comes from open peer review. In the problem identification step, pre-publication of the identified problem could be used to give both practitioners and researchers the opportunity to provide critical feedback on whether it is worth pursuing or not. This feedback could come in the form of realigning the focus, or making it clear it is not worth pursuing, or has already been solved. This is particularly useful when a problem has been identified from the literature. An example from the literature is Mustafa et al. [42] who provided an open feedback forum around the problem they identified, so feedback could be gathered from the practitioners they were working with. There are no OS outputs that fit with this step.

Design and Build: DSR seeks to build artefacts that help solve the problem that has been stated [4, 49]. Such artefacts can consist of constructs, models, methods, instantiations, design principles, technological rules, and/or design theories [36]. These get created in the design and build phase, where Peffers et al. [4] defines it as *"determining the artifact's desired functionality and its architecture and then creating the actual artefact"*. Kuechler and Vaishnavi [46] say it is at this step that the *"tentative direction(s) for artifact generation explored in the suggestion phase are made concrete through construction and iterative refinement"*, and Sein et al. [45] state it is the *"initial design of the IT artifact, which is further shaped by organizational use and subsequent design cycles"*.

Open source is an OS input that DSR researchers can apply here. If the artefact(s) to be built is in the form of a software application, DSR researchers can utilise open source software that is freely available to help design and build their artefact(s). The literature review highlighted that this is a practice already adopted by DSR researchers. For example, Schmeil et al. [50] developed two open worlds called UNIworld and ShanghAI, building on two open source platforms, Open Wonderland and OpenSim, respectively. While Meth et al. [40] built an artefact called REMINER, using open source components, along with components they built themselves. There are no OS outputs that fit with this step.

Evaluation: Evaluation consists of evaluating the artefact to see if has achieved its intended goal of solving the identified problem, or not [4, 45]. Peffers et al. [4] describes it as *"observe and measure how well the artifact supports a solution to the problem"*, while Sein et al. [45] state *"evaluation assesses whether the intended outcomes were realized"*. Kuechler and Vaishnavi [46] offer no definition of evaluation. Evaluation can be done in many ways, such as experiments, observations, or field studies, and is dependent on the problem environment and the artefact itself. It is also an iterative step, where the researchers can decide to take the lessons learned and return to the design and build activity to improve the artefact, or they can move to the next activity.

There are two OS inputs that can be adopted here. The first comes from open data, where DSR researchers can use data that is freely available to evaluate their artefacts. For example, Fedorschak et al. [43] collected open data to use to evaluate the three artefacts they built (mixing some of it with proprietary data). The second input is open peer review, which can occur in two ways. First, DSR researchers can make their evaluation process available in a pre-publication review, and have their peers critically evaluate the method. Such reviews could help improve the rigor of the evaluation method (often an area of criticism for DSR research). There was no example from the literature of this being done but it is an important component of OS as it is making one of the steps of the scientific process more transparent. Second, DSR researchers can make their artefact available for practitioners to evaluate, which could be a form of evaluation for the artefact itself. Again, no explicit examples of this was identified in the literature.

There is one OS output from this phase, in the form of open source software. If a researcher develops an artefact in the form of a software application, they can make it available on an open source platform for others to use. This does not have to be the finished artefact, or it can even be a component of it. An example of this is Coenen et al. [39] who developed an information system, making it available on GitHub under the GPL3 license, where it can be downloaded or contributed to.

Contributions: Once the design cycles are complete, the contributions of the study should be communicated to academic and/or practitioner outlets [5, 51]. Contributions can be made in the form of prescriptive and/or descriptive knowledge as material artefacts, or at more abstract levels [36]. Peffers et al. [4, p. 56] define this as *"communicate the problem and its importance, the artifact, its utility and novelty, the rigor of its design, and its effectiveness to researchers and other relevant audiences such as practicing professionals, when appropriate"*. Sein et al. [45] have this step under *"Formalization of Learning"* and describe it as researchers *"outline the accomplishments realized in the IT artifact and describe the organizational outcomes to formalize the learning"*. Kuechler and Vaishnavi [46] have the step *"Conclusion"* in their process model but do not explain what this entails.

There is one OS input that can be adopted. This comes in the form of open peer review, where DSR researcher can make the pre-publication of their articles available for feedback from practitioners and/or researchers. This feedback could then be considered before submitting it for publication (no example was identified from the literature). There are two OS outputs that can be applied. The first output is in the form of open data. Here, DSR researchers can make the data that they generated during their project freely available for others to use. This is already being discussed in the literature where Mustafa and Sjöström [52] propose design principles on how to make such data accessible. This can improve the verifiability and reproducibility of DSR projects. Further, such data could be useful to other researchers in their own studies, improving the reusability of the data. The second OS output comes in the form of open access, where researchers would need to consider whether to go with a "green" or "gold" publisher. In terms of a green publisher, they may publish in a non-open access journal but with the explicit permission that they can archive the article to an online repository. If a "gold" publisher is chosen, the article is immediately made available by the publishers in an open access mode, and the researchers may retain their copyrights.

One observation made while mapping the OS concepts to the DSR process model, was that OS only considers artefacts in the form of software applications. For example, when DSR researchers look to open source platforms in their initial design and build phase, it is only useful if they are developing some form of software artefact.

Further, when they have completed their design cycles, and wish to make their artefact openly available, it is again only possible if they have developed an artefact in the form of an application. However, as has been mentioned, DSR artefacts can be in the form of constructs, models, methods, instantiations, design principles, technological rules, and design theories. Further, if researchers develop an artefact and decide to publish it in a paid for journal, how can they make their artefact(s) available for their intended audiences, i.e. practitioners? It seems counterintuitive to develop an artefact to solve a problem practitioners have, but not make that artefact available for them to use. Thus, the open artefact is an emerging concept needed by DSR researchers wanting to adopt OS practices, and is explained next.

4.2   Open Artefact

While there can be different contributions from DSR studies, one of the most important is that of the artefact. And while we've discussed how DSR researchers can make their publications available through open access practices, there is little discussion on how they can make their artefact(s) openly available for use by academics and practitioners outside of reading these publications. Further, from an OS perspective, only one type of artefact is considered and that comes in the form of software applications made available through open source platforms. However, when the artefact is in a different form, there is no understanding on how it can be made openly available. This has resulted in the emerging concept of the open artefact.

The open artefact can be defined as *"DSR artefacts that can be accessed online for free, with an open license that allows use, inspection, modification and reuse"* (adapted from Pontika et al. [14] and Gill and Hevner [53]). This expands on the concept of open source, to incorporate the other types of DSR artefacts that can be shared in an open way. And by having them openly available, it could help increase the use of the artefact (s) for its intended purposes, and encourage the evolution of the design [53]. It also provides an opportunity for these artefacts to be adapted, and/or applied, in different scenarios than the researcher(s) had intended, leading to the potential of new research opportunities. Lastly, it delivers on one of the goals of DSR, and that is by making the artefact open, knowledge is more accessible to practice.

There is much work required to making the open artefact more practical. First, the open source inputs and outputs in Fig. 2 should be replaced by the open artefact. Second, a valid license needs to be created that researchers can apply when they make their artefacts openly available. This would also have to adhere to the rules that paid for publishers apply when researchers submit their articles for publication, i.e. if you publish a framework you created, do you still have permission to make the artefact openly available? Third, there is also an opportunity to design and develop an open artefact platform that allows DSR researchers to make their artefact(s) available. Such a platform could provide practitioners and researchers with access to these open artefacts when looking at problems in their own organisations or studies. Fourth, it could provide researchers with the feeling that their research is having a real practical impact. In agreement with Gregor and Hevner [36], we believe the open artefact *"could mean that important and relevant work will reach a wider audience, dissemination of which contributes to both research and professional practice"*.

5   Conclusion

The aim of this article is to stimulate a discussion amongst DSR researchers about open science practices in DSR. This is a discussion we believe is necessary, and by providing an understanding of where these OS practices can be adopted into our DSR process models, it is one DSR researchers can start to have, helping to better promote and disseminate scientific knowledge. Further, we believe the open artefact is a necessary step, both from an academic and practitioner view, where they can use, inspect, modify and reuse, this knowledge. From an academic perspective, if artefacts are not made available for inspection, falsification of them is questionable. And that means we enter the philosophy of science space where one could argue that DSR is not scientific (because it is not falsifiable). From a practitioner perspective, by having access to artefacts that have been built to solve real-world problems, they can apply such knowledge to their own problems without the need of having to access, read, and try to understand academic publications. In terms of future research, the suggested DSR process model with OS concepts needs to be applied in a real DSR project, helping to confirm, or improve, the model, and build our understanding of OS in DSR. The open artefact needs to be developed further, and can provide an interesting perspective for the open science community that hasn't yet been considered. Further, building a platform that can host such artefacts, with an open license that allows for it, needs to be developed. There are also some limitations to this study. First, Web of Science does not contain all articles of the journals and conferences in this study. However, the 479 articles used provides a good representation of DSR research. Second, it is possible some articles discussed the concepts of OS without using the terms explicitly. A more detailed review of the literature identified will be required to identify if this is true.

In practicing open science for this study two concepts have been applied. First, a preprint of the article has been made openly available on OSF. OSF provides a digital object identifier (a DOI is a persistent identifier to the content). This preprint can be accessed at https://www.doi.org/10.31219/osf.io/ye6xp. Further, the dataset used has also been made openly available at OSF which can be accessed at https://www.doi.org/10.17605/OSF.IO/3HGQ9. This dataset consists of a concept matrix of the 479 DSR articles that were reviewed, and the evidence for each time an article mentioned one of the OS concepts. It also provides a concept matrix of the 11 articles that were used to build the understanding of the OS concepts, and the evidence that was taken from each of these articles to build this understanding. This dataset can be used by others to validate the findings we have in this study, or can be used for their own projects.

References

1. Baskerville, R.: What design science is not. Eur. J. Inf. Syst. **17**(5), 441–443 (2008)
2. Nagle, T., Sammon, D., Doyle, C.: Insights into practitioner design science research. In: Maedche, A., vom Brocke, J., Hevner, A. (eds.) DESRIST 2017. LNCS, vol. 10243, pp. 414–428. Springer, Cham (2017). https://doi.org/10.1007/978-3-319-59144-5_25
3. Hevner, A.: A three cycle view of design science research. Scand. J. Inf. Syst. **19**(2), 87–92 (2007)

4. Peffers, K., Tuunanen, T., Rothenberger, M.A., Chatterjee, S.: A design science research methodology for information systems research. J. Manage. Inf. Syst. **24**(3), 45–77 (2007)
5. Nagle, T., Sammon, D., Doyle, C.: Meeting in the middle: bridging the practice research divide from both sides. In: ECIS, Research Paper, p. 158 (2016)
6. Wellcome open access policy. https://wellcome.ac.uk/funding/guidance/open-access-policy. Accessed 10 Feb 2019
7. Bill & Melinda Gates Foundation open access policy frequently asked questions. https://www.gatesfoundation.org/How-We-Work/General-Information/Open-Access-Policy/Page-2. Accessed 10 Feb 2019
8. Tennant, J.P., et al.: A multi-disciplinary perspective on emergent and future innovations in peer review. F1000Res. **6**, 1151 (2017)
9. Tennant, J.P., Waldner, F., Jacques, D.C., Masuzzo, P., Collister, L.B., Hartgerink, C.H.: The academic, economic and societal impacts of open access: an evidence-based review. F1000Res. **5**, 632 (2016)
10. Garcia-Penalvo, F.J., García de Figuerola, C., Merlo, J.A.: Open knowledge: challenges and facts. Online Inf. Rev. **34**(4), 520–539 (2010)
11. Demchenko, Y., Zhao, Z., Grosso, P., Wibisono, A., De Laat, C.: Addressing big data challenges for scientific data infrastructure. In: 2012 IEEE 4th International Conference on Cloud Computing Technology and Science (CloudCom), pp. 614–617. IEEE (2012)
12. De Roure, D., et al.: myExperiment: defining the social virtual research environment. In: IEEE Fourth International Conference on eScience, 2008. eScience 2008, pp. 182–189. IEEE (2008)
13. Munafò, M.R., et al.: A manifesto for reproducible science. Nat. Hum. Behav. **1**(1), 0021 (2017)
14. Pontika, N., Knoth, P., Cancellieri, M., Pearce, S.: Fostering open science to research using a taxonomy and an eLearning portal. In: Proceedings of the 15th International Conference on Knowledge Technologies and Data-driven Business, p. 11. ACM (2015)
15. Ross-Hellauer, T.: What is open peer review? A systematic review. F1000Res. **6**, 588 (2017)
16. Chambers, C.D., Dienes, Z., McIntosh, R.D., Rotshtein, P., Willmes, K.: Registered reports: realigning incentives in scientific publishing. Cortex **66**, A1–A2 (2015)
17. Chambers, C.D.: Registered reports: a new publishing initiative at Cortex. Cortex **49**(3), 609–610 (2013)
18. Rajpert-De Meyts, E., Losito, S., Carrell, D.T.: Rewarding peer-review work: the Publons initiative. Andrology **4**(6), 985–986 (2016)
19. Kraker, P., Lex, E., Gorraiz, J., Gumpenberger, C., Peters, I.: Research data explored II: the anatomy and reception of figshare. arXiv preprint arXiv:1503.01298 (2015)
20. Allen, L., Dawson, S.: Scholarly publishing for the network generation. Insights **28**(1), 57–61 (2015)
21. Harnad, S., et al.: The access/impact problem and the green and gold roads to open access. Serials Rev. **30**(4), 310–314 (2004)
22. Fact sheet: Open Access in Horizon 2020. https://ec.europa.eu/programmes/horizon2020/sites/horizon2020/files/FactSheet_Open_Access.pdf. Accessed 08 Feb 2019
23. Bailey Jr., C.W.: Open access bibliography: liberating scholarly literature with e-prints and open access journals. Association of Research Libraries, Washington, DC (2005)
24. Fecher, B., Friesike, S.: Open science: one term, five schools of thought. In: Bartling, S., Friesike, S. (eds.) Opening Science, pp. 17–47. Springer, Cham (2014). https://doi.org/10.1007/978-3-319-00026-8_2
25. Molloy, J.C.: The open knowledge foundation: open data means better science. PLoS Biol. **9**(12), e1001195 (2011)

26. Lerner, J., Tirole, J.: The open source movement: Key research questions. Eur. Econ. Rev. **45**(4–6), 819–826 (2001)
27. González, A.G.: Open science: open source licenses in scientific research. NCJL Tech. **7**, 321 (2005)
28. European Commission website. http://ec.europa.eu/research/openscience/index.cfm?pg= openaccess. Accessed 08 Feb 2019
29. Wasko, M., Teigland, R., Leidner, D., Jarvenpaa, S.: Stepping into the internet: new ventures in virtual worlds. MIS Q. **35**(3), 645–652 (2011)
30. Siponen, M., Willison, R.: A critical assessment of IS security research between 1990–2004. In: ECIS 2007 Proceedings (2007)
31. Bandara, W., Miskon, S., Fielt, E.: A systematic, tool-supported method for conducting literature reviews in information systems. In: ECIS 2011 Proceedings (2011)
32. Abbasi, A., Sarker, S., Chiang, R.H.: Big data research in information systems: toward an inclusive research agenda. J. Assoc. Inf. Syst. **17**(2), 1–32 (2016)
33. Germonprez, M., Kendall, J.E., Kendall, K.E., Mathiassen, L., Young, B., Warner, B.: A theory of responsive design: a field study of corporate engagement with open source communities. Inf. Syst. Res. **28**(1), 64–83 (2016)
34. Hjalmarsson, A., Rudmark, D.: Designing digital innovation contests. In: Peffers, K., Rothenberger, M., Kuechler, B. (eds.) DESRIST 2012. LNCS, vol. 7286, pp. 9–27. Springer, Heidelberg (2012). https://doi.org/10.1007/978-3-642-29863-9_2
35. Malgonde, O., Hevner, A.: Finding evidence for effectual application development on digital platforms. In: Maedche, A., vom Brocke, J., Hevner, A. (eds.) DESRIST 2017. LNCS, vol. 10243, pp. 330–347. Springer, Cham (2017). https://doi.org/10.1007/978-3-319-59144-5_20
36. Gregor, S., Hevner, A.R.: Positioning and presenting design science research for maximum impact. MIS Q. **37**(2), 337–356 (2013)
37. Samuel-Ojo, O., et al.: Meta-analysis of design science research within the IS community: trends, patterns, and outcomes. In: Winter, R., Zhao, J.L., Aier, S. (eds.) DESRIST 2010. LNCS, vol. 6105, pp. 124–138. Springer, Heidelberg (2010). https://doi.org/10.1007/978-3-642-13335-0_9
38. Hariharan, A., et al.: Brownie: a platform for conducting NeuroIS experiments. J. Assoc. Inf. Syst. **18**(4), 264 (2017)
39. Coenen, T., et al.: An information system design theory for the comparative judgement of competences. Eur. J. Inf. Syst. **27**(2), 248–261 (2018)
40. Meth, H., Mueller, B., Maedche, A.: Designing a requirement mining system. J. Assoc. Inf. Syst. **16**(9), 799 (2015)
41. Kowatsch, T., et al.: Design and evaluation of a mobile chat app for the open source behavioral health intervention platform MobileCoach. In: Maedche, A., vom Brocke, J., Hevner, A. (eds.) DESRIST 2017. LNCS, vol. 10243, pp. 485–489. Springer, Cham (2017). https://doi.org/10.1007/978-3-319-59144-5_36
42. Mustafa, M.I., Sjöström, J., Lundström, J.E.: An empirical account of fitness-utility: a case of radical change towards mobility in DSR practice. In: Tremblay, M.C., VanderMeer, D., Rothenberger, M., Gupta, A., Yoon, V. (eds.) DESRIST 2014. LNCS, vol. 8463, pp. 289–303. Springer, Cham (2014). https://doi.org/10.1007/978-3-319-06701-8_19
43. Fedorschak, K., Kandala, S., Desouza, K.C., Krishnamurthy, R.: Data analytics and human trafficking. In: Tremblay, M.C., VanderMeer, D., Rothenberger, M., Gupta, A., Yoon, V. (eds.) DESRIST 2014. LNCS, vol. 8463, pp. 69–84. Springer, Cham (2014). https://doi.org/10.1007/978-3-319-06701-8_5
44. Nunamaker, J.F., Chen, M., Purdin, T.: Systems development in information systems research. J. Manage. Inf. Syst. **7**(3), 89–106 (1990)

45. Sein, M., Henfridsson, O., Purao, S., Rossi, M., Lindgren, R.: Action design research. MIS Q. **35**(1), 37–56 (2011)
46. Kuechler, B., Vaishnavi, V.: On theory development in design science research: anatomy of a research project. Eur. J. Inf. Syst. **17**(5), 489–504 (2008)
47. Mullarkey, M.T., Hevner, A.R.: An elaborated action design research process model. Eur. J. Inf. Syst. 1–15 (2018)
48. Walls, J., Widmeyer, G., El Sawy, O.: Building an information system design theory for vigilant EIS. Inf. Syst. Res. **3**(1), 36–59 (1992)
49. Hevner, A., March, S., Park, J., Ram, S.: Design science in information systems research. MIS Q. **28**(1), 75–105 (2004)
50. Schmeil, A., Eppler, M.J., de Freitas, S.: A structured approach for designing collaboration experiences for virtual worlds. J. Assoc. Inf. Syst. **13**(10), 836 (2012)
51. vom Brocke, J., et al.: Tool-Support for Design Science Research: Design Principles and Instantiation (2017)
52. Mustafa, M.I., Sjöström, J.: Design principles for research data export: lessons learned in e-health design research. In: vom Brocke, J., Hekkala, R., Ram, S., Rossi, M. (eds.) DESRIST 2013. LNCS, vol. 7939, pp. 34–49. Springer, Heidelberg (2013). https://doi.org/10.1007/978-3-642-38827-9_3
53. Gill, T.G., Hevner, A.R.: A fitness-utility model for design science research. In: Jain, H., Sinha, A.P., Vitharana, P. (eds.) DESRIST 2011. LNCS, vol. 6629, pp. 237–252. Springer, Heidelberg (2011). https://doi.org/10.1007/978-3-642-20633-7_17

Performant Peer Review for Design Science Manuscripts: A Pilot Study on Dedicated Highlighters

Oscar Díaz, Jeremías P. Contell[✉], and Haritz Medina

ONEKIN Web Engineering Group,
University of the Basque Country (UPV/EHU), San Sebastián, Spain
{oscar.diaz,jeremias.perez,haritz.medina}@ehu.eus

Abstract. Peer review is under pressure. Demand for reviews is outstripping supply where reviewers tend to be busy people who contribute voluntarily. Authors highly value reviews, yet complain about the time it takes to get feedback to the point of putting research timeliness at stake. Though part of the review process has been moved to the Web, the review itself is still often conducted with the only help of a yellow highlighter, physical or digital. This work looks for more performant highlighters that account for the review specifics. Peer review does not stop at spotting the manuscript (de)merits, it also strives for manuscript improvement and gatekeeping. These functions are conducted within an often tacit research-quality framework, and frequently in a discontinuous way. Unfortunately, when it comes to support review practices, current facilities fall short. This work introduces a set of requirements for review-dedicated highlighters. These requirements are instantiated and evaluated through *Review&Go*, a color-coding highlighter that generates a review draft out of the reviewer's highlighting activities. The aim is to offer representational guidance to enhance context/cognitive awareness so that reviewers can exert less effort while offering valuable and timely reviews.

Keywords: Peer review · Annotation · Design Science Research

1 Introduction

Peer review is under scrutiny [9]. Although widely supported by researchers [17], reviewing is not without opponents who claim current reviewing to be "slow, costly, ineffective, biased, easily abusable, anti-innovatory or largely a lottery" [18]. Three stakeholders are impacted: authors, readers and journals. Authors are deprived from getting useful advice to improve their research [7, 13], often leading to further submissions without modifying manuscripts, and as a result, to a waste of reviewers' effort [9, 26]. Readers consume sub-standard papers, and, in the worst cases, fraudulent or incorrect work is published due to gatekeeping errors [6, 20]. Finally, journals have their *raison d'être* undermined, i.e. the prompt dissemination and recognition of knowledge advances [6]. Different causes can be blamed for this situation: (1) lack of transparency in the process [6, 20], (2) lack of agreement about what constitutes good reviewing [9, 18, 20, 26], (3) lack of skills and reviewing experience [9, 13], and

© Springer Nature Switzerland AG 2019
B. Tulu et al. (Eds.): DESRIST 2019, LNCS 11491, pp. 61–75, 2019.
https://doi.org/10.1007/978-3-030-19504-5_5

(4), lack of time [3]. The latter is identified as a main area of discontent in a survey among active reviewers who report "an average of 14 reviews per year at 5 h each" [26]. According to another 2009 study [27], there are estimated to be about a number of 1.5 million articles per year with a grown at about 2.5–3% per year. Do the maths and peer review emerges as a "black hole" of academic efforts. And this scenario frequently leads to reviewing being undertaken "without sufficient care" [19, 20]. This calls for assistance in reconciling efficiency and effectiveness in peer review.

Peer review limitations have been addressed with a revolutionary or evolutionary perspective. The former include: incentivize good peer reviewing by rewarding their best reviewers [4] or revealing reviewers' identities [26]. Alternatively, evolutionary solutions do not change current practices but provide some kind of support: online reviewing for reducing the workload and speeding the communications between authors, editors and reviewers [25]; training programmers for young scientists to develop peer reviewing skills [3]; collaborative annotation upon the same manuscript rather that annotation being scattered across dedicated review documents [10]. Our approach is also evolutionary insofar as supporting existing practices. Specifically, we look into dedicated annotation for more efficient (fighting back lack of time) and effective (facing lack of care or expertise) reviewing feedback.

Annotation is the process whereby content is enhanced with marks or comments to highlight, complement and enrich some of its aspects. Before the digital age, annotation was conducted manually, and usually, individually. Now, different tools permit to annotate digital content, either locally (e.g. Acrobat Reader) or in a collaborative manner in the Web (e.g. Diigo). Yet, reviewing is not just annotation. Peer review is governed by a reference frame that informs about what a good manuscript should contain. This reference frame underpins highlighting and commenting. Hence, reviewing calls for annotation to be *guided* insofar as reviewers look for hints within the manuscript that sustain or contradict this frame (e.g., is the significance of the problem being established?). But this guide is domain specific, i.e. each research methodology has its own (sometimes, tacit) checklist. Unfortunately, current annotation tools (e.g. Acrobat Reader) are general purpose, and do not capture the specifics of annotating for review. This raises the following question:

What should a review-dedicated annotating tool be like? What benefits would such tools bring to peer review?

To provide an answer to these questions, we are informed by theories on providing good feedback [15]. Though initially proposed for student assignment, their principles can also be useful in a reviewing setting. In addition, configurability and familiarity become main non-functional requirements. The former due to reviewing being a diverse practice [20]. Even within the same field, criteria might vary. As for familiarity, smooth adoption advocates for not being disruptive w.r.t. traditional annotation tools. At this regard, our base comparison is with Acrobat Reader.

This research follows the Design Science Research (DSR) paradigm, in that it develops a new purposeful artifact to address a significant general problem, i.e. the limited support for reviewing in existing annotation tools. The work follows the five-step DSR Process Model of [23]. Awareness of Problem came from the literature, specially the survey conducted in [26]. Suggestion was derived from our previous work on Strategic Reading for students [5] (Sect. 2). Development was undertaken in an iterative approach of prototyping different aspects of the purposeful artifact (Sect. 3). Evaluation thus far has been formative in nature (Sect. 4). We start by characterizing the practice of peer review.

2 Peer Review: The Practice and the Needs

This Section characterizes the practice of peer review in terms of

- activities involved. Reviewing intermingles three key activities: strategic reading, feedback giving and summarizing,
- actor profile. Reviewing is knowledge intensive, hence conducted by well-educated people with tight agendas,
- setting. Reviewers continue to be volunteers working under stringent time constraints, but now working online.

On reporting about the state of affairs on peer review, Ware noticed that main areas of discontent include: "concerns at the length of time taken by the process; some concerns at the burdens imposed by reviewing commitments; and concerns about bias and lack of fairness" [26]. This reveals a tension between time and quality. If this is the problem, then solutions should attempt to facilitate one without overlooking the other. As in other areas of human activity, this calls for software assistance that supports the more routine activities of peer review (facing timeliness) so that reviewers can focus on the most added-value tasks (facing quality). This section identifies a set of meta-requirements for this sort of tools. The goal: performant reviewing, i.e. producing quality reports in an efficient way.

2.1 MR1: Support for Bespoke Review Frameworks

Peer review plays a gatekeeping function: passing judgement on whether a paper should be published at all [21]. This involves *strategic reading*. Strategic reading conceives reading as a process of constructing meaning by interacting with text. While reading, individuals use their prior knowledge along with clues from the text to construct meaning, and place the new knowledge within this frame [14]. Mimicking this definition, we can refer to "*strategic reviewing*" as a process of pinpointing evidences in the manuscript, and place them into a review framework to weight the merits of the manuscript. This definition implies the existence of a *review framework* that organizes and drives the review process. But, what review framework?

Review quality measurement is about quantifying to what extent a manuscript possesses desirable characteristics. Similar to software quality frameworks, we can distinguish between *quality characteristics* (e.g. relevance) and their *measurable attributes* (e.g. adoption and use of the new artifact by real organizations). Yet, reviewing is a diverse practice [20]. Even within the same field, quality criteria might vary. DSR is a case in point. In his survey about quality of DSR, Venable observed that there exists a lack of consensus concerning how research should be assessed [24]. Thus, review frameworks tend to be rather subjective. Though general principles apply, personal preferences and background might certainly tinge the review. This calls for review frameworks to be customizable.

2.2   MR2: Support for Quality Feedback

Peer review plays a manuscript-improvement function: providing comments that make the published paper better than the submitted manuscript. About 90% of researchers overall thought the main area of effectiveness for peer review would be in improving the published paper by providing constructive feedback to authors [9, 26]. For student assessment, good practices have been compiled about quality commenting [15, 16]. Next, we rephrase these attributes for the practice of reviewing:

- Specific: pointing to paragraphs in the manuscript where the feedback applies,
- Timely: provided in time along the conference/journal deadline,
- Contextualized: framed with reference to methodological criteria of ample support within the community,
- Selective: commenting in reasonable detail on two or three aspects that the author can do to improve the manuscript, distinguishing major concerns (i.e., those that threaten the validity of the study) from minor concerns that can be corrected (e.g., an additional analysis).

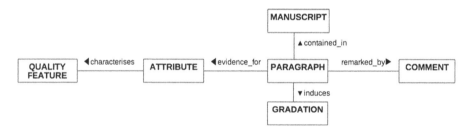

Fig. 1. Concepts involved in quality feedback.

Figure 1 depicts a conceptual model for reviewing as a process of spotting text paragraphs in manuscripts. Along the "specific" mandate, the model places "*paragraph*" in the middle. Along the "contextualized" mandate, paragraph highlighting responds to a purpose: pinpointing evidences of *quality*. Along the "selective" mandate, highlighting should be supplemented by *comments* as well as a *gradation* that sets the mood of the comment (e.g., minor vs. major). Support should be given to capture these elements as indicators of quality feedback.

2.3   MR3: Support for Review Summarization

Peer review is about grading. While strategic reading helps spot the merits, reviewing is about weighting whether those merits on balance deserve publication. When it comes to reviewing, the question is not whether the manuscript ticks off all the items of the *review framework*, but whether the manuscript holds enough merits to be worth publishing. And merits might not weigh all the same. For instance, good English is certainly a desirable feature. Yet, most authors agree that minor spelling and grammatical errors, thought they can be distracting, they should not decide the manuscript's fate [13].

More complex is the scenario where the weight of merits depends on the type of work. DSR is a good example. Gregor and Hevner illustrate this situation for manuscripts in the invention quadrant [8]. Here, "reviewers find it difficult to cope with the *newness*". Here, concerns about the design being insufficiently grounded in kernel theories, the design not being rigorously evaluated, or there being no new contribution to theory made via the design can be excused due to its newness [8]. In a similar scenario, Venable states "a potential resolution that I suggest here is to use a cumulative model that adds up the value of the DSR work's contribution to some (but not necessarily all) of the various criteria, rather than the subtractive model inherent in a check-list approach (where all criteria not met fully count against the research)". This suggests reviewing not being merely the gathering of the manuscript's merits, but a *subjective assessment* of whether existing merits are sufficient. Thus, mechanisms are needed to support review summarization.

2.4 MR4: Provide a Head Start for Review Writing

Peer review is time-consuming [13]. The overall average (median) time spent by reviewers per article is about 5 h (mean 8.5 h) [26]. Certainly, this very much depends on the manuscript's size, and how detailed the report is. If the report has to be specific, timely, contextualized and selective, then five hours do not seem that long.

A frequent practice is for reviewers first annotate the manuscript, take some notes, and once the manuscript is read, produce the report. This might require reviewers moving back-and-forth between the manuscript and the note editor, threatening the reading focus. In this scenario, a head-start might be provided by obtaining a draft out of the annotations already taken in the manuscript. In a limited manner, Acrobat Reader already accounts for this. It generates a text document with a list of the comments upon the PDF at hand [1]. This is a start, though certain limitations apply: no reference to the comment's target (i.e. the manuscript's paragraphs); no reference to the comment's purpose (i.e. the review frame); no reference to the comment's gradation (i.e. minor vs. major); no a sensible way of clustering comments, just the comments ordered chronologically. This is not a complaint. Acrobat Reader is general purpose, not a dedicated visor for reviewing. Dedicated visors can however go a long way in automating transcript tasks by automatically framing reviewers' comments in terms of the review frame or the gradations.

2.5 MR5: Account for Prompt Resumption

Peer review tends to be a fragmented activity. Reviewers do not always find easy to dispose of 5 h straight to conduct the review. Support should then be given to resume reviewing activity. At this respect, ubiquity and offline support are also important since it is not rare for reviewers to work at home, and even, when traveling. Facilities should be provided for reviewers to resume the reviewing state prior to the interruption.

2.6   MR6: Account for Familiarity

People like to stay in their comfort zone and they tend to be reluctant to fiddle around with new Graphical User Interfaces (GUI) [12]. More to the point, if the tool is sporadically accessed, then users might forget the GUI's gestures from their last interaction. This might well be the case of peer review. According to Ware's survey, active reviewers reporting an average of 14 reviews per year. This is a bit above once a month, a frequency not high enough to risk convoluted GUIs where reviewers might forget the tool's springs. Chances are reviewers are familiarized with Acrobat Reader. Hence, easy adoption advices dedicated highlighters to mimic Acrobat Reader gestures.

So far, we conjecture that an artifact design that fulfills meta-requirements above would have utility to speed up reviewing without compromising quality. Next, this theory is tested out through a purposeful artifact: *Review&Go*.

3   Purposeful Artifact

This section describes an expository instantiation of the aforementioned meta-requirements. The outcome is a dedicated highlighter for PDF manuscripts that outputs draft reviews out of annotation activities conducted upon manuscripts: *Review&Go*. Implementation wise, *Review&Go* is a Chrome's plug-in. It is available for download at the Chrome's Web Store[1], and a demo video is available[2]. Table 1 outlines the features of the artifact that realize each of the meta-requirements. The Section is structured along these requirements.

3.1   Bespoken Review Frameworks

Reading for reviewing has a first endeavor: spotting manuscript merits. For this reading to be "strategic", reviewers use their prior knowledge along with clues from the text to construct meaning, and place the new knowledge within a domain specific frame. *Review&Go* makes the case for DSR. The question is what would this frame be for DSR?

To answer this question, we resort to [24] where DSR authors are surveyed about properties determining research works' quality. We selected those aspects with the highest agreement among the DSR community, and arranged them along three quality characteristics: Rigor, Relevance and Design. We do not claim this list to be exhaustive, not even correct. *Review&Go* offers it as a first option that can latter be tuned to the personal taste of the reviewer at hand. The key point is that *Review&Go* resorts to these quality criteria for color-coding highlighting (see Fig. 2). That is, highlighting not only collects but also typifies evidences along the *review framework*. This default framework can be customized at wish by changing the sidebar's button labels. As a bonus, a "typo" button permits to spot misprints that will next be automatically listed at the end of the report (see Sect. 3.4).

---

[1] https://chrome.google.com/webstore/detail/hgiannlbfceoomjmcgedbmkfeblbcogi.

[2] https://rebrand.ly/reviewAndGo-video.

Table 1. Fleshing out the theory in *Review&Go*.

Meta-requirement: provide support for…	Instantiation: *Review&Go* realization by…
Bespoken review frameworks	Color-coding highlighter
Quality feedback	Highlight-framed comments with gradations & reference finder
Review summarization	Canvas
Head-start for report writing	Draft generation
Prompt resumption	Back-to-last-annotation button & canvas
Customizability	Customizable color codes
Familiarity	Preservation of Acrobat Reader gestures

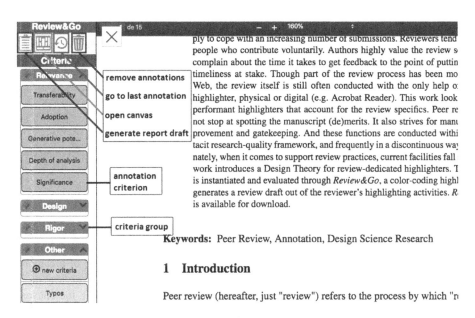

ply to cope with an increasing number of submissions. Reviewers tend people who contribute voluntarily. Authors highly value the review s complain about the time it takes to get feedback to the point of puttin timeliness at stake. Though part of the review process has been mo Web, the review itself is still often conducted with the only help o highlighter, physical or digital (e.g. Acrobat Reader). This work look performant highlighters that account for the review specifics. Peer re not stop at spotting the manuscript (de)merits. It also strives for man provement and gatekeeping. And these functions are conducted withi tacit research-quality framework, and frequently in a discontinuous way nately, when it comes to support review practices, current facilities fall work introduces a Design Theory for review-dedicated highlighters. T is instantiated and evaluated through *Review&Go*, a color-coding highl generates a review draft out of the reviewer's highlighting activities. *R* is available for download.

Keywords: Peer Review, Annotation, Design Science Research

1 Introduction

Peer review (hereafter, just "review") refers to the process by which "n

Fig. 2. *Review framework* is realized through a color-coding highlighter.

3.2 Provide Support for Quality Feedback

Along the conceptual model in Fig. 1, quality feedback qualifies evidences (i.e. highlights) through comments and gradations. *Review&Go* permits to attach this information by double-clicking upon the highlight at hand (see Fig. 3). Guidelines also recommend to complement comments with references to the literature [26]. To this end, *Review&Go* includes a reference finder where typed keywords are passed to the DBLP API[3]. Just a click for the full-reference to be included in the report (see Sect. 3.4).

---

[3] https://dblp.uni-trier.de/faq/13501473.

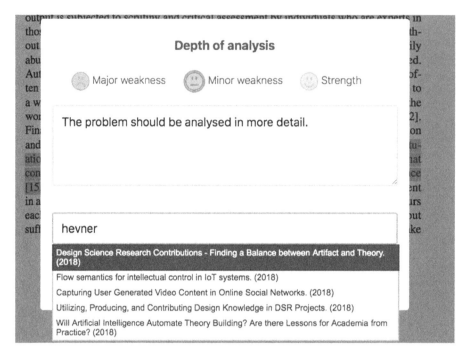

Fig. 3. Double-click on a highlight for the comment box to pop up. Besides the comment, grades and references can be introduced.

3.3 Support for Review Summarization

As the revision progress, reviewers might need to have an overview of the situation so far. This comes in handy when the final decision should be taken, but also if the reading is resumed after some days off. Johannesson and Perjons suggest the use of a canvas whenever there is a need to get a compact and easily understandable overview of a Design Science project [11]. Reviewing is one of these scenarios. In [11], the canvas outlines work in progress: the artifact under consideration, the problem it addresses, the knowledge base used, etc. By contrast, reviewing is not about constructing but the other way around: "de-constructing" the manuscript, i.e. brushing away the narrative to get the bare essentials of DSR milestones. On these premises, *Review&Go* generates a canvas out of the highlights gathered so far (see Fig. 4). A brief glance serves to apprehend which DSR aspects have been tackled, and those that have been left out. Worth noticing, paragraphs have been turned into hyperlinks. On clicking, reviewers can move back to the PDF to see the paragraph in context.

3.4 Provide a Head Start for Review Writing

Once being annotated, the manuscript itself is a good conduit for the review. Yet, using manuscript structure to organize reviewers' comments might not be the most effective way. *Review&Go* supplements PDFs with a report draft (see Appendix). Two ways to

Relevance	Adoption			Generative potential	Transferability
	Depth of analysis				
	"Different causes canbe blamed for this situation: (1) lack of transparency in the process[18,5], (2) lack ofagreement about what constitutes good reviewing[18,16,24,8], (3) lack of skills and re-viewing experience [11,8], or (4) lack of time."			Significance	
Design	Artefact	Evaluation	Solution comparison		
	"It is available for download at the Chrome'sWeb Store"		"Is Review&Go perceived to be better than conducting the review through Acrobat Reader"		
		Novelty			
	Behavior explanation				
Rigor	Justificatory knowledge	Meta-requirements	Research methods		
	Meta-design	Nascent Theory	Testable hypotheses		

Fig. 4. A canvas generated out of the highlights: regions stand for quality attributes; content corresponds to manuscript paragraphs; background colors denote the gradation.

arrange comments are available: attribute-based or grade-based. The former organizes comments along quality attributes. By contrast, the grade-based option arranges comments by strengths and weaknesses. No matter the way, comments are always framed by the associated highlighted paragraph and the manuscript page which holds that paragraph. Finally, typos and references are added at the end of the draft (see Appendix). The draft is structured in accordance with guidelines in [9]. Being text, drafts can now be copy&pasted into the editor at wish for completion.

3.5 Account for Prompt Resumption

A review can be conducted along different days, distinct places, and even, multiple copies of the manuscript. No matter the setting, reviewers should be able to go back to their reviewing at the point they left it. *Review&Go* exhibits some features that facilitate resumption. Being Web-based, *Review&Go* naturally supports ubiquity. Following Web-annotation standards, *Review&Go* faces annotation portability so that annotations can be overlaid on top of manuscript copies other than the ones on which annotations were first conducted[4]. These aspects facilitate going back to annotations (i.e. "the annotation state") but they do not restore "the mental state". To this end, the aforementioned canvas can

---

[4] This is achieved using Hypothes.is library. Implementation details are outside the scope of this paper.

help. *Review&Go*'s canvas can be obtained at any time to display the annotations collected so far. After some hours/days off, reviewers can display the canvas to restore "the mental state" before interruption. In addition, a button is provided to the last annotation being made so that reading can continue after this point.

3.6 Account for Familiarity

Basically, this requirement aims to preserve Acrobat Reader's gestures for highlighting, commenting and overviewing. Next paragraphs abound on how this non-functional requirement impacted *Review&Go* design.

Highlighting. Acrobat Reader supports two modes. Sporadic mode: select target paragraph; next, click *highlight* button. Continuous mode: select *highlight* button; next, keep selecting paragraphs that are readily highlighted. Likewise, *Review&Go* supports two modes: the continuous mode for quality characteristics (i.e. Rigor, Design and Relevance), and the sporadic mode for the attributes.

Commenting. Once on a highlighted paragraph, Acrobat Reader adds comments by double-clicking. So does *Review&Go*. Difference stems from the comment canvas. Acrobat Reader's holds date, author and the text. *Review&Go*'s supports the gradation, the comment itself, and the reference-finder box. In accordance with reviewing practices, no trace of date or authorship.

Overviewing. Acrobat Reader offers a list-of-comment tab that behaves as an index: click on one of the comments to move to the document's paragraph where this comment was made. The *Review&Go* counterpart is the canvas (see Fig. 4). But the canvas is not just an index. It is intended to offer a quick glimpse of the manuscript's merits by clustering annotations by reviewing criteria. In so doing, it promotes a quick glance of the strengths (green background) and limitations (red or yellow background) of the manuscript.

To conclude, this Section argues about *Review&Go* being a purposeful artifact that fleshes out the meta-requirements put forward in Sect. 2. For each meta-requirement, we introduce an enabler (see Table 1). If we can demonstrate that *Review&Go* has utility for its purpose, then we will provide a first support of this theory. This moves us to next Section.

4 Evaluation

This section reports on a formative evaluation for *Review&Go*. The evaluation was planned through the GQM (Goal, Question, Metric) paradigm [2].

Goal. The purpose of this study is to *predict* the adoption of *dedicated highlighters* for improving *reviewers' effort* and *review quality* from the point of view of *reviewers* in the context of a *conference manuscript revision*.

Questions. To better profile what is meant by "predict", we resorted to a reduction of Roger's model of Diffusion of Innovations that includes only those constructs consistently related to Technology Adoption Model (TAM): relative advantage, complexity and compatibility [22]. Specifically, three general questions are posed:

- Is *Review&Go* perceived to be better than conducting the review through Acrobat Reader? (Relative Advantage)
- Is *Review&Go* perceived to be consistent with the existing values, needs, and past experiences of Acrobat Reader? (Compatibility)
- Is *Review&Go* perceived to be difficult to use? (Complexity)

Metrics. Each of these questions is next refined in terms of the Design Principles that guide *Review&Go* (see Fig. 5): relative advantage (questions 1 to 9), compatibility (questions 10 to 12) and complexity (questions 13 to 17). The Cronbach's alpha values of the three dimensions were 0.77, 0.71 and 0.71, implying acceptable reliability of the questionnaire. Finally, metrics are derived from the subjects' answers as a normalization of good perception (i.e. *Agree, Strongly Agree*) vs. the total number of answers. Hence, "1" will stand for the highest perception. Next, we provide details of the evaluation.

Subjects. Participants were recruited locally. For participants to qualify as "reviewers", they should have experience in reviewing papers, specifically, along the DSR methodology. Six lecturers and three post-grads qualified. Participants were given a brief introduction to *Review&Go* where a sample manuscript was reviewed.

Methodology. Subjects were asked to review a paper from previous editions of DESRIST. Papers were selected based on claiming the use of DSR as the research methodology. To check out resumption utilities, revision was interrupted for 20 min so that the short-term memory was reset. Once the testing session was over, participants were asked to fill in a questionnaire that rates different aspects of *Review&Go* along a five point Likert scale (see Fig. 5). The questionnaire builds upon constructs consistently related to technology adoption behavior: relative advantage, complexity and compatibility [15]. In addition, open comments were also welcome.

Results. Figure 5 outlines results using a Diverging Stacked Bar Chart. These charts are recommended where the primary interest is in the total count (or percent) to the right or left of the neutral answer (i.e. 'No Opinion'). The breakdown into strongly or not is of lesser interest so that the primary comparisons do have a common baseline of zero. Resulting metrics are added at the end of each question along the formula:

(#Agree + #StronglyAgree)/#Subjects.

Discussion. In general, users perceive *Review&Go* as providing a relative advantage w.r.t. using Acrobat Reader highlight facilities (questions 3 and 7 in Fig. 5). Next, *Review&Go* gestures were considered quite consistent with those of Acrobat Reader (questions 10 to 12) except the way of obtaining overviews. Some additional comments follow.

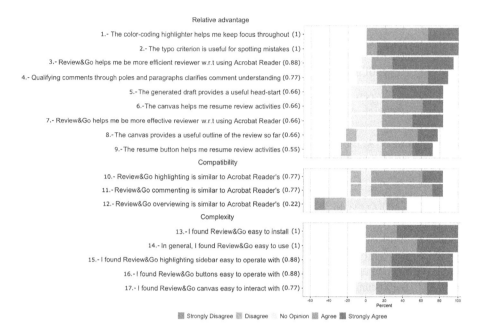

Fig. 5. Diverging Stacked Bar Chart for the Perceived-Adoption Questionnaire using a 5 point Likert scale.

First, highlights are often used. It is a way to pinpoint meaningful paragraphs. Yet, subjects felt a bit overwhelmed with the 15 quality attributes offered as a default. Some of them preferred to focus first on the main quality categories (i.e. *Relevance*, *Design* and *Rigor*), and next, move down to the measurement attributes in subsequent readings, if necessary. In the same vein, five subjects introduced their own quality criteria (e.g. *'understandability'*). This suggests that customizability is certainly a must for this kind of color-coding highlighters. A subject suggested "review-criteria cartridges" that, provided by Journals and Conferences, could automatically configure the highlighter.

Second, surprisingly, the "typo" button to effortless report misprints was the highest in the rank. Subjects also appreciated color-coding and the draft generator as a transcript utility (no need for manual copy&paste) but also as a way to have comments arranged along grades. Two subjects observed the inability to introduce comments without associated highlighted paragraph. This prevents general observations from being captured if no related paragraph exists.

Third, the canvas received a neutral punctuation. Subjects appreciated its role as an index on top of the manuscript highlights but with not so much enthusiasm. Its role as a resumption utility was not really appreciated, more likely due to failure in re-creating a realistic scenario where the manuscript size and real evaluation needs would lead to longer reviewing times, and hence, making more compelling the need for resumption support. One subject observed the interest of the canvas for article documentation as a sort of bibliographic record.

5 Conclusions

The peer review system is under pressure, partially due to an increase in the number of submissions. To improve reviewers' productivity, we advocate to move beyond Acrobat-Reader-like facilities to dedicated highlighters that account for review specifics. We introduce meta-requirements for dedicated highlighters. These requirements are being formatively tested out through *Review&Go*. Results are certainly promising but far from being conclusive. It should be noted the sole reliance on subjective measures as a limitation of our study.

Next follow-on is to evaluate *Review&Go* in realistic settings. At this respect, approaching PC chairs is on the radar. PC chairs have most interest in improving reviews for attracting submissions and enhancing authors' satisfaction. By providing a "review-criteria cartridge", PC chairs can tune *Review&Go*'s color codes, facilitating review harmonization and, hence, pooling sessions.

Acknowledgements. This work is supported by the University of the Basque Country under contract US17/13. Haritz Medina enjoys a grant from the same University.

Appendix: Review Draft Automatically Generated Out of Reviewer Annotations

<Summarize the work>
   STRENGTHS:

   - the proposed solution is clear and convincing.
   * (Page 6): "It is available for download at the Chrome's Web Store".
      The availability of the artefact is a plus.
   - the artefact has been compared with extant solutions.
   * (Page 12): "Is Review&Go perceived to be better than conducting the review through Acrobat Reader". The comparison with Acrobat Reader is pertinent.

   MINOR WEAKNESSES:

   There is a minor point that should be clarified. The paper seems to overlook the 'why' and focus too much on the 'what'.
   * (Page 1): "Different causes can be blamed for this situation: (1) lack of transparency in the process [18, 5], (2) lack of agreement about what constitutes good reviewing [18, 16, 24, 8], (3) lack of skills and re-viewing experience [11, 8], or (4) lack of time".
      The problem should be analysed in more detail.
   I would encourage the authors to look at the following papers: [1]

TYPOS:

- (Page 1): "raison d'etre"

REFERENCES:
[1] Richard Baskerville, Abayomi Baiyere, Shirley Gregor, Alan R. Hevner, Matti Rossi: Design Science Research Contributions - Finding a Balance between Artifact and Theory. (2018)
<Comments to editors>

References

1. Adobe: Importing and exporting comments (2017). https://helpx.adobe.com/acrobat/using/importing-exporting-comments.html. Accessed 22 Mar 2019
2. Basili, V.R., Caldiera, G., Rombach, H.D.: Goal question metric paradigm. Encycl. Softw. Eng. **1**, 528–532 (1994)
3. Clarke, M.: Reducing the peer-reviewer's burden (2010). http://blogs.nature.com/peer-to-peer/2010/05/reducing_the_peerreviewers_bur_1.html. Accessed 22 Mar 2019
4. DeMaria, A.N.: Peer review: the weakest link. J. Am. Coll. Cardiol. **55**(11), 1161–1162 (2010)
5. Díaz, O., Contell, Jeremías P., Venable, J.R.: Strategic reading in design science: let root-cause analysis guide your readings. In: Maedche, A., vom Brocke, J., Hevner, A. (eds.) DESRIST 2017. LNCS, vol. 10243, pp. 231–246. Springer, Cham (2017). https://doi.org/10.1007/978-3-319-59144-5_14
6. Enago: Experts' take on peer review evaluation (PRE) (2018). https://www.enago.com/academy/experts-take-on-peer-review-evaluation/. Accessed 22 Mar 2019
7. Grant, R.P.: On peer review (2010). http://occamstypewriter.org/rpg/2010/04/15/on_peer_review. Accessed 22 Mar 2019
8. Gregor, S., Hevner, A.R.: Positioning and presenting design science research for maximum impact. MIS Q. **37**(2), 337–355 (2013)
9. Hames, I.: Peer review in a rapidly evolving publishing landscape. In: Academic and Professional Publishing, pp. 15–52. Elsevier (2012)
10. Hanson, B., Panning, J., Townsend, R., Wooden, P.: Annotation tool facilitates peer review. In: EOS, vol. 98 (2017)
11. Johannesson, P., Perjons, E.: An Introduction to Design Science. Springer, Cham (2014). https://doi.org/10.1007/978-3-319-10632-8
12. Lawrence, M.: Familiarity: A UX consideration (2017). https://blog.endpointmedia.co/familiarity-a-ux-consideration-5e8fe0913551 (accessed 22 Mar. 2019)
13. Lovejoy, T.I., Revenson, T.A., France, C.R.: Reviewing manuscripts for peer-review journals: A primer for novice and seasoned reviewers. Ann. Behav. Med. **42**(1), 1–13 (2011)
14. McEwan, E.K.: Seven Strategies of Highly Effective Readers: Using Cognitive Research to Boost K-8 Achievement. Corwin press, Thousand Oaks (2004)
15. Nicol, D.: From monologue to dialogue: improving written feedback processes in mass higher education. Assess. Eval. High. Educ. **35**(5), 501–517 (2010)
16. Nicol, D.: Good designs for Written Feedback to Students. McKeachie's Teaching Tips: Strategies, Research, and Theory for College and University Teachers, pp. 108–124. Cengage Learning (2010)

17. Publishing Research Consortium (PRC): Peer review survey 2015 (2016). http://bit.ly/prcsurvey2015. Accessed 22 Mar 2019
18. Smith, R.: What is peer review? is peer review effective? classical peer review: an empty gun. Breast Cancer Res. **12**(Suppl 4), 13 (2010)
19. Spyns, P., Vidal, M.-E.: Scientific Peer Reviewing. Practical Hints and Best Practices. Springer, Cham (2015). https://doi.org/10.1007/978-3-319-25084-7
20. Tennant, J.P., Dugan, J.M., Graziotin, D., et al.: A multi-disciplinary perspective on emergent and future innovations in peer review. F1000Research **6**, 1151 (2017)
21. Tenopir, C., et al.: Research Publication Characteristics and Their Relative Values: A (2010)
22. Tornatzky, L.G., Klein, K.J.: Innovation characteristics and innovation adoption-implementation: A meta-analysis of findings. IEEE Trans. Eng. Manage. EM **29**(1), 28–45 (1982)
23. Vaishnavi, V.K., Kuechler, W.: Design Science Research Methods and Patterns: Innovating Information and Communication Technology. CRC Press, Boca Raton (2015)
24. Venable, John R.: Five and ten years on: have DSR standards changed? In: Donnellan, B., Helfert, M., Kenneally, J., VanderMeer, D., Rothenberger, M., Winter, R. (eds.) DESRIST 2015. LNCS, vol. 9073, pp. 264–279. Springer, Cham (2015). https://doi.org/10.1007/978-3-319-18714-3_17
25. Ware, M.: Online submission and peer-review systems. Learn. Publish. **18**(4), 245–250 (2005)
26. Ware, M.: Peer review: recent experience and future directions. New Rev. Inf. Netw. **16**(1), 23–53 (2011)
27. Ware, M., Mabe, M.: The STM report: An overview of scientific and scholarly journals publishing (2009). https://www.stm-assoc.org/2009_10_13_MWC_STM_Report.pdf. Accessed 22 Mar 2019

Leveraging Machine-Executable Descriptive Knowledge in Design Science Research – The Case of Designing Socially-Adaptive Chatbots

Jasper Feine$^{(\boxtimes)}$, Stefan Morana, and Alexander Maedche

Institute of Information Systems and Marketing (IISM),
Karlsruhe Institute of Technology (KIT), Karlsruhe, Germany
{jasper.feine,stefan.morana,
alexander.maedche}@kit.edu

Abstract. In Design Science Research (DSR) it is important to build on descriptive (Ω) and prescriptive (Λ) state-of-the-art knowledge in order to provide a solid grounding. However, existing knowledge is typically made available via scientific publications. This leads to two challenges: first, scholars have to manually extract relevant knowledge pieces from the data-wise unstructured textual nature of scientific publications. Second, different research results can interact and exclude each other, which makes an aggregation, combination, and application of extracted knowledge pieces quite complex. In this paper, we present how we addressed both issues in a DSR project that focuses on the design of socially-adaptive chatbots. Therefore, we outline a two-step approach to transform phenomena and relationships described in the Ω-knowledge base in a machine-executable form using ontologies and a knowledge base. Following this new approach, we can design a system that is able to aggregate and combine existing Ω-knowledge in the field of chatbots. Hence, our work contributes to DSR methodology by suggesting a new approach for theory-guided DSR projects that facilitates the application and sharing of state-of-the-art Ω-knowledge.

Keywords: Design science research · Descriptive knowledge ·
Prescriptive knowledge · Ontology · Chatbot · Conversational agent

1 Introduction

Design Science Research (DSR) seeks to design, build, and evaluate socio-technical artifacts that extend the boundaries of existing knowledge in order to address unsolved problems in a new and innovative way or to solve known problems in a more effective manner [1–3]. The knowledge used to inform a DSR project can be divided into two broad areas: descriptive knowledge (Ω-knowledge) and prescriptive knowledge (Λ-knowledge) [1, 2, 4]. The first describes "the what knowledge about natural phenomena and the laws and regularities among phenomena" [2, p. 343]. Its primary purpose is to inform and justify the research question and the assumed relationships [2]. The second consists of the "how knowledge of human-built artifacts" [2, p. 343]. It includes artifacts and design theories that address a similar research problem from the

© Springer Nature Switzerland AG 2019
B. Tulu et al. (Eds.): DESRIST 2019, LNCS 11491, pp. 76–91, 2019.
https://doi.org/10.1007/978-3-030-19504-5_6

past. Overall, both knowledge areas are important as "the success of a design research project is predicated on the research of the team in appropriately drawing knowledge from both Ω and Λ to ground and position the research" [2, p. 343].

Since access to existing prescriptive knowledge that can be (re-)used in the design of a new artifact is limited [1], DSR scholars often rely on Ω-knowledge and (kernel) theories in order to follow a theory-guided artifact construction [2]. However, as in any other research domain, it requires a lot of effort to aggregate and apply the existing Ω-knowledge, which restricts its application in DSR. One reason is the data-wised unstructured textual nature of scientific publications [5] (problem 1). Scientific knowledge communication largely depends on "text production, reading and interpretation" [6, p. 1] and follows a document-centered knowledge exchange [5]. Moreover, there is a lack of comparable identifiers for terminologies, definitions, and concepts among research areas [5]. This makes the extraction of relevant components more difficult and requires a lot of creativity and rigor [5, 7]. As a consequence, Ω-knowledge with a clear structure can be of great value but does not solve the Ω-knowledge application problem alone [5]. The aggregation, combination, and application of many phenomena and relationships described in the Ω-knowledge base can be very complex (problem 2) [5]. Many of the empirical results interact or exclude each other, which makes it quite difficult to choose the right pieces of knowledge for a foundation of the design. Therefore, approaches that leverage computing resources to aggregate and combine the existing knowledge base could support researchers in their DSR project. However, there is currently only very limited machine support, which makes access to scientific publications very difficult [5]. As a consequence, DSR researchers face the challenge that "the creation, reading and processing of scientific literature is currently tying up an extremely high cognitive capacity" [5, p. 2]. Thus, solutions should simplify the application, (re-)use, and sharing of existing Ω-knowledge in DSR. Hence, we articulate the following research question:

How to transform descriptive Ω-knowledge into a machine-executable representation in order to simplify knowledge access in design science research projects?

To answer this research question, we first present our DSR project in which we experienced both problems outlined above. In our DSR project we investigate the design of socially-adaptive chatbots and have identified large amounts of publications that deliver descriptive Ω-knowledge. However, this knowledge was not directly accessible (problem 1) and much of the empirical evidence interacted or excluded each other which made an application quite complex (problem 2). To address both problems in our DSR project, we followed a two-step approach to transform Ω-knowledge into machine-executable design knowledge. We instantiated a system that aggregates and combines existing Ω-knowledge. Hence, this paper contributes to DSR methodology by suggesting a new approach for a theory-guided design that facilitates the application and sharing of existing Ω-knowledge in DSR. From a more practical point of view, this enables building artifacts based on state-of-the-art and up-to-date Ω-knowledge.

2   Conceptual Foundations

2.1   Types of Knowledge in DSR

Knowledge in DSR projects can be distinguished into two broad areas, namely Ω-knowledge and Λ-knowledge [2]. Ω-knowledge comprises descriptive and explanatory knowledge and evolves from a behavioristic-oriented research approach [1]. It consists of the *"what-knowledge"* about natural, artificial, and human-related phenomena and their sense-making relationships [2]. It includes (kernel) theories that consist of *"any descriptive theory that informs artifact construction"* [2, p. 340] and therefore provides the theoretical basis for DSR projects (i.e., sometimes also referred to as justificatory knowledge [2]). The other knowledge area (i.e., Λ-knowledge) comprises applicable and prescriptive knowledge and evolves from a design-oriented research approach [1]. It consists of the *"how-to-knowledge"* about artifacts designed by humans such as constructs, models, methods, instantiations, and design theories [2]. Figure 1 provides a more detailed description of different types of Ω- and Λ-knowledge in DSR [2].

Descriptive Ω - knowledge		Prescriptive Λ - knowledge				
Phenomena	Sense-making	Constructs	Models	Methods	Instantiations	Design theory
Description of natural, artificial, and human-related phenomena.	Knowledge of the sense-making relationships among phenomena.	Vocabulary and symbols to define and understand problems & solutions.	Designed representation of problem and solution.	Algorithms, practices, and recipes for performing a task.	Physical realization that act on the natural world.	Abstract, coherent body of prescriptive knowledge that describes the principles of form and function.

Fig. 1. DSR knowledge base and definitions following Gregor and Hevner [2].

From a DSR knowledge consumption perspective, researchers draw valuable information from both knowledge areas [2, 4]. On the one side, Ω-knowledge informs and justifies the research question and assumed relationships and builds the foundation for an artifact [2, 4]. On the other side, Λ-knowledge provides existing artifacts and design theories that address a similar research problem from the past [2, 4].

From a DSR knowledge contribution perspective [4], contributions to Ω-knowledge increase the understanding of the world, whereas contributions to Λ-knowledge increase the understanding of technological innovations [1, 2]. In this context, two research streams evolved that either emphasized their contribution on design theories or on innovative artifacts [2]. However, various discussion in the past have led to the common understanding that both types of contributions are valuable and intertwined [2, 4].

2.2 Structures of Knowledge

Knowledge can be captured in structured (e.g., databases), semi-structured (e.g., XML), or unstructured (e.g., natural language) data [8]. A typical knowledge management problem is the difficulty to access and extract knowledge that is captured in unstructured text-based data such as in scientific publications [7]. Nevertheless, scientific knowledge communication depends on *"text production, reading and interpretation"* [6, p. 1] and therefore largely relies on document-centric information flows [5]. This leads to problems as the scientific output in the form of text-based articles has almost doubled in the last ten years [5]. As a result, *"scientists spend a large part of their time reviewing literature, presenting their own research in document form and [...] working independently on very similar research results"* [5, p. 2].

To address this problem, various initiatives aimed to augment the scientific knowledge communication process in order to simplify the access and extraction of existing knowledge. For example, in the IS domain there is an ongoing effort to provide concepts and tools in order to systematically capture constructs and their relationships [9, 10]. Some approaches leverage nomological networks that identify potential pathways for theory integration and development [9]. Therefore, researchers screen variables of functional and structural components from past quantitative research publications and identify shared variables. Then they connect these with each other in a nomological network in order to reduce theory fragmentation and to identify similar phenomena across disciplines [9]. Other approaches leverage tools to automatically identify construct identity in literature reviews and meta-analyses in order to recognize whether two constructs refer to the same real-world phenomenon [10]. These tools are a valuable extension to support experts as they leverage computing resources and natural language processing algorithms. Particularly in the DSR contexts, initiatives aim to develop tool support in order to help researcher and practitioners to structure, manage, and present the multi-faceted nature of DSR projects including the resulting design knowledge and artifacts [11, 12]. In the field of computer science, various communities (e.g., knowledge engineering, description logics, logic-based databases) investigated approaches for decades to structure and capture knowledge in a machine-executable form. In this context, ontologies are considered as an important enabler to establish a shared common understanding and to enable a (re-)use of knowledge [13]. Ontologies are conceptual models that provide a controlled vocabulary to describe a set of concepts and relations of a domain [8]. Based on the ontological conceptualization, a knowledge base is a repository that links classes in the ontology to individual instances [14]. Thus, such an approach enables a machine-executable expression of meanings and concepts that can be directly processed [15].

As a consequence, ontological approaches have been applied in various domains [13]. Efforts are made to use ontologies to accumulate scientific knowledge in medicine [14] or to store user characteristics in user models [16]. In addition, the Semantic Web Initiative [15] proposed standards to make existing knowledge on the Web more available. Therefore, various standards have been defined including the RDF data model, the RDF Schema (RDFS) and the Web Ontology Language (OWL), as well as the SPARQL Protocol And RDF Query Language (SPARQL) [8]. They enable the description of concepts, provide rich sets of operators, and further allow the use of a reasoner to check for mutually consistency and to recognize which concepts fit under which definitions [17]. In addition, various software packages exist that support various ontology languages and enable the editing of ontologies. One of the most famous open-source ontology software packages is Protégé developed at Stanford university [18]. It is used in various research projects such as clinical decision support systems, collaborative ontology development, and many others [18].

3   DSR Project: Designing Socially-Adaptive Chatbots

In our DSR project, we focus on designing chatbots. Chatbots are software-based systems that converse with humans via the use of text or speech based natural language [19]. They are assumed to solve the app overload, reduce costs, and enhance customer experience and are used in several contexts (e.g., customer service, energy feedback, collaboration systems) [19–22]. However, many chatbots failed as the interactions did not feel natural [23]. In this context, various studies revealed that humans react to chatbots in a similar way as humans usually react in interpersonal communication [24, 25]. To describe this phenomenon, Nass and colleagues have introduced the Computer are Social Actors (CASA) paradigm which states that human-computer interaction is fundamentally social and natural [24, 26]. Social behavior is always triggered whenever the computer exhibits sufficient cues that can be associated with the behavior or appearance of human beings (e.g., natural language, gender, response delay) [24, 27]. Therefore, scholars often refer to these cues as *social cues* [28]. As humans constantly adapt their social cues (e.g., adapt their formality of speech according to the conversation partner), chatbots could also adapt their social cues to the user, task, and context in order to make the interaction more natural and to increase user satisfaction.

To achieve this goal, we conduct a DSR project and suggest the development of socially-adaptive chatbots that adapt their social cues to an interaction. This is a promising approach as adaptive systems have shown to enhance user satisfaction [16] and performance [29] in other contexts. Therefore, we followed established DSR guidelines and reviewed existing knowledge about social cues by conducting a literature review [30]. In our literature review, we identified various relevant publications across domains (e.g., chatbots, dialog systems, embodied conversational agents). However, we identified only few publications that provide prescriptive Λ-knowledge for the design of socially adaptive chatbots. The vast majority of identified publications describes phenomena of social cues and/or explains the reason for these phenomena. Thus, a large body of research appears to be hidden in the textual nature of publications delivering Ω-knowledge.

To reveal and apply the existing Ω-knowledge, it is necessary to identify and extract relevant descriptions of phenomena and relationships from empirical results. However, it is not clear how the extracted Ω-knowledge should be represented and how it could subsequently be (re-)used in the design of socially-adaptive chatbots (problem 1). Furthermore, much of the revealed empirical findings interact and exclude each other. For example, Sah and Peng [31] showed that a user is more willing to disclose intimate information in a health context when a chatbot addresses the user directly and personally. However, others revealed that a direct address in a financial context can also have a negative effect on information disclosure [32]. Thus, both publications provide different recommendations to increase information disclosure depending on the context. This becomes even more complicated when we further account for different user variables such as demographics (e.g., age, gender), geography (e.g., country of origin), and usage behavior (e.g., sporadic users, experienced users) [33]. As a result, it is very complex to aggregate, combine, and apply the existing Ω-knowledge to investigate social cues of chatbots (problem 2). Thus, both problems limit researchers and designers to efficiently access and apply the existing body of knowledge in order to design socially-adaptive chatbots.

4   Leveraging Machine-Executable Ω-Knowledge for Designing Socially-Adaptive Chatbots

To address both problems introduced above, we present our approach to simplify access to existing Ω-knowledge in the design of socially-adaptive chatbots. Our approach leverages the use of machine-executable Ω-knowledge and is outlined below.

4.1   Step 1: Transform Ω-Knowledge into Prescriptive Design Rules

To address problem 1, we aimed to transform Ω-knowledge embedded in textual publications in a consistent and prescriptive format. One of the main vehicles to convey prescriptive design knowledge in the IS discipline are design principles and technological rules [34]. They are statements *"that prescribes what and how to build an artifact in order to achieve a predefined design goal"* [34, p. 4040]. Chandra et al. [34] propose to include three components in order to articulate purposeful prescriptive design knowledge: These include (1) the actions made possible through the artifact, (2) information about the properties making the action possible, and (3) boundary conditions for when it will work. With this, we could define prescriptive design rules that help designers to achieve a specific outcome in a specific situation (e.g., to achieve X and you believe you are in Y, then design the social cue like Z) [4]. Thus, in step 1, we suggested to transform existing Ω-knowledge into prescriptive social cue design rules.

To perform step 1, we reviewed each publication for (1) outcomes of a social cue design (e.g., positive attitude towards chatbot), (2) types of investigated social cue design characteristics (e.g., formal clothing), and (3) factors that influence the outcomes of a social cue design characteristic (e.g., user, task, context). With all three components, we were able to state a purposeful prescriptive social cue design rule. In case a publication described a direct cause-and-effect relationship without any uncertainty (e.g., do X to achieve Z), we defined an abstract boundary condition, e.g., based on the user types (e.g., user profession: *students*), study type (e.g., experimental task: *desert survival problem*), or the overall domain (e.g., context domain: *service domain*). To illustrate the overall process, Fig. 2 shows two examples that are explained below.

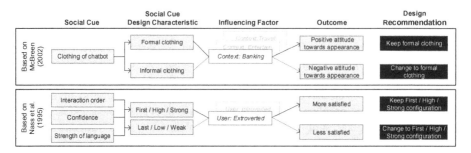

Fig. 2. Exemplary development of prescriptive social cue design rules.

In the first example, McBreen [35] showed that different clothing styles of a chatbot (i.e., formal, informal) lead to different outcomes (i.e., attitude towards chatbot) depending on the context of the interaction (i.e., banking, entertainment, travel). Thus, we derived the prescriptive social cue design rule that the clothing style of a chatbot should fit to the interaction context in order to maximize the user attitude towards the chatbot. In the second example, Nass et al. [36] showed that design characteristics of a specific set of social cues (i.e., interaction order, confidence level, strength of language) lead users to assume that the chatbot possesses a specific personality (i.e., extroverted, introverted). In addition, they showed that users are more satisfied when the chatbot's personality matches their own. Thus, we derived the rule that the design of the interaction order, confidence level, and strength of should match the personality of the user in order to maximize user satisfaction. Finally, we derived over 150 prescriptive social cue design.

In the next step, we faced the problem that a manual aggregation, combination, and application of the developed knowledge is highly complex (problem 2). Various prescriptive social cue design rules provide different design recommendations for different influencing factors. To showcase this, Table 1 displays the prescriptive social cue design rules for selecting the design characteristic of only one social cue, namely the chatbot's gender. The 18 derived social cue design rules illustrate that a manual design selection for only one social cue is already a challenging task.

Table 1. Prescriptive social cue design rules for selecting the gender of a chatbot.

Social cue design	Influencing factor	Outcome	Ref.
Gender: *male*	User Gender: *female* Chatbot role: *tutor bot*	Positive impact on user performance and effort	[37]
Gender: *female*	User Gender: *male* Chatbot role: *tutor bot*	Positive impact on user performance and effort	[37]
Gender: *male*	Platform: *website*	Less attribution of negative stereotypes	[38]
Gender: *female*	Chatbot role: *Q&A agent*	Positive impact on comfort, confidence and enjoyment	[39]

(continued)

Table 1. (*continued*)

Social cue design	Influencing factor	Outcome	Ref.
Gender: *male*	Chatbot role: *job interview*	Higher perceived power, trust, and expertise	[40]
Gender: *female*	Chatbot role: *job interview*	Higher perceived likeability	[40]
Gender: *female*	Chatbot role: *job interview* User Personality: *agreeable & trusting users*	Higher willingness to listen to chatbot persona	[41]
Gender: *male*	Chatbot role: *job interview* Personality: *extraverted & neurotic users*	User is less likely to inflate themselves	[41]
Gender: *female*	Frustration of user: *high due to errors*	Increases impact of affective excuses to reduce frustration	[42]
Gender: *male*	Chatbot role: *stereotypical male jobs*	Positive impact on satisfaction score	[43]
Gender: *female*	Chatbot role: *stereotypical female jobs*	Positive impact on satisfaction score	[43]
Gender: *male*	Chatbot role: *tutor bot*; Feedback type: *negative*	Positive impact on learning performance	[44]
Gender: *female*	Chatbot role: *tutor bot*; Feedback type: *positive*	Positive impact on learning performance	[44]
Gender: *female*	Context: *sales*; Product gender: *female*	Positive belief in the credibility of advice	[45]
Gender: *male*	Context: *sales*; Product gender: *male*	Positive belief in the credibility of advice	[45]
Gender: *female*	Conversation topic: *love and relationships*	Positive impact informative rating	[24]
Gender: *male*	Conversation topic: *technology*	Positive impact informative rating	[24]
Gender: *male*	Feedback type: *positive and negative evaluation*	Positive impact on competence and friendliness	[24]

4.2   Step 2: Make Prescriptive Design Rules Machine-Executable

To address problem 2, we aimed to increase application of the previously derived prescriptive social cue design rules. Therefore, we suggested to transform the design rules into a machine-executable representation. This enables researchers and designers to leverage computational resources to aggregate and combine existing knowledge. Therefore, we relied on ontological models and suggested to conceptualize the previously derived design rules in a prescriptive social cue design rule ontology and explicitly instantiate each rule in a knowledge base. Subsequently, we built a social cue configuration system that leverages computing resources and enables researchers and designers to apply and share the derived knowledge base.

To perform step 2, we first followed the ontology engineering process proposed by Ostrowski et al. [46] and conceptualized all design rules in a prescriptive social cue design rule ontology. We used Protégé to develop the ontology in order to check for consistencies among the classes and properties [17]. Therefore, we first defined the main classes of a social cue design rule (i.e., social cue design rule, social cue, influencing factor, outcome). Second, we defined subclasses for each identified social cue design (e.g., chatbot clothing, chatbot gender), influencing factor (e.g., user age, task complexity, context domain), and outcome (e.g., attitude towards the chatbot, user satisfaction). Next, we defined properties which describe attributes of instances of the classes and the relations to other instances [46] (i.e., a social cue design rule has social cue, has influencing factor, and has outcome). Finally, we conceptualized all relevant classes and relationships of a prescriptive social cue design rule. To increase readability, we simplified and aggregated the classes and properties and display a simplified ontology in Fig. 3.

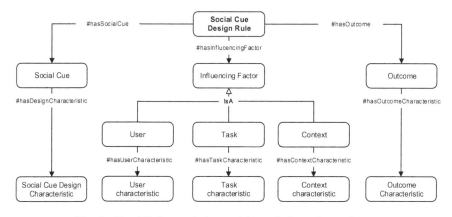

Fig. 3. Simplified prescriptive social cue design rule ontology.

In the next step, we developed a prescriptive social cue design rule knowledge base by creating several instances that capture individual empirical findings from the identified publications. Therefore, we reviewed each prescriptive social cue design rule and identified instances of each rule (e.g., clothing design characteristic: *formal*; context characteristic: *banking,* attitude towards the chatbot: *positive*). Next, we defined instances of the social cue design rule class, each of which holds specific properties concerning a particular rule (e.g., *rule 1* has clothing design characteristic *formal,* has context characteristic *banking,* and has a *positive* attitude towards the chatbot). After this, we were able to query the knowledge base in order to list all relevant prescriptive social cue design rules which fulfill a specific configuration condition (e.g., select *all* social cue design characteristics from the prescriptive social cue design rules where the context characteristic is *banking* and the attitude towards the chatbot is *positive*). The resulting output includes all social cue design characteristics that meet the query conditions (e.g., chatbot clothing should be *formal* according *to rule 1* and chatbot age should be *old* according to *rule 3*). However, the resulting design recommendations can contain conflicts as they might violate potential disjoint assumptions (e.g., *rule 2* proposes the chatbot gender to be *male* whereas *rule 5* proposes a *female* chatbot name). In such a case, researchers need to resolve the conflicts by reviewing both publications from which the design rules originated. Thus, it is important to provide researchers with relevant background information about the underlying reference of each design rule in order to review and resolve conflicts for a specific configuration. Finally, we built a prototypical chatbot social cue configuration system that enables user to access, configure, and query the developed design recommendations (see Fig. 4).

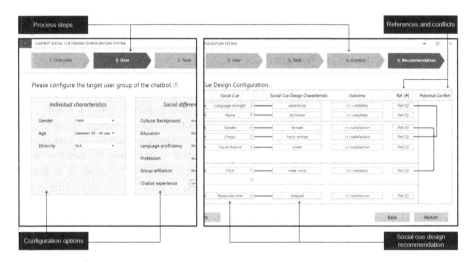

Fig. 4. Prototypical chatbot social cue configuration system. (Color figure online)

The chatbot social cue configuration system follows a four step configuration process: first, designers can configure the desired outcome of the chatbot social cue design (e.g., attitude towards chatbot: *positive*). In the next three steps, designers can configure assumed influencing factors (e.g., context: *banking*). Finally, the system queries the knowledge base and displays prescriptive social cue design recommendations (e.g., clothing of chatbot: *formal*). Potential design conflicts are highlighted with a red line and users can click on the reference buttons to review the corresponding reference. As a consequence, our chatbot social cue configuration system can simplify the access to relevant Ω-knowledge (problem 1) and helps to aggregate, combine, and resolve the complexity of existing Ω-knowledge (problem 2).

5   Discussion

Current state-of-the-art knowledge is typically captured in scientific publications that represent knowledge in natural language. Hence, researchers are faced with two problems: first, researchers need to deal with the data-wise unstructured textual nature of scientific publications (problem 1). Second, several knowledge pieces can influence or exclude each other which makes an aggregation and combination very complex (problem 2). Thus, both problems restrict the application and sharing of Ω-knowledge in DSR. To address both problems, we proposed a two-step approach to generate machine-executable design knowledge that simplifies access to relevant Ω-knowledge in DSR. We applied the two-step approach in our DSR project to publications that investigate the outcomes of social cues of chatbots. Therefore, we transformed descriptive Ω-knowledge about social cues of chatbots into prescriptive social cue design rules (step 1). Next, we built a prescriptive social cue design rules ontology and knowledge base in order to develop a prototypical chatbot social cue configuration system (step 2). This enables researchers and designers to easily query the existing knowledge base and reduces manual effort to aggregate and combine social cue design rules. A graphical interface that links the rules to the underlying references further decreases the time to resolve any conflicts.

To apply the proposed two-step approach, researchers need to elaborate its suitability beforehand, as it cannot be applied in every context and to every type of descriptive knowledge. Therefore, researchers need to assess whether they can identify the three components needed to articulate purposeful prescriptive design knowledge, i.e., (1) actions made possible through the artifact, (2) information about the properties making the action possible, and particularly (3) boundary conditions for when it will work [34]. To demonstrate that the two-step approach can also be applied in other contexts, we exemplary applied the two-step approach to three publications that contribute valuable knowledge for the design of adaptive systems in other domains (i.e., cross-cultural websites [16], PC games [47], education systems [48]). Therefore, we performed step 1 and reviewed the publications for the three relevant information in order to define purposeful prescriptive design rules [34] (see Fig. 5).

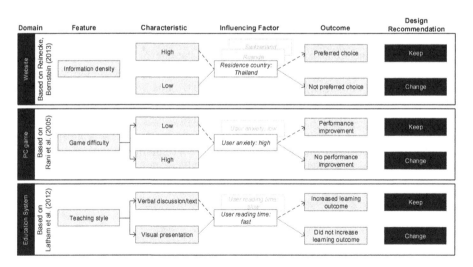

Fig. 5. Prescriptive design rules for other types of adaptive systems.

In the first example, Reinecke and Bernstein showed [16] that (1) user prefer different website designs (2) in terms of information density (3) depending on the user's cultural origin. After identifying the three information, we were able to derive a prescriptive design rule, i.e. adapt the information density of a website to the cultural origin of a user. In addition, Rani et al. [47] investigated in a computer game context how an adaptation of the game's difficulty to the user's anxiety level can improve performance. Moreover, Latham et al. [48] showed that the teaching style of an education system impacts learning outcomes depending on the user's reading time. Both findings can be transformed into prescriptive design rules for the design of games or education systems depending on an influencing factor (i.e., anxiety level, reading time).

After transforming the Ω-knowledge into prescriptive design rules, we can perform step 2 and make the derived design rules machine-executable. Therefore, we can conceptualize the identified classes (e.g., website design rule, website information density, cultural origin, outcome), define properties (e.g., has information density, has cultural origin, has outcome), and instantiate the knowledge base by reviewing each prescriptive design rule (e.g., website design rule *rule 1* has information density *high*, has cultural origin *Thailand*, and has the outcome *preferred choice*). Finally, a website configuration system could query this knowledge base in order to reveal the optimal design features of a website for specific users (e.g., select *all* design characteristics from the prescriptive design rules where the user origin is *Thailand* and the design matches the user's *preferred choice*). Finally, a website configuration system could display the optimal design characteristics (e.g., information density should be *high*), which enables researchers to efficiently access, query, and (re-)use existing Ω-knowledge for the design of websites.

Consequently, we showed that the proposed approach can also be applied to simplify access to knowledge of other adaptive systems. We argue that the transformation of descriptive Ω-knowledge into a machine-executable form can be of high value for almost any field, as it allows scholars to efficiently retrieve, apply, and share design-relevant Ω-knowledge. However, our proposed approach to transform descriptive Ω-knowledge into machine-executable design rules is not free of limitations. First, we did not evaluate the approach with researchers and practitioners to see whether they accept such an artifact as well as finally trust and use the artifact. Although we applied the proposed two-step approach to other publications, future research should investigate the application and adoption of the proposed two-step approach in a controlled experiment or focus group assessment. Second, the approach does not account for causality. It only aggregates empirical cause-and-effect relationships without questioning the underlying theoretical assumptions [49]. Thus, it does not *"identify the causal claims upon which proposed design principles or theories are founded"* [50, p. 8]. Therefore, future approaches should capture the underlying theoretical foundations. Third, the aggregation of empirical results leads to a loss of precision, which could lead to an incompatible comparison of two identical labels, e.g., the construct *perceived threat* could refer to different phenomena and instances in two different publications. Therefore, future approaches should conceptualize constructs on an item level. Fourth, the initial transformation of textual knowledge in an ontology model and knowledge base requires extensive preprocessing to structure such data in a machine-executable way [13]. Therefore, future research can address this problem by developing solutions to enhance knowledge collection. Finally, the proposed two-step approach can only be used to support the scientific design process. It is not intended to replace the manual knowledge extraction process, since the iterative process of research, going back and forth in small steps, is a mandatory prerequisite for innovation and creativity. However, a simplified access to the existing knowledge-base will support researchers and practitioners to efficiently leverage existing knowledge in their DSR project.

6   Conclusion

In this paper we present a two-step approach that makes existing Ω-knowledge more applicable in DSR projects. Therefore, we propose to transform descriptive Ω-knowledge into machine-executable representation. This enhances the application of existing Ω-knowledge and facilitates the (re-)use and sharing of already extracted knowledge pieces. In addition, we show that the two-step approach is not only limited to the specific context of socially-adaptive chatbots. Hence, researchers and designers can apply our approach to simplify knowledge access in their DSR projects. This facilitates a theory-guided artifact design process and supports building a more comprehensive body-of-knowledge in the field of IS and beyond.

References

1. Hevner, A., Vom Brocke, J., Maedche, A.: Roles of digital innovation in design science research. Bus. Inf. Syst. Eng. **6**, 39 (2018)
2. Gregor, S., Hevner, A.R.: Positioning and presenting design science research for maximum impact. MIS Q. **37**, 337–355 (2013)
3. Hevner, A.R., March, S.T., Park, J., Ram, S.: Design science in information systems research. MIS Q. **28**, 75–105 (2004)
4. Drechsler, A., Hevner, A.R.: Utilizing, producing, and contributing design knowledge in DSR projects. In: Chatterjee, S., Dutta, K., Sundarraj, R.P. (eds.) DESRIST 2018. LNCS, vol. 10844, pp. 82–97. Springer, Cham (2018). https://doi.org/10.1007/978-3-319-91800-6_6
5. Auer, S.: Towards an open research knowledge graph (2018). https://doi.org/10.5281/zenodo.1157185
6. Marcondes, C.H.: From scientific communication to public knowledge: the scientific article web published as a knowledge base (2005)
7. Davenport, T.H., de Long, D.W., Beers, M.C.: Successful knowledge management projects. Sloan Manag. Rev. **39**, 43–57 (1998)
8. Staab, S., Studer, R.: Handbook on Ontologies. Springer, Heidelberg (2019). https://doi.org/10.1007/978-3-540-92673-3
9. Hovorka, D.S., Larsen, K.R., Birt, J., Finnie, G.: A meta-theoretic approach to theory integration in information systems. In: 46th Hawaii International Conference on System Sciences (HICSS), pp. 4656–4665 (2013)
10. Larsen, K.R., Bong, C.H.: A tool for addressing construct identity in literature reviews and meta-analyses. MIS Q. **40**, 529–551 (2016)

11. Morana, S., et al.: Tool support for design science research-towards a software ecosystem: a report from a DESRIST 2017 workshop. In: Communications of the Association for Information Systems, vol. 43 (2018)
12. vom Brocke, J., et al.: Tool-support for design science research: design principles and instantiation. SSRN Electron. J. 1–13 (2017). https://doi.org/10.2139/ssrn.2972803
13. Maedche, A., Motik, B., Stojanovic, L., Studer, R., Volz, R.: Ontologies for enterprise knowledge management. IEEE Intell. Syst. **18**, 26–33 (2003)
14. Larsen, K.R., et al.: Behavior change interventions: the potential of ontologies for advancing science and practice. J. Behav. Med. **40**, 6–22 (2017)
15. Berners-Lee, T., Hendler, J., Lassila, O.: The semantic web. Sci. Am. **284**, 34–43 (2001)
16. Reinecke, K., Bernstein, A.: Knowing what a user likes: a design science approach to interfaces that automatically adapt to culture. MIS Q. **37**, 427–453 (2013)
17. Horridge, M.: A Practical Guide To Building OWL Ontologies Using Protégé 4 and CO-ODE Tools Edition 1.3. University of Manchester (2011)
18. Musen, M.A.: The protégé project: a look back and a look forward. AI Matters **1**, 4–12 (2015)
19. Dale, R.: The return of the chatbots. Nat. Lang. Eng. **22**, 811–817 (2016)
20. Gnewuch, U., Morana, S., Maedche, A.: Towards designing cooperative and social conversational agents for customer service. In: Proceedings of the 38th International Conference on Information Systems (ICIS). AISel, Seoul (2017)
21. Gnewuch, U., Morana, S., Heckmann, C., Maedche, A.: Designing conversational agents for energy feedback. In: Chatterjee, S., Dutta, K., Sundarraj, R.P. (eds.) DESRIST 2018. LNCS, vol. 10844, pp. 18–33. Springer, Cham (2018). https://doi.org/10.1007/978-3-319-91800-6_2
22. Rietz, T., Benke, I., Maedche, A.: The impact of anthropomorphic and functional chatbot design features in enterprise collaboration systems on user acceptance. In: 14. Internationale Tagung Wirtschaftsinformatik (WI 2019) (2019)
23. Mimoun, M.S.B., Poncin, I., Garnier, M.: Case study—embodied virtual agents. An analysis on reasons for failure. J. Retail. Consum. Serv. **19**, 605–612 (2012)
24. Nass, C., Moon, Y.: Machines and mindlessness. social responses to computers. J. Soc. Issues **56**, 81–103 (2000)
25. Feine, J., Morana, S., Gnewuch, U.: Measuring service encounter satisfaction with customer service chatbots using sentiment analysis. In: 14. Internationale Tagung Wirtschaftsinformatik (WI 2019) (2019)
26. Nass, C., Steuer, J., Tauber, E.R.: Computers are social actors. In: Proceedings of the SIGCHI Conference on Human Factors in Computing Systems, pp. 72–78. ACM, New York (1994)
27. Gnewuch, U., Morana, S., Adam, M., Maedche, A.: Faster is not always better: understanding the effect of dynamic response delays in human-chatbot interaction. In: Proceedings of the 26th European Conference on Information Systems (ECIS), Portsmouth, 23–28 June 2018
28. Fogg, B.J.: Computers as persuasive social actors. In: Persuasive Technology: Using Computers to Change What We Think and Do, pp. 89–120. Morgan Kaufmann Publishers, San Francisco (2002)
29. Hurst, A., Hudson, S.E., Mankoff, J., Trewin, S.: Automatically detecting pointing performance. In: Proceedings of the 13th International Conference on Intelligent User Interfaces, Gran Canaria, pp. 11–19. ACM (2008)

30. Webster, J., Watson, R.T.: Analyzing the past to prepare for the future. Writing a literature review. MIS Q. **26**, xiii–xxiii (2002)
31. Sah, Y.J., Peng, W.: Effects of visual and linguistic anthropomorphic cues on social perception, self-awareness, and information disclosure in a health website. Comput. Hum. Behav. **45**, 392–401 (2015)
32. Puzakova, M., Rocereto, J.F., Kwak, H.: Ads are watching me. Int. J. Advertising **32**, 513–538 (2013)
33. Catrambone, R., Stasko, J., Xiao, J.: ECA as user interface paradigm. In: Ruttkay, Z., Pelachaud, C. (eds.) From Brows to Trust. HIS, vol. 7, pp. 239–267. Springer, Dordrecht (2004). https://doi.org/10.1007/1-4020-2730-3_9
34. Chandra, L., Seidel, S., Gregor, S.: Prescriptive knowledge in IS research: conceptualizing design principles in terms of materiality, action, and boundary conditions. In: 48th Hawaii International Conference on System Sciences, pp. 4039–4048 (2015)
35. McBreen, H.: Embodied conversational agents in E-commerce applications. In: Dautenhahn, K., Bond, A., Cañamero, L., Edmonds, B. (eds.) Socially Intelligent Agents. Multiagent Systems, Artificial Societies, and Simulated Organizations, vol. 3. Springer, Boston (2002). https://doi.org/10.1007/0-306-47373-9_33
36. Nass, C., Moon, Y., Fogg, B.J., Reeves, B., Dryer, D.C.: Can computer personalities be human personalities? Int. J. Hum Comput Stud. **43**, 223–239 (1995)
37. Kraemer, N.C., Karacora, B., Lucas, G., Dehghani, M., Ruether, G., Gratch, J.: Closing the gender gap in STEM with friendly male instructors? On the effects of rapport behavior and gender of a virtual agent in an instructional interaction. Comput. Educ. **99**, 1–13 (2016)
38. Brahnam, S., de Angeli, A.: Gender affordances of conversational agents. Interact. Comput. **24**, 139–153 (2012)
39. Niculescu, A., Hofs, D., van Dijk, B., Nijholt, A.: How the agent's gender influence users' evaluation of a QA system. In: International Conference on User Science and Engineering (i-USEr) (2010)
40. Nunamaker, J.E., Derrick, D.C., Elkins, A.C., Burgoon, J.K., Patton, M.W.: Embodied conversational agent-based kiosk for automated interviewing. J. Manag. Inf. Syst. **28**, 17–48 (2011)
41. Li, J., Zhou, M.X., Yang, H., Mark, G.: Confiding in and listening to virtual agents. In: Proceedings of the 22nd International Conference on Intelligent User Interfaces - IUI, pp. 275–286. ACM Press (2017)
42. Hone, K.: Empathic agents to reduce user frustration. The effects of varying agent characteristics. Interacting Comput. **18**, 227–245 (2006)
43. Forlizzi, J., Zimmerman, J., Mancuso, V., Kwak, S.: How interface agents affect interaction between humans and computers. In: Proceedings of the 2007 Conference on Designing Pleasurable Products and Interfaces, pp. 209–221. ACM, New York (2007)
44. Hayashi, Y.: Lexical network analysis on an online explanation task. Effects of affect and embodiment of a pedagogical agent. IEICE Trans. Inf. Syst. **99**, 1455–1461 (2016)
45. Beldad, A., Hegner, S., Hoppen, J.: The effect of virtual sales agent (VSA) gender – product gender congruence on product advice credibility, trust in VSA and online vendor, and purchase intention. Comput. Hum. Behav. **60**, 62–72 (2016)
46. Ostrowski, L., Helfert, M., Gama, N.: Ontology engineering step in design science research methodology: a technique to gather and reuse knowledge. Behav. Inf. Technol. **33**, 443–451 (2014)

47. Rani, P., Sarkar, N., Liu, C.: Maintaining optimal challenge in computer games through real-time physiological feedback. In: Proceedings of the 11th International Conference on Human Computer Interaction, vol. 58 (2005)
48. Latham, A., Crockett, K., McLean, D., Edmonds, B.: A conversational intelligent tutoring system to automatically predict learning styles. Comput. Educ. **59**, 95–109 (2012)
49. Durand, R., Vaara, E.: Causation, counterfactuals, and competitive advantage. Strateg. Manag. J. **30**, 1245–1264 (2009)
50. Hovorka, D.S., Gregor, S.: Untangling causality in design science theorizing. In: 5th Biennial ANU Workshop on Information Systems Foundations, pp. 1–16 (2010)

Work-Integrated Learning as an Outcome of Using Action Design Research in Practice

Amir Haj-Bolouri[1]([⊠]), Christian Master Östlund[1], Matti Rossi[2],
and Lars Svensson[1]

[1] School of Economics, Business, and IT, University West, Trollhättan, Sweden
{amir.haj-bolouri, christian.ostlund,
lars.svensson}@hv.se
[2] Information Systems, Aalto University, Helsinki, Finland
matti.rossi@aalto.fi

Abstract. This paper highlights Work-Integrated Learning (WIL) as an outcome of using Action Design Research (ADR) in practice. We argue that ADR is a subtype of Design Science Research (DSR) and a prominent method for facilitating mutually beneficial collaboration between academia and practice. Subsequently, we tie our work around ADR and WIL to the Scandinavian school of IS-research and worker participation, by emphasizing reflective practice on both researcher and practitioner side. We demonstrate this through two empirical cases and four case episodes. Consequently, the cases highlight building, intervention, and evaluation in the areas of civic orientation and county administration. The narrative around each case focuses on ADR-activities that mediate reflection and learning through iterative cycles. Outcomes from the cases are reported as WIL-outcomes and finally, we conclude this paper by briefly suggesting two implications for future relevant research.

Keywords: Action Design Research · Work-Integrated learning ·
Reflective practice · Design Science Research

1 Introduction

Information Systems (IS) is an applied research discipline that has a history of believing in bridging scientific rigor with practical relevance. This generally concerns the adoption and improvement of methodologies and theories that help IS-researchers produce and bridge practical outcomes with theoretical contributions. A number of scientific and practitioner commentaries call for research approaches and methodologies that incorporate a dual mode of contribution through collaborative projects between practice and academia. Examples of this kind of work can be found in Action Research (AR) [1, 2], which aims for knowledge development through collaboration and intervention in real-world settings. Similarly, the paradigm of Design Science Research (DSR) in IS aims to produce efficient artifacts that support human activities [3–6]. Other examples include Practice Research (PR) [7], Collaborative Practice Research (CPR) [8], Engaged Scholarship (ES) [9, 10], Participatory Design (PD) [11, 12], and Action Design Research (ADR) [13].

© Springer Nature Switzerland AG 2019
B. Tulu et al. (Eds.): DESRIST 2019, LNCS 11491, pp. 92–107, 2019.
https://doi.org/10.1007/978-3-030-19504-5_7

The ADR-method in particular has gained increasing attention among IS researchers [14, 15]. In essence, the underlying philosophy of ADR advocates that the researchers shall start an ADR-project by emphasizing a specific problem or objective that is situated within a specific and real setting [e.g. 16]. From there on, the researchers engage with members of an ADR-team, which is constituted of stakeholders, such as, practitioners, and end-users [13]. A central aspect of the ADR-philosophy is thus sufficient collaboration between academia and practice. Such collaboration is organized and executed through iterative cycles of ADR-activities (e.g. building and evaluation of technologies, organizational intervention), which bridge a contribution of practical outcomes with theoretical outputs. In turn, a continuous process of reflection and learning is incorporated through mutual involvement between representatives of academia and practice [17]. An ADR-project is thus organized and performed through a collaboration between academia and practice, rather than being performed as an isolated research endeavor. The ADR-method provides a framework for participation that is organized into four stages (shown in Fig. 1).

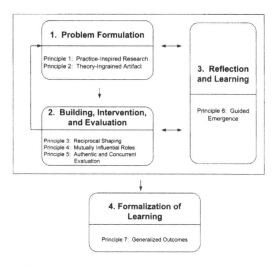

Fig. 1. ADR method: stages and principles [13]

Previous ADR-studies [16–23] motivate and verify the utility of ADR from perspectives of continuous process of building, intervention, and evaluation of sufficient artifacts that solve situated problems (e.g. organizational issues); iterative cycles of reflection and learning that are incorporated across various stages of ADR and producing generalizable learning outcomes and sharing those with representatives of both academia and practice. In this paper we argue that these perspectives of ADR implicitly incorporate a continuous learning process that enables a reciprocal knowledge transfer among scholars and practitioners. We frame this kind of learning outcome as Work-Integrated Learning (WIL) [24, 25], because it is organized and executed within the realms of (a) working environment through a process of being pro-active toward a reflective practice, intervention, and learning [26, 27] - rather than being formally detached from it.

The rationale and motivation behind discussing ADR from the perspective of WIL, can be summarized in the following arguments:

> **Collaboration** and *participation* are essential components of a practice-driven IS-research approach [8, 12, 28–32]
>
> **Collaboration, participation,** and *organizational intervention*, are discussed in WIL-related research [24, 25, 33, 34] as driving factors that engage practitioners in reflective learning processes at work
>
> **ADR facilitates collaboration and participation** through cyclical iterations of producing practical outcomes (e.g. building and evaluating IT-artifacts) that are bridged with formalized research outputs (e.g. design principles). Consequently, ADR emphasizes *organizational intervention, reflection and learning*, as key components of an ADR-cycle.

These arguments support the idea that practice centered research methods, such as ADR, support WIL implicitly, but can be made explicit through ADR-method development where interaction, reflection and collaboration between researchers and practitioners is designed to support mutual work-integrated learning. We will attempt to do so in this paper to achieve the following two objectives:

1. To initiate a discussion about ADR that concern humans, knowledge, learning, and work, as well as building and evaluation of sufficient artifacts.
2. To introduce WIL as an outcome of ADR where activities for reflection and formalization of learning is designed to support organizational transformation as well as supporting the further development of ADR.

The paper is structured as follows: first we will provide a general introduction to WIL as a research domain that studies the relations between humans, knowledge, learning, and work. Then, we will frame and discuss aspects of WIL within the IS-literature. We will in particular emphasize the participatory component of WIL and tie it to the longer perspective of Scandinavian approach to IS and worker participation. After that, we will demonstrate WIL as a practical outcome of ADR through case specific scenarios. Finally, we will provide a concluding discussion.

2 Work-Integrated Learning

At its core, WIL emphasizes a range of approaches and strategies that integrate theory with practice within a designed education curriculum [35]. WIL as a research domain is not solely constrained to the objective of bridging practice with theory through formalized education. Rather, WIL emphasizes the relations between humans, knowledge, learning, and work, as study phenomena. WIL concepts highlight how approaches and methods can be used to integrate learning processes with work activities to bridge different professions. Early works of Lave and Wenger [36] and Wenger [37] discussed foundations of WIL from the perspectives of situated learning and communities of practice, where members of a community share a collective activity in which a common interest binds them together through mutual engagement and the sharing of collective resources such as routines, tools, and notions. Learning was consequently defined as a social process of collaboration, engagement, and participation in everyday activities in and between communities of practice [36, 37]. Subsequently, learning derives from the socio-cultural theory of learning (see e.g. [38] for an early discussion), and has been utilized in different constellations of WIL-related research [24, 25, 34–37].

Billett [24, 25] in particular, elaborates WIL from the aspects of collaboration, engagement, and participation, by emphasizing how workplaces provide opportunities for learning, and how that is integrated with work activities through guidance of advanced members within a community of practice. Billet [24] problematizes how participation in a professional community can increase levels of expertise through gradual and continuous learning process at work, and highlights the importance of designing for pedagogically rich activities [39] where agentic participants (40) from different communities can maximize the potential for mutual learning in a joint endeavor (e.g. researchers and practitioners in an ADR-project). WIL has been outlined and profiled by [41] as follows:

Development of 'hard' and 'soft' skills at work
Developing multi-tasking skills at work
Promoting knowledge at work through formal and informal learning processes
Promoting new technologies at work that incorporate learning activities
Engaging practitioners in processes of reflective learning at work
Establishing a knowledge-sharing culture through participation and co-participation
Intrapersonal and interpersonal learning.
Transformative and reflective learning

We note that all eight points implicitly depend on structures for diffusion of WIL in research and that practice organizations are in place to support transformative learning where the outcome of ADR catalyzes persistent organizational development [42]. We will, in the next section, continue to elaborate on these characteristics from the perspective of the Scandinavian School of IS-research and worker participation.

3 Scandinavian School of IS-Research and Worker Participation

Early works within the Scandinavian school of IS-research [11, 28, 43–46] emphasized the design process (of sufficient systems) as intertwined with a subsequent participation of workers. Ehn [28] for instance, scrutinized the human activity of designing computer artifacts that are useful to people in their daily activity at work, by emphasizing opportunities and constraints for industrial democracy and quality of work. Others such as Greenbaum and Kyng [46], elaborated essentials of how users can be involved through participation and cooperation during the design process, in order to collectively design computer systems that support and sustain the working environment of users. This underlying philosophy of engaging and involving users as co-participants of the design process, is the foundational pillar of Participatory Design (PD), which has its roots in Scandinavia and which has been (and still is) frequently incorporated in IS-research.

PD aims at designing efficient and sufficient IT-artifacts, by involving prospective users (and other stakeholders) in the design process. According to Bratteteig and Wagner [12], [32] PD differs from other user or human-centered design approaches, because PD emphasizes users as co-designers or co-participants during all phases of the design process. Enabling collaboration and allowing different 'voices' (e.g. researchers, designers, users) to be heard, is inherently incorporated by the PD-philosophy. This is implicitly explicated by Robertson and Wagner [47, p. 65] as follows:

> The Core Principle of PD is that people have a basic right to make decisions about how they do their work and indeed any other activities where they might use technology. This is also the most contested aspect of PD, its most directly stated ethical commitment and its main point of different to more mainstream user- or human-centered design approaches.

Scandinavian projects that incorporated prior notions of PD [11, 28, 48, 49] for more information), also developed an *Action Research* (AR) approach, emphasizing active co-operation between researches and workers of the organization to help improve the workers' work situation. This approach is built on the workers' own experiences, needs and requirements, incorporated through in situ collaboration between researchers and workers. However, in current times, IT-artifacts enable people to work at different places (e.g. home, office) and time, making the landscape of work a complex arena for designers and researchers to incorporate through traditional PD-approaches [50].

Participatory philosophy is incorporated by several current IS-research approaches (e.g. *Engaged Scholarship, Collaborative Practice Research, ADR*) inspired by the Scandinavian school of IS-research. Subsequently, early theories of action, organizational learning, and reflective practice [51, 52], are ideas that have been adopted and integrated into the designated stage of *reflection and learning* in the ADR-framework. Several recent extensions of ADR [53, 54] have attempted to elaborate the *participatory* aspect with an emphasis on cycles of reflective learning through practice.

We argue that ADR is highly inspired by the Scandinavian philosophy of IS-research with a particular interest for incorporating reflective practices and learning through action, design, and participation. Such characteristics (*participation, reflection, learning, practice*) are also central to WIL.

4   Two Empirical Cases of Producing WIL as an Outcome of ADR

This section outlines two cases where WIL was produced as an outcome of ADR. Both cases were conducted separately from each other and the principle researchers of the cases (author 1 and author 2) were not involved in each other's case. We will thus, for each separate case, elaborate and highlight two specific episodes that concern how WIL was produced as an outcome of utilizing ADR. A summary of each case's empirical setting is depicted in Table 1.

Table 1. The empirical setting of both cases

Case	Description
Case 1 – Designing e-learning solutions for the civic orientation program	The empirical setting of the first case was at a municipality in Sweden. The municipality was responsible for supporting the integration work of newly arrived immigrants in Sweden, also known as *newcomers*. The integration workers organize and perform civic orientation for a large and heterogeneous group of newcomers (e.g. newcomers from Somalia, Syria etc.). In turn, through participation in the civic orientation program, the newcomers learn fundamental knowledge about society such as: what is democracy, what are the laws in Sweden, what is the education like, etc. through classroom teachings
Case 2 – Designing a national work-integrated e-learning platform	The setting of the second case is the county administration in the Western part of Sweden. Essentially, the county administration is a government authority that ensures decisions made by the government and parliament are carried out locally in each of the 21 counties. Hereby the county administration serves as a link between the people and the municipal authorities on the one hand and the government, parliament and other central authorities on the other hand. Within the study, the county administration in the Western part of Sweden launched a project called the *Academy of County Administrations* aiming at creating a national platform for work integrated e-learning where the expertize from different counties would be made available

4.1 Case 1 – Designing an E-Learning Platform for the Civic Orientation Program

The primary reason for designing e-learning solutions for the civic orientation program was due to the need of distributing and making the program available nationwide. This had to do with the large influx of newcomers in Sweden as well as the need of performing the program through a flexible that combine different e-learning solutions – e.g. different pedagogies (e.g. e-learning, blended learning), different modes of performing civic orientation (e.g. online, classroom). More importantly, an essential part of this case concerned how to support the integration workers and extend their knowledge base (e.g. professional roles, areas of responsibility) through work-integrated learning. Different counties and municipalities in Sweden organize and provide civic orientation in non-standardized ways, meaning that they do not share a common base of knowledge domain (e.g. skills, competencies, education).

The integration workers had different professional roles with different areas of responsibilities. Some of them were employed on full time basis, whereas some of them were employed at part time basis. Additionally, they originate from different parts of the world and are thus heterogeneous with regards to their background, age, gender, culture, and worldviews in general. Therefore, a crucial challenge within the case concerned how to design e-learning solutions that are adaptable toward the integration workers' different communities of practice. In order to address this challenge, and to incorporate their WIL continuously, certain WIL-activities were organized and conducted within the realm of the ADR-stages. These activities are summed up through two different episodes as follow.

Episode 1

The first episode took place during the ADR-stage of ***building, intervention, and evaluation (BIE)*** in 2014. This stage incorporated ***reflection and learning*** as an integrated part through a participatory workshop. The workshop was organized and conducted at the municipality together with a total of 10 integration workers. During the workshop, a framework (also referred to as a *platform*) of e-learning solutions was introduced, demonstrated, tested, and evaluated in situ with the integration workers. The integration workers were thus encouraged to (1) interact with the e-learning solutions, which consisted of different kind of technologies (e.g. cloud services, video conferencing, administrative tools etc.), (2) reflect on how well the solutions and their features were mapped with the integration workers' daily tasks and responsibilities, and (3) 'translating' their experiences into future needs and refinements of the framework.

During the workshop, we combined an active process of reflection and learning with testing and evaluation of the framework, by (1) demonstrating the features and letting the integration workers test them; (2) observing their interaction with the framework; (3) collecting feedback through a roundtable discussion at the end of the workshop. The workshop was documented through notes and video recording. Excerpts from the roundtable discussion are depicted in Table 2.

Table 2. Excerpts and analysis from the participatory workshop

Excerpts	Analysis
I like the idea of combining different simple technologies to organize and prepare my sessions… it seems that this platform can be adapted and used at different levels of complexity… which is good, but requires more knowledge about the different features. (Tutor)	Sense-making of the IT-tools and their relevance occur through early incremental testing and in situ evaluation

(*continued*)

Table 2. (*continued*)

Excerpts	Analysis
In the beginning I thought that the platform features were too trivial and not sufficient... especially from the perspective of coordinating content and sessions... but then after this workshop and the discussions... I feel that the features are easy to understand and adapt to... even for a person that is not an IT expert like me... this is important, especially because we at the integration center have different IT skills... and also because we need to teach future employees how the platform works... so I like the adaptable feeling of the features. (Coordinator)	Sense-making of the IT-tools and their relevance occur through early incremental testing and in situ evaluation
The security features seem to be easy to administrate... I mean, because we need to administrate different users I guess... ranging from being tutors, to newcomers... from this perspective, the features need to be easy to understand and adapt to... and it seems that they are adaptable enough to different kind of users in the system. (Coordinator)	Sense-making of the IT-tools and their relevance toward different users occur through early incremental testing and in situ evaluation

Based on insights from analysis and experiences of the workshop, we share a summary of what we consider being the WIL outcome:

- **WIL outcome – active learning and sense-making**: the workshop facilitated dialogues and a social process of sense-making, which enabled the integration workers to not only learn how to use the provided e-learning solutions, but also to learn the underlying meaning and relevance of the framework toward their roles and areas of responsibilities. Analysis of the excerpts indicate that early incremental testing and in situ evaluation, incorporates sense-making through a continuous and attached process of reflection and learning. This is an implication of encouraging active learning through participation and involvement of the integration workers, rather than treating them as passive recipients of implemented technologies. Here, we consider that WIL was produced through ADR due to active *participation* and *sense-making* during the stage of **building, intervention, and evaluation**. ADR did thus produce work-integrated learning as a practical outcome of the participatory workshop activities. In retrospect – we believe the workshops to be pedagogically rich activities [39], where the shared responsibility of the agenda contributed to making all participants agentic learners [40], and set the stage for transformative learning [42].

Episode 2

The second episode took place during the *building, intervention, and evaluation* stage in 2015. This stage was incorporated the stage of *reflection and learning* as an integrated part and was manifested through a set of workplace training sessions at the municipality. A total of 6 sessions were held with each session focusing on a particular training theme (depicted in Table 3).

Table 3. Workplace training sessions

Training session	Purpose	Participants
Training Sessions 1, 2, 3	To demonstrate, test, and learn collaborative features for distributing and publishing non-standardized online-learning content, together with underlying teaching pedagogies that support the features. The scope of these sessions was provided on a very fundamental level, with a simple structure and facts about the nature and purpose of the collaborative features. Participants were encouraged to test the features systematically within the frame of each session and ask questions sporadically when needed. These three sessions lasted for three hours per session	- 15 integration workers - 1 researcher
Training Sessions 4, 5	To demonstrate, test, and learn administrative features for producing, coordinating, sharing, and maintaining civic orientation content (both standardized and non-standardized). Participants were encouraged to test the features systematically within the frame of each session and ask questions sporadically when needed. These two sessions lasted for two hours per session	- 6 integration workers - 2 scholars - 1 researcher
Training Session 6	To elaborate extended roles of practitioners by introducing and explaining new areas of responsibilities. Here, the participants became familiar with new concepts and words, which help them understand their new responsibilities better. The new roles were introduced as system roles. The session lasted for three hours	- 12 integration workers - 2 scholars - 1 researcher

The first **three training sessions** focused on systematically training tutors and providing them fundamental knowledge about relevant system features that support their work with organizing and conducting civic orientation sessions in dual settings (e.g. classroom and digital setting). During the sessions, the researcher demonstrated all of the system features and encouraged the tutors to test and interact with the features continuously. The integration workers were basically provided with a tablet or laptop to interact with the artifact features. The approach of this session was inspired through informing literature [55–58] that promotes direct interaction between participants and technology, and which advocates an open philosophy for thinking about and discussing input from the participants as a reflective practice [26, 51, 52]. Thus, the participants were encouraged to reflect and provide input as they were interacting with the system.

The **fourth and fifth training sessions** focused on systematically training the content producers and coordinators and providing them advanced know-how about how to produce, coordinate, share, maintain, update, distribute, and publish civic orientation content. At this stage, a dichotomy was made between standardized content and non-standardized content, where standardized content was addressed as the formal course book or PowerPoint slides, whereas the non-standardized content was addressed as content that a unique tutor, in collaboration with content producers, can create and implement in their unique course sites. Essential artifact features of this purpose were presented and tested during the sessions. The integration workers were provided with a tablet or computer to interact with and test the features.

The **sixth and final training session** focused on introducing and explaining extended roles and areas of responsibility. This concerned extending and re-defining the integration workers' current roles with respect to new system roles, which concern new areas of responsibility for managing and administering the instantiated platform. The new areas of responsibility included adopting system roles that focus on various aspects of maintaining components of the platform's technical architecture, as well as its system layers. The session ended with an open discussion about the organizational implications of introducing new roles, and how such implications may affect the current organizational prerequisites.

In light of the workplace training activities and their outcomes, we highlight the WIL-outcome of the second episode as follows:

- **WIL outcome – workplace training and on-site learning:** the workplace training sessions are explicit examples of how WIL can be produced as a practical outcome of ADR. Here, the stage of *reflection and learning* was directly incorporated into the workplace training sessions by enabling learning to take place at the integration workers' workplace (on-site learning), mapped together with their different roles, responsibilities, and daily working routines.

The training sessions were thus not detached from their reality of work (as for instance formalized sessions of education may be). Instead, it was integrated with their work and each session highlighted and provided the integration workers with a relevant body of knowledge. Consequently, a reflective practice was facilitated through questions, dialogues, and a continuous process of interaction, which allowed the integration workers to reflect about their extended roles, responsibilities, and what bearing new concepts and words (e.g. e-learning, distance education) have toward their own practice of integration work.

We claim that this aspect of supporting a reflective practice through ADR, is a part of producing WIL as an outcome. The BIE-activities in an ADR-project are indeed candidates for what Billet [39] calls pedagogically rich activities. Subsequently, the experiences from the civic-orientation case, strengthened a view that the designed artifact can serve as a boundary object [37] that fosterers intra- and inter-professional transformative learning [42].

4.2   Case 2 – Designing a Nationwide Work-Integrated E-Learning Platform

The primary reason for initiating this case was the negative experiences from a large competence development project that was launched because the Swedish Parliament decided that there should be a nationally unified environmental policy. As a consequence, adjacent counties were forced to collaborate to a greater extent than before and the policy change effected work practices throughout all areas of the county administrations. To address this, all 21 county administrations developed learning materials and arranged courses in various forms. The problem was that this was done in parallel with each other, with virtually no coordination or cooperation. The large shared costs for all these separate learning initiatives constituted a strong incentive to create a national platform for online education where experts from different counties could collaborate in developing digital courses. We will as follows highlight the WIL-outcomes of this case through two the subsequent case episodes (episode 3 and 4).

Episode 3
The initial ADR-team within the case consisted of two senior researchers, a PhD student, and three representatives from the County administration of Western part of Sweden (HR Manager, IT-manager, and an IT-expert). In addition, the project group reported to a reference group with representatives from the other participating county administrations. There was a need for increased skills in online searching expressed by employees through special interest groups and the project group decided that the first e-training initiative should be on the theme *Searching the WWW*. It was expressed by the representatives from the County administration that the e-training solution had to be flexible so that using it would not interfere with the employees' daily work.

   During this first ADR-cycle, the goal was to develop a design concept for web-based lectures that could be used on other e-training courses. The initial problem phase exposed that there was a lack of research that acknowledges the complexity of the interplay that technology and pedagogy create when designing systems for learning and training in the workplace. A literature review [59–61] resulted in design-oriented theories and frameworks in a school setting, but eventually the authentic e-learning by Herrington et al. [60] was chosen to guide the design in stage of *building*, *intervention*, and *evaluation*.

   Based on the pedagogical design framework of authentic e-learning [57] and the design frameworks for the interaction design and usability [62–64], a pilot system was built and tested in the IT environment at the county administration. After initial tests of different tools done by the researchers the choice fell on an XML based synchronization language called SMIL. SMIL gave a developer great freedom concerning layout and re-usability of the content. To run a SMIL application a standalone application such as the Ambulant Player had to be installed on the computer. A pilot system was built using SMIL and was evaluated throughout the *reflection and learning* stage, which was facilitated through a workshop with the representatives from the county administration. In light of this stage, we consider the WIL-outcome as follow

- **WIL outcome – reciprocal shaping of an e-training solution:** The workshop made it evident that the e-training system had to be re-designed so that it would run on one of the applications already available in the IT infrastructure of the county administration. This workshop resulted in the design principle - the limitations and opportunities of the organizational and infrastructural context must be carefully considered as a frame for the design of e-training. A new version using embedded HTML was then developed, implemented and evaluated in two more design cycles. Again, the episode demonstrates how the designed artefact can work as a catalyst for learning across the boundaries between researchers and practitioners and their respective contexts [42]. It is also a good illustration of how tentative design principles can be confirmed, rejected and/or developed [65] through pedagogically rich work-integrated learning interactions.

Episode 4
During the second ADR-cycle of designing the e-training system, the county administration approached the researchers of the ADR-team, since their IT department were about to start building the e-training system. The reason for this was that the county administration was migrating to one common IT milieu on a national level at the time of the study. This meant that e.g. using only one email client throughout the organization instead of the local counties choosing their own. For some counties this meant a big change in reference to system beings used in the everyday practice and for others already using a lot of the systems being implemented in the new common IT milieu it only meant minor changes.

The particular WIL outcome of this cycle is highlighted as follow:

- **WIL outcome – employee preparation:** In order to prepare the employees throughout the different counties for this change of IT milieu, an e-training system–technologies used to automate IT and business processes in general - would be developed and made available to them before the new IT milieu would be implemented. This was done throughout the building, intervention, and evaluation of the second ADR-cycle, where the authentic e-learning and interface framework were presented and discussed with the developing team during a workshop at the county administration. During this stage, reflection and learning, the team decided to develop and implement the e-training system guided by design-oriented theories of authentic e-learning and the lessons learned from the evaluations from the first cycle - e.g. by addressing the issues with collaboration and articulation by encouraging the employees to discuss any questions they would have with colleagues. The pedagogically rich activity is when developers meet with researchers to jointly make sense of how the guidelines could be translated to a new situation [39].

5 Concluding Remarks

In this paper, we have argued and demonstrated how and why work-integrated learning can be seen as an outcome of using ADR in practice. This is one critical element of engaging with practitioners and keeping them engaged and delivering knowledge outcomes for them from an ADR project. Subsequently, we have (1) initiated a discussion about ADR from a dual perspective that concern humans, knowledge, learning, and work, as well as building and evaluation of sufficient artifacts; (2) introduced WIL as an outcome of ADR and a research domain that incorporate IS-research through relevant concepts and theories of work and learning, and (3) emphasizing that WIL in an ADR-project involves both the learning and transformative practices in the participating practices, as well as the researchers' learning in terms of method development of all four stages in the ADR-cycle.

We argue that ADR is a prominent method for bridging the gap between academia and practice, and that ADR incorporates typical characteristics (e.g. *participation, collaboration, organizational intervention, transformative learning*) of both WIL and the Scandinavian school of IS-research and worker participation. Consequently, we have demonstrated this through four case episodes, where ADR was retrospectively analyzed as a way to produce WIL outcomes. We do also suggest that, by fostering a participatory philosophy, ADR enables organizations and practitioners a continuous process of reflection and learning, which incorporates a reflective practice and challenges of transformative/expansive learning among practitioners. Additionally, we argue that our work is one of the few within the DSR-literature that highlights ADR from the perspective of WIL, and that this research may initiate further curiosity and interest within the DSR-community, about the relation between ADR and WIL-especially for future ADR-researchers.

Finally, our retrospective analysis of the cases has pointed out two implications for further research: (1) how ADR-cycles can be staged to better support diffusion and transformation of ideas and artifacts in participating organization, and (2) how an emphasis on learning feedback can be returned into the development of ADR-method. We believe that these implications can be problematized on a general basis for the utilization of ADR in practice, and that insights from such an endeavor would benefit overall discussions around the utilization of DSR-methods in general. The latter issue could advance through DSR-cases that explicitly highlight learning outcomes as an integrated element of building and evaluating IT-artifacts within organizations, because essential parts of any given DSR-project are (principally at least) to, solve real world problems and to produce academic body of knowledge that incorporates practical project outcomes. Our research is a step towards that direction and we hope that future method-focused research in DSR will derive inspiration from our work.

References

1. Baskerville, R., Myers, M.: Special issue on action research in information systems: making: IS research relevant to practice – foreword. MIS Q. **28**(3), 329–335 (2004)
2. Davison, R.M., Martinsons, M.G., Kock, N.: Principles of canonical action research. Inf. Syst. J. **14**, 65–86 (2004)
3. Walls, J., Widmeyer, G., El Sawy, O.: Building an information systems design theory for vigilant EIS. Inf. Syst. Res. **3**(1), 36–59 (1992)
4. Hevner, A.R., March, S.T., Park, K.: Design research in information systems research. MIS Q. **28**(1), 76–105 (2004)

5. Gregor, S., Jones, D.: The anatomy of a design theory. J. Assoc. Inf. Syst. (JAIS) **8**(5), 312–335 (2007)
6. Peffers, K., Tuunanen, T., Rothenberger, M., Chatterjee, S.: A design science research methodology for information systems research. J. Manag. Inf. Syst. **24**(3), 45–77 (2008)
7. Goldkuhl, G.: The research practice of practice research: theorizing and situational inquiry. Syst. Signs Actions **5**(1), 7–29 (2011)
8. Mathiassen, L.: Collaborative practice research. Inf. Technol. People **15**(4), 321–345 (2002)
9. Van de Ven, A.: Engaged Scholarship: A Guide for Organizational and Social Research. Oxford University Press, New York (2007)
10. Mathiassen, L., Nielsen, P.A.: Engaged scholarship in IS research. Scand. J. Inf. Syst. **20**(2), 1 (2008)
11. Ehn, P., Kyng, M.: The collective resource approach to systems design. In: Computers and Democracy, pp. 17–57 (1987)
12. Bratteteig, T., Wagner, I.: Spaces for participatory creativity. CoDesign **8**(2-3), 105–126 (2012)
13. Sein, M., Henfridsson, O., Purao, S., Rossi, M., Lindgren, R.: Action design research. MIS Q. **35**(1), 35–56 (2011)
14. Haj-Bolouri, A., Purao, S., Rossi, M., Bernhardsson, L.: Action design research as a method-in-use: problems and opportunities. In: Designing the Digital Transformation: DESRIST 2017 Research in Progress Proceedings of the 12th International Conference on Design Science Research in Information Systems and Technology, Karlsruhe, Germany, 30 May–1 June. Karlsruher Institut für Technologie (KIT) (2017)
15. Haj-Bolouri, A., Purao, S., Rossi, M., Bernhardsson, L.: Action design research in practice: lessons and concerns. In: European Conference on Information Systems, ECIS 2018, Portsmouth, UK, 23rd June–28th 2018 (2018)
16. Mullarkey, M.T., Hevner, A.R.: Entering action design research. In: Donnellan, B., Helfert, M., Kenneally, J., VanderMeer, D., Rothenberger, M., Winter, R. (eds.) DESRIST 2015. LNCS, vol. 9073, pp. 121–134. Springer, Cham (2015). https://doi.org/10.1007/978-3-319-18714-3_8
17. Keijzer-Broers, W.J.W., de Reuver, M.: Applying agile design sprint methods in action design research: prototyping a health and wellbeing platform. In: Parsons, J., Tuunanen, T., Venable, J., Donnellan, B., Helfert, M., Kenneally, J. (eds.) DESRIST 2016. LNCS, vol. 9661, pp. 68–80. Springer, Cham (2016). https://doi.org/10.1007/978-3-319-39294-3_5
18. Lempinen, H., Rossi, M., Tuunainen, V.K.: Design principles for inter-organizational systems development – case hansel. In: Peffers, K., Rothenberger, M., Kuechler, B. (eds.) DESRIST 2012. LNCS, vol. 7286, pp. 52–65. Springer, Heidelberg (2012). https://doi.org/10.1007/978-3-642-29863-9_5
19. Mustafa, M.I., Sjöström, J.: Design principles for research data export: lessons learned in e-health design research. In: vom Brocke, J., Hekkala, R., Ram, S., Rossi, M. (eds.) DESRIST 2013. LNCS, vol. 7939, pp. 34–49. Springer, Heidelberg (2013). https://doi.org/10.1007/978-3-642-38827-9_3
20. Maccani, G., Donnellan, B., Helfert, M.: Action design research in practice: the case of smart cities. In: Tremblay, M.C., VanderMeer, D., Rothenberger, M., Gupta, A., Yoon, V. (eds.) DESRIST 2014. LNCS, vol. 8463, pp. 132–147. Springer, Cham (2014). https://doi.org/10.1007/978-3-319-06701-8_9
21. Miah, S., Gammack, J.: Ensemble artifact design for context sensitive decision support. Aust. J. Inf. Syst. **18**(2) (2014)
22. McCurdy, N., Dykes, J., Meyer, M.: Action design research and visualization design. In: Proceedings of the Sixth Workshop on Beyond Time and Errors on Novel Evaluation Methods for Visualization, BELIV 2016, pp. 10–18 (2016)

23. Haj-Bolouri, A.: Designing for adaptable learning. Doctoral Dissertation, University West (2018)
24. Billett, S.: Learning through work: workplace affordances and individual engagement. J. Work. Learn. **13**(5), 209–214 (2001)
25. Billett, S.: Workplace participatory practices: conceptualizing workplaces as learning environments. J. Work. Learn. **16**(6), 312–324 (2004)
26. Schön, D.: Educating the Reflective Practitioner. Jossey-Bass, San Francisco (1987)
27. Cole, R., Purao, S., Rossi, M., Sein, M.: Being proactive: where action research meets design research. In: International Conference on Information Systems (ICIS), Las Vegas, Nevada, USA (2005)
28. Ehn, P.: Work-oriented design of computer artifacts. Doctoral Dissertation, Arbetslivscentrum (1988)
29. Bjerknes, G., Bratteteig, T.: User participation and democracy: a discussion of Scandinavian research on system development. Scand. J. Inf. Syst. **7**(1), 1 (1995)
30. Schuler, D., Namioka, A. (eds.): Participatory Design: Principles and Practices. CRC Press, Boca Raton (1993)
31. Kensing, F.: Methods and Practices in Participatory Design. ITU Press, Copenhagen (2003)
32. Brockbank, A., McGill, I., Beech, N.: Reflective Learning in Practice. Gower Publishing, Burlington (2002)
33. Engeström, Y., Kerosuo, H.: From workplace learning to inter-organizational learning and back: the contribution of activity theory. J. Work. Learn. **19**(6), 336–342 (2007)
34. Fuller, A., Unwin, L., Felstead, A., Jewson, N., Kakavelakis, K.: Creating and using knowledge: an analysis of the differentiated nature of workplace learning environments. Br. Educ. Res. J. **33**(5), 743–759 (2007)
35. Patrick, C.-J., Peach, D., Pocknee, C., Webb, F., Fletcher, M., Pretto, G.: The WIL (Work-Integrated Learning) Report: A National Scoping Study. Australian Learning and Teaching Council (ALTC). Queensland University of Technology, Brisbane (2008)
36. Lave, J., Wenger, E.: Situated Learning: Legitimate Peripheral Participation. Cambridge University Press, Cambridge (1991)
37. Wenger, E.: Communities of Practice: Learning, Meaning, and Identity. Cambridge University Press, Cambridge (1998)
38. Vygotsky, L.S.: Socio-cultural theory. In: Mind in society (1978)
39. Billett, S.: Implications for practice. In: Mimetic Learning at Work, pp. 83–103. Springer, Cham (2014)
40. Engeström, Y.: Expansive learning at work: toward an activity theoretical reconceptualization. J. Educ. Work. **14**(1), 133–156 (2001)
41. Malloch, M., Cairns, L., Evans, K., O'Connor, B.N.: The SAGE Handbook of Workplace Learning. Sage Publications, Thousand Oaks (2010)
42. Akkerman, S.F., Bakker, A.: Boundary crossing and boundary objects. Rev. Educ. Res. **81**(2), 132–169 (2011)
43. Nygaard, K.: Tasks, roles, and interests of information systems specialists in the 1980s. Lecture at CREST Course (1979)
44. Flensburg, P.: Personlig Databehandling: Introduktion, Konsekvenser, Möjligheter. Lund Universitet (1986)
45. Bjerknes, G., Ehn, P., Kyng, M.: Computers and Democracy: A Scandinavian Challenge. Avebury, Aldershot (1987)
46. Greenbaum, J., Kyng, M.: Design at Work: Cooperative Design of Computer Systems. Erlbaum Assoc, Hillsdale (1991)
47. Robertson, T., Wagner, I.: Engagement, representation and politics-in-action. In: Simonsen, J., Robertson, T. (eds.) The Handbook of Participatory Design, pp. 64–85 (2012)

48. Bodker, K., Kensing, F., Simonsen, J.: Participatory IT Design: Designing for Business and Workplace Realities. MIT Press, Cambridge (2004)
49. Bødker, S.: Creating conditions for participation: conflicts and resources in systems development. Hum. Comput. Interact. **11**(3), 215–236 (1996)
50. Beck, E.: P for political - participation is not enough. SJIS **14** (2002)
51. Argyris, C., Schön, D.A.: Organizational Learning: A Theory of Action Perspective. Addison-Wesley, Reading (1978)
52. Schön, D.A.: The Reflective Practitioner: How Professionals Think in Action. Basic Books, New York (1983)
53. Bilandzic, M., Venable, J.: Towards a participatory action design research: adapting action research and design science research methods for urban informatics. J. Community Inform. (2011)
54. Haj-Bolouri, A., Bernhardsson, L., Rossi, M.: PADRE: a method for participatory action design research. In: Parsons, J., Tuunanen, T., Venable, J., Donnellan, B., Helfert, M., Kenneally, J. (eds.) DESRIST 2016. LNCS, vol. 9661, pp. 19–36. Springer, Cham (2016). https://doi.org/10.1007/978-3-319-39294-3_2
55. Berge, Z.L.: Obstacles to distance training and education in corporate organizations. J. Work. Learn. **14**(5), 182–189 (2002)
56. Lee, M.C.: Explaining and predicting users' continuance intention toward e-learning: an extension of the expectation–confirmation model. Comput. Educ. **54**(2), 506–516 (2010)
57. Kraiger, K., Ford, J.K.: The expanding role of workplace training: themes and trends influencing training research and practice. In: Koppes, L.L. (ed.) Historical Perspectives in Industrial and Organizational Psychology, pp. 281–309 (2006)
58. Tynjälä, P., Häkkinen, P., Hämäläinen, R.: TEL@ work: toward integration of theory and practice. Br. J. Educ. Technol. **45**(6), 990–1000 (2014)
59. Hung, D.W.L., Chen, D.: Situated cognition, vygotskian thought and learning from the communities of practice perspective: implications for the design of web-based e-learning. Educ. Media Int. **38**(1), 3–12 (2001)
60. Herrington, J., Reeves, T.C., Oliver, R.: A Guide to Authentic E-Learning. Routledge, New York (2010)
61. Hardless, C.: Designing Competence Development Systems. Department of Informatics, Göteborg University, Göteborg (2005)
62. Norman, D.A.: The Design of Everyday Things. Doubleday, New York (1988)
63. Nielsen, J.: Designing Web Usability: The Practice of Simplicity. New Riders, Indianapolis (2000)
64. Rogers, Y., Sharp, H., Preece, J.: Interaction Design: Beyond Human Computer Interaction, 3rd edn. Wiley, Hoboken (2011)
65. Östlund, C.: Design for e-training. Copenhagen Business School (2017)

Extending Design Science Research Through Systems Theory: A Hospital System of Systems

Richard J. Tarpey[1]([✉]) and Matthew T. Mullarkey[2,3]

[1] Management Department, Jones College of Business,
Middle Tennessee State University, Murfreesboro, TN, USA
Richard.tarpey@mtsu.edu
[2] Information Systems and Decision Sciences Department,
MUMA College of Business, University of South Florida, Tampa, FL, USA
mmullarkey@usf.edu
[3] Workwell: Research Unit for Economic and Management Sciences,
North-West University, Potchefstroom, South Africa

Abstract. Labor planning and allocation are critical success factors for hospitals in today's low margin, competitive healthcare environment. This research investigated the design and evaluation of an innovative labor planning and allocation system co-created with a practitioner team responsible for nursing labor management across departments in multiple hospitals within a North American hospital system. The research found a unique means to extend Design Science Research theory and practice using a Systems Theory approach to the design, build and evaluation of innovative labor allocation information and management systems within the existing hospital systems. The "system of systems" approach identified conflicting structures of management processes that prevented system balancing feedback loops from operating efficiently. An elaborated Action Design Research (eADR) method used a guided, emergent approach to redesign the structure, roles, and tasks of labor planning and allocation within this system of systems framework. The instantiated innovative nursing labor-management model was shown to benefit from its theory-ingrained approach to deliver a significantly improved labor allocation outcome for each level of the system.

Keywords: Design Science Research · Systems theory ·
elaborated Action Design Research · Hospital labor management

1 Introduction

Hospitals in the United States operate in a low margin environment. For-profit and non-profit hospitals are all under pressure to control costs while simultaneously improving patient care, which has been demonstrated to be impacted by hospital staffing levels [1–3]. Labor is typically the largest hospital organizational expense; therefore, efficient and effective utilization is key to successful operational performance. Successful utilization, however, is challenged by labor management processes which rarely develop around high-level system structures. These processes and behaviors typically evolve from the

© Springer Nature Switzerland AG 2019
B. Tulu et al. (Eds.): DESRIST 2019, LNCS 11491, pp. 108–122, 2019.
https://doi.org/10.1007/978-3-030-19504-5_8

lower system (departmental) structures creating organizational silos for labor planning and allocation.

In these labor-management silos, department leaders are prone to developing "us vs. them" or "self-protection" mentalities as noted in organizational behavior literature [4]. The inter-department competition for labor resources caused by a narrow focus on individual departmental success can result in sub-optimization of the utilization of labor across the service line or hospital system. These disconnected departmental labor systems come into conflict with system-managed processes in the hospital that require interdependence and inter-dependability such as the management of patient flow.

Patients routinely flow across the hospital landscape driven by care requirements. The labor needed to serve these patients and the associated allocation information becomes "bound" at the department level resulting in significant loss of productive time. In some cases, patient care can be compromised, as extraordinary efforts (over-time, on-call staffing, floating staffing, etc.) are employed to ameliorate the inherent homeostasis. The research effort focused on diagnosing the systemic challenges of operating with greater efficiency and efficacy in the nursing labor allocation between departments given dynamic patient flows in a large hospital system.

2   Research Design

The initial problem diagnosis identified a gap that existed between the desire to optimize the Labor Planning and Allocation Cycle (LPAC) and the actual resultant staffing as compared to dynamic patient flows in hospitals. The project team was composed of a principal investigator, vice-president nursing labor management, and nursing department chairs for several departments and hospitals within the macro-hospital system.

The practitioners' initial objective was to document an understanding of critical inputs to LPAC components, knowledge generated and shared within and between each component, work and task structure that impact knowledge creation and sharing, and organizational structures that facilitate confirming and corrective interventions. The team postulated that this understanding could subsequently be leveraged to re-shape the Systemic LPAC as the framework for designing new work and organizational structures/systems to facilitate system performance and outcome improvement.

The team recognized that existing technology systems automating tasks failed to account for several dynamic factors affecting the actual allocation of the right nurse at the right time to the right patient care requirement. Unaddressed factors include real-time human judgment, inter-departmental communication, nursing supervisory interaction, patient demand adaptation, and labor information systems feedback.

2.1   Research Method

The complexity of this objective required a research method that went beyond the typical anecdotal observations and explanations of why planned nursing labor rarely met the real-time nursing labor need on a department by department basis. The team chose to derive empirical evidence using a research method grounded in action research that involved multiple interventions with practitioners in situ. The interventions co-created and co-evaluated multiple artifacts to diagnosis and design a future-state Systemic LPAC that optimized the balance between nursing labor, cost, and patient outcomes based less upon a "plan" and more upon "dynamic" real-time daily patient flows.

The research moved beyond an inter-departmental and centralized policy approach to the conduct of the Labor Planning and Allocation Cycle (LPAC) within a hospital by using a systemic approach. Moreover, rather than optimizing the individual components of workload forecasting, scheduling, and allocation separately, this research considered all three components within their interdependent, dynamic, cyclical systemic nature and sought to analyze the impact of the component interactions, organization structure, knowledge creation/sharing and human interactions involved within the work tasks. The research objective was to generate a new LPAC management model artifact that leveraged a systemic optimization of organizational structures, work tasks and human interactions based upon patient flow to create improved outcomes.

Not sure exactly what the ideal LPAC system would look like, the project team employed an elaborated Action Design Research (eADR) [5] method to ensure the guided emergence of an innovative artifact – the Systemic LPAC – that was evaluated and improved through interventions in situ with practitioners. Embedding researchers within the practitioner environment provided the opportunity to iteratively design and refine artifacts at the time of use within the LPAC cycle. Through the iterative use – define, build, evaluate, learn, reflect process – these artifacts were found to become increasingly more relevant and contribute more toward a viable solution.

The team asked the following research questions:

1. What will a better future look like with a Systemic LPAC deployed in a typical hospital?
2. How will a systems approach driven by patient flow and not limited by departmental structures lead to greater optimization of the balance between nursing labor, nursing satisfaction, and patient outcomes?
3. How can an understanding of systems theory guide the design and evaluation of labor-management information systems that are more likely than current systems to meet these nursing labor requirements?

2.2   Diagnosis

The hospital's leadership teams previously recognized the problem within the context of hospital operations. Sufficient data concerning labor cost, staff scheduling/allocation, staff dissatisfaction, and patient outcomes existed to recognize that a problem existed. In spite of large investments in technology over the years, the hospitals routinely failed to meet objectives in all of these categories. The challenge was that no documented artifact existed providing a model for addressing the disconnect between systemic hospital systems and labor management. Therefore, the research entered the eADR method with a defined problem, but no theoretical framing for the inefficiencies that existed. The project first executed the eADR Problem Diagnosing (PD) stage to involve both researcher and practitioner in the understanding of the underlying system theory concepts believed to be causing the inefficiencies observed. In partnership, researchers and hospital leadership outlined the overarching objective to investigate a structure of LPAC management to optimize outcomes. Fulfilling this objective required an intervention over multiple iterative artifact designs, builds, and evaluations in situ.

Subsequent iterative phases were executed to design the conceptual framework based on the systems theory approach and to formulate the artifact before the iterative building and the implementing stages (refer to Fig. 1). In the first pass through the process in Fig. 1, iterative cycles developed and documented the LPAC Management Model outlining the specifics of roles, responsibilities, critical data elements, communication paths, etc. The resulting draft model was then "built" via hiring and training of resources to fill the newly defined roles and then "implemented" in a test set of departments. The researcher-practitioner team then performed intensive iterations of performance analysis pre- and post-implementation state. Learning from this exercise was fed back into the top of the process loop to validate the mapping of the theoretical foundation to begin the next round of implementations. Looping through the steps in Fig. 1 was repeated multiple times to add subsequent departments, service lines, and ultimately hospitals. Researchers and practitioners evaluated and learned at each stage to continuously refine specific aspects of the artifact to address identified challenges and exploit improvement opportunities.

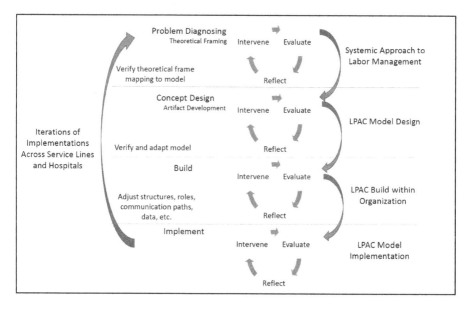

Fig. 1. eADR method applied to LPAC model development

3   Theory-Ingrained Design: A Systems Theoretical Framework

Subsystems disconnected from surrounding subsystems present a significant opportunity for transformative thinking to leverage a systems view of any operation. There has been significant precedent work applying a system view to the patient side of the equation in the form of patient flow and patient throughput analysis, but the same rigor is not present in the labor side of the equation. Academic studies and practitioners have relentlessly focused on the individual components of the LPAC within a similar narrowly focused environment (e.g., single department or service line) absent any form of system perspective [6–9]. The majority of these studies have centered on investigating how to automate human work within the processes of the individual LPAC functions. A research gap exists in the form of a lack of investigation of the LPAC components as lower function subsystems operating within multiple higher subsystems. Value exists in analyzing each function individually. However, there is greater value in studying the collection of functions as they naturally exist within the larger complex hospital system.

Since the 1950s, researchers have recognized the importance of viewing organizations as highly integrated collections of multiple layers of interdependent, dynamic sub-systems that form a whole that is greater than the sum of its parts [10–12]. More recently, researchers have applied a system perspective on hospital operations in multiple studies toward understanding the impact of systems on patient movement through the facility and the quality of care [13–15]. This research provides an incomplete view of the total equation, however. As patients move, resources must also move within the same set of systems reacting to patient needs in higher-layer balancing feedback loops. Healthcare resources are potentially less interchangeable between departments due to specialized skills, yet opportunities exist to move resources where competencies allow. To fully understand the flows and interactions, one must view the labor side of the equation from the same system perspective as impacted by the surrounding environment.

In a simplified diagram of a single departmental labor allocation subsystem (Fig. 2), there are two main flows, patients and staff. Patient stock represents the department workload that needs to be in balance with staff inventory. Various balancing feedback loops regulate flows of patients and staff. Intervening controls applied to the flows include adjustments of staff and patients via movement into or out of the department (staff call in, call out, floating, patient admissions, transfers, and discharges). Considering patients must come from and go to other replicated subsystems, a disconnect exists where patients flow between subsystems, but labor is constrained (siloed) within each subsystem. The team posited that balancing feedback loops break down in these scenarios resulting in more frequent and longer periods of imbalance leading to inefficiencies that can impact cost and patient care.

The objective was to create a model of management that would re-engage feedback loops and balance the multiple layers of systems across the hospital through the timely intervention of corrective actions for flow control. To develop this method, various conceptual frameworks as foundations were considered to find a more robust framework than business process modeling to be able to include both social and technical interactions of process actors. The sociotechnical system (STS) model provided an ideal framework. Trist and Bamforth first discussed this concept in the early 1950s as a way to describe organizations' ability to integrate social and technological subsystems [16]. Organizations include two main subsystems: a social subsystem including people, attitudes, individual relationships, and group relationships; and a technical subsystem including processes, structures, tools, and knowledge [17]. The overall success of an organization is related to the organization's ability to align and optimize these subsystems [14]. Human Systems Interaction (HSI) theory which includes the basic assumption that most components of work include interaction between human beings, technology, and other aspects of the surrounding environment contributed an additional framework [18]. Concepts from both of these theories guided documentation efforts around each participant's interactions with other participants, technology, critical data elements, and the surrounding environment.

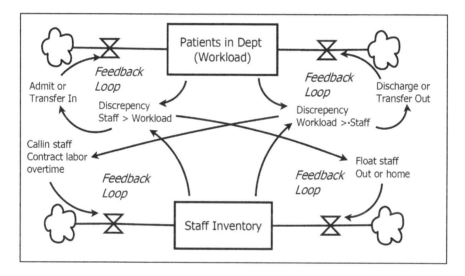

Fig. 2. Simplified labor allocation stock and flow diagram

When seeking to address findings regarding the failure of task automation to improve the outcome performance of the LPAC significantly, concepts from Human Interaction Management (HIM) developed by Harrison-Broninski proved to be useful. HIM guides the imperfect solutions provided by technology built around automated processes serving as the sole mechanism for information exchange. Automated processes alone ignore large parts of knowledge sharing and human interactions that enhance solutions generated in tasks that are consistently unique requiring creativity and real-time adaptability. Observations indicated that LPAC work tasks are not routine and therefore not conducive to being represented by pre-sequenced activities.

Participants (actors) who take on roles within the processes of the system are known as role participants. These role participants undertake work tasks in the LPAC in a manner where they prioritize what to work on, seek knowledge to creatively solve problems and adapt to ever-changing criteria that affect the parameters of the problems to be solved as described by Harrison-Broninski [19]. Observations also indicated that successful task completion is more dependent on the role participant's experience, ability to interact with others and known systems, and ability to seek out relevant information. The context of this research is the integration of human beings, processes, knowledge, and technology across departments and service lines of a hospital to create a model that provides role participants with guidance regarding whom to interact with, what knowledge or resource to exchange, and what tasks to complete. This concept includes the consideration of both technical and social subsystems in which this new model will operate in as well as the many human-human and human-systems inter-actions involved with forecasting, scheduling and staffing.

3.1   The Hospital as a System

The domain of this research lies within the disconnect between flows moving across multiple subsystems and flows bound within a single subsystem. The concept of a "system of systems" as described by Silva-Martinez is particularly attractive for conceptualizing this concept within a hospital [18]. One can view the overall hospital as a high-level system with multiple lower layers of subsystems. The lower layer subsystems consist of service lines and departments as illustrated in Fig. 3 (nursing direct care units only). Including ancillary care departments and flows would provide much more complexity to the illustration. The dotted lines in Fig. 3 represent possible patient flow paths across multiple departments and service lines. The pathway through these subsystems is not consistent, but unique to each patient based on illness, acuity, and care needs. Each of the different layers of subsystems is indicated beginning with the hospital inpatient system (first-layer system) down to the fourth-layer subsystem consisting of individual depart-ment labor forecasting, scheduling, and staffing functions. Patients and resources flow between these subsystems including multiple integrations of technological (e.g., infor-mation, data, knowledge) and social (e.g., relationships, attitudes) components.

Figure 4 provides a more focused visualization of the disconnects present across both departments and service lines when labor management is sub-optimized at the departmental level. Technological and social integration connections are severed in these instances while patient flow continues between departments. Isolating one of the subsystems creates imbalances in knowledge and resources, interrupting necessary feedback loops that are critical to keeping the hierarchical subsystems in balance.

3.2   Labor Forecasting, Scheduling, and Staffing Subsystem

The objectives of labor planning and allocation functions are adequate planning, scheduling, and staffing employees (inventory) to cover patient needs (workload). In this subsystem, inputs (human capital, technology, and information) are transformed to pro-duce multiple outputs (patient care services, financial results, information) (refer to Fig. 5). In a siloed approach, this subsystem is balanced by department leadership to optimize results for the one department representing the pre-project state in the test hospitals. Balancing occurred with little consideration given for departmental connections and interdependencies. Communication between departments was nonexistent during the forecasting and scheduling phases and limited to house supervisor coordination of staff at the last minute just before and during the shift while staffing.

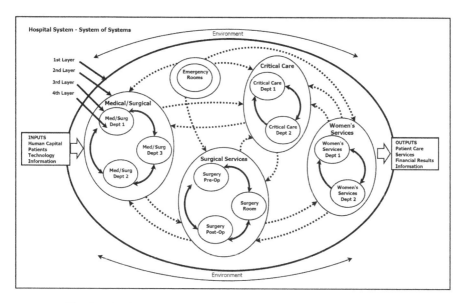

Fig. 3. Hospital organizational structure system of system complexity

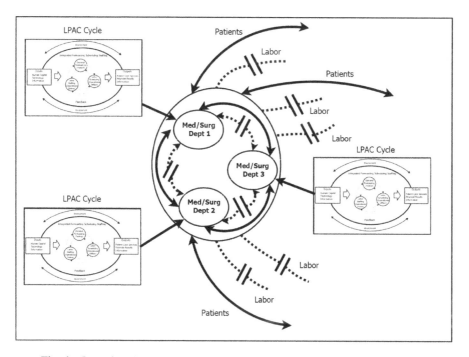

Fig. 4. Operating departments or service line isolation from higher-layer systems

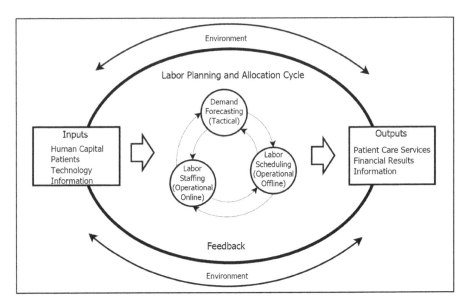

Fig. 5. Labor Planning and Allocation Cycle (LPAC)

The three phases of the LPAC are cyclical. They repeat in a regular cadence beginning with forecasting workload, creating a forecast-based labor schedule, and staffing the department-based patient/departmental needs. These activities are sequential to some degree, yet highly interdependent. Outcomes of each function have the potential to impact and alter activities in downstream and upstream functions since outputs become inputs to downstream tasks and consumed in upstream tasks as feedback [20]. These interactions are significant since they determine the effort level of most tasks. For example, more work effort in the scheduling phase can compensate for an inaccurate workload forecast. Likewise, an ineffective or inefficient schedule can be overcome in the staffing phase but will require more effort to find or reallocate staff at the last minute. Essentially, higher effort in subsequent phases can compensate for poor outcomes in a previous phase (refer to Fig. 6).

4   LPAC Model Design and Evaluation

Worksession participants conceptually captured each task, role, data element, IT system, and communication channel involved providing the framework for the initial draft of the artifacts. Artifact development efforts accommodated aspects of both formal and informal integration mechanisms as described by Glover et al. to provide role participants guidance on where critical knowledge can be found to execute given tasks [13]. The artifacts were intended to serve two main objectives. First, it was important that the artifacts guide role participants as to where task-specific critical data resided whether it be in systems or retained with other participants. The premise was that in the pre-implementation state, role participants made decisions without the benefit of complete information resulting in the majority of sub-optimization.

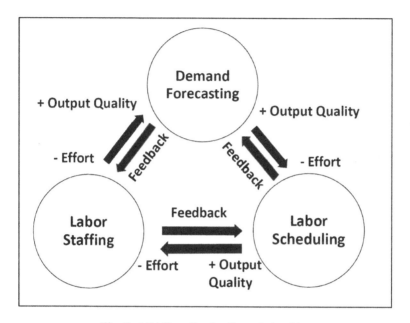

Fig. 6. LPAC quality & effort relationships

The LPAC model documentation method included the use of the Role Activity Diagram (RAD) methodology for the documentation of roles, tasks, and knowledge sharing due to the tool's intuitive nature for modeling processes and interactions [21, 22]. The documentation was extended to include Interaction Model Cards (IMC) to visualize and understand human-human and human-system interaction critical to the successful outcomes of the work [23]. The advantage of these methodologies was that information was created regarding where information for solutions exists rather than detailed process map documentation attempting to provide pre-determined but likely non-optimal solutions. This aspect of the documentation was meant to coincide with the fluid and dynamic environments of each of the functions giving role participants necessary guidance, but also the flexibility to be creative and develop custom solutions to challenges presented. In this manner, generalized artifacts were developed to apply beyond a single type of environment without the need for modifications. This strategy also created artifacts that were resistant to obsolescence.

Figure 7 provides an example of a RAD after multiple cycles of design, build, implement for forecasting and scheduling and an example of an associated IMC for one of the processes. These illustrate the various work roles across the top and details the functions in which each role is involved. The diagram also illustrates examples of knowledge and information flow further documented within the IMCs. The IMC details the goal, participants, responsible role, interactions (human-human and human-system) required, touchpoints required, and knowledge shared and used in the process. The interactions documented during this process were critical in designing both the job roles and the work structures of the resource planning office. As the forecasting, scheduling and staffing functions for each service line of the hospitals moved into the central planning office; the management model was reviewed, analyzed, and refined based on prior experiences and learning. The resulting process was a continuous verification effort reinforcing the artifacts over multiple iterations.

5 LPAC Model Build and Implementation

The developed model was subsequently "built" through the hiring, training, and setup of the resource planning center. The center first transitioned a small set of departments into the new model as a "pilot" for several cycles of forecast, schedule and staff activities. After much learning and reflection, the researcher-practitioner team revisited the artifacts for modifications to address problematic areas. Once the team reached consensus on the modifications, another implementation phase was executed to transition more departments. At the beginning of each phase, the researcher-practitioner team validated prior stage results and the artifact via participant discussions, department leader interviews and evaluation of LPAC key performance metrics in each LPAC function. Revisions were made to address the weaknesses identified.

Each of the roles and functions was crafted to facilitate human-human and human-systems interactions including touchpoints and potential intervention points. The RADs, IMCs, and system diagram artifacts guided work tasks, role responsibilities, and interaction points for each of the various functions whether human or system in nature. They also provided support for training resources in the new central planning roles ensuring staff understanding and transition to managing labor across subsystems.

Assessment of final implementation across the three LPAC functions revealed metric performance improvement within each function. In workload forecasting, 20 out of 24 departments showed improvement. In scheduling, a majority of departments showed improvement across three performance metrics involving schedule completeness. Both facilities had high-performance pre-implementation in commitment scheduling and pattern healthiness. Post-implementation measurements showed no degradation in this performance. In staffing, 21 out of 24 departments showed improvement. Taken in summary the research team was able to conclude that performance improvement was evident with the new model.

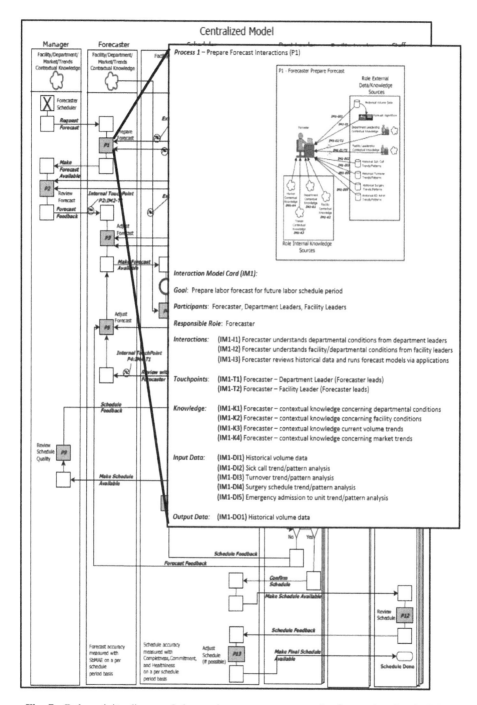

Fig. 7. Role activity diagram & interaction management cared – forecasting & scheduling

6 Conclusion

This project resulted in the development of a Systemic LPAC Management Model artifact. The artifact defines roles and the critical technological and social components and interactions driving the dynamic performance of the forecasting, scheduling and staffing phases of the LPAC. Role Activity Diagrams and Interaction Management Cards detailed each technological and social interaction involving critical data and information element flows necessary for the performance of the phase tasks. This documentation allowed for a thoughtful model design leveraging each value-added interaction.

These artifacts were used to move the LPAC management model away from a sub-optimized department labor focus to a systemic focus seeking to balance labor across the numerous subsystems where needs exist. The dynamic management of nursing labor at the system and sub-system levels better matched the real-time patient flow which occurred at these same levels. The new LPAC management model provided the opportunity for balancing feedback loops to operate more efficiently to keep the patient workload and staff capacity in balance. The overall goal of ensuring that the right amount of staff was in each department to accommodate patient needs adhered to the contention that adequate staffing positively impacts quality patient care. Departments in the post-implementation state operated with the correct staff to match their staffing plan more often than during the pre-implementation state. While departments operated less frequently short-staffed, they also operated less frequently over-staffed and thereby better achieved labor cost control.

It is important to note that while significant improvement was achieved through the implementation of the new LPAC management model and operating from the systemic perspective, many variables can impact each LPAC phase. Internal factors such as staff vacancies, staff willingness to volunteer overtime, bed capacity, and patient throughput are just a few variables that can impact how accurately staffed a department is for a given shift. Additionally, many external factors can impact results such as local incidents (e.g., large freeway accident) or regional incidents (e.g., flu outbreak, hurricane). One of the key objectives of the LPAC management model is to provide adaptability for processes to react to these less foreseeable and unpredictable events. The model is intended to provide for continuous model adaptations and evolutions.

7 Contributions and Future Research Direction

The artifact developed in this project provides an important first step to address the main challenge identified during the implementation of the new model. Existing technology was unable to support the work of the new role participants due to critical data elements spread across multiple disparate systems. Non-value-added time was wasted repeatedly seeking and gathering critical data and information. The theory-ingrained, practice-inspired artifact provides an initial roadmap containing the critical data elements and participant interactions necessary to define supporting technology to optimize system-based labor forecasting, scheduling, and staffing.

The model addresses an organizational capability within labor management from a new perspective viewing the capability from a systems perspective removing the siloed approach. The research addressed the problem through multiple, successive interventions involving both researchers and practitioners in situ. The artifact also resulted in an innovative change in the strategy of the implementing organization. The project transitioned labor management from the sub-optimized department perspective to a system-based management model and is now an adopted organizational strategy. While much work remains to develop technology to support the new model, this research takes the first step down the path of efficient, effective system-based labor management in hospitals.

The research found a unique means to extend Design Science Research theory and practice using a systems theory approach to the design, build and evaluation of innovative labor allocation information and management systems within the existing hospital systems. The "system of systems" approach identified two conflicting structures of management processes that prevented system balancing feedback loops from operating efficiently and subsequently contributing to poor labor allocation outcomes. An elaborated Action Design Research (eADR) method used a guided, emergent approach to redesign the structure, roles, and tasks of the labor planning and allocation within a system of systems framework. The instantiated innovative nursing labor-management model designed, built and evaluated in situ through this approach proved to be practice-inspired and benefited by its theory-ingrained artifact design and evaluation.

Several items of interest limited this research. Design, testing, and implementation involved multiple service lines and departments but included only two hospitals. Therefore, the potential scalability and generalization across a larger number of hospitals was left to be studied. Existing technology did not fully support the concepts of higher-layer LPAC systems management and decision support causing significant amounts of manual work to be performed. Further research is needed to develop information systems artifacts that can support both technological and social interactions and improved decision support. These new IS artifacts could then form the basis of the technological system required to test the management methodology artifacts further.

The second opportunity of future research is to more thoroughly investigate the sociological impact of new LPAC models across the staff, leader, and patient perspective. Additional practitioner environments should be tested to determine if the new model performs with differing levels of support from leadership and staff. Additionally, this project focused mainly on the staff and department leaders involved with executing the tasks of the LPAC. Future research should also investigate the impact on nursing staff, leaders and patients as a result of the LPAC functions. The potential impact on patient satisfaction and quality of care are interesting future areas to explore.

References

1. Mark, B.A., Harless, D.W., McCue, M., Xu, Y.: A longitudinal examination of hospital registered nurse staffing and quality of care. Health Serv. Res. **39**(2), 279–300 (2004)
2. Needleman, J., Buerhaus, P., Mattke, S., Stewart, M., Zelevinsky, K.: Nurse-staffing levels and the quality of care in hospitals. N. Engl. J. Med. **346**(22), 1715–1722 (2002)
3. Welton, J.M.: Hospital nursing workforce costs, wages, occupational mix, and resource utilization. J. Nurs. Adm. **41**(7/8), 309–314 (2011)

4. Ashforth, B.E., Mael, F.: Social identity theory and the organization. Acad. Manag. Rev. **14**(1), 20–39 (2016)
5. Mullarkey, M.T., Hevner, A.R.: An elaborated action design research process model. Eur. J. Inf. Syst. **28**(1), 6–20 (2019)
6. Castillo-Salazar, J.A., Landa-Silva, D., Qu, R.: Workforce scheduling and routing problems: literature survey and computational study. Ann. Oper. Res. **239**(1), 39–67 (2016)
7. Defraeye, M., Van Nieuwenhuyse, I.: Staffing and scheduling under nonstationary demand for service: a literature review. Omega (UK) **58**, 4–25 (2016)
8. Park, S.H., Blegen, M.A., Spetz, J., Chapman, S.A., De Groot, H.A.: Comparison of nurse staffing measurements in staffing-outcomes research. Med. Care **53**(1), e1–e8 (2015)
9. Van Den Bergh, J., Belien, J., De Bruecker, P., Demeulemeester, E., De Boeck, L.: Personnel scheduling: a literature review. Eur. J. Oper. Res. **226**(3), 367–385 (2013)
10. von Bertalanffy, L.: An outline of general systems theory. Br. J. Philos. Sci. **1**(2), 134–165 (1950)
11. Boulding, K.: General systems theory-the skeleton of science. Manag. Sci. **2**(3), 197–208 (1956)
12. Meyer, R.M., O'Brien-Pallas, L.L.: Nursing services delivery theory: an open system approach. J. Adv. Nurs. **66**(12), 2828–2838 (2010)
13. Glover, W., Li, Q., Naveh, E., Gross, M.: improving quality of care through integration in a hospital setting: a human systems integration approach. IEEE Trans. Eng. Manag. **64**(3), 1–12 (2017)
14. Marsilio, M., Torbica, A., Villa, S.: Health care multidisciplinary teams: the socio-technical approach for an integrated system-wide perspective. Health Care Manag. Rev. **42**(4), 303–314 (2017)
15. Tay, H.L.: Examining trade-offs in hospital operations using a systems approach in an acute care setting. Int. J. Bus. Inf. **11**(2), 264–284 (2016)
16. Pasmore, W., Shani, A., Francis, C., Haldeman, J.: Sociotechnical systems: a North American reflection on empirical studies of the seventies. Hum. Relat. **32**(12), 1179–1204 (1982)
17. Shani, A.B., Grant, R.M., Krishnan, R., Thompson, E.: Advanced manufacturing systems and organisational choice: a sociotechnical system approach. Calif. Manag. Rev. **34**(4), 91–111 (1992)
18. Silva-Martinez, J.: Human systems integration: process to help minimize human errors, a systems engineering perspective for human space exploration missions. Reach **2**(2–4), 8–23 (2016)
19. Harrison-Broninski, K.: Human Interactions: the Heart and Soul of Business Process Management, 1st edn. (2005)
20. Hulshof, P.J.H., Kortbeek, N., Boucherie, R.J., Hans, E.W., Bakker, P.J.M.: Taxonomic classification of planning decisions in health care: a structured review of the state of the art in OR/MS. Health Syst. **1**(2), 129–175 (2012)
21. Ould, M.A.: Business Processes: Modeling and Analysis for Re-Engineering and Improvement. Wiley, Hoboken (1995)
22. Phalp, K.T., Henderson, P., Walters, R.J., Abeysinghe, G.: RolEnact: role-based enactable models of business processes. Inf. Softw. Technol. **40**(3), 123–133 (1998)
23. Seo, W., Yoon, J., Lee, J., Kim, K.: A state-driven modeling approach to human interactions for knowledge intensive services. Expert Syst. Appl. **38**(3), 1917–1930 (2011)

Design Science Research Applications in Healthcare

Designing a Machine Learning Model to Predict Cardiovascular Disease Without Any Blood Test

Arin Brahma[1,2(✉)], Samir Chatterjee[1], and Yan Li[1]

[1] Claremont Graduate University, Claremont, CA 01711, USA
{arin.brahma, samir.chatterjee, yan.li}@cgu.edu
[2] Loyola Marymount University, Los Angeles, CA 90045, USA

Abstract. Healthcare in the USA is struggling with alarming levels of hospital readmission. Cardio Vascular Disease (CVD) has been identified as the most frequent cause. While the factors related to high hospital readmission are complex, according to prior research, early detection and post-discharge management has a significant positive impact. However, the widening gap between the number of patients and available clinical resources is acutely aggravating the problem. A solution that can effectively identify well patients at risk of future CVDs will allow focusing limited clinical resources to a more targeted set of patients, leading to more widespread early detection, prevention and disease progression management. This in turn, can reduce CVD-related hospital readmissions. Moreover, if the patient data required by such a solution can be collected without any blood test or invasive procedure, the addressable patient population can be vastly expanded to include home care, remote, and impoverished patients while delivering cost savings of the invasive procedures. Using a Design Science Research (DSR) approach, this research has led to the design and development of a machine learning based predictor artifact capable of identifying patients with future CVD risks. The performance of this predictor artifact, as measured by the area under the receiver operating characteristic (ROC) curve, is 0.859. The sensitivity or recall is 85.9% at probability threshold of 0.5. The significant differentiating feature of this artifact lies in its ability to do so without any blood test or invasive procedure.

Keywords: Cardiovascular disease · Design science research · Machine learning · Healthcare

1 Introduction

Cardio Vascular Disease (CVD) is a global public health problem involving very high levels of morbidity or mortality. According to the World Health Organization (WHO) 2017 Fact Sheet [1], CVD's are the number one cause of deaths globally, with an estimated 17.7 million deaths from CVD in 2015, representing 31% of all global deaths. According to the Heart Disease and Stroke Statistics – 2017 Update [2] by the American Heart Association (AHA), on the basis of 2011 to 2014 data, an estimated 92.1 million American adults suffer from one or more forms of CVD, that currently

© Springer Nature Switzerland AG 2019
B. Tulu et al. (Eds.): DESRIST 2019, LNCS 11491, pp. 125–139, 2019.
https://doi.org/10.1007/978-3-030-19504-5_9

claim more lives each year than cancer and chronic lower respiratory disease (CLRD) combined. On an average, about 2200 Americans die of CVD each day. As per the CDC website, it is also the number one cause of death in the United States. In 2011, the AHA estimated that by 2030, 40.5% of the US population would have some form of CVD [2].

While the morbidity and mortality numbers are alarming, the economic burden of this global pandemic is equally staggering. In the United States alone, the direct annual medical costs of CVD were projected to reach $818 billion by 2030 [2]. A big contributor to this staggering cost is heart failure-related hospitalization and readmissions that require inpatient care. Although currently there are several strategies that attempt to solve this problem (e.g., nurse interventions, triage by qualified health workers, etc.), the challenges with implementing such interventions could be related to the ever-expanding gap between the number of CVD patients and the number of qualified health personnel. There is an acute current and projected shortage of skilled healthcare professionals globally. WHO (2013) estimates that, based on a threshold of 4.45 skilled health professionals per 1000 population, the need-based shortage of healthcare workers globally is about 17.4 million. If the trend continues the global need-based shortage of healthcare workers is projected to be over 14 million by 2030 [3]. Therefore, there is a need to identify strategies, processes, and technologies that have the potential to proactively and automatically identify patients at risk of CVD and target limited clinical resources only towards the identified ones. Prior literature published on this topic indicate that, when reliable patient physiologic data is made available, expert systems and artificial intelligence (AI) technologies have the potential to identify patients at risk, and trigger interventions [4–7].

This strategy will also expand the reach of the solution to an expanding population of home-monitored, remote and financially challenged patients. Recent advancements of Bluetooth technology enabled wireless medical data collection devices allow efficient data collection from in-home self-care patients. However, this efficiency also leads to an increased data load at the end of the hospitals and healthcare providers. They now need to deal with a higher volume of patient data coming in from the tele-monitored patients, that they didn't have to handle in the past. Moreover, since the burden of carefully reviewing each patient's data, identifying patients needing interventions, and making treatment decisions remained with the healthcare professionals and performed manually, this deluge of new data can overwhelm and stretch providers' resources. This leads to further justification of the need for automatically analyzing information and identifying patients at risk. There is an increased interest in the researchers and innovators to solve this problem using artificial intelligence and machine learning. Evidence found in literature reveals that application of machine learning can improve cardiovascular risk prediction [8–12].

Past research in the category of CVD prediction and identification of strong predictors include a recent 2017 publication by Weng et al. [8], in which the authors presented evidence that machine learning based CVD prediction models improve upon American Heart Association's 2013 CVD risk prediction model based on statistical techniques. It is noteworthy that such models routinely include one or more blood test related features, such as HDL cholesterol, LDL cholesterol, triglycerides, C-reactive protein, serum fibrinogen, gamma GT, serum creatinine, and HbA1c etc. In reality, collecting these details for patients under in-home care or in remote locations is often an additional obstacle, expensive, and renders such prediction models less usable in such scenarios. However, this brings us to the question, if an effective and useful CVD predictive model can be built that does not require any blood test or other invasive tests. We believe this is a gap our research can help in addressing.

Our exploratory research began with the goal of building an AI/Machine Learning (ML) based CVD predictor instantiated artifact, with predictive performance better than the designs existed at present. However, during the iterative design and evaluation cycles of this research, we discovered that, along with the traditional blood test or invasive test based features, a good number of features related to patient's demographics, lifestyle, quality of life, and medical history are consistently appearing within the group of strong predictors. We further noted that, Kerver et al. [13] demonstrated direct correlation between various diet, their constituent food groups, and various blood test based biomarkers, that are routinely used as predictors of CVDs. Diets and food habits are reflections of individual lifestyle, culture, living conditions, quality of life etc. Inspired by these observations, we revised the design goals to focus on building a CVD prediction model that can, not only deliver a strong predictive ability in comparison with the previous models, but accomplish that by using only non-invasive features such as, demographics, lifestyle, quality of life, medical history, and other anthropometric measurements.

The uniqueness of this research can be summarized as follows:

- Applicability for in-home and remote area patients significantly expands the scope of the addressable target CVD patient population, which otherwise would not be possible
- No blood test or invasive lab based data collection procedure needed
- The model identifies patients with CVD risks using only sixteen demographic, lifestyle, quality of life, medical history and anthropometric measurement features
- ML-based predictor model artifact integrated with data input computer interface artifact
- Model training (knowledge seeding) using extensive CVD data of 5804 patients obtained from the National Heart Lung and Blood Institute (NHLBI) representing patients pooled from diverse cohorts in the United States
- Potential implications in reducing CVD-related hospitalization and readmission rates.

The remainder of this paper is organized in the following manner. We begin with a discussion on CVD and its risk factors to familiarize the audience with the subject domain so that an overall context and applicability of this research can be established. We will present our analysis of past work in the specific area of this research and the gap this research is trying to fill. Then we present the research methodology, data used, and the design process. The design science theories that ground the design and the study will be briefly described in this context. The design section will provide details of each iterative design cycle and explain how knowledge discovered from the data and insights from current knowledge led to various revisions of the design goals and their implementation strategies over multiple design cycles. Following that, we will describe our methods of model evaluation, testing, and external validation. Finally, we conclude this paper by discussing the limitations, contributions, and future research opportunities in the field of CVD.

2   Understanding CVD and Associated Risk Factors

2.1   Cardiovascular Disorder or Disease (CVD)

WHO defines CVD as a group of disorders of the heart and blood vessels, and they include the following diseases [14].

- Coronary heart disease – disease of the blood vessels supplying the heart muscle;
- Cerebrovascular disease – disease of the blood vessels supplying the brain;
- Peripheral arterial disease – disease of blood vessels supplying the arms and legs;
- Rheumatic heart disease – damage to the heart muscle and heart valves from rheumatic fever, caused by streptococcal bacteria;
- Congenital heart disease – malformations of heart structure existing at birth;
- Deep vein thrombosis and pulmonary embolism – blood clots in the leg veins, which can dislodge and move to the heart and lungs.

Diseases of the heart, or heart disease (HD), which is a subset of CVD, alone accounts for about 30% of the people affected by CVD. AHA statistics (2017) shows that out of 92.1 million American Adults affected by some form of CVD, 27.6 million has been diagnosed with HD [2]. Heart Diseases may lead to various forms of heart failure, coronary heart diseases (CHD), heart attack or myocardial infarctions (MI), strokes and several other outcomes. Out of 27.6 million people affected by HD, 16.5 are diagnosed with CHD, which is about 60%.

To put this in context, the data set used by this research, obtained from National Heart Lung and Blood Institute (NHLBI), captured the following five heart diseases as CVD outcome: coronary heart disease (CHD), congestive heart failure (CHF), myocardial infarction (MI) or heart attack, stroke, and angina. All of these outcomes, except stroke, are types of heart diseases. Stroke is cardiovascular disease (CVD), but not a heart disease (HD). The CVD risks identified by the model developed in this research cover these five specific cardiovascular diseases.

2.2   CVD Risk Factors and Current Risk Assessment Models

CVD risk scoring models are not new and traditionally they are developed using statistical methods. In 1998, Framingham CHD risk scoring model was developed, and since then many more were developed and used in clinical practice. The most recent scoring model published by American Heart Association (AHA) and American College of Cardiology (ACC) in 2013, was developed using state-of-the-art statistical methods. The 2013 atherosclerotic cardiovascular disease (ASCVD) Risk Assessment report from ACC/AHA [15] describes the methodology in great detail. ACC/AHA defines ASCVD as "nonfatal myocardial infarction or coronary heart disease (CHD) death or fatal or nonfatal stroke". The latest ACC-AHA ASCVD risk prediction model has been made available as a Web application for the practitioners. As evidenced by the Web application on ACC website [16], the latest model uses nine risk factors: Age, Sex, Race, Systolic BP, Total Cholesterol, HDL Cholesterol, History of Diabetes, Smoker, and On Hypertension Treatment.

Another emerging approach to CVD risk prediction is based on the application of AI/Machine Learning. Evidence found in literature reveals that application of machine learning can improve cardiovascular risk prediction [8–12] over traditional methods. In a recent 2017 publication by Weng et al. [8], the authors presented evidence that machine learning based CVD prediction models improve upon the statistical predictive model by American Heart Association's 2013 ASCVD risk prediction model. However, such work has not been translated into instantiated artifact designs that can be applied at the point of service to benefit the clinical practices. As noted in the prior section, current CVD risk prediction models, including the ones based on AI/ML, routinely include one or more blood markers such as, HDL cholesterol, LDL cholesterol, triglycerides, etc.

3 Requirements and Design Goals

The discussion above leads to the need for an instantiable predictor artifact that can predict long term (within 15 years or less) CVD prediction risk of well patients with strong predictive performance. A well patient is defined as someone who does not have past recorded history of any of the CVD related episodes, procedures, or known conditions. Discoveries during the design cycles led us to include in our design goals, an additional requirement of the artifact to predict CVDs without using any blood test or any invasive test data. As literature demonstrated superior performance of AI/Machine Learning based predictors over the traditional statistical models, we aimed to adopt the AI/Machine Learning based approach to design and build such an artifact in this research. In addition to designing the predictive artifact, this research also aims to instantiate the predictor artifact in the form of a software object and integrate the same with an user interface artifact that will allow entering a target patients predictive features. The patient data entered through this user interface artifact interacts with the back-end predictor model artifact and generates specific predictions. The predictions are displayed on computer screen to the user via the user interface artifact. To ensure usability and minimize data entry efforts by the clinicians, we imposed a requirement of keeping the number of predictive features below 20, without compromising on its predictive performance.

For a general "order of magnitude" comparison and to benchmark our model's performance, we will designate the performance of the 2017 AI/machine learning based CVD prediction model published by Weng et al. [8] as the reference baseline model. It is important to note that our model and the referenced benchmark model have differences with respect to the data used, population demographics, features used, and the definition of the CVD classifier in terms of specific CVD included. However, the domain, target outcome, model goals, and methods are close enough for an order of magnitude general comparison, but the underlying conditions are different enough to establish if one model is better performing than the other in absolute terms. The published performance data of this reference model is presented in Table 1 below.

Table 1. Reference model (Weng, et al.) performance as a design goal

Select performance measures	Model algorithms	
	Random forest	Logistic regression
AUC (c-Statistic)	0.745	0.76
Recall	65.30%	67.10%
Fl-Score	Not available	Not available

4   Research Method and the Design Process

Design science research (DSR) approach was followed in building the predictor artifact. Hevner and Chatterjee [17] explain that DSR is an iterative process that includes
iterative phases of relevance cycle, rigor cycle, and design cycle. Continual and iterative build and evaluate activities in the design cycle mark one of the significant
characteristics of DSR methodology. Problem identification, motivation, and the design
goals, as identified from analysis of the context, are described in the earlier sections.
The target artifact - the CVD predictor, was designed, developed, evaluated, and
improved through a series of three iterative design cycles as discussed below in detail.

4.1   Common Elements of the Design Process

The Data. The source of the data used in the research is National Heart Lung and
Blood Institute (NHLBI) of the United States [18]. To develop this dataset NHLBI
recruited the participants from nine existing epidemiological studies related to heart and
respiratory diseases, in which cardiovascular risk factors had already been collected
previously. Hence, the data set is made up of 5804 unique patient records with 1990
features. Five CVD outcomes (CHF, MI, Stroke, CHD, and Angina) are included in the
features. Longitudinal data about the patients were collected in four cycles, with first
data collection in 1995, two subsequent visits between 1995 and 2003, and CVD
outcome collection until 2011. Inclusion criteria of the cohort members were age 40
years or older; no history of treatment of sleep apnea; no tracheostomy; no current
home oxygen therapy.

Data Extraction. Based on the design requirements, 5099 patient records are
extracted from the original data sets of 5804 records after eliminating patients with
prior CVD history or conditions. Once the final set of features are decided, more
records were dropped for the purpose of addressing missing data and outliers, leading
to a balance of 2128 patient records for model building. We avoided imputation for
missing values and preferred dropping the records whenever possible and necessary.

Model Training, Scoring, and Validation. The balance 2128 patient records were
split into training (70%) and testing (30%) data based on randomized stratified split.
For model training 5-fold random stratified data partitioning is used to reduce overfitting risks among other measures. The trained model was scored using 638 patient
records (test data) previously unseen by the trained model. The scoring results were
used to calculate model performance statistics or test results.

4.2   Design Cycles

DSR Design cycles draw inputs from the contextual environment of the research project or the relevance cycle, specifically with respect to the problem identification and motivation. This in turn, translates into the initial or revised objectives of the design cycle. Within each design cycle a version of the artifact prototype is designed and developed and improved iteratively by incorporating the evaluation feedbacks. In the process, if the design objective gets revised, a new design cycle is initiated. Three design cycles were involved in building the CVD predictor artifacts as discussed below in detail.

Design Cycle 1. Design cycle 1 focused on exploring and discovering the NHLBI clinical data sets with the goal of finding a set of predictive features and ML algorithm (a predictive model) that can further improve the CVD predictive ability (as measured by c-statistic) in relation to our baseline reference model. We also wanted to explore if the predictive features of such a model would be different from those of the baseline model. The steps involved in the design cycle 1 is illustrated in detail in Fig. 1 below. Initial data discovery involved developing a domain understanding of each feature, meaningful grouping into factor groups, and generating descriptive statistics of the features to examine distribution, missing values, outliers etc. Through this effort, 62 features, organized in 5 groups, were extracted, as presented in Table 3.

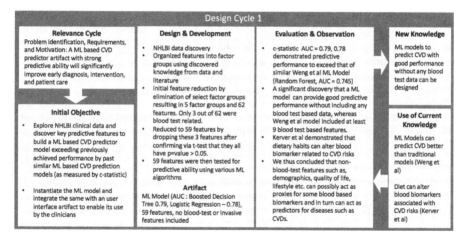

Fig. 1. Design cycle 1: gaining new knowledge through artifact development

We noted that out of 14 body measurement features, only 3 required blood test (triglycerides, hdl, and cholesterol). Patient data for rest of the 62 features can be gathered non-invasively. We performed a t-test to investigate the significance difference for these three blood test related features in regards to the two target outcome groups. The t-test results are displayed in Table 2 below.

Table 2. t-Test for group difference for blood-test related features

Feature	t-Test (0–1 group difference): p-value (95% confidence)	Significant? (<0.05)
Triglyceride	0.4995	No
Hdl	0.0842	No
Cholesterol	0.0754	No

These observations motivated us to drop the blood test related features altogether leading to a total of 59 features. At this stage we wanted to explore how 59 features would perform in terms of predictive ability. For an evaluation, we developed two ML algorithm based models using this data - logistic regression and boosted decision tree. The c-statistic - area under the curve (AUC) for the models were 0.78 and 0.79 respectively, thereby already signifying that these 59 features, even without any blood test data, have the potential to be good predictors, relative to the baseline model of Weng et al. (AUC = 0.745, random forest). This was a significant discovery. We could explain this result drawing from the knowledge of the existing the literature:

- Kerver et al. [13] demonstrated that dietary habits can alter blood biomarkers associated with CVD risks
- Weng et al. [8] demonstrated that ML based models can effectively predict CVDs.

Hence, it appeared possible that features related to demographics, lifestyle, quality of life etc. may act as proxies for some blood test based predictors. This understanding inspired us to revise our research objective at this point to building a CVD predictive model without any blood test related features. However, we aimed to reduce the number of features further to make it more comparable to the baseline model of Weng et al. (30 features). This revision of our research objective led to the second design cycle which is presented in the next section.

Design Cycle 2. In this design cycle (Fig. 2) we apply a wrapper model for feature selection from the 59 features shortlisted in design cycle 1. In literature, wrapper models were shown effective for decision trees induction. In this technique, the feature selection process uses (wraps around) specific algorithms and uses the algorithms' feature importance score to rank the features for the purpose of shortlisting and selection. In our case, we used the feature selection wrapper around random forest algorithm. This means we ran all 59 features through the random forest algorithm and obtained the feature importance score generated by the algorithm. Then we selected the top 25 features based on the descending feature importance score. Table 3 presents the top 25 feature importance scored list of features out of 59.

In the next step this list of 25 features (shortlisted based on feature importance score) were ran through logistic regression and random forest models to gauge and compare the predictive performance of this set as exposed to two very different types of classifiers. AUCs for this run were 0.76 and 0.81 for logistic regression and random forest models respectively. As the performance of the random forest algorithm appeared to be promising, to further improve the performance, we used manual step-wise add/drop experiments using random forest. This experimentation resulted in 23 features with AUC score of 0.84 with random forest and 0.745 with logistic regression. We concluded that for our given data set, random forest will continue to outperform logistic regression and hence decided to build the final model using random forest. This strong performing feature set is presented below in Table 4.

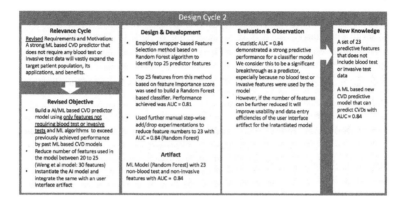

Fig. 2. Design cycle 2: new knowledge revising design goals and strategies

Table 3. Wrapper based selection: top 25 from random forest feature importance score

	Feature	Score		Feature	Score
1	Age	0.360387	14	Health limits bending, kneeling, or stooping row	0.001552
2	Health Limited Social Activities	0.212619	15	Forced Expiratory Volume in one sec in liters	0.001383
3	Forced Vital Capacity of Lung in liters	0.016976	16	Cups of tea intake on a regular day	0.001257
4	Average Systolic blood pressure	0.015142	17	Hip measurement in centimeters	0.001189
5	Height in centimeters	0.010669	18	Have a lot of energy during the past 4 weeks	0.001094
6	Neck circumference in centimeters	0.006996	19	Average glasses of soda (with caffeine) per day	0.000681
7	Self Reported Hypertension	0.006917	20	Difficulty performing work during the past 4 weeks	0.000558
8	Lifetime cigarette smoking in pack-years	0.006004	21	Self Reported Sinus Trouble	0.000499
9	waist circumference in centimeters	0.005399	22	Felt tired in past 4 weeks	0.000485
10	Marital Status	0.003785	23	Average Body Mass Index	0.00022
11	Education Level	0.003228	24	Been a happy person during the past 4 weeks	0.00019
12	Cups of Coffee intake on a regular day	0.002734	25	Diabetes status	0.000058
13	Bodily pain during the past 4 weeks	0.002163			

Table 4. List of 23 features after manual step-wise add/drop optimization

1	Age	13	Lifetime cigarette smoking in pack-years
2	Race	14	Number of hours drive each day
3	Marital Status	15	Frequency of drive
4	Education Level	16	Self Reported Sinus Trouble
5	Height in centimeters	17	Cough most days
6	Weight in kilograms	18	Self Reported Hypertension
7	Neck circumference in centimeters	19	Health Limited Social Activities
8	Waist Circumference in centimeters	20	Health limits bending, kneeling, or stooping now
9	Hip measurement in centimeters	21	Felt tired in past 4 weeks
10	Average Body Mass Index	22	Been a happy person during the past 4 weeks
11	Cups of tea intake on a regular day	23	History of Diabetes
12	Cups of Coffee intake on a regular day		

Encouraged with this result, we decided to validate our features with an external domain expert (cardiologist) to discover any further scope for improvements. We anticipated that if the number of features can be further reduced without comprising the predictive performance, it will make the interaction of the user interface artifact with the ML model more efficient and usable by the clinical practitioners. This led us to the final design cycle which is described in the following section.

Design Cycle 3. At this design cycle (Fig. 3) the objective was to make further possible improvements of the model by incorporating feedback from an external expert (cardiologist), while also validating the usefulness and real life applicability of such a solution.

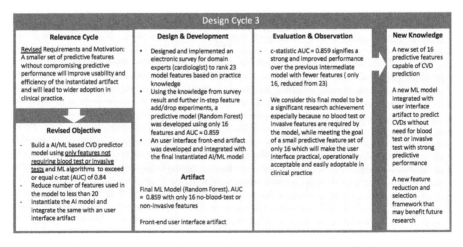

Fig. 3. Design cycle 3: final artifacts and knowledge contributions

4.3   Evaluation

We conducted a simple 5 question electronic survey with a cardiologist at a renowned large private hospital in California. The survey result is summarized in Table 6. Incorporating the feedback on the predictive features of the model, we attempted another round of manual stepwise feature add/drop experiments and arrived at a final list of 16 features. We constructed a random forest based model based on these 16 features. The predictive performance of this model is presented in Table 5.

Table 5. Final model performance (16 features, random forest)

	Random forest	
	This research	Weng et al.
AUC (c-Statistic)	0.859	0.745
Recall	85.90%	65.30%
Precision	77.40%	Not available
Accuracy	76.90%	Not available
F1 Score	0.814	Not available

Table 6. Cardiologist survey result summary

Interveiwee Profile	Cardiologist at a renowned large private hospital in California
Survey Tool / Platform Used	SurveyMonkey
Date of Response	26-Nov-18

	Survey Questions	Response
Q1.	But do you believe predicting CVD using just the 23 features without any blood test or other lab tests could be possible?	Yes, it is possible
Q2.	Which FIVE of the 23 features do you believe has the STRONGEST relationship to CVD?	1. Lifetime smoking in Pack-Years 2. History of diabetes 3. Self-reported hypertension 4. Limitation of social activities in past 4 weeks 5. Current limitations in bending, kneeling, or stooping
Q3.	Which FIVE of the 23 features do you believe has WEAKEST relationship to CVD?	1. Number of cups of coffee daily 2. Number of cups of tea daily 3. Frequency of driving 4. Coughing history
Q4.	If such a prediction tool were integrated with your EHR computer system in your practice enabling your system to predict CVD using only the above information without requiring any blood test or special lab test with acceptable level of accuracy. How useful do you think it would be in YOUR clinical practice	Highly useful
Q5.	Let's say that this model gives you just two data points once the above patient information is entered: (a) if the patient is at CVD risk within next 15 years, and (b) what is the % risk of such an event. Is this information actionable? If it is, what actions you are likely to take based on the above information when a patient is identified to be at risk by this model?	1. Discuss with patient 2. Address modifiable risk factors 3. Counsel weight loss where appropriate 4. Optimize risk factor modification 5. Focus on aggressive targets

4.4   Final Artifacts

The final ML based predictor model based on 16 features and random forest ML algorithm is instantiated in Microsoft Azure ML Studio cloud platform. A cloud based fully functional user interface prototype has been developed and instantiated. The user

136   A. Brahma et al.

interface provides a front end to the back-end ML predictor model and allows entry of patient data and display of the prediction results. The model displays two responses: (1) CVD Risk: 1 or 0, and (2) A percentage probability of the risk. The 16 features of the final ML model artifact is described in detail in Table 7.

4.5   IT Platforms and Tools Used

We used various combinations of IT platforms and tools to maximize computational efficiencies. For the data exploration, merging, cleaning, and transformation tasks we used Excel, Python, and SQL. For ML model building, experimentations, and instantiation we used Microsoft Azure ML cloud platform. For statistical analysis Stata desktop was used. During the model building stages, we used algorithms and

Table 7. Final set of 16 model feature descriptions

	Feature description	Feature options/type	Feature category		Feature description	Feature options/type	Feature category
1	Age in years	Numeric	Demographics	11	During the past 4 weeks, has your health limited your social activities (like visiting with friends or close relatives)?	1: All of the time 2: Most of the time	Quality of Life
2	Race	1: White 2: Black 3: Other		12	Does your health now limit you in this activity, and if so, how much: Bending, kneeling, or stooping	1: Yes, limited a lot 2: Yes, limited a little 3: No, not limited at all	
3	Marital Status	1: Married 2: Widowed 3: Divorced/separated 4: Never married 5: Unknown/refused		13	During the past 4 weeks, how much of the time; did you feel tired?	1: All of the time 2: Most of the time 3: A good bit of the time 4: Some of the time 5: A little of time 6: None of the time	
4	Education level in years of education	1: Less than 10 years of education 2:11–15 years of education 3:16–20 years of education 4: More than 20 years of education		14	During the past 4 weeks, how much of the time; have you been a happy person?	1: All of the time 2: Most of the time 3: A good bit of the time 4: Some of the time 5: A little of time 6: None of the time	

Table 7. (*continued*)

	Feature description	Feature options/type	Feature category		Feature description	Feature options/type	Feature category
5	Weight in Kg	Numeric	Body Measurements	15	Lifetime cigarette smoking in pack years	Numeric	Lifestyle
6	Waist circumference in centimeters	Numeric					
7	Hip measurement in centimeters	Numeric		16	How many cups of tea (with caffeine) do you drink on a regular day?	Numeric	
8	Neck circumference in centimeters	Numeric					
9	History of Diabetes	0: No 1: Yes	History				
10	Self reported hypertension	0: No 1: Yes					

techniques such as randomized k-fold stratified partitioning, level 1 and 2 regularization, data value normalization and standardization, and hyperparameter tuning for optimizing performance and ruggedizing the model against potential overfitting issues.

4.6   Feature Selection Methodology Summary

This research has developed a unique and custom feature selection methodology that allowed selection and reduction of features ultimately to 16 highly predictive features. This step by step process is summarized and illustrated in Fig. 4 below. We consider this feature selection methodology to be another addition to the body of knowledge.

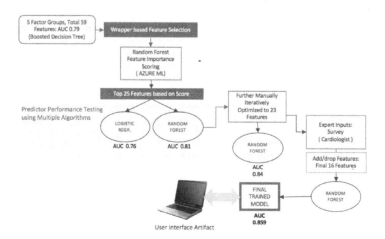

Fig. 4. Feature selection methodology

5   Limitations and Future Research Opportunities

While ML based prediction artifacts have been demonstrated to solve many problems, they have their limitations. Often, there are uncertainties about the potential performance of a ML model when it is exposed to unseen data. A high-performing model in the test environment can be under-performing in real life situations due to problems related to overfitting, data deficiencies, or assumption violations. Hence, external validity or generalization is a challenge for such models. For example, the model developed in this research is specifically built using NHLBI data sets. It is hard to generalize the model for all other data sets. This means for operationalization, such models must be tested and refined continually with additional data sets from various situations over a period of time, before the generalization of the model can be assumed. However, this also creates future research opportunities. We also want to highlight that the select 16 feature set which is the foundation of the model's performance, may not be the only or necessarily the best performing feature set. There may be several other feature combinations that may produce equal or better performance. Future research can uncover such possibilities. Additionally, because of the nature of the underlying data set, this model currently can be said to predict 15 year CVD risks. We believe the usefulness of the model can be further enhanced if the risk prediction horizon were 10 years or less.

6   Conclusion

This research has led to the design and development of a high performing CVD predictor artifact that does not require any blood test or invasive patient data, based on machine learning approach. The model demonstrates an impressive discriminating ability with AUC of 0.859. It also meets the design goal of a high recall rate, delivering a value of 85.9%. The F1-score of 0.814 signifies the models balanced capability in identifying true positives and true negatives. This performance not only far supersedes our reference model benchmark goals, but it also denotes a strong AUC with respect to the biomedical domain in general. The most distinguishing feature of the artifact is that it does not require any blood test or invasive test based patient data. If future research in this area are able to establish strong external validity of this model, it will be a breakthrough in the field of CVD prediction, implications of which is far reaching including reduction in CVD related rehospitalization, early detection, prevention, and healthcare cost in general. Additionally, the benefits of such an artifact can be extended to remote, in-home, and impoverished patients in a significant and impactful way.

Acknowledgment. Co-author Dr. Chatterjee was funded in part by a fellowship from the Schoeller Research Center of Nuremberg, Germany. We would also like to thank Dr. Luanda Grazette of USC Keck School of Medicine for helping us with the knowledge of cardiology domain.

References

1. World Health Organization. Cardiovascular Diseases (CVD) Fact Sheet. https://www.who. int/en/news-room/fact-sheets/detail/cardiovascular-diseases-(cvds)
2. Benjamin, E.J., et al.: Heart disease and stroke statistics-2017 update: a report from the American Heart Association. Circulation **135**(10), e146–e603 (2017)
3. World Health Organization: Global strategy on human resources for health: Workforce 2030 (2016)
4. Colantonio, S., Martinelli, M., Moroni, D., Salvetti, O., Chiarugi, F., Emmanouilidou, D.: A decision support system for aiding heart failure management. In: 2009 Ninth International Conference on Intelligent Systems Design and Applications 2009, pp. 351–356. IEEE (2009)
5. Seto, E., Leonard, K.J., Cafazzo, J.A., Barnsley, J., Masino, C., Ross, H.J.: Developing healthcare rule-based expert systems: case study of a heart failure telemonitoring system. Int. J. Med. Inform. **81**(8), 556–565 (2012). https://doi.org/10.1016/j.ijmedinf.2012.03.001
6. Sourla, E., Sioutas, S., Syrimpeis, V., Tsakalidis, A., Tzimas, G.: CardioSmart365: artificial intelligence in the service of cardiologic patients. Adv. Artif. Intell. **2012**, 2 (2012)
7. Zhang, J., Goode, K.M., Rigby, A., Balk, A.H., Cleland, J.G.: Identifying patients at risk of death or hospitalisation due to worsening heart failure using decision tree analysis: evidence from the Trans-European Network-Home-Care Management System (TEN-HMS) study. Int. J. Cardiol. **163**(2), 149–156 (2013)
8. Weng, S.F., Reps, J., Kai, J., Garibaldi, J.M., Qureshi, N.: Can machine-learning improve cardiovascular risk prediction using routine clinical data? PLoS ONE **12**(4), e0174944 (2017)
9. Choi, E., Schuetz, A., Stewart, W.F., Sun, J.: Using recurrent neural network models for early detection of heart failure onset. J. Am. Med. Inform. Assoc. **24**(2), 361–370 (2016)
10. Das, R., Turkoglu, I., Sengur, A.: Effective diagnosis of heart disease through neural networks ensembles. Expert Syst. Appl. **36**(4), 7675–7680 (2009)
11. Mortazavi, B.J., et al.: Analysis of machine learning techniques for heart failure readmissions. Circ. Cardiovasc. Qual. Outcomes **9**(6), 629–640 (2016)
12. Dai, W., Brisimi, T.S., Adams, W.G., Mela, T., Saligrama, V., Paschalidis, I.C.: Prediction of hospitalization due to heart diseases by supervised learning methods. Int. J. Med. Inform. **84**(3), 189–197 (2015)
13. Kerver, J.M., Yang, E.J., Bianchi, L., Song, W.O.: Dietary patterns associated with risk factors for cardiovascular disease in healthy US adults. Am. J. Clin. Nutr. **78**(6), 1103–1110 (2003)
14. World Health Organization: Types of Cardiovascular disease. https://www.who.int/ cardiovascular_diseases/en/cvd_atlas_01_types.pdf
15. Goff, D.C., et al.: 2013 ACC/AHA guideline on the assessment of cardiovascular risk: a report of the American College of Cardiology/American Heart Association Task Force on Practice Guidelines. J. Am. Coll. Cardiol. **63**(25 Part B), 2935–2959 (2014)
16. ASCVD Risk Estimator Plus. http://tools.acc.org/ASCVD-Risk-Estimator-Plus/#!/calculate/ estimate/
17. Hevner, A., Chatterjee, S.: Design Research in Information Systems: Theory and Practice, vol. 22. Springer, New York (2010). https://doi.org/10.1007/978-1-4419-5653-8
18. Sleep Heart Health Study. https://sleepdata.org/datasets/shhs

Development and Evaluation of a Web Application for Prenatal Care Coordinators in the United States

Beenish Moalla Chaudhry[1]([✉]), Louis Faust[2], and Nitesh V. Chawla[2]

[1] University of Louisiana at Lafayette, Lafayette, LA 70504, USA
`beenish.chaudhry@louisiana.edu`
[2] University of Notre Dame, Notre Dame, IN 46556, USA

Abstract. Technology-based solutions have been developed to enhance competencies of maternity health workers (MHWs) in the developing countries, but there has been a limited exploration of such tools in the developed world. We developed a web-based application to support care coordination tasks of the prenatal care coordinators (PNCCs) in U.S. using a 3-phase methodology. During the first phase, following key functionalities were identified in collaboration with an expert panel: assessment, information prescription, collaborative calendar, and secure messaging. The second phase was about iterative and incremental development of the app with the expert panel using modular design and easy to use interfaces. This led to the development of a password-protected PHP web application based on a MySQL database. An outside panel consisting of sixteen PNCCs evaluated the tool and provided feedback on perceived benefits, risks and concerns. The evaluators thought that the app could be help them save resources, empower clients, identify risks, maintain continuity of care and simplify documentation. However, they expressed concerns about feasibility of the tool, implementation cost, compliance with guidelines, security issues related to storage of client data and complexity of managing a paperless system. Concerns of MHWs in the developed and developing countries have a significant overlap, hence there is an opportunity for the developed world to learn from research targeted for the developing world. To address some specific concerns of the MHWs in the developed world, we recommend further ethnographic work assuming an activity theoretic approach with the target users.

Keywords: Pregnancy · Community-based · Health workers ·
Care coordination · Usability · Evaluation · Web-based · Connected

1 Background and Significance

In the United States, 90% of the total infant deaths (death of children less than one year old) every year take place in low socio-economic communities [1]. Most of these deaths are linked to poor birth outcomes like pre-term births and low birth weights that can be avoided through adequate prenatal care and health education. The maternity health workers (MHWs) in U.S. known as the prenatal care coordinators (PNCCs), typically work with low-income women to increase their access to these preventative

© Springer Nature Switzerland AG 2019
B. Tulu et al. (Eds.): DESRIST 2019, LNCS 11491, pp. 140–156, 2019.
https://doi.org/10.1007/978-3-030-19504-5_10

measures. They, typically, conduct risk assessments to arrange personalized, culturally competent and cost-effective health and social care for the target population. They also play a vital role in providing health education, increasing knowledge and promoting behavior change in at-risk women. And, most importantly, they provide socio-emotional support by acting as guides across the entire care continuum – prenatal to postpartum to parenthood.

However, these essential health workers face many challenges in providing quality care to their clients and practicing to their full competencies. The continuity of care from community to facility and across all stages of conception is difficult to maintain because of limited resources and complex psychosocial realities of their clients. Limited resources mean that many PNCCs are still utilizing antiquated and error-prone methods in their practices, such as paper and pen for case management, phone calls for communicating with clients and fax machines for sharing data with a diverse array of maternity health actors. These time-consuming methods can put considerable constraint on PNCCs, who typically manage a high client-load involving complex medical regulations requiring long hours and low pay. Their target population constitutes women with low-wage jobs, unpredictable work schedules and demanding employers. Moreover, majority of their clients live in rural areas, have limited resources and face complex psychosocial realities such as multiple children, unpredictable childcare, abusive domestic situations, etc. [17]. These factors, ultimately, prevent PNCCs from connecting with their clients to provide need-based support and maintain continuity of care.

Researchers have been investigating how technologies can be used to empower MHWs and help them overcome some of these challenges in the context of the developing countries. (Since titles, profiles and duties of PNCCs vary enormously across countries, we use the term maternity health workers in our literature review). It has been shown that digital health technologies such as mobile apps are effective in increasing self-efficacy and health knowledge of MHWs in rural areas of the developing world [2, 3]. MHWs are ready and willing to adopt such innovations but they are often concerned about complexity of such tools and training required to adopt them [4, 5]. Well-designed systems can reduce training cost and time, but they require the inclusion of end-users in the design and evaluation during system development. This is because complexity issues, overlooked by developers, are often brought to light by the end-users [6, 7]. The research, however, shows that aligning software design with the requirements of MHWs is extremely challenging due to their unpredictable work environments, privacy and security issues involved in storing and sharing data, and technical know-how of the target users [8]. Hence, adoption of technological tools by MHWs relies heavily on the perceived usability, value, security and social influence of these tools, along with their ease of integration into the existing workflow [9, 10].

Tools that have demonstrated feasibility and acceptance in rural MHWs of the developing world include mobile prenatal monitoring applications, decision support systems and clinical backup software [11, 12]. Electronic health records (EHRs) are accepted by MHWs when they support clinical practice and successfully address challenges related to scalability, individualized patient care, and remote data collection [13]. MHWs also prefer EHRs when they provide structure to the interviewing procedures and support accurate data collection and organization of information [14]. But, due to usability challenges, adoption of EHRs has been low among the MHWs [15].

Overall, the existing work shows that when MHWs' needs are prioritized in the development of technologies, MHWs generally find technologies easy to use and are willing to integrate them into their workflows.

A major limitation of the existing work is that the majority of it was conducted in the developing countries. The technology design needs of the low-resource community-based MHWs, such as PNCCs, in the U.S. are relatively under-explored. Given that these regions, differ greatly in terms of health workers' literacy levels, clinical protocols as well as socio-political structures, it may not be possible to translate the developing world-entered findings to the developed world. Research is, therefore, warranted to establish needs, behaviors and motivations of MHWs in the developed world. In the U.S., this urgency is compounded due to the advent of new health care payment models, which is driving the major health systems to work in collaboration with smaller community-based organizations to improve health care quality and patient experience at reduced costs. Therefore, understanding how technologies can be developed to help these players overcome existing challenges and practice to their full competencies is becoming increasingly relevant.

In this paper, we attempt to address this gap by presenting a case study about the implementation of an interactive web-delivered application that was developed to support the preventative and supportive care practices of low-resource PNCCs in the United States. We describe our implementation process and present our findings by discussing the concerns and challenges perceived by the PNCCs in using the developed system.

2   Context

In 2013, the state-wide Perinatal Collaborative – consisting of representatives from the local health department, leadership and PNCCs from a community hospital child birthing unit, the county Women, Infant and Children (WIC) offices, county minority health coalitions, the United Way and other community-based agencies, and researchers from our home institution – assembled around the question of addressing disparities in infant mortality rates. The goal of the Collaborative was to understand how the strengths of the PNCCs could be enhanced to prevent preterm birth rates and improve the health of pregnant women, infants, and children from low-income communities in the region.

A recurring observation amongst PNCCs of the Collaborative was that most of their Medicaid-eligible low-income pregnant clients had smartphones and preferred to be contacted through text or social media by the coordinators. This naturally stirred interest in understanding how this medium could be utilized to solve the issue at the table. The researchers of our home institution led a brainstorming session with the Collaborative to conceptualize a connected health system consisting of a mobile app for pregnant women and an app for the PNCCs. The system would empower PNCCs to support mothers during pregnancy and prevent them from getting lost as they transitioned from face-to-face prenatal visits to everyday life where they continued to face changing needs. To summarize, a system was needed to help PNCCs offer personalized services and maintain continuity of care at greater efficiencies and reduced costs.

3   Methods

Using the principles of community-based participatory research, we devised a 3-step methodology to develop the proposed application for the PNCCs. A corresponding mobile application connected to this web application has been developed for mothers and has been described in a separate publication [20].

3.1   Phase 1. Key Functionalities

The goal of this phase was to reach consensus regarding the key features of the tool that was conceptualized by the Collaborative. The researchers at our home institutions organized a panel of experts, consisting of local PNCCs (n = 3) and social workers (n = 3), who had also participated in the statewide discussion. Social workers were included because they worked alongside the local PNCCs and shared the workload by providing many overlapping services [16]. We conducted three face-to-face discussions with the panel over a period of three months and augmented the process via email discussions. With respect to developing the application for PNCCs, the panel was asked to consider the following questions: (1) What essential aspects of the PNCCs' workflow should be included in the initial implementation? (2) What major limitations/barriers in care coordination should be addressed? (3) Which device/medium would be suitable for this application?

3.2   Phase 2. Application Development

Application Development. Once we reached a consensus regarding the key functionalities and target medium/device for the proposed tool, we adopted Rapid Application Development (RAD) approach to iteratively and incrementally develop the application with the involvement of the expert panel. We used this approach because frequent changes to the application design were expected due to the highly collaborative nature of the development. The development lasted for over eighteen months during which we organized several feedback sessions with the expert panel. The goal of each session was to iterate on one key functionality by identifying problems, confirming content and improving designs of the existing prototype.

Interface Designs. For each key functionality, we first reach a consensus regarding its interface designs. This process, typically, started with us soliciting feedback on rough paper sketches that were then gradually transformed into interactive wire-frames using a web-based tool called Moqups. About 2–3 group discussions were conducted to finalize user interfaces for one functionality for a total of 10–12 discussions. Each discussion session lasted for 1–2 h and focused on 1–2 usage scenarios. The experts interacted with the prototypes, asked questions, discussed related scenarios and provided suggestions to improve the designs. The interfaces were then converted into web pages using HTML, CSS and JavaScript/jQuery.

Application Architecture. Once user interfaces for each functionality were stabilized, we proceeded to code the app. We used PHP with MySQL database as the programming language. We adopted Model-View-Controller (MVC) architecture with a separate data manipulation layer to develop the desired functionalities. The advantage of this programming paradigm is that it keeps the presentation of data separate from the methods that interact with the data by using three components: (a) models consist of business entities that work with the data access objects to fetch and return data from the database in usable formats, one model and one data access object is created for each business entity; (b) controllers handle requests, process data returned from models and load views to send in response; and (c) views are display templates that are sent in the response to the web browser. Each component of MVC acts independently of each other and makes the code easily reusable.

Usability Evaluation. Following its implementation, each functionality was usability tested by the expert panel using a think aloud approach. Our goal was to encourage participants to vocalize their thoughts, feelings and opinions as they interacted with the prototype. Participants were asked to complete various scenarios with the functionality in question, while commenting on the visual layout of the screens and the way functionalities were supported by the interfaces. If a participant did not vocalize her interactions during the evaluation, we used prompts and semi-structured interviewing technique to collect the requisite data. One researcher observed participant's interactions and recorded the solicited feedback during the usability testing sessions.

3.3   Phase 3. Acceptance Evaluation

The purpose of this phase was to understand benefits, risks, and concerns of the developed application as perceived by the target users. Originally, we had planned to conduct the evaluation with the original expert panel, however, due to state's decision to cut funding to prenatal programs, our partnership abruptly ended sometime during phase 2. Therefore, we reached out to other pregnancy organizations for gather required feedback on the developed application. At the same time, we were looking for organizations who would be interested in pilot-testing the web application at their sites. We targeted community-based organizations who served low-income, Medicaid-eligible pregnant or postpartum women both in our vicinity and other states. Over 250 email invites were sent to various organizations across the country; only sixteen accepted the invitation to evaluate the system.

Study Design. Depending on where the participants were located, a face-to-face or a Skype meeting was arranged to conduct the evaluation study, which consisted of three phases: (a) orientation; (b) demonstration; and (b) feedback. The orientation phase consisted of debriefing participants with the purpose of the study and obtaining informed consent. During the demonstration phase, we walked participants through the main functionalities of the app, such as adding alerts on the dashboard, prescribing information and sending reminder notifications from the web app to the mobile app. One researcher noted down participants' comments and feedback that were voiced by participants during the demonstration. The demonstration lasted for 1–2 h. At the end of the demonstration, we provided participants with an evaluation package consisting of a set of open-ended questions to solicit their feedback on perceived benefits, risks and concerns of using the application. The package also included instructions for logging into the application and a brief overview of the functionalities. We expected participants to engage in a self-guided exploration of the application after the meeting ended and fill out the feedback form that was supposed to be sent back to us. Everyone who emailed back the completed feedback form was sent an electronic $20 gift card.

Participants. Every participant was a female and described herself as a PNCC or a social worker. Nine participants had completed post-graduate degrees, three had a college degree and four described themselves as having a trade apprenticeship/diploma in the field of maternal and child health. The average years of experience was 10.7 years (range 2–23 years). Participants described their clients as culturally and ethnically diverse women from low-income and low educational (<=12th grade) backgrounds. Everyone rated herself as an expert computer user, using a variety of computer applications every day. Eleven participants reported using multiple software such as Word, Excel, Access to manage client cases. Everyone had used or was currently using social media and emails to communicate with her clients.

4 Analysis

Throughout the research, huge amount of qualitative data was collected. The first two authors used qualitative content analysis using Taylor-Powell and Renner approach to structure the data and sort out important insights [21]. We, first, independently coded all the qualitative data and then, met to compare their codes. Whenever there was a difference in coding, discussion ensued until some consensus was reached. The agreed upon codes were categorized into themes, which continued to get refined through discussion. Whenever possible, we shared the identified themes with our collaborators and refined our analysis based on their feedback.

5 Results

5.1 Phase 1. Key Functionalities

The qualitative discussions with the expert panel led to the identification of four key functionalities for the proposed application.

Client's Care Journey. We learned that one PNCC (or social worker) works with one client throughout her pregnancy and is responsible for providing information, services and resources based on client's needs or provider's recommendations. PNCCs accomplish this by meeting with clients several times during their pregnancies. During each meeting, a PNCC assesses the client using structured questionnaires and documents recommendations for follow-up care. *"We take very detailed notes in order for the client to receive the best case-management services. We use them to determine follow-up services and when the next appointment should be made. Even if a client was contacted over phone, we take detailed notes about when the call was made and what* *was discussed."* The app, therefore, needed to collect both structured and unstructured data generated during a client encounter. The structured data consisted of state-recommended assessments, while the unstructured data consisted of narrative notes taken by PNCCs during each visit.

Communication. Besides regular face-to-face meetings, PNCCs used Facebook, phone calls and text messaging to answer clients' queries, perform informal check-ins and provide reminders about upcoming appointments and classes. PNCCs wanted to integrate all types of communication at a single location so they could easily visualize and report how a client's care journey has been evolving over her pregnancy. *"Prenatal care workers should be supplied with devices that will allow them to communicate easier on a daily basis for documentation."* Furthermore, they wanted a communication medium that was accessible to their clients. The challenge with phone calls and text messaging was that clients frequently changed their phone numbers or ran out of minutes. And, PNCCs considered Facebook to be insecure for sharing medical information because it harvested clients' data for marketing purposes. They suggested building a secure messaging component within the application itself, so they would not have to rely on external software for communication purposes. *"I would love to have a chat or an in-app messaging feature that would allow moms to send me a message during their pregnancy, so they don't have to wait for an appointment. And, also allow me to get in touch with them whenever I need to do so."*

Information Exchange. The panel identified the importance of information prescriptions, consisting of educational content and referral information, in delivering a patient-centered care, but acknowledged that current method of providing referral information had some limitations. First, such prescriptions were being made on paper, which were typically easily lost or thrown away. *"We generally provide things that they need help with such as housing, transportation etc. The only issue is that people don't keep paper around for too long and lose the information in the trash."* Second, the panel wanted to know how clients used and implemented the prescribed information in their everyday lives. For example, PNCCs wanted to know: Whether a client followed their recommendations and met with the referrals? How was their experience? What problems did they encounter and what further support did they need? Did clients read the recommended articles? Do they need further guidance on understanding or implementing the new knowledge? To address these problems, the panel wanted the system to allow PNCCs to make digital information prescriptions that could be sent directly to client's smartphone. Based on the clients' usage of this information, the system should update PNCCs with necessary details such as, client has met with the referrals, client needs further follow-up or client has missed an appointment, etc.

Collaborative Calendar. PNCCs informed us that one of their major day-to-day activities was contacting clients to remind them about upcoming appointments and/or beneficial educational events. Currently, this was being done through phone calls, text messages or social media. The PNCCs wanted to manage clients' schedules, and suggested that the system should allow them to schedule events and reminders for clients by giving PNCCs direct access to client's personal calendars. *"I would like to access my client's calendar so I can arrange meetings or set reminders for her without* *having to wait for her to return my calls."* Related to this, PNCCs also wanted a scheduling system that would allow them to manage their daily activities, set reminders and stay on task. *"If a client tells me that she is having her GTT done on a certain day. I want to be triggered the day after, to check in to see if she did the test and was it OK."*

Target Device. There was some debate about whether the application should be a mobile application or a web application. Ultimately, the panel voted in favor of a web application for the following reasons: (a) a web-based system could be easily accessed on multiple devices, such as desktops, laptops and tablets; (b) the identified key functionalities were typically performed during office visits for which a mobile was unnecessary; (c) data entry tasks for assessment were too complex for the small screen of a mobile device; and (d) laptops could be easily connected to the personal hotspots enabled on phones, if WiFi was needed but not available during home visits.

5.2   Phase 2. Application Development

Application Development. The final application is a web-based password-protected PHP application built on top of a MySQL database. It can send and receive data from a mobile application that is used by clients. (The client mobile app has not been described in this manuscript). To support key functionalities of the web app, following main functions were written: Register a Client, Assess and Prescribe, Add Events and Secure Messaging. Table 1 shows the functionalities supported by the developed functions.

Table 1. Key functionalities versus app functions.

Key functionalities	Supporting functions
Client's care journey	Register a Client, Create Survey, Assess & Prescribe
Communication	Secure Messaging
Information exchange	Client Events, Get Data, Assess & Prescribe
Collaborative calendar	Add Events, Client Events

Register a Client is the core functionality that enables PNCCs to enroll a client into the system using her name and email address. Once a client is enrolled, the app automatically generates a personal page from where PNCCs can initiate and manage case management tasks for the client, including risk assessment, narrative notetaking, secure messaging, and referral and education prescriptions, etc. PNCCs can also create mobile app accounts for clients. And once a client has installed the mobile app on her phone, she begins to receive prescriptions, reminders and messages from her PNCC.

The *Assess and Prescribe* function generates risk factors as well as education and referral recommendations using the structured assessment data (that are collected by PNCCs via web forms on the website). The interface gives PNCCs the flexibility to update/modify risk factors and knowledge recommendations using her own judgement. Once she is satisfied, she clicks the send button and the information (i.e. referral details, links to articles) are delivered to client's app. This information is also recorded in the web app's database and is visible from the client's personal page. A complementary function called *Get Data* allows PNCCs to view the client's follow-up activities, by displaying the data uploaded by the client's mobile app. This visualization allows PNCCs to determine follow-up care for the client.

The *Add Events* functions allow PNCCs to add appointments and events to a shared calendar (shared with other PNCCs and clients), along with helpful notes and reminders. The function allows PNCCs to decide whether an event should be shared with all the clients, a specific client or with other PNCCs. She can also use this function to set self-reminders about upcoming events and appointments. Events that are shared with clients appear on their mobile apps' calendars, where clients can reset reminder times and make further modifications. PNCC's private events or reminders appear on the application's main page and can be deleted or marked completed when no longer needed (Fig. 1). *Client Events* function updates the portal database to indicate events/reminders changes made by the client on her mobile app.

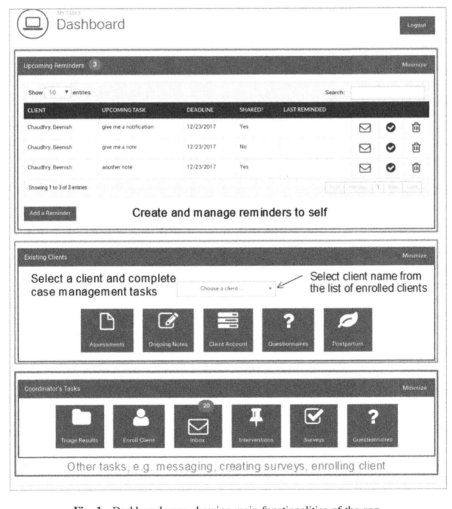

Fig. 1. Dashboard page showing main functionalities of the app.

The *Secure Messaging* function controls all the information that is exchanged between the PNCC portal and the client mobile app. It allows PNCCs to send in-app messages and (phone) notifications to their clients, to encourage engagement in care plans, to perform casual wellness checks, to remind about an upcoming appointment, to solicit notes from a scheduled appointment, etc. In collaboration with other functions, this function also delivers prescriptions such as referral appointment details, referral information, article links, etc. to clients' phones. PNCCs can create and save message templates on the web app and customize them based on needs. This function also helps PNCCs initiate message threads with other PNCCs to coordinate activities, etc. Finally, they can exchange messages and client reports with referrals directly.

In addition, functions were created to enable PNCCs to curate content and build database of referrals to prepare themselves with a wide array of resources. A registration function was created to enable the PNCC supervisor to request an account for herself by providing her name and email. Once her account is approved, she can create additional accounts for her staff using their names and email addresses. Figure 1 shows the main page of the developed application with access to case management tasks.

Modifications After Usability Evaluations. We made five types of modifications to the web application after think-aloud usability evaluations. First, participants requested us to use colored codes to distinguish positive and negative feedback generated by the web application. We changed all positive feedback to appear in green and negative feedback to be in red. Second, participants wanted to minimize data-entry tasks on the structured data collection forms. They suggested replacing text fields with dropdown lists, checkboxes, list views, etc. wherever possible. Algorithms were also added to further control follow-up questions and minimize data-collection tasks. Third, we added client-side validations to the web-forms and session variables to prevent data loss when questionnaires were saved to the database. Fourth, we made all client management tasks accessible from the main page, in addition to including them on the client's account page, since participants wanted multiple pathways to enter these functionalities.

Finally, we introduced a few new features and functionalities within the application. We wrote algorithms to automate risk identification, and referral and education recommendation. We also created a new function called *Create Survey* to enable PNCCs to send and receive surveys to client's mobile apps. For example, if a PNCC wants to screen a client for postpartum depression, she can do it remotely by creating the Edinburgh Postnatal Depression Scale on her web app and then e-send it to her client's mobile app. We also enhanced the *Secure Messaging* function to enable PNCCs to send group messages (and information e-prescriptions) to clients with similar needs.

5.3   Phase 3. Acceptance Evaluation

Based on the qualitative analysis, we identified following benefits, risks and concerns raised by the participants. Although not specifically asked, participants also recommended additional functionalities for the application.

Benefits. *Saving resources.* Participants stated that digital information prescriptions will help them save resources such as time and paper. Posting events digitally would mean that PNCCs are not spending several hours every month mailing paper calendars to their clients and have more time to care for their clients. *"One benefit I am seeing is saving paper handouts by sending e-articles."* Participants also pointed out that digital information will not be easily lost or forgotten, and consequently, they will not have to waste time re-prescribing this information to their clients. Many participants also noted that the app is a big improvement over existing systems that are old, slow, and require long hours for data entry.

Documentation. Participants who were still using paper to manage their cases commented that the application will simplify documentation and data organization tasks. And, ultimately it will help them create reports and analyze outcomes. *"It would allow me to keep patient's electronic file with all the information pertaining to prenatal care and a list of referrals made for patients. Ultimately, this will help create reports."* Participants also stated that communication via the app will automate a major reporting requirement. *"I love that messages can be sent for both clients and referrals. This allows for documentation of a major prenatal care requirement."*

Client Empowerment. Participants pointed out that the app would make it easier for them to convey important information to clients who are not always easy to find or fail to respond to their attempts to connect. They will be able to empower clients with all the needed resources while respecting their privacy and desired autonomy. Many participants acknowledged that clients and families often become frustrated when PNCCs make multiple attempts to connect with them to increase their engagement. And, sometimes they even discontinue participation in the program altogether. *"This helps eliminate multiple emails/texts to families that might be frustrating to them and may no longer want to participate due to us being a nuisance."*

Risk Identification. Participants pointed out that the app's interface presents an efficient and easy way to identify risks that are often ignored by the mainstream healthcare system or overlooked due to inefficient and time-consuming systems. *"One major benefit of this app is that it allows for easy identification and care of risk factors that might not be addressed by conventional care givers. I feel as though efforts are either duplicated or missed due to the fact that we have to manually review patient's narrative notes to determine what has and has not been addressed."* They also commented that with better knowledge of their patient's risks, they will be empowered to speak to other providers and influence client's care.

Continuity of Care. Participants stated that if they were to adopt this system, they would use be able to use all the available features to improve continuity of care and ensure that the client is not getting lost in the referral process. They also commented that this app will make life easier for their clients, since they would not have to commute to PNCC office for every meeting. They will be able to provide reports about meeting by answering the surveys from the comfort of home. Ultimately, this will put less burden on clients and they will be more likely to complete the program.

Risks and Concerns. *Cost.* Since majority of the participants belonged to a non-profit organization that were supported by time-limited grants, they all expressed concerns about the cost of the app. They reminded us that if they were going to adopt the system, it would probably have to coincide with their next funding cycle, when they could build the cost of the app (as long as it is reasonable) into the budget. They also preferred subscribing to a service as opposed to adopting a free open source one, because subscriptions came with tech support that was valued by participants. *"The decision to adopt this app would depend on the cost to us as providers as well as our clients. We work in a health department, so funds are usually limited."* Participants also stated that their clients are typically low-income individuals who have limited minutes on their smartphones. The would not be feasible to them, if it is consuming too much mobile data to receive notifications from the PNCCs.

Security. Since participants belonged to health entities, they reminded us that they are required by the law to protect patient's health data. Almost everyone wanted to know what mechanisms had been incorporated within the app to protect clients' data. And, they commented that the level of security offered by the app will ultimately dictate whether they will adopt this app or not. *"Security as far as HIPAA will be a biggy, otherwise it seems low risk."*

Shared System. Many participants explained that their clients are often moved from one location to another to provide them relevant services. Therefore, they stated that their agency would adopt a system that has the capability to share data with multiple locations. *"We are a statewide agency, so if a pregnant patient moves to another location, the care manager in that county needs to pick her up where the other care manger left off. If this system is not state-wide and just practice-based, this would be valuable information that another case manager would need."*

Compliance. Many participants were concerned whether the tool complied with the Medical Assistance (MA) requirements. According to MA rules, providers must follow certain protocols and collect specific data items to receive reimbursement for the services they are providing to eligible patients. Many participants also pointed out that the MA requirements likely varied across states, so the system would have to be flexible to accommodate differences. *"Everything is MA guidelines driven, so anything that is not on the website that MA requires for documentation would not be helpful for us. As far as just caring for patients, this website would be very useful. I would love to see a mock MA audit of this app done by someone. If the app could be individualized to specific state's MA requirements, it would be helpful."*

Uncertainty. Participants expressed concerns about moving to a totally paperless system, even though they acknowledged that a digital system can offer far more benefits, including data organization and direct communication. The uncertainties stemmed from not knowing how long it would take to get used to a paperless system and what would be involved in the management of the tool. *"One concern is that moving to paperless forms is challenging. What will be the backup procedures and what will happen during the down time? But I can see how this makes it easier to send reminders about appointments and doctors."*

Client Limitations. Participants pointed out that this system would not work with clients who have limited internet access. *"WiFi accessibility is low in rural areas. Not all families have computers, but most do have smart phones, but their dollar minutes may be limited."* Some participants also pointed out that some of their clients may not have the organizational and cognitive skills that are necessary to stay up to date with an app and its communication features. Many participants also stated that they would not adopt a system, unless another group of PNCCs have already tested it and found it effective with a similar patient population. *"I won't know what to expect until it is tried out in real time. Different patient populations respond differently. I would love to see it tried out by someone."*

Feature Requests. *Care plans.* Participants recommended that the app should allow them to automatically generate care plans based on the identified risks. *"The care plan is a big part of prenatal care and documentation. I did not see any generated care plans from the identified risks."* Moreover, they recommended integrating care plans within the risk assessment module, that is, going from assessment to risk identification to care plan generation to education or action (referral). This aligned with the MA requirement of documenting all the steps. Participants indicated that a client's signature on the care plan is also needed and, ultimately, clients should have access to them on their apps.

Distinguishing Referrals. Participants also pointed out that it is important that the system makes a distinction between a formal and an informal referral. The MA guidelines require a follow-up for every formal referral, but this is not necessary for an informal referral. *"Sometimes, we just give clients contact information without a formal referral. MA requires documentation of follow-up for every referral, which we may not have for informal referral. Therefore, it would be more useful for us to have the option to distinguish the two."*

Risk Follow-Up. Participants also requested a further refinement to the risk identification algorithm. They wanted the system to also determine the severity of the risk and explicate follow-up requirements. Participants explained that these metrics are usually based on an individual patient and, therefore, sophisticated calculations can help make these decisions with accuracy. *"Identify which risk factors need further follow up, i.e. ppd/dv issues; level of risk depends on the patient unless you have a scale."*

Wider Integration. The participants pointed out that they should be treated as an important part of the health care system, as they collect data that can benefit other health actors involved in the care of the same individual. Therefore, they suggested that the app should extended to integrate with health care systems, including EHRs, of other health actors. They should be able to communicate with the wider health care system and also share essential health information with them. *"We should be able to communicate with other health care providers working with the same client."*

Reporting Capability. Many participants suggested that the web application should allow them to generate reports, so they can report back to their funders and other stakeholders in case of audits. *"I would like to see reporting capability and tracking information. Example, how many moms in 1st trimester who had a referral to where they did follow up, how many appointments were kept. Generate csv or excel sheets so we can create reports in case of an audit.* " Other thought that it would be a great help if the system could be customized to communicate with other databases they were using to report to funders and other stakeholders.

6 Discussion

User involvement during development of a new technology is imperative to ensure solutions meet users' needs and abilities [20]. In this paper, we present a 3-step research and development methodology that we used to involve community-based PNCCs in the development of a tool to support their care coordination activities. Due to the absence of steady research partners, only the first two phases of design and development were conducted with the same expert panel. A different group of PNCCs was recruited in the final phase, which was both advantageous and disadvantageous for this project. One advantage was that it helped us identify issues that were not raised by the original expert panel. In particular, risks, concerns and feature requests raised by the outside evaluators broadened our understanding of the target users and their contexts. The original panel may not have been very skeptical because they were involved in building the application from the scratch and appreciated the incremental development approach. On the flip side, the potential benefits identified by the outside evaluators provides feasibility of moving ahead with a pilot study. The disadvantage was that we could not find partners who were willing to pilot-test a partially developed app and become research and development partners. Instead, PNCCs wanted the feasibility validation to come from other PNCCs as well as higher authorities, such as the state's health department. Moreover, there were budgetary issues related to the management of the research project that could not be addressed without a major grant won by us or our future research partners.

Our research was conducted with a small but diverse group of PNCCs, representing different regions and contexts within the U.S. Yet, we found that many of their concerns with using technology for care of pregnant women are similar to those of the MHWs in the developing world. In particular, security and privacy concerns related to storing and sharing of patient data are universal. And, complicated because a variety of health actors are involved in the care of one individual. We also found that the major prenatal care tasks performed by the PNCCs in the U.S. have many similarities to those performed by the MHWs in many developing countries. For example, Chawani and Ngoma identified referral, follow-up, counsel and education as the four main activities of MHWs in Malawi [4] and these activities are similar to PNCCs' tasks in our studies. Moreover, like the rural areas in the developing world, technical issues as well as financial and personal circumstances of the population create numerous challenges with the usage of mobile Internet and data. These similarities imply that there are ample opportunities to learn from the research efforts conducted in the developing world. For example, synchronous integrated voice recognition (IVR) platforms constitute one type of technologies that has been successful in resource-limited settings [19] of the developing world, but they have not been evaluated in the context of the developed world.

On the other hand, in comparison to MHWs in the developing world, PNCCs in our studies saw monitoring clients' usage of prenatal services and overall health beyond scheduled meetings essential for providing timely care and preventing pregnancy complications. This requirement may be related to the health insurance system in the U.S., where pregnant women living below the poverty line are eligible to receive maternity care benefits under the government instituted health insurance called Medicaid. In order to ensure that their reimbursement benefits under Medicaid remain covered, community-based organizations need proof of the effectiveness of their services. Hence, their desire for more intense monitoring and surveillance of clients. The novelty of the developed application lies within this area as well. That is, the system enables PNCCs to monitor clients and intervene into their lives at any place and time as long as clients are sharing this information. The success of this approach, however, is complicated by the existence of diverse cultural and ethnic minorities among low-income communities in the U.S., who may respond differently towards the target application due to various reasons. Therefore, there is a need for a systematic evaluation of this or a similar application with different populations.

Other challenges and concerns uncovered by this work have received relatively limited coverage by the related work. Specifically, our research shows that PNCCs in the U.S. are required to follow and document a strict protocol encompassing all stages of enrollment in the prenatal programs according to the MA guidelines. The evaluators in our study recommended enhancing the existing task flow from assessment to care plan to education or referral to follow-up. Particularly, they wanted the system to provide them assurances that they are hitting all the MA requirements. Additionally, PNCCs stated the need for an integrated system that would bring all maternity health actors involved in the care of one individual at a single location to collaborate. In theory, this seems possible, however, in reality, different health actors are not always carefully coordinated. In U.S., the links among government funded services, private physicians, and other service systems such as welfare and housing are weak or nonexistent. Therefore, achieving optimal benefits possible through a coordinated effort of different health actors with a technology-based system will be a challenging endeavor. The goal of this research, however, was to develop a minimal viable product to support communication between PNCCs and pregnant women, we did not seek to integrate every functionality into this implementation. Further development of this tool would require alignment with existing protocols and guidelines, which would require ethnographic work assuming an activity theoretic approach with the target population.

7   Conclusion

There is a significant overlap of the activities of MHWs in the developed and developing countries, hence there is an opportunity to leverage the research work conducted in the developing world. To address some specific concerns of the MHWs in the developed world, we recommend further ethnographic work assuming an activity theoretic approach with the target users.

References

1. Olson, M.E., Diekema, D., Elliott, B.A., Renier, C.M.: Impact of income and income inequality on infant health outcomes in the United States. Pediatrics **126**(6), 1165–1173 (2010)
2. Agarwal, S., Perry, H.B., Long, L.A., Labrique, A.B.: Evidence on feasibility and effective use of mHealth strategies by frontline health workers in developing countries: systematic review. Tropical Med. Int. Health **20**(8), 1003–1014 (2015)
3. Lee, S., Chib, A., Kim, J.N.: Midwives' cell phone use and health knowledge in rural communities. J. Health Commun. **16**(9), 1006–1023 (2011)
4. Chawani, M.S., Ngoma, C.: Use of mobile technology to support provision of community-based maternal and neonatal care in developing countries. In: HEALTHINF, pp. 260–267 (2011)
5. Zakane, S.A., et al.: Guidelines for maternal and neonatal point of care: needs of and attitudes towards a computerized clinical decision support system in rural Burkina Faso. Int. J. Med. Informatics **83**(6), 459–469 (2014)
6. Hakkinen, H., Korpela, M.: A participatory assessment of IS integration needs in maternity clinics using activity theory. Int. J. Med. Informatics **76**(11), 843–849 (2007)
7. Psaila, K., Fowler, C., Kruske, S., Schmied, V.: A qualitative study of innovations implemented to improve transition of care from maternity to Child and Family Health (CFH) services in Australia. Women Birth **27**(4), e51–e60 (2014)
8. Velez, O., Okyere, P.B., Kanter, A.S., Bakken, S.: A usability study of a mobile health application for rural Ghanaian midwives. J. Midwifery Women's Health **59**(2), 184–191 (2014)
9. Byomire, G., Maiga, G.: A model for mobile phone adoption in maternal healthcare. In: IST-Africa Conference, pp. 1–8. IEEE (2015)
10. Speciale, A.M., Freytsis, M.: mHealth for midwives: a call to action. J. Midwifery Women's Health **58**(1), 76–82 (2013)
11. Dunsmuir, D., et al.: Development of mHealth applications for pre-eclampsia triage. IEEE J. Biomed. Health Informatics **18**(6), 1857–1864 (2014)
12. Martinez, B., et al.: Agile development of a smartphone app for perinatal monitoring in a resource-constrained setting **11**(1) (2017)
13. Mahunnah, M., Taveter, K.: A scalable multi-agent architecture in environments with limited connectivity: case study on individualised care for healthy pregnancy. In: 7th IEEE International Conference on Digital Ecosystems and Technologies (DEST), pp. 84–89 (2013)
14. Deldar, K., Tara, F., Bahaadinbeigy, K., Khajedaluee, M., Tara, M.: A data model for teleconsultation in managing high-risk pregnancies: design and preliminary evaluation. JMIR Med. Inform. **5**(4), e52 (2017)
15. Hawley, G., Janamian, T., Jackson, C., Wilkinson, S.A.: In a maternity shared-care environment, what do we know about the paper hand-held and electronic health record: a systematic literature review. BMC Pregnancy Childbirth **14**(1), e52 (2014)
16. Chaudhry, B.C., Faust, L., Chawla, N.V.: Towards an integrated mHealth platform to support prenatal care coordinators who serve low income communities. In: ACM 12th International Conference on Pervasive Computing Technologies for Healthcare, pp. 118–127 (2018)

17. Hughson, J.A., Marshall, F., Daly, J.O., Woodward-Kron, R., Hajek, J., Story, D.: Health professionals' views on health literacy issues for culturally and linguistically diverse women in maternity care: barriers, enablers and the need for an integrated approach. Aust. Health Rev. **42**(1), 10–20 (2018)
18. Spencer, M.S., Gunter, K.E., Palmisano, G.: Community health workers and their value to social work. Soc. Work **55**(2), 169–180 (2010)
19. Kazakos, K., et al.: A real-time IVR platform for community radio. In: Proceedings of the 2016 CHI Conference on Human Factors in Computing Systems, pp. 343–354 (2016)
20. Kyng, M., Dekan, K.P.: Users and computers - a contextual approach to design of computer artifacts (1999)
21. Powell, E.T., Renner, M.: Analyzing Qualitative Data. University of Wisconsin-Extension Program Development and Evaluation Cooperative Extension Publications, Madison (2003)

Development of a Smart Glass Application for Wound Management

Kai Klinker[✉], Manuel Wiesche, and Helmut Krcmar

Chair for Information Systems, Technical University of Munich,
Boltzmannstraße 13, 85748 Garching, Germany
kai.klinker@in.tum.de

Abstract. Treatment of chronic wounds is a challenging task for health care professionals. When treating chronic wounds, accurate documentation of wound development via photos, measurements, and written descriptions are crucial for monitoring the healing progress over time and choosing the right wound treatment. Currently, however, wound documentation is often perceived as inaccurate and incomplete. In this research, we follow a user-centered design science approach to develop a smart glass-based wound documentation system to support healthcare workers. Through ethnographic fieldwork, interviews and prototype tests with focus groups, we find that smart glass applications hold potential for improving the wound documentation process because they allow for hands-free documentation at the point of care.

Keywords: Augmented Reality · Health care · Wound management ·
Design science · Smart glasses

1 Introduction

As more and more time in healthcare is being spent on administrative tasks, there is less time for direct patient care [1]. Using smart devices to provide information access for service processes at the point of care (POC) is therefore a promising endeavor to improve outcomes and reduce administrative burdens [2].

Within our research, we focus on wound management, as an exemplary service process within health care. Treatment of chronic wounds is a challenging task in health care [3]. In Germany, annually, 2–3 million patients receive wound treatment. Among those, about 900000 suffer from chronic wounds [4]. When treating chronic wounds, accurate documentation of the wound development via photos, measurements, and written descriptions are crucial for monitoring the healing progress over time [5]. Currently, health care facilities often employ digital cameras and hand-written documentation, which are cumbersome and time-consuming to use [6]. Moreover, the documentation often does not meet quality standards.

Augmented Reality (AR) smart glasses, such as the Microsoft HoloLens, are a new generation of smart devices that have the potential to transform healthcare processes and healthcare management in general [7, 8]. Their main advantage is that they can be operated hands-free, thus allowing healthcare workers to use both hands for their work while having access to an information system [9].

© Springer Nature Switzerland AG 2019
B. Tulu et al. (Eds.): DESRIST 2019, LNCS 11491, pp. 157–171, 2019.
https://doi.org/10.1007/978-3-030-19504-5_11

Despite their potential, research on the usage of smart glasses in the service sector is still at a very early stage. In order to build an artifact that supports the wound management process, we follow the Design Science Research (DSR) guidelines proposed by Hevner et al. to iteratively develop smart glass applications and evaluate them with health care professionals [10].

2   Research Approach

The aim of our research is to improve digital support for the wound management process in the health care sector using a design science approach. Throughout our research, we followed the guidelines for Design Science Research (DSR) as described by Hevner [10]. The DSR approach consists of relevance, rigor and design cycles. The rigor cycle provides past knowledge to the research project and ensures that the designs produced are research contributions [10, 11]. The design cycle is the heart of any design science research project [10]. This cycle of research activities iterates more rapidly between the construction of an artifact, its evaluation, and subsequent feedback to refine the design further [10]. Finally, the relevance cycle typically initiates DSR with an application context that not only provides the requirements for the research as inputs but also defines acceptance criteria for the ultimate evaluation of the research results [10].

Figure 1 depicts how relevance, rigor, and design cycles were employed in our research. As suggested by Hevner, we started with a relevance cycle by discussing challenges of the current wound management process with healthcare professionals in focus group meetings and by shadowing them during their daily activities [10]. Thereafter, we conducted a rigor cycle by reviewing the scientific literature on wound management, technology acceptance, and smart glasses. Building upon this, we conducted three design cycles. In each design cycle, we built and tested prototypes in order to gain insights into how process support for wound documentation should be designed in order to improve the workflow of the wound managers. Each of the cycles is described in more detail in the following sections.

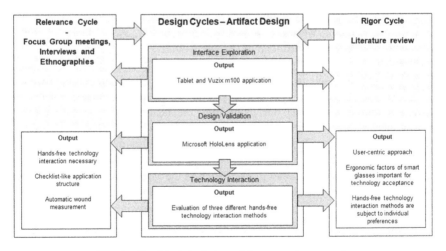

Fig. 1. Graphical depiction of the research approach

3 Related Work (Rigor Cycle)

In order to accomplish our objectives and to help understand the potential likelihood of success of different technology designs being considered, we turned to three major streams of research that we felt could inform our thinking: (1) Technology Adoption (2) Wound Management and (3) Augmented Reality smart glasses. First, we review the literature on Technology Adoption and employee satisfaction in order to understand the factors that are crucial for the adoption of wound documentation artifacts in health care settings. Next, we turn to the literature on Augmented Reality and 3D User interfaces and discuss their relevance to our work. Finally, we discuss the characteristics of the wound documentation process that have been discussed in scientific literature.

3.1 Technology Acceptance and Employee Satisfaction

Many models and theories for technology acceptance have been adopted from sociology and psychology and tested over the last decades [12]. The best-known ones are the Technology Acceptance Model, the Unified Theory of Acceptance and Use of Technology (UTAUT) [12]. In our research, we decided to use UTAUT, because it was originally developed to explain the technology acceptance and use behavior of employees [13]. UTAUT has been used before in several instances to predict define and enhance use [14]. The UTAUT questionnaire measures factors like performance expectancy, effort expectancy and social influence of individuals to use an artifact. These constructs predict an individual's intention to use the artifact, which in turn predicts actual use.

Satisfaction refers to the perceived discrepancy between prior expectation and perceived performance after consumption – when performance differs from expectation, dissatisfaction occurs [15]. The service profit chain directly links employee satisfaction to customer satisfaction [16]. Increasing employee satisfaction is therefore likely to improve overall service quality.

3.2 Wound Management

Chronic wounds pose a major problem in healthcare. Annually 2–3 million German patients need wound treatment, of which approximately 900000 patients suffer from chronic wounds, which is defined by a treatment period of more than eight weeks [4].

For the treating physician, it is obligatory to provide accurate documentation of the wound process [5]. The documentation is not only required by German law but also serves as a basis for care quality assessment [5]. Yet, there is a lack of clear direction and agreement on what tools to use for wound documentation [17].

The documentation improves wound treatment outcomes because it enables healthcare professionals to assess how the wound has changed over time and relations between interventions and outcomes become evident [17]. This enables professional therapy planning and ensures the best possible care for the patient. Moreover, standardized wound treatment documentation helps to shift from practice- to evidence-based wound treatment [18].

The current wound documentation process is complicated to execute for nursing staff and can lead to serious problems. These include the transmission of germs. This can happen via the surfaces of digital cameras or similar devices, which are used for image capture of wounds [6]. Nurses may touch devices numerous times during the day without washing their hands, potentially spreading germs to others [19].

Moreover, the actual recording of the photograph is challenging for the nursing staff. Often, several nurses are required for such documentation, which makes it a time-consuming endeavor and adds to their workload. For hygienic reasons, the documentation is typically written in the station room after the wound treatment is completed and is therefore not done in a timely manner [17]. This requires nurses to remember specific details about the wound until they reach the station room. The resulting wound documentation is often described as inaccurate [17, 18].

Many POC documentation systems, such as Physician-order entry systems or smartphone and tablet applications have been tested in the context of wound management [20]. However, POC systems whose functionality mismatches the workflow are not valued by healthcare workers [20]. A reoccurring problem with existing POC systems is that healthcare workers cannot use them when they do not have their hands free or need to perform aseptic procedures [21]. Smartphones and laptops are not well suited for documentation at the POC, because they should not be touched while the practitioner's hands are sterile or soiled. In contrast to hand-held devices, smart glass applications can be used hands-free. Information is displayed in the user's field of view and technology interaction can be done through hands-free interaction modalities such as voice commands or eye blinking.

3.3   Requirements for Smart Glasses in Health Care

Some smart glasses make use of Augmented Reality (AR) while others just display information that resides statically in front of the user's eyes. The goal of AR is to bring additional information as seamlessly as possible into the view of a user [22]. This is done by adding real-time interactive virtual three-dimensional (3D) elements into the user's real-world environment [23]. AR smart glasses have been tested in various service-related contexts. For instance, they have been used for collaboration scenarios, minimal-invasive surgery, displaying assembly instructions or supporting workers to pick the right parts from a shelf in logistics [24].

Irrespective of whether a smart glass uses AR or not, users need to be able to interact with their smart glass. Since such devices are typically operated in mobile and 3D-environments, established interaction paradigms such as keyboard, mouse or the Windows Icons Menus Pointers (WIMP) are not a good fit for this technology [25]. Instead, physical 3D-interaction concepts like gestures, hand pointing, ray-casting with hand-held devices, eye blinking, gazing or audio-based interaction concepts like speech commands or natural language processing can be used [26, 27].

Several of these modalities have been discussed for septic-safe contexts [28]. Septic-safe technology interaction needs to occur without touching the device [28–31]. During surgery, there may occur numerous scenarios over which a physician could be cut off from the availability of individual modalities for technology interaction. Surgeons could have their throat indisposed generally or momentarily, preventing the use of voice commands. Moreover, surgeons also often have both of their hands involved during the operation, so a technology interaction system based on hand gestures should not be used as a base interface [28].

Several of the design principles for smart glasses in the scientific literature focus on improved social acceptability. Instead of designing all-purpose smart glasses, smart glass designs should rather focus on clear, task-oriented usage to allow users to see them as a dedicated aid in a specific work environment [31]. In addition, knowledge about the intended use of smart glasses and about the actions performed with the device is crucial when it comes to user acceptance since it helps to reduce objections [31].

Apart from paying attention to social acceptability, it is also crucial to focus on user experience when designing wearable healthcare systems [32]. A wearable health system should be lightweight, easy-to-use, secure, effective, reliable, low power consuming, scalable, cost-efficient, of embedded intelligence, and able to keep a connection with a remote medical station [32]. Moreover, a bad performance can also trigger negative usability perceptions. Sultan et al. suggest that application reaction times should not exceed two seconds [33].

4 Relevance Cycle

To design an application for a specific use case, it is essential to first analyze the underlying process in detail. This allows the best possible understanding of the current application domain, any limitations, user needs, or general problems. Based on this, requirements can be determined which are to be met by the implemented application. A triangulation of ethnographic research, expert interviews and focus group meetings was used in collaboration with several nursing homes and hospitals to gain an initial understanding of the health care domain and the wound management process. More details on the triangulation approach and its results are described below.

4.1 Research Procedure

Ethnographic studies were carried out in one hospital (40 h total) and in two nursing homes (60 h each) in Germany. In some health care facilities wound management is delegated to dedicated wound management experts, while in other facilities wound management is integrated into the daily routine of the staff of a ward. Throughout the ethnographic studies, we had the opportunity to watch 14 different health care workers throughout their daily work.

In two cases, health care workers specializing in wound care were accompanied during their daily work. The other 12 health care workers were followed as part of multi-day internships in health facilities. Since our studies took place in facilities run by different health care providers, different types of documentation processes could be observed. Observations were captured in field notes for later analysis. In addition, 8 formal and various informal interviews were conducted with wound experts and other members of the staff.

The questions for the formal interviews were pre-formulated in a semi-structured interview guide and served as a basis for discussion during the interviews. Building upon these insights a focus group meeting was conducted in order to discuss the results and to get input for a concept of a first prototype. The goal of the relevance cycle was a detailed understanding of the current process of wound documentation as well as the associated requirements for the application to be developed. Tables 1 and 2 provide an overview of the interview partners and facilities in which the ethnographic studies were conducted.

Table 1. Requirements for hands-free interaction derived from the scientific literature

Requirement	Description
LRQ1: Hands-free interaction	Interaction needs to occur without touching the device [28–31]
LRQ2: Multi-modal interaction	Some interaction modalities might not be available [28]
LRQ3: Task orientation	Task orientation can improve technology acceptance [31]
LRQ4: Wearability	Lightweight, comfortable and noninvasive [32]
LRQ5: Interactivity	Minimalistic, intuitive interface for low cognitive effort [32]
LRQ6: Security	Secure authentication and data storage [30, 32]
LRQ7: Effectiveness	The system should perform well and robust under all circumstances [32, 33]
LRQ8: Low power consumption	Efficient algorithms extend battery life [28, 32]
LRQ9: System validation	New systems should be compared to existing procedures [32]

4.2   Results of the Relevance Cycle

Although the general process is similar in most facilities, in practice, the wound documentation process often differs in some details among facilities managed by different care providers. Moreover, information system support of the process was very heterogeneous. While in some facilities, the patient's wound data was recorded with paper files, other facilities use special software.

The ethnographies showed that the wound documentation is divided into two parts: Initial and continuous documentation. Initial documentation is done only once, when a wound is first detected and includes data such as the location of the wound and the reason it occurred. The continuous documentation is conducted repeatedly at regular time intervals and includes measurements of several wound parameters (e.g., length, width and color of the wound). The documentation is performed in a very structured manner and is often based on checklists. The interval at which patients' wounds are documented should not exceed one week and occur additionally whenever bandages are changed or when significant changes to the wound are noticed. A typical sequence of steps for continuous wound documentation is shown in Fig. 2. The orange-marked blocks indicate process steps which experts consider to have the potential for digital support.

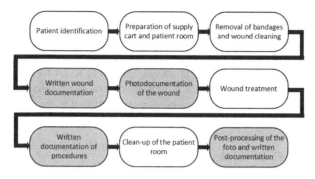

Fig. 2. Overview of the wound management process (Color figure online)

4.3 Discussion

During the focus group meeting and the interviews, several requirements for a digital wound management solution were discussed. The results are summarized in Table 2. Experts confirmed that hands-free interaction is necessary for documentation at the POC and emphasized that they often need both hands to stabilize the patient during wound treatment. One especially challenging part of the documentation process is to take pictures of the wound while stabilizing the patient. Wound managers would thus welcome an artifact that can take pictures of the wound while they stabilize the patient with both hands. Wound treatment can be painful for the patient. In order to divert attention from pain and to create a trusting atmosphere, wound managers often engage in conversations with the patient while they treat the wound. In order to enable conversations with the patient, a digital wound management application should thus demand as little cognitive effort as possible. Quite a lot of healthcare workers in Germany have migrated from other countries and speak with an accent. If hands-free technology interaction is implemented using voice commands it is important that it also works robustly for non-native speakers. Finally, wound documentation is currently often filled in incompletely or inaccurately. Documenting at the POC and making all input fields mandatory were seen as a potential solution to improve documentation outcomes.

Table 2. Requirements for hands-free interaction derived from field research

Requirements	Description
FRQ1: Photo functionality	It should be possible to take pictures of wounds
FRQ2: Hands-free documentation	Both hands are needed for stabilizing the patient during continuous documentation
FRQ3: Low cognitive effort	It should be possible to communicate with the patient while documenting
FRQ4: Easy to learn and to use	The application should support the process without making it more complicated
FRQ5: Language barrier	Voice commands should work for users with accents
FRQ6: Compliance with regulations	Wound documentation should be complete and accurate

5 Artifact Design (Design Cycle)

The technology acceptance literature and our insights from the relevance cycle suggest that usefulness and ease of use are important prerequisites for acceptance of a digital wound management application. Therefore we decided to focus on designing a digital solution that improves the workflow of wound managers. We followed a user-centered approach by building upon the design requirements identified in the rigor and relevance cycle.

5.1 First Design Cycle – Interface Exploration

In this first design cycle, we were especially focusing on the challenge of finding a balance between usability and hands-free use. While interaction paradigms for tablets, smartphones, and PCs are well established and known to the general public, hands-free interaction modalities such as voice commands and hand gestures are known to a lesser extent. While selecting among a limited set of options works robustly for hands-free modalities like voice commands, more complex tasks such as filling free text input fields are complicated and error-prone.

Suggestion and Development. We decided to tackle this challenge by using a combination of devices. The initial part of the wound documentation was implemented on a tablet device. The interaction paradigms of tablets and smartphones are well known to most health care workers and it is easier to type names and select wound locations on such an interface. Since the initial documentation only needs to be done once and could be performed in the patient room before hands are disinfected, this seemed to be a rational approach.

The continuous part of the documentation can be implemented using predefined selection options. Users are not required to insert free-text input. Therefore we implemented the continuous part of the documentation as a hands-free application on a Vuzix m100 smart glass. The Vuzix m100 is a monocular smart glass that displays visual information via a little prism that is placed in front of one eye. A checklist-like structure was used to guide users through the wound documentation process. Figure 3 shows an overview of the sequence of screens.

Evaluation. The application was tested with the focus group that had already been consulted in the relevance cycle. It consisted of 8 wound management experts. The experts had the opportunity to try out the prototype application extensively and give feedback. Several practice runs were conducted using a dummy doll. Overall, the approach of using a combination of tablet and smart glass application was well received. Using voice commands to interact with the smart glass worked robustly, even for non-native speakers, and the experts made positive remarks about the simplicity and usability of the application. The sequential checklist-like structure of the application allowed them to focus on one aspect of the documentation at a time inducing only very little cognitive load.

While the experts were not concerned that the application might induce high levels of cognitive load they were unsure how patients would react to them speaking voice commands. Moreover, the ergonomics of the Vuzix m100 were criticized.

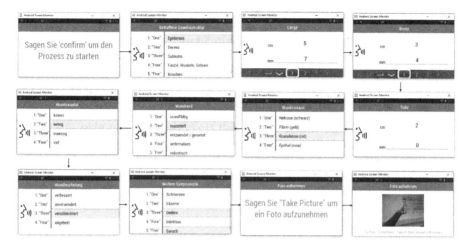

Fig. 3. Overview of the sequence of screens in the Vuzix m100 application

The one-sided weight distribution and unstable design prevent the display remaining rigidly in place. This requires the user to touch the prism and put it back to the right place whenever the head is tilted, which is not possible after hands have been disinfected. Moreover, experts that normally would wear eyeglasses had difficulties reading the display because they were not able to wear their normal glasses together with the Vuzix m100.

Finally, the experts wished that the smart glass had a function that would help them measure the size of the wound without having to use their hands. In the current process, paper rulers are used for this purpose. The experts explained that it is difficult to hold the paper rulers in place while taking a picture of the wound. In addition, the use of a ruler carries the risk of transmitting germs into the wound and is difficult to handle while stabilizing a patient.

Discussion. While the overall concept of splitting up the documentation to a tablet and a smart glass for balancing usability with hands-free capabilities was supported, several new requirements were discovered throughout the evaluation. They are summarized in Table 3.

Table 3. Refined requirements for a digital wound management application

Requirements	Description
RRQ1: Ergonomics	Smart glasses need to remain in place rigidly
RRQ2: Usable with normal eyeglasses	It should be possible to wear normal eyeglasses together with a smart glass
RRQ3: Automatic wound measurement	A software feature that measures the length and width of the wound would be very helpful
RRQ4: Alternative to voice commands	Voice commands are good for hands-free use but there should be an alternative modality in case a patient feels uncomfortable with it

5.2   Second Design Cycle – Design Validation

Building upon the insights of the first design cycle we tested new smart glass designs with improved ergonomics and looked into ways how an automatic wound measurement feature could be implemented. While previous work indicates that gesture-based interaction is not a good solution for surgeons [32], we wanted to test whether this also holds for the process of wound management.

Suggestion and Development. The Microsoft HoloLens is a smart glass that weighs considerably more than the Vuzix m100 but remains in a rigid position on the head and allows users to wear their normal eyeglasses. It provides built-in gesture-based interaction and voice commands that work robustly. Moreover, it has built-in depth sensing capabilities that make it possible to measure the size of a wound.

We replicated the continuous wound documentation application designed for the Vuzix m100 on the Microsoft HoloLens (see Fig. 3). Moreover, we implemented a wound measurement feature, which allows the user to measure the length and width of a wound without a paper ruler. The picture on the right side of Fig. 4 shows a nurse wearing the Microsoft HoloLens. The picture on the left shows how the wound measurement feature looks like from the user's perspective.

Fig. 4. Wound measurement feature form the user's perspective

Evaluation. We tested the application with the same expert focus group that had been consulted in the first design cycle. Additionally, we evaluated it in a workshop with five wound management experts from a different care provider. The experts liked the measurement function and the possibility to complete the entire process in the patient's room without having to use their hands. They found the ergonomics of the Microsoft HoloLens to be much better suited for their purposes. Despite weighing significantly more than the Vuzix m100, the HoloLens is more comfortable to use, because the weight is well-balanced and it remains rigidly attached to the head even when the head is tilted. Moreover, it is possible to wear normal eyeglasses together with the HoloLens which makes it easier to read the displayed information.

The experts were skeptical that the gesture-based approach would be feasible in practice for two reasons. First of all, they found it tiring to hold one arm outstretched for prolonged periods of time. Second, they preferred to have both hands available for treating the patient. While experts liked the usability of the audio based technology interaction via voice commands they repeated their concerns that some patients might not accept it. They wished for a technology interaction modality that allows them to use smart glasses while working hands-free without having to use audio-based technology interaction.

Discussion. Overall, the wound management application was well received and the requirements pertaining to ergonomics and hands-free wound documentation could be addressed with the Microsoft HoloLens. However, gesture-based technology interaction was not seen as a viable solution to complement voice commands.

5.3   Third Design Cycle – Technology Interaction

The overall structure and design of the artifact had been confirmed in the evaluations of the first two design cycles. However, technology interaction using only voice commands was not considered appropriate in every situation. Moreover, the application had so far only been evaluated in group settings. This is a weakness because participants of the evaluations might have been reluctant to voice criticism openly. Therefore we decided to focus on testing alternative technology interaction methods and to validate the overall system design in an experimental setting with individual users to assess health care worker's willingness to use the developed artifact.

Suggestion and Development. The 3D user interface literature proposes quite a few methods for technology interaction. However, many of them are not fit for the hands-free context of wound management (e.g. hand gestures and hand-held devices). Foot pedals have been used for technology interaction in operation rooms, but are not useful for wound management, because foot pedals would have to be present in every patient room [21]. We decided to test whether eye blinking is an appropriate technology interaction method. This method does not interfere with the wound manager's work and is not likely to disturb patients. Moreover, research suggests that eye blinks can be detected reliably by inwards facing cameras in smart glasses [34].

The Microsoft HoloLens does not have inward facing cameras, but future generations of smart glasses are likely to make use of them for eye calibration [34]. In order to test whether eye blinking is a promising modality for technology interaction in hands-free contexts, we decided to employ a Wizard-of-Oz approach [35]. Throughout the evaluation, a trial manager would watch the participant's eyes and clicked on a Bluetooth device whenever the participant blinked twice with both eyes.

Evaluation. We tested voice commands and eye blinking as technology interaction methods in a within-subject experiment with healthcare workers. We recruited 45 healthcare workers with wound management experience at four hospitals, three ambulant and two stationary healthcare providers. The sample comprised 33 women (73.3%) and 12 men (26.6%). The average age of the nurses was 40.48 years (standard deviation (SD) = 12.03) and they had 16.20 years of experience on average (SD = 11.63).

Overall, a total of two manipulated scenarios and one baseline scenario were presented to subjects: (1) the wound documentation process currently in use at the healthcare facility; (2) The HoloLens application using voice commands and (3) the HoloLens application using eye blinking.

The experiment was conducted in quiet rooms at the healthcare facilities. In each of the experimental treatments, participants were asked to document different wounds that we had printed on paper using the experimental documentation artifact.

Data was collected using a closed online questionnaire. It contained questions on: Demographic Data, Performance Expectancy (4 items), Effort Expectancy (4 items), Patient Influence (2 items), Behavioral Intention (3 items), nurses' satisfaction (4 items) and open comment sections after each treatment. Participants needed about 5 min on average to fill out one part of the questionnaire. Participants were asked to fill out one part of the questionnaire after each treatment. Moreover, the time needed to complete a treatment was taken for later analysis.

Results. Data associated with technology acceptance and satisfaction outcomes were analyzed with a repeated-measure ANOVA test with three within-subject factors as independent variables: The tool wound managers are using in their current process (1), voice commands (2) and eye blinking (3) using the wound management application on the HoloLens. To test differences between the treatments contrast tests, based on the Wilcoxon signed-rank test were used [36]. All significant results (p < .05) of the contrast tests are reported in the "Comparison"-column of Table 4. In addition, Table 4 also reports means, variances and completion times. Due to problems with the logging system on the HoloLens only n = 33 datasets could be used for the evaluation of the completion times. In addition, the completion times of the current process were not measured during the experiment.

Table 4. Experiment results (p-value significance level: *.05, **.01, ***.001). Completion times are reported in seconds, while all other variables are 7-point Likert scales.

Outcomes	(1) Current process		(2) Voice commands		(3) Eye blinking		Comparison
	M	SD	M	SD	M	SD	
Performance Expectancy	4.33	1.33	4.94	1.55	5.47	1.42	3 > 1***, 2 > 1*
Effort Expectancy	5.08	1.15	5.34	1.42	5.74	1.24	3 > 1**
Patient Influence	4.76	1.34	4.52	1.65	5.08	1.41	No significant effects
Behavioral Intention	4.15	1.59	4.87	1.50	5.19	1.44	3 > 1**, 2 > 1*
Satisfaction	3.89	1.58	5.09	1.42	5.63	1.27	3 > 1***, 2 > 1***, 3 > 2*
Completion times	NA	NA	124.66	90.02	85.94	32.59	3 > 2***

6 Conclusion and Outlook

This research makes several contributions. First, we present design recommendations for wound documentation systems. We find that such systems need to be usable hands-free and documentation needs to take place at the POC. Health care workers need to stabilize and interact with the patient while measuring the wound's size and taking a photo of it.

These restrictions imply that the usage of smart glasses is a good fit for the task. Smart glasses can be used hands-free and it can be used in mobile contexts. Using a Design Science Research approach we iteratively developed a smart glass and tablet application that helps wound managers to document wounds. Furthermore, we test eye blinking, voice commands and hand gestures for hands-free interaction with smart glasses. We find that voice commands and eye blinking yielded more favorable technology acceptance outcomes than the documentation systems currently in place in health care facilities. Moreover, participants were significantly faster using eye blinking compared to voice commands.

Future research could build upon the presented design recommendations to digitize further processes in the health care sector. Moreover, digital support using hands-free technology interaction with smart glasses could also be used for processes in other fields, such as machine maintenance or customer service. Future research on hands-free technology interaction is needed to develop intuitive interaction paradigms for smart glasses. Making interaction with smart glasses feel as natural as using a smartphone would open their use to a plethora of application fields.

One weakness of this research is that patients were not involved in the evaluation of the developed artifact. A promising avenue for future research is to evaluate how caregivers' use of smart glasses affects patient's trusting beliefs. Such insights could be valuable for designing new smart glasses and establishing usage guidelines.

Acknowledgments. This research and development project is/was funded by the German Federal Ministry of Education and Research (BMBF) within the Program "Innovations for Tomorrow's Production, Services, and Work" (ARinFLEX: 02K14A080) and managed by the Project Management Agency Karlsruhe (PTKA). The author is responsible for the contents of this publication. We would especially like to thank Dorothee Wittek and the numerous employees of the Johanniter for supporting our research.

References

1. Vollmer, A.-M., Prokosch, H.-U., Bürkle, T.: Identifying barriers for implementation of computer based nursing documentation. Stud. Health Technol. Inform. **201**, 94–101 (2014)
2. van Rooij, T., Marsh, S.: eHealth: past and future perspectives. Per. Med. **13**, 57–70 (2016)
3. Klinker, K., Wiesche, M., Krcmar, H.: Conceptualizing passive trust: the case of smart glasses in healthcare. In: European Conference on Information Systems (2019)
4. Schubert, I., Köster, I.: Epidemiologie und Versorgung von Patienten mit chronischen Wunden. Eine Analyse auf der Basis der Versichertenstichprobe AOK Hessen/KV Hessen. Modul (2015)

5. BVMed - Bundesverband Medizintechnologie e.V.: Informationsbroschüre Wirtschaftlich-keit und Gesundheitspolitik Einsatz von hydroaktiven Wundauflagen (2015)
6. Block, L., et al.: SuperNurse: nurses' workarounds informing the design of interactive technologies for home wound care (2017)
7. Klinker, K., Fries, V., Wiesche, M., Krcmar, H.: CatCare: designing a serious game to foster hand hygiene compliance in health care facilities. In: Twelfth International Conference on Design Science Research in Information Systems and Technology, pp. 20–28 (2017)
8. Przybilla, L., Klinker, K., Wiesche, M., Krcmar, H.: A human-centric approach to digital innovation projects in health care: learnings from applying design thinking. In: Pacific Asia Conference on Information Systems (PACIS), Yokohama (2018)
9. Klinker, K., et al.: Structure for innovations: a use case taxonomy for smart glasses in service processes. In: Multikonferenz Wirtschaftsinformatik (MKWI 2018), pp. 1599–1610 (2018)
10. Hevner, A.R.: A three cycle view of design science research. Scand. J. Inf. Syst. **19**, 4 (2007)
11. Hevner, A.R., March, S.T., Park, J., Ram, S.: Design science in information systems research. Manag. Inf. Syst. Q. **28**, 6 (2008)
12. Venkatesh, V., Morris, M.G., Davis, G.B., Davis, F.D.: User acceptance of information technology: toward a unified view. Manag. Inf. Syst. Q. **27**, 425–478 (2003)
13. Venkatesh, V., Thong, J.Y.L., Xu, X.: Consumer acceptance and use of information technology: extending the unified theory of acceptance and use of technology. Manag. Inf. Syst. Q. **36**, 157–178 (2012)
14. Wills, M., El-Gayar, O., Benett, D.: Examining healthcare professionals' acceptance of electronic medical records using UTAUT. Issues Inf. Syst. **IX**, 396–401 (2008)
15. Oliver, R.L.: A cognitive model of the antecedents and consequences of satisfaction decisions. J. Mark. Res. **17**, 460 (1980)
16. Loveman, G.: Employee satisfaction, customer loyalty, and financial performance. J. Serv. Res. **1**, 18–31 (1998)
17. Ding, S., Lin, F., Gillespie, B.M.: Surgical wound assessment and documentation of nurses: an integrative review. J. Wound Care **25**, 232–240 (2016)
18. Gillespie, B.M., Chaboyer, W., St John, W., Morley, N., Nieuwenhoven, P.: Health professionals' decision-making in wound management: a grounded theory. J. Adv. Nurs. **71**, 1238–1248 (2015)
19. Thomas, C.M., McIntosh, C.E., Edwards, J.A.: Smartphones and computer tablets: friend or foe? J. Nurs. Educ. Pract. **4**, 210–217 (2013)
20. Wüller, H., Behrens, J., Klinker, K., Wiesche, M., Krcmar, H., Remmers, H.: Smart glasses in nursing–situation change and further usages exemplified on a wound care application. Stud. Health Technol. Inform. **253**, 191–195 (2018)
21. Hatscher, B., Luz, M., Elkmann, N., Hansen, C.: GazeTap : towards hands-free interaction in the operating room. In: Proceedings of the 19th ACM International Conference on Multimodal Interaction, pp. 243–251 (2017)
22. Schwald, B., de Laval, B.: Training and assistance to maintenance in an augmented reality environment. Int. Conf. human-computer Interact. Cogn. Soc. Ergon. Asp. **11**, 1121–1125 (2003)
23. Azuma, R.: A survey of augmented reality. Presence Teleoperators Virtual Environ. **6**, 355–385 (1997)
24. Evans, G., Miller, J., Pena, M.I., MacAllister, A., Winer, E.: Evaluating the Microsoft HoloLens through an augmented reality assembly application (2017)
25. Jacob, R.J.K., Girouard, A., Hirshfield, L.M., Horn, M.S.: Reality-based interaction: a framework for post-WIMP interfaces, pp. 201–210. Portal.acm.org (2008)

26. Huck-Fries, V., Wiegand, F., Klinker, K., Wiesche, M., Krcmar, H.: Datenbrillen in der Wartung: Evaluation verschiedener Eingabemodalitäten bei Servicetechnikern. In: Informatik 2017. Lecture Notes in Informatics (LNI), Chemnitz (2017)
27. Bowman, D.A., et al.: 3D user interfaces: new directions and new perspectives. In: Computer Graphics and Applications, pp. 1–19 (2008)
28. Czuszynski, K., Ruminski, J., Kocejko, T., Wtorek, J.: Septic safe interactions with smart glasses in health care. In: 37th Annual International Conference of the IEEE Engineering in Medicine and Biology Society (EMBC), pp. 1604–1607. IEEE (2015)
29. Aldaz, G., et al.: Hands-free image capture, data tagging and transfer using Google Glass: a pilot study for improved wound care management. PLoS ONE 10, e0121179 (2015)
30. Mitrasinovic, S., et al.: Clinical and surgical applications of smart glasses. Technol. Health Care 23, 381–401 (2015)
31. Zhao, Y., Heida, T., van Wegen, E.E.H., Bloem, B.R., van Wezel, R.J.A.: E-health support in people with Parkinson's disease with smart glasses: a survey of user requirements and expectations in the Netherlands. J. Parkinsons Dis. 5, 369–378 (2015)
32. Meng, Y., Choi, H.-K., Kim, H.-C.: Exploring the user requirements for wearable healthcare systems. In: 13th IEEE International Conference on E-health Networking Applications and Services (Healthcom), pp. 74–77. IEEE (2011)
33. Sultan, N.: Reflective thoughts on the potential and challenges of wearable technology for healthcare provision and medical education. Int. J. Inf. Manage. 35, 521–526 (2015)
34. Itoh, Y., Klinker, G.: Interaction-free calibration for optical see-through head-mounted displays based on 3D Eye localization. In: 3DUI, pp. 75–82 (2014)
35. Maulsby, D., Greenberg, S., Mander, R.: Prototyping an intelligent agent through Wizard of Oz. In: ACM SIGCHI Conference on Human Factors in Computing Systems, pp. 277–284 (1993)
36. Wilcoxon, F.: Individual comparisons of grouped data by ranking methods. J. Econ. Entomol. 39, 269 (1946)

MyLung: Design and Testing
of a Mobile-Based Assistive Technology
for COPD Patients

Riad Alharbey[1]([envelope]) [iD] and Samir Chatterjee[2] [iD]

[1] University of Jeddah, Jeddah 21959, Kingdom of Saudi Arabia
`ralharbi@uj.edu.sa`
[2] Claremont Graduate University, Claremont, CA 91739, USA
`Samir.chatterjee@cgu.edu`

Abstract. Chronic Obstructive Pulmonary Disease (COPD) is one of those progressive diseases that deteriorate lung functions. When patients cannot breathe, nothing else in their lives matters. Moreover, a lack of relevant and updated information about the causes and consequences of the disease can exacerbate the problems of health literacy, information accessibility, and medical adherence. The objective of this study is to design an innovative mobile-based assistive technology through the lens of design science research (DSR). This IT artifact includes three integrative modules that have not been introduced before in the literature: education, risk reduction, and monitoring. The evaluation study uses mixed methods to thoroughly understand how the assistive mobile-based technology can influence patients' behavioral intention to change their lifestyle. The contribution of this study is the innovative IT artifact that functions as a complete solution for patients and their caregivers. We also discuss few design principles that capture knowledge about designing mobile-based technology and demonstrate the impact of the use of this mobile-based artifact by patients with COPD and their caregivers.

Keywords: Assistive technology · Patient empowerment · COPD · mHealth

1 Introduction

Chronic Obstructive Pulmonary Disease (COPD) is a prevalent disease worldwide that is responsible for the major cause of morbidity and mortality [1]. COPD is a group of obstructive lung diseases that encompasses multiple conditions and shares two common factors: airflow limitation and unusual inflammations in the lung. Patients with COPD experience symptoms, including chronic cough, sputum production dyspnea, chronic sputum, hyperinflation, and wheezing [1]. Several factors are responsible for triggering COPD symptoms. These are based on two categories: lifestyle (typically long-term smoking) and occupational or environmental factors. Patients with COPD are susceptible to the risk of frequent episodes or exacerbations. According to [2], exacerbation is defined as "sustained worsening of the patient's condition from the stable state and beyond normal day-to-day variations that is acute in onset" (p. 47).

© Springer Nature Switzerland AG 2019
B. Tulu et al. (Eds.): DESRIST 2019, LNCS 11491, pp. 172–188, 2019.
https://doi.org/10.1007/978-3-030-19504-5_12

Because COPD conditions have a long-term effect, patients frequently suffer from complications and require constant education and awareness to promote better empowerment. Education empowerment increases patients' knowledge of matters associated with their conditions. Patients with chronic diseases should receive an effective education on how to actively manage their conditions on a daily basis. Equipping patients with education empowerment mechanisms about their chronic conditions, such as understanding the consequence of risks and in receiving timely guidelines, is associated with improved self-management and self-control of disease. These mechanisms will positively help patients change their behaviors about managing their disease conditions [3]. The consequences of COPD are aggravated when patients cannot access adequate and relevant information about the disease. Access to the relevant information leads to increase awareness about the risk factors related to COPD [4]. The consequences of COPD can be better managed with information technology, in particular, mobile health (mHealth) and telemedicine. mHealth technologies can enable a variety of technical features that facilitate better education and self-management for patients with COPD [5] that, in turn, persuade patients to change their behavioral intentions toward self-care.

COPD can lead to behavioral problems [3] that increase the threat of disease progression. Those problems are related to daily lifestyle and medication taking behaviors. The behavioral problems occur as a result of lacking access to appropriate skills and knowledge that help patients better manage their conditions. Moreover, patients with COPD are always in the condition of anxiety, which causes depression and distress. When patients become panicked about the fear of becoming breathless, they cannot be easily motivated to engage in self-care behavioral activities. In order to trigger the behavioral intention, change can be established by advocating a proper practice of COPD disease-related skills such as inhalation techniques. Additionally, lifestyle behaviors can be accomplished when patients receive recommendations about outdoor pollution hazards, smoking cessation techniques and regular exercises. Relevant knowledge and skills help develop a self-efficacy that increases patients' confidence in their abilities to perform behavioral actions.

Patient education and self-management processes face three broad categories of obstacles that hinder patients with COPD conditions from receiving healthcare information they need [6]. The first category is related to barriers to performance of learning tasks. These barriers include inadequate health literacy, language, culture, and financial problems. The second set of barriers is related to accessibility to patient education programs. These include transportation problems, physical symptoms (e.g., fatigue, pain, and aging), and lack of awareness of existing patient education programs. The last category of barriers refers to the poor environment and setting where the education and self-management programs are taking place. In fact, these obstacles can be mitigated when behavioral empowerment is included in the education and self-care process. Knowledge alone is not equal to power [7]. Patients are empowered when they feel that they can and want to use the knowledge.

This study aims to develop an innovative mobile-based technology that offers complete solution for patients with COPD. The problem space and solution space are investigated through the lens of design science research [8]. The innovative design introduces three modules with complete and integrated features. The design offers education, risk reduction, and monitoring modules in one artifact we call MyLung. The effectiveness and better use of this IT artifact supports patients with COPD with self-awareness and self-management mechanisms. With self-awareness, patients can understand and learn about COPD and its relevant consequences. With self-management, patients are empowered with useful means to help them better monitor their symptoms and receive suggestions and notifications when risks are imminent. That is, the design should be able to persuade patients to change their behavioral intentions toward self-care. Research problems are investigated through the lens of design science research (DSR) [8, 9]. Design science research helps to understand patients' needs and creates an effective assistive technology to fulfill those needs. DSR researchers generate knowledge from the use of IT artifacts [10]. Therefore, the questions of this study drive the design process to create an effective IT artifact. The main question is: how could an integrated assistive mobile-based technology be designed to improve patient's understanding of COPD (knowledge about the risk factors and consequences of COPD), and to increase patient behavioral intention toward self-care? Can it be effective?

2 Background and Related Work

2.1 Information Access

Patients with chronic conditions experience emotional and physical pain in their lives. However, this pain most of the time is temporary. For patients with chronic conditions, pain can be progressive and often continuous. Patients with COPD require access to a variety of resources to help them understand the consequences of the disease [4]. Additionally, access to proper knowledge and information resources allows patients to manage a wide array of complications along with their disease. The complications may include limited physical activity, breathlessness, and anxiety, among other things. Educating patients with chronic diseases about risk and managing chronic conditions requires access to knowledge to assist them in many aspects. Healthcare organizations and medical insurance can help these patients by offering them the information they need, providing self-management tools, and establishing Web sites or Web-based technologies that enable patients to communicate with the hospital, clinical staff, and care givers [11]. Access to relevant information allows patients with COPD to receive support and encouragement that assists those patients to perform self-care tasks.

Access to healthcare information and educational resources become a challenge for patients with COPD because of the barriers that prevent easy delivery of information. These barriers result from physiological factors relevant to patients, environmental setting and cost of educational programs [6]. Physiological barriers play a major part on how a patient with COPD is able to perceive and process health information. As COPD symptoms develop, physical pain and emotional distress increase, making it difficult for the patients to process information. Patients therefore have low motivation to search for information. The physical illnesses limit mobility and capability to sit and be receptive to the learning [12].

Inadequate health literacy, culture and language are the obstacles related to patients' characteristics that lead to reduced information access. Health literacy is defined by the Department of Health and Human Services (DHHS) as "the degree to which [patients] have the capacity to obtain, process, and understand basic health information and services needed to make appropriate health decisions" (p. 1) [13]. Lack of health literacy is related to understanding the content of the health educational intervention. Some patients with chronic conditions are able to read and write in the context they are familiar with, but struggle to understand the unfamiliar vocabulary and concepts in health-related content [6].

Patients with COPD can access information and learn through booklets and leaflets. These materials are handed to patients when they visit their doctors or they receive them through postal mails from their medical insurance [14]. Unfortunately, these traditional materials can hardly address the barriers to information access. In fact, the traditional materials (i.e., booklets and leaflets) are not convenient because they are not reachable anytime and anywhere. Patients want access to current and updated medical information in the most convenient manner wherever they go [14]. Moreover, traditional patient education and self-management tools cannot change patients' behavior although they can improve the patients' knowledge of COPD.

2.2   Patient Empowerment

The philosophy behind empowerment is based on the assumption that to be healthy, patients should be able to "bring about changes" [15]. In fact, this change is not only about altering the state of patients' personal behaviors, but also changing their social situations and the environmental settings that influence their lives. As mentioned earlier, the consequences of COPD have a wide variety of negative effects. Not only do these effects deteriorate patients' health, but also, they weaken social relationships that lead to social isolation. In fact, these issues are cumbersome for patients and their caregivers, especially when these issues become daily life experiences. As a matter of fact, the empowerment education mechanism should focus on the experience of living with COPD. The empowerment education mechanism should seek to increase patients' independence and expand freedom of choice [16]. Educational and self-management mobile-based solutions should be designed to reflect upon patients' daily lives activities.

The elements of educational empowerment should be manifested as features in the mobile-based artifact. These features are based on the use of behavioral language [15]. Behavioral language can be embedded in the motivational educational content that encourages patients with COPD to take behavioral actions and make choices. In the context of this research, there will be two integrated IT mobile-based interventions. The first one is the educational application that empowers patients with the skills and knowledge they need to change their behavior. The content of the application is designed to persuade and motivate patients to take health actions using related behavioral language. The second IT mobile-based intervention is a self-management tool that allows patients to monitor their symptoms and to receive notifications about imminent risks.

2.3   Related Work

Telemonitoring and mHealth technologies are a relatively new field in COPD research [17]. Tabak et al. [18] reported a pilot study on the use of a telehealth program for patients in the stable stage of COPD. The telehealth program consisted of different features including web-based exercise and self-management of COPD exacerbations. The system helped patients measure their physical activities via an accelerometer-based activity sensor. The physical activities were presented on the web portal. As the exacerbation management, patients were asked to fill in their diary on the web portal which, in turn, fed the decision algorithm to detect the exacerbation. Even though the study provided a solution to manage patient exacerbations, the design of the system lacked simplicity. In the same vein, Hardinge et al. [19] reported findings of a six-month cohort study of COPD patients' use of a mobile-based (mHealth) app. The mHealth app adapted in the study run on an Android tablet. The application was designed by a multi-disciplinary team that included primary care physicians, respiratory nurses, a secondary care respiratory physician, a psychiatrist, and engineers. The application allows patients to self-report their symptoms. The results of both studies show no promising results on the effectiveness of the app usage. The failure to detect a significant effect on adherence to daily activities may be attributed to the process of designing solution that lack motivation and engagement mechanisms. Additionally, both designs lack employing empowerment and behavioral motivation elements.

3   Theoretical Grounding

This research seeks to develop an innovative assistive technology intervention that improves quality of life for patients with COPD. To develop effective healthcare interventions, the design should facilitate and trigger the desired behavior change directly and indirectly. Glanz and Bishop [20] suggest that healthcare interventions are more effective when they are based on social and behavior theories than those which are not. It is also suggested that the strongest healthcare intervention can be designed from multiple theories which, in turn, lead to a unique contribution. Therefore, the process of building the IT artifact should be grounded on the body of knowledge or theories related to behavioral science that includes theories about persuasion and empowerment. With those theories, the features of the IT artifact are designing to influence patient's attitudes and behaviors.

The innovative assistive technology in this research is built with the lens of the design science paradigm which will be described in the following section. Theories that are applied in the design science approach are used as references to guide the design. Since design entails "product" and "process" [21], the theories grounding the study involve both types. According to Walls et al. [21], the role of theories in the design of a product is to govern the design requirements whereas in the design of a process the role of theories is to govern the design process itself [21]. As can be seen in Fig. 1, the Health Belief Model (HBB) was selected from the medical discipline as a kernel theory to guide the design product while the Behavior Change Support System (BCSS) [24] was selected as the kernel framework to guide the design process.

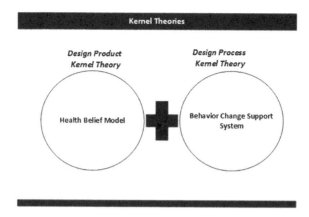

Fig. 1. Theoretical foundations

3.1 Health Belief Model (HBM)

The HBM is the most commonly adopted model in healthcare promotion, risk prevention and health education [20]. The Health Belief Model (HBM) is a psychological model that attempts to explain and predict health behaviors. This is done by focusing on the attitudes and beliefs of individuals. Those beliefs are triggered by a range of interpersonal and environmental factors that affect health behavior. The HBM states that recommended actions and decisions about health behavior are influenced by perceived benefits and barriers perceptions [22]. The perceptions in the HBM are categorized into four constructs, perceived: susceptibility, severity, benefits and barriers. Moreover, the model has been expanded to include three more constructs: cues to action, motivating factors, and self-efficacy. This study embeds perceived-severity and self-efficacy. Perceived severity refers to belief about severity and seriousness that result from disease progression. When a patient with COPD knows that exposure to outdoor pollution could put them in the hospital, in this case, the perception of the outdoor pollution become serious. In the same vein, when patients know that a stay in a hospital last a week or longer, this can influence their perception of the seriousness of the disease as leading to job loss. Self-efficacy refers to patients' belief in their ability to perform behavioral tasks. Patients will not be following guidelines or performing tasks unless they realize they can do so. In fact, the mobile-based intervention could not be successful if the patients' confidence in their ability to perform tasks, such as daily exercising, is low. To design an effective IT artifact, implementing elements related to self-efficacy is crucial for patients with COPD to comply with self-management tasks.

3.2 Behavior Change Support System (BCSS)

A behavior change support system (BCSS) is a sociotechnical information system that is designed and developed to help users form, alter or reinforce attitudes and behaviors without using resources of coercion and deception [23]. The goal of the BCSS is to develop an information system that leads to positive behavioral and psychological outcomes. To design an effective persuasive technology, designers and researchers should consider two important steps of analysis, namely, analysis of intended outcomes and changes, and analysis of its persuasive potential [23]. Oinas-Kukkonen and Harjumaa [24] describe a wide range of BCSS features. Those are classified into four categories, namely, primary task support (focus on primary activities), dialogue support (features aim at simplification to achieve the desired goal), system credibility support (features aim to design an authentic and believable system) and social support (features aim to leverage social behaviors). Primary task principles include tailoring, tunneling, and self-monitoring, among other things.

4 Research Approach

4.1 Method and the Build Phase

The design of the MyLung app follows design science research (DSR) [8, 9]. The research design comprises two design cycles, as illustrated in Fig. 2. The first cycle in this research project is referred to as a prototype design cycle; the second cycle is referred as the final design cycle. The first design cycle was the prototype design, which started by defining a specific research problem. The research problem focuses on issues related to educational empowerment and lack of information accessibility for patients with COPD. To establish problem awareness, an initial literature review was conducted guided by the research problem in order to introduce a set of meta-requirements. To determine the gap in the literature, four domains were considered from the problem space; namely, information access, patient educational empowerment, chronic disease management, and mobile health. Guided by the problem awareness step, we used the health belief model (HBM) theory and behavioral change support system (BCSS) principles to govern both the design requirements and the design process. Using knowledge gained from the literature and kernel theories, preliminary design requirements were conceptualized.

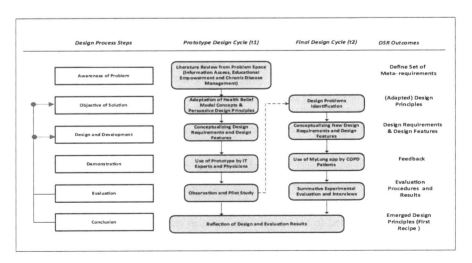

Fig. 2. Design cycles

Subsequently, the design requirements were translated into designed features for prototype implementation. A demonstration session was then conducted with a COPD physician, in which he examined the prototype and provided more design requirements that fit patients' needs. To collect more feedback on the effectiveness and usability of the mobile-based prototype, we conducted a focus group interview with IT and health-related experts. During the focus group session, each participant observed the prototype and offered feedback through an online survey.

The new requirements and feedback initialized a new design cycle for better implementation of innovative mobile assistive technology design. In the second design cycle, the adapted requirements were conceptualized to guide development of final designed features. Thus, we returned to the literature and consulted the BCSS principles to address new suggested requirements. The design features were implemented to improve quality of life for COPD patients. These features were designed to provide a solution within one IT artifact, which we called MyLung. The IT artifact includes an educational module, a risk reduction module, and a monitoring module. It works both on Android and IOS platforms. Educational module is designed to increase a patient's level of understanding about COPD by providing reliable educational videos and information. The risk reduction module is comprised of features that empower patients

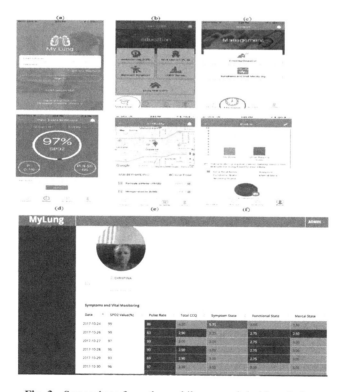

Fig. 3. Screenshots from the mobile app and dashboard view

with ways to avoid risk-related factors. The monitoring module has features that allow patients to self-monitor their symptoms and vitals including peripheral capillary oxygen saturation (SpO2). SpO2 value is entered through a medical device via a Bluetooth low-energy connection. It also provides a dashboard that helps caregivers and physicians intervene before exacerbations occur. Figure 3 shows screenshots of the mobile-based app that was used by real patients with COPD.

4.2   Evaluation

The evaluation study started after obtaining Institutional Review Board (IRB) approval from Claremont Graduate University. The evaluation study used a mixed-method approach, sequential explanatory design—that is, quantitative data were collected first from the questionnaires that were distributed through "Qualtrics"; and then qualitative data were collected in semi-structured interviews. A purposive sampling was used to select COPD patients who visited a pulmonary medicine clinic in southern California. With purposive sampling, patients were selected based on the research criteria listed below. Subsequently, patients were assigned to two groups without knowing their behavioral intentions and their knowledge about COPD. One group was the intervention group that received the MyLung app. Another group was a control group that received booklet-based information. We randomly assigned 15 patients to each group. Nine patients dropped from the study, leaving a final sample of 21 patients (11 patients in the intervention group and 10 in the control group). Patients were elderly on average; 9% were between 33 to 44 years old; 6% were between 45 to 54 years old; 33% were between 55 to 64 years old; 19% were between 65 to 74 years old; and 33% were older than 75 years old. Fifty-two percent of those patients were female. All spoke English at least somewhat fluently, and they were fairly educated, with 10% having bachelor's degrees, 38% having associate degrees or at least some college education, 42% having a high school diploma, and 10% having less than a high school diploma. We started the subject recruitment process and collected the data in October 2017. The inclusion criteria include:

1. Patient should be diagnosed with COPD.
2. Patient should have acceptable literacy level to read and deal with a smartphone.
3. Patient should have a smartphone, Android-based or iPhone.

Patients in the intervention group downloaded the MyLung app from Google Play or the Apple App Store, received iHealth Pulse Oximeter, and participated in a training session. During the training, we made sure that patients were able to connect the app with the pulse oximeter, and to understand the app features. Additionally, patients who were assigned to the intervention group were given instruction guides on how to use the MyLung features, whereas patients in the control group were given a booklet comprised of traditional educational material about COPD. Prior to the training session and to taking part in the experiment, patients in both groups had to complete a pre-survey. The survey consisted of 11 questions. The survey was administered to patients with COPD to measure their awareness level and knowledge of COPD, self-efficacy, perceived severity, and overall intention to engage in a healthy behavioral style. The post-survey was sent to the patient one month after the recruitment day. Every patient in both groups received a questionnaire as an exit survey that was similar to the pre-survey. The results from the quantitative analysis introduced several follow-up interviews using in the qualitative study. The qualitative analysis yielded rich insight into phenomena related to app experience and behavioral change for patients with COPD.

5   Results and Analysis

5.1   Quantitative Results

The paired-sample t-test revealed that the difference in the awareness level score before and after using the MyLung app in the intervention group was significant (M = 3.28 versus 4.56, t(10) = 6.062, p < 0.001). In the same vein, the independent sample t-test revealed that the difference in the awareness level score between the intervention group and the control group was significant after using the MyLung app (M = 4.56 versus 3.31, t(19) = 4.80, p < 0.001). As can be seen in Table 1, a paired-sample t-test revealed that the difference in the self-efficacy score before and after using the MyLung app in the intervention group was significant (M = 3.11 versus 5.56, t(10) = 2.96, p = 0.014). Also, the independent sample t-test (see Table 2) revealed that the difference in the self-efficacy score after using the MyLung app between intervention group and control group was significant (M = 5.56 versus 3.66, t(19) = 2.8, p < 0.012). Although there were marginal differences in the perceived severity score between groups before and after using the app, statistical methods showed that the difference between mean scores was not significant. As shown in Table 1, a paired-sample t-test revealed that the difference in the perceived severity score before and after using the MyLung app in the intervention group was not significant (M = 3.03 versus 3.28, t(10) = 0.540, p = 0.601). In the same vein, the independent sample t-test (see Table 2) revealed that the difference in perceived severity score after using the MyLung app between intervention group and control group was not significant (M = 3.28 versus 2.96, t(19) = 0.864, p = 0.389). As can be seen in Table 1, a paired-sample t-test revealed that the difference in the behavioral intention score before and after using MyLung app in the intervention group was significant (M = 2.91 versus 4.55, t(10) = 3.212, p = 0.009). However, the independent samples t-test (see Table 2) showed that the difference in behavioral intention score after using the MyLung app between intervention group and control group was not significant (M = 4.55 versus 3.60, t(19) = 2.05, p = 0.054). This result might be related to small numbers of subjects. Additionally, Table 2 reveals that there is no significant difference in all measurements before and after receiving the booklet-based training (the control). This result concludes that booklets has no impact on patients' awareness and behavioral determinants.

Table 1. Pre-post comparisons within groups

Measure	Control (n = 10)			Intervention (n = 11)		
	Mean Before	Mean After	Mean of difference	Pre-Mean	Post-Mean	Mean of difference
Awareness level	3.33	3.31	.02 (p = .95 ns)	3.28	4.56	1.28 (***p = .001)
Self-efficacy	4.00	3.66	0.34 (p = .380 ns)	3.11	5.56	2.45 (**p = .014)
Perceived-severity	2.52	2.95	0.43 (p = .131 ns)	3.03	3.28	0.25 (p = .601 ns)
Behavioral intention	3.10	3.60	0.50 (p = .343 ns)	2.91	4.55	1.64 (**p = .009)

Note: ns = not significant

Table 2. Comparison between groups on post survey measurements

Measure	Mean for intervention group	Mean for control group	Mean difference	Levene's Test		t	Sig. (2-tailed)
				F	Sig.		
Awareness level	4.56	3.31	1.25	3.77	.067	4.79	p < .001
Self-efficacy	5.56	3.66	1.90	1.62	.218	2.78	p = .012
Perceived severity	3.28	2.95	0.33	1.23	.281	0.86	p = .398 ns
Behavioral intention	4.55	3.60	0.95	4.32	.051	2.05	p = .054 ns

Note: ns = not significant;
N = 11 for the intervention group & N = 10 for the control group

5.2 Qualitative Results

Patients for the qualitative study were obtained from the same sample as the quantitative sample. The method used to determine the number of interviews was theoretical saturation. The first interviewee was a smoker (P13). I selected this patient because I found that she used the smoking cessation tool in MyLung for only a few days. The analyzed data of this interview suggested conducting more interviews with other patients. The collected interview data were compared to previous data collected. The threshold to stop selecting more patients was based on knowing what had been learned from previously analyzed data. In total, four semi-structured interviews were conducted with four patients and their caregivers. We conducted a qualitative thematic analysis to extract key themes from the qualitative data. Thematic analysis is defined by Bryman [25] as a process of identifying meaningful patterns from the qualitative data. Each pattern relates to a theme that is built using the process of coding interview transcripts [25, 26]. Thematic analysis is used in information systems research for different purposes. IS researchers adapt thematic analysis to understand an interesting phenomenon that is connected to information systems [27]. Additionally, thematic analysis is used in the design science paradigm to evaluate the effectiveness of the IT artifact [28, 29].

The process of the analysis started by coding the interview transcripts using a computer-assisted qualitative data analysis system, NVivo. In this study, the coding started by capturing information related to a patient's empowerment and user experience. Then, we related and categorized codes that emerged into sub-themes to obtain a comprehensive view of the information. Finally, we related sub-themes to each other and, then we defined a theme for each sub-theme category. This process ended by identifying four themes: patient empowerment, quality of life and user experience.

Patient Empowerment. Patient empowerment refers to the process of seeking knowledge about patients' health, and motivating them to take responsibility for their own health [30]. Patient empowerment can be established by increasing patients' attention to their COPD symptoms. P14 noted that his attention to COPD symptoms increased after using the MyLung app. He noted:

It [the app] helped me to pay a little more attention to the symptoms. I am the type that will just ignore them.

Not only does the MyLung app increase patients' attention to their COPD symptoms, but also it influences caregivers' attention in order to avoid imminent COPD episodes. Likewise, the caregiver of P14 explained her attention this way:

Yeah, it was kind of giving me a warning to kind of pay attention. I had two days of that, and that was the first two days I put him on his antibiotic, and then it stopped giving the warnings after he started to feel a little bit better.

Because of the decline in their daily activity, patients with COPD are socially isolated. The MyLung app encourages caregivers to be more proactive, and to provide support to their loved ones. The results show that when caregivers interact with the MyLung dashboard, they feel closer to their patients. This fact was noted by a caregiver of P3:

I've dealt with a lot of health issues with both ... both my husband and my dad ... and honestly, this is the scariest one, and so it was nice to go back ... When he started not feeling good, I'm looking through everything you had on there.

Patients can be empowered by their COPD physicians through education, counseling, and patient-centered care [31]. Moreover, the COPD physician can empower patients with an early health decision before a COPD exacerbation occurs. This decision can be delivered through a dashboard that presents patients' symptoms and vitals to the COPD physician. Patients with COPD feel empowered when a COPD physician receives their information daily. P6 described her reaction to this relationship:

[I]f my doctor was receiving that information, that kind of made me feel a little better. You know, like if he was to see something that wasn't normal, or if something was too high or too low.

Health-Related Quality of Life. By using the MyLung app, health-related quality of life can be improved for patients with COPD. Health-related quality of life is an outcome that can be determined by patient's behavior regarding self-management activities. According to [32], behavioral change is considered a major factor for improving health outcomes in patients with COPD.

P6 explained how her behavior changed in order to avoid outdoor air pollution. She noted:

> *I try to stay inside. Well, I'm not outside a whole lot anyway, but yeah, if it's in red I just try to stay inside more than I normally would.*

Another patient with COPD, P3, changed her health life style after using the MyLung app. She modified her dietary habits and performed more breathing exercises. She commented about these adjustments:

> *Things you didn't know before, you learn, and you can apply them..., eating healthier, number one. [And], trying to exercise more.*

Health-related quality of life can also be determined by the outcome of the patient symptoms. A patient noticed an improvement in her breathing capacity, which was enabled by avoiding risk factors and engaging in breathing exercises provided by the MyLung app. P6 explained how her breathing capacity developed for the positive:

> *It [the app] helps me with my breathing ...*

Likewise, P13 noticed that her COPD symptoms decreased after taking the medication. The notification messages sent to her indicated that her symptom state was higher than normal. She commented on this data:

> *The only thing that has changed is the cough. That decreased a lot once I got the medication. That's why I changed to that one.*

User Experience. User experience occurs when a patient interacts with the app. User experience is defined as the consequence of user expectation of system services within which the interaction occurs, including pleasure and enjoyment [33, 34]. An intuitive design helps patients to access educational information with the least effort, and complete entering their COPD symptoms quickly. To this end, we ensured that user experience involved tapping through as few screens as possible. P14 commented on his experience while he was interacting with the education module:

> *[T]he education part was the least complicated because everything was just right there.*

Although P14 faced some issues connecting the pulse oximeter device to the app, his overall experience with the app's usability was positive:

> *I think overall, it was easy to use. The only issue [I] ever had was sometimes connecting the device on the finger to the thing. It took a while. Sometimes going in and out, to connect. But other than that, it was very easy to use.*

The intuitive design made patients satisfied with the app content, practicality, and educational module that comprised of texts and videos. P3 explained how she was satisfied with the app content:

> *...it's good educational-wise for people with COPD, so you learn things that you didn't know before. I just thought it was a good ... I think it's a good app.*

Likewise, P6 noted her over all experience:

They're very helpful and I was very satisfied.

Educational information is delivered to the COPD patient in many ways, to ensure he or she has reusable content. The app content includes texts, images, and videos; that is, the app content has been organized in whatever way the patient wants or needs to consume it. P3 explained how she benefited from educational tips by applying them to managing her conditions.

> *[In]the educational parts, you can go back and watch the educational part and it'll give you tips as to how to manage your breathing, what to do, you know, for COPD exacerbation if you're not knowledgeable, and use those tips and kind of monitor, and use the tips, and they're helpful like that.*

Moreover, patient experience with the application's usability can be evaluated by having effective notification messages that warn patients before a COPD exacerbation occurs. These messages can guide patients and their caregivers to take action. P3 explained her experience upon receiving the notification messages.

> *...it [the notification message] helps me monitor my oxygen, and it just seems to be very helpful.*

Likewise, P14 commented on his reaction to push notifications:

Well, I definitely like the warning because at least I know to keep a closer eye...

Although most of the COPD patients were satisfied with the app, two patients encountered some challenges using its pulse oximeter device. These challenges related to both Bluetooth connectivity and reading precision. Occasionally, P14 faced some issues connecting the pulse oximeter device to the app. He commented:

> *The only issue [I] ever had was sometimes connecting the device on the finger to the thing. It took a while. Sometimes going in and out, to connect.*

Female patients who were wearing nail polish might have received inaccurate readings from the pulse device. That is, nail polish can be problematic for obtaining a reliable reading—particularly for COPD patients who are wearing black, green, or blue nail polish [35]. Over the course of time, using MyLung, P3 noticed that her SpO2 values were not true when she was wearing nail polish. She thought the pulse oximeter device didn't work properly. She described her experience:

> *Well sometimes it doesn't work if you have fingernail polish on... Not annoying, you just have to maneuver your finger.*

6 Discussion and Conclusion

The objective of this study is to design and build an innovative assistive mobile-based technology for patients with COPD. Through the lens of a design science research paradigm, this study provides a complete solution to increase awareness levels and to promote self-care management for patients with COPD. With this solution, patients are empowered with knowledge and skills that help them to understand the consequences of the disease, and hence increase their intentions to engage in health behavioral tasks. The solution is delivered as one IT artifact that includes three integrative modules: education module, risk reduction module, and monitoring module. The novelty of this design stems from the fact that it is the first mobile app that introduces features to help patients discover and make use of COPD solutions based on the behavioral change support system (BCSS) framework and health belief model (HBM) constructs. The results of the evaluation study provide evidence that confirm that the MyLung app is effective in increasing patient understanding of COPD and its consequences. This finding draws an inference that the design of this app leads to significant increases in awareness level. When awareness level increases, patients can learn more about COPD, and modify behavior such as smoking cessation. Additionally, the study confirms that the MyLung app influences patients' confidence to perform health-behavioral tasks. This finding draws another inference confirming that the design increases self-efficacy for patients with COPD. The design encourages management skills, in many ways considering different levels of health literacy. IT artifact itself can have a great impact on society and hospital resources. When patients are empowered with relevant skills to self-manage their conditions at home, the hospital readmission rate will be lowered.

We discuss few design principles as another type of contribution in this research study. Design principles are defined as prescriptive statements that aim to capture knowledge about designing and building other artifacts related to the same class [36, 37]. Those statements are represented as generalized statements that are externalized from the tacit knowledge of designing the assistive mobile-based artifact, MyLung. We propose the design principles following Chatterjee's first recipe [38]. The design principles are:

> **DP1**: *The design of assistive technology should empower patients with respiratory diseases with integrated means that increase their awareness level, and bolster their intentions.*
> **DP2**: *The design should reduce effort that patients spend with regard to use, entering their health-related readings data and updating existing ones.*
> **DP3**: *The design should aid patients to communicate their symptoms with other supporting elements (such as caregivers) in their health environment.*

These design principles allow us to make some recommendations to IS practitioners who design and develop assistive technology systems for patients with respiratory diseases. These systems should recognize an empowerment mechanism that helps patients to change their behaviors. Systems can include updated and timely educational content that increases patient knowledge about any respiratory disease. Patients can receive information about imminent risks as notification messages. Information system practitioners can integrate the awareness tool and educational tool with a self-management mechanism to promote better self-care activities.

Our findings and the design principles have implications for assistive technology design, research on chronic condition management, and health care. The results of this study can inform health informatics design research.

References

1. Celli, B.R., et al.: Standards for the diagnosis and treatment of patients with COPD: a summary of the ATS/ERS position paper. Eur. Respir. J. **23**(6), 932–946 (2004)
2. Burge, S., Wedzicha, J.A.: COPD exacerbations: definitions and classifications. Eur. Respir. J. **21**(41), 46s–53s (2003)
3. Worth, H., Dhein, Y.: Does patient education modify behaviour in the management of COPD? Patient Educ. Couns. **52**(3), 267–270 (2004)
4. Brown, F.M.: Inside every chronic patient is an acute patient wondering what happened. J. Clin. Psychol. **58**(11), 1443–1449 (2002)
5. Kumar, S., et al.: Mobile health technology evaluation the mHealth evidence workshop. Am. J. Prev. Med. **45**(2), 228–236 (2013)
6. Beagley, L.: Educating patients: understanding barriers, learning styles, and teaching techniques. J. Perianesth. Nurs. **26**(5), 331–337 (2011)
7. Joseph-Williams, N., Elwyn, G., Edwards, A.: Knowledge is not power for patients: a systematic review and thematic synthesis of patient-reported barriers and facilitators to shared decision making. Patient Educ. Couns. **94**(3), 291–309 (2014)
8. Hevner, A., Chatterjee, S.: Design Science Research in Information Systems. Springer, New York (2010). https://doi.org/10.1007/978-1-4419-5653-8
9. Hevner, A.R., March, S.T., Park, J., Ram, S.: Design science in information systems research. MIS Q. **28**(1), 75–105 (2004)
10. Simon, H.A.: The Sciences of the Artificial. MIT Press, Cambridge (1996)
11. Newman, S., Steed, L., Mulligan, K.: Self-management interventions for chronic illness. Lancet **9444**, 1467–1468 (2004)
12. Mueller, J., Davies, A., Harper, S., Jay, C., Todd, C.: Widening access to online health education for lung cancer: a feasibility study, pp. 1–4 (2016)
13. DHSS: National action plan to improve health literacy (2010). https://health.gov/communication/HLActionPlan/pdf/Health_Lit_Action_Plan_Summary.pdf. Accessed 08 Nov 2016
14. Carré, P.C., et al.: The effect of an information leaflet upon knowledge and awareness of COPD in potential sufferers. Respiration **76**(1), 53–60 (2008)
15. Feste, C., Anderson, R.M.: Empowerment: from philosophy to practice. Patient Educ. Couns. **26**(1), 139–144 (1995)
16. Roberts, K.J.: Patient empowerment in the United States: a critical commentary. Health Expect. **2**(2), 82–92 (1999)
17. Cruz, J., Brooks, D., Marques, A.: Home telemonitoring in COPD: a systematic review of methodologies and patients' adherence. Int. J. Med. Inf. **83**(4), 249–263 (2014)
18. Tabak, M., VanderValk, P., Hermens, H., Vollenbroek-Hutten, M., Brusse-Keizer, M.: A telehealth program for self-management of COPD exacerbations and promotion of an active lifestyle: a pilot randomized controlled trial. Int. J. Chron. Obstruct. Pulmon. Dis. **9**, 935 (2014)
19. Hardinge, M., et al.: Using a mobile health application to support self-management in chronic obstructive pulmonary disease: a six-month cohort study. BMC Med. Inform. Decis. Mak. **15**(1), 46 (2015)
20. Glanz, K., Bishop, D.B.: The role of behavioral science theory in development and implementation of public health interventions. Annu. Rev. Public Health **31**, 399–418 (2010)
21. Walls, J.G., Widmeyer, G.R., El Sawy, O.A.: Building an information system design theory for vigilant EIS. Inf. Syst. Res. **3**, 36–59 (1992)

22. Rosenstock, I.M., Strecher, V.J., Becker, M.H.: Social learning theory and the health belief model. Health Educ. Behav. **15**, 175–183 (1988)
23. Oinas-Kukkonen, H.: A foundation for the study of behavior change support systems. Pers. Ubiquitous Comput. **17**(6), 1223–1235 (2013)
24. Oinas-Kukkonen, H., Harjumaa, M.: Persuasive systems design: key issues, process model, and system features. Commun. Assoc. Inf. Syst. **24**(1), 28 (2009)
25. Bryman, A.: Social Research Methods. OUP, Oxford (2012)
26. Fereday, J., Muir-Cochrane, E.: Demonstrating rigor using thematic analysis: a hybrid approach of inductive and deductive coding and theme development. Int. J. Qual. Methods **5**(1), 80–92 (2006)
27. Gregory, P., Barroca, L., Taylor, K., Salah, D., Sharp, H.: Agile challenges in practice: a thematic analysis. In: Lassenius, C., Dingsøyr, T., Paasivaara, M. (eds.) XP 2015. LNBIP, vol. 212, pp. 64–80. Springer, Cham (2015). https://doi.org/10.1007/978-3-319-18612-2_6
28. Neuhauser, L., Kreps, G.L., Morrison, K., Athanasoulis, M., Kirienko, N., Van Brunt, D.: Using design science and artificial intelligence to improve health communication: ChronologyMD case example. Patient Educ. Couns. **92**, 211–217 (2013)
29. Schnall, R., Rojas, M., Travers, J., Brown, W., Bakken, S.: Use of design science for informing the development of a mobile app for persons living with HIV. In: AMIA Annual Symposium Proceedings 2014, pp. 1037–1045 (2014)
30. Kuijpers, W., Groen, W.G., Aaronson, N.K., van Harten, W.H.: A systematic review of web-based interventions for patient empowerment and physical activity in chronic diseases: relevance for cancer survivors. J Med Internet Res. **15**(2), e37 (2013)
31. McAllister, M., Dunn, G., Payne, K., Davies, L., Todd, C.: Patient empowerment: the need to consider it as a measurable patient-reported outcome for chronic conditions (2012)
32. Bourbeau, J.: Integrated disease management for adults with chronic obstructive pulmonary disease (2014)
33. Dirin, A., Nieminen, M.: mLUX: usability and user experience development framework for M-learning. iJIM **9**(3), 37–51 (2015)
34. Choi, W., Tulu, B.: Effective use of user interface and user experience in an mHealth application. In: Proceedings of the 50th Hawaii International Conference on System Sciences (2017)
35. Hakemi, A., Bender, J.A.: Understanding pulse oximetry, advantages, and limitations. Home Health Care Manag. Pract. **17**(5), 416–418 (2005)
36. Sein, M., Henfridsson, O., Purao, S., Rossi, M., Lindgren, R.: Action design research. MIS Q. **35**(1), 37–56 (2011)
37. Chandra Kruse, L., Seidel, S., Purao, S.: Making *Use* of design principles. In: Parsons, J., Tuunanen, T., Venable, J., Donnellan, B., Helfert, M., Kenneally, J. (eds.) DESRIST 2016. LNCS, vol. 9661, pp. 37–51. Springer, Cham (2016). https://doi.org/10.1007/978-3-319-39294-3_3
38. Chatterjee, S.: Writing my next design science research master-piece: but how do i make a theoretical contribution to DSR? In: ECIS2015 Completed Research Papers: Proceedings of 23rd ECIS Conference, Munster, Germany, vol. 28 (2015)

Design Science Research Applications in Data Science

Citizen Data Scientist: A Design Science Research Method for the Conduct of Data Science Projects

Matthew T. Mullarkey[1,2(✉)], Alan R. Hevner[1], T. Grandon Gill[1],
and Kaushik Dutta[1]

[1] Information Systems and Decision Science Department, Muma College of
Business, University of South Florida, Tampa, USA
{mmullarkey,ahevner,grandon,duttak}@usf.edu
[2] Extraordinary Research Scientist, Workwell: Research Unit for Economic &
Management Sciences, North-West University, Potchefstroom, South Africa

Abstract. Firms are seeking to gain greater understanding of and insights into more and more massive quantities of data collected and stored in disparate public and private databases. To effectively and efficiently deploy project resources to the data science search activity and to consequently build and evaluate innovative artifacts, firms are finding that a Design Science Research (DSR) approach can extend into the Data Science (DS) project domain through an iterative, evaluative project management method for the diagnosing, design, implementation, and evolution of data science artifacts. Importantly, DSR also provides a guided, emergent search paradigm that can be integral to finding hidden insights in massive data where the problem and solution domains are both frequently poorly understood at the outset of the DS inquiry. This article examines a case for using the elaborated action design research (eADR) method to inform the DS project management (PM) approach in situ with a Fortune 100 Global Manufacturer. The innovative DS PM approach resulted in multiple innovative DS solution artifacts built and evaluated by a dozen DS PM teams at the firm over the first two years of the DS PM deployment.

Keywords: Design science · Data science · Action design research ·
Digital innovation · Informal learning · Data science project management

1 Introduction

There comes a point in any (successful) technology where the use of the technology moves from the laboratory of the expert and into the domain of the practitioner. A point where those with domain expertise can easily learn and deploy the technology to solve problems where those problems exist – not in the lab but in practice. A point where the knowledgeable domain expert assumes ownership of the innovative technology and applies it to create significant, positive change heretofore too difficult, too costly, too time consuming, and too persistent to be resolved in practice. Often the ease of use of this innovative technology occurs due to a fortunate intersection of improved

© Springer Nature Switzerland AG 2019
B. Tulu et al. (Eds.): DESRIST 2019, LNCS 11491, pp. 191–205, 2019.
https://doi.org/10.1007/978-3-030-19504-5_13

processing speed, tool maturation and simplified user interfaces and the development of a robust method for the deployment of the technology in projects in practice.

In this paper we provide evidence of an approach organizations can take to deploy data science technologies through a design science research (DSR) informed data science project management method that empowers domain experts to design and conduct data science projects that generate innovative artifacts and competitive intelligence. We show that data science (DS) has evolved to the point where its collective technologies can be relatively easily understood and deployed by any domain expert due to the addition of simplified interfaces for many of the DS tools, increases in enterprise and desktop computing capacity, and improved enterprise access to structured and unstructured, public and private data. We pair the tools and data to a DSR inspired method that focuses on the creation and evaluation of interesting (often innovative) artifacts at every level of abstraction.

Our work in situ with a Fortune 100 global advanced manufacturing company extended the boundary of DSR theory and practice through the development of a DS method that we combined with the state-of-the-art GUI interfaces in data science tools and the computing capability and massive data present in the organization to allow this organization to truly develop their own "citizen" data scientists.

1.1 Motivation

As big data and data analytic tools have become increasingly available, a critical shortage of trained data scientists has become evident (Markow et al. 2017). In fact, data science has been singled out as the area where the greatest STEM shortage exists (Lohr 2017). The problem is particularly acute in areas such as manufacturing, where the availability of data is huge but which also lacks the potential large pay days associated with financial services, which currently employs the lion's share of trained data scientists.

A significant aspect of the challenge of acquiring suitable data scientists derives from the fact that effective analysis of big data involves two distinct areas of expertise: expertise in the tools and techniques of data science and expertise in the domain into which it is to be applied. Facing this shortage, GCM[1] - a multi-national manufacturing company located in Florida, USA, producing products such as circuit boards, with annual revenue of over $18 billion—decided to flip the problem. Rather than hiring data scientists and then teaching them the business, the company would take existing employees who already know their respective domains and train them in relevant data science techniques.

To do so, they enlisted the aid of DSR-trained researchers who developed a project-focused curriculum that taught domain experts a guided, emergent search project management method employing the latest DS tools and data analysis techniques using an adult learning-by-doing approach, referred to as the Citizen Data Scientist Program (CDS Program). After running the CDS Program for two years, DSR researchers gained significant insights into the manner in which DSR theory and practice can

---

[1] GCM is a fictitious company name used for anonymity.

extend to the conduct of DS discovery of hidden insights through the iterative design, build, and evaluation of DS artifacts from diagnosing, to design, finally to implementation of innovative DS instantiations.

1.2 Theoretical Foundation: DSR and Informal Learning

Theories and processes from DSR drive both the underlying philosophy and project management method of the CDS Program and also inform how the designed artifacts are created and evaluated over the course of any given CDS Program project. We consider the following research questions:

(1) How can DSR (and specifically the elaborated Action Design Research (eADR) method) inform the conduct of DS projects?
(2) How can the conduct of DSR informed DS projects be implemented by domain experts in an organization?
(3) How will the design and evaluation of artifacts produced in successive iterative eADR cycles aid organizational understanding of DS project contributions?

2 DSR and the DS Project

The scientific foundations of design underpin our understanding and representation of both the problem and solution domains toward achieving intellectual merit and real-world impacts in our research. Design science research (DSR) seeks to enhance technology and science knowledge bases via the creation of innovative artifacts that solve problems and improve the environment in which they are instantiated. The results of DSR include both the newly designed artifacts and a fuller understanding of why the artifacts provide an enhancement (or, disruption) to the relevant application contexts (Hevner et al. 2004). Among the key research challenges of the design scientist is how best to ground and to perform the search for a design solution that satisfies the problem constraints (i.e. requirements) while achieving the desired goals (i.e. aspirations and opportunities). The research process supports the simultaneous building of a problem space and a solution space; both of which grow in completeness and evolve through the multiple iterations. The guided, emergent gain in understanding and representational accuracy of both spaces is the long-term objective of a DSR project.

We identify two dominant approaches for these search processes. In rational, stable environments, kernel theories of behavior can be called upon to predict how a particular design artifact will perform in the application environment. A search for a good solution is based on these reliable predictions of system behaviors. This is the school of Predictive Planning and its success is dependent on the ability to predict the future evolution of the application environment. A second approach moves away from predicting the future and emphasizes adaptive learning based on applying incremental, controlled search methods. The use of non-predictive controls supports a more agile, but riskier, search process that may or may not lead to satisfactory ends. This approach is the school of Adaptive Learning and its success is less sure but can be used with problem environments that are fast changing and have greater amounts of uncertainty.

Good data science, like all science, needs to be built on a methodical approach. To effectively and efficiently deploy project resources to the data science search activity and consequently build and evaluate innovative artifacts, the CDS Program is grounded in the DSR approach combined with action research in the industrial environment. The novel approach provides an iterative, evaluative method for the diagnosing, design, implementation, and evolution of data science artifact creation.

The second element of the philosophy driving the CDS Program is the need to move data science from the lab to practice—a major concern for GCM. The table that follows highlights ways in which this knowledge transfer is currently occurring. The key was to develop training programs that capitalized on this transference (Table 1).

Table 1. Knowledge transfer in DS from lab to practice.

DS in the lab	DS in practice
Tool innovation & deployment	Method innovation & deployment
Specialized software and hardware	Ubiquitous software on existing hardware
Deep disciplinary knowledge	Deep domain knowledge
Technical user interface	"Civilian" user friendly interface
Close to the research gap question	Close the domain specific question
Demonstrate clever investigations	Create a competitive advantage
Demonstrated by gain in knowledge	Demonstrated return on investment
Limited, experimental use	Widespread, predictable use

We take an evidence-based approach to suggest that data science has evolved to the point where its collective technologies can be relatively easily understood and deployed by any domain expert due to the normal evolution of a methodological approach, simplified interfaces, computing capacity, and access to data needed to move from the domain of the expert scientist to the praxis scientist. Our analysis of the prior examples of the process of moving from research and science to problem solving and practice identified a logical evolution of technologies from the lab to the workbench. (i.e. six sigma Motorola & GE) When we move from the theoretical to the practical an innovative technology formed through research can be said to transition from theoretical into practical use via a wider set of engaged researchers and actual practitioners. In so doing, the technology moves from the lab and into practice addressing and solving sticky, wicked problems in real-world application domains.

2.1   Data Science: A Search Process

Given the inherent complexity and fast-paced nature of current and future application environments, data scientists will increasingly move away from the limitations of kernel theory predictions to the more adaptive solution search approaches of fast design iterations under the intellectual control of the data scientist teams.

Extensive search for applicable theories upon which to ground design and predict behaviors is unlikely to be fruitful in complex system environments. It is better for the team to begin immediately performing iterative cycles of building and refining the solution artifacts in a controlled manner. Later, upon reflection of the design results, identification and extension of relevant theories can occur (Gregor and Hevner 2013).

In fact, we find that significant data science projects are grounded in interesting questions that explore the inherent variation in the data in all of its 'glory' to gain (competitive) insights into the underlying behaviors and then capitalize on that intelligence to design systems that automatically display that information in ways that inform improved decision making. We demonstrate the rigorous use of adaptive science of design principles in the project's use of DSR's action design research (ADR) methods (Sein et al. 2011; Mullarkey and Hevner 2015, 2019) as described below.

In the CDS program, the GCM citizen data scientist teams perform iterative elaborated ADR cycles. Within each cycle, the team refines the relevant data problem, creates an artifact for practice intervention, evaluates its impacts, reflects on the emerging design principles, and generates the learning outcomes from that cycle.

2.2   Citizen Data Scientist Program

Gartner (Moore 2017) defines "a citizen data scientist as a person who creates or generates models that use advanced diagnostic analytics or predictive and prescriptive capabilities, but whose primary job function is outside the field of statistics and analytics." With the help of citizen data scientists, an organization can transform itself into a data-driven organization. In a data-driven organization, every decision is a hypothesis at the beginning of the decision-making process. Such a hypothesis is tested based on historical data and then applied to decisions in organizations. In organizations where data science activities are entrusted to only a few individuals who are experts on data science techniques but have little or no knowledge of the business, it becomes challenging to promote data-driven decisions at every level and every division of the organization.

Contrary to this, in an organization full of citizen data scientists, every decision-maker is equipped with data-driven decision-making tools and thus can follow this hypothesis-testing route in their daily activities. Employees from diverse backgrounds and organizational silos (accounting, finance, operations, manufacturing, information technology, human resource) are trained on data analytic tools and can lead data-driven decision-making processes.

Our research team identified the following skill-sets required to drive a data-driven decision-making project:

- Project Management methodology with a focus on DSR processes to manage DS projects
- Knowledge of data management to store and manage data
- Knowledge of inferential statistics and hypothesis testing to analyze the data
- Knowledge of data visualization techniques to explain the data
- Knowledge of predictive and prescriptive modeling and automation techniques
- Knowledge of decision support and business process improvement integration

Based on the above, the schedule of the 16-week citizen data science (CDS) program follows in Fig. 1.

Citizen Data Science Program Outline

Prior to Week One: Group formation and Project Plan definition.

Citizen Data Science Week One: Diagnosis
Day 1: Project Management Session 1: (8 hr)
Day 2: Statistics and Visualization Session 1: (8 hr)
Day 3: Data Management Session 1: (8 hr)
Day 4: Visualization using PowerBI session: (8 hr)
Day 5: End of week Presentations: (4hr)

Prior to Week Six: Upload Project Status Report and Video

Citizen Data Science Week Six: Design
Day 1: Visualization & Modeling Session 2: (8 hr)
Day 2: Statistics Session 2: (8 hr)
Day 3: Data Management Session 2: (8 hr)
Day 4: Predictive Modeling Session 2: (8 hr)
Day 5: End of week Presentations: (4hr)

Prior to Week Eleven: Upload Project Status Report and Video

Citizen Data Science Week Eleven: Implementation
Day 1: Modeling Session 3: (8 hr)
Day 2: Modeling Session 4: (8 hr)
Day 3: Modeling Session 5: (8 hr)
Day 4: Deploying DS Projects on Amazon AWS & MS Azure (8 hr)
Day 5: End of week Presentations: (4hr)

Prior to Week Sixteen: Upload Project Status Report and Video

Citizen Data Science Week Sixteen: Final Project Presentations

Fig. 1. 16-week training schedule for CDS Program.

2.3   CDS Session Design

Kolb (1985) states, "Most learning for adults occurs in natural settings as opposed to formal situations and institutions." Following this, we applied a project driven adult learning approach for this program. Students start the program with a project goal and, by the end of the program, the student attempts to complete the project with the help of tools and techniques learned in the program to achieve the initial goal. Each module in the program includes multiple hands-on exercises that allow students to try the tools and techniques taught in the class immediately.

We incorporated a learner-centered teaching approach in the program, which is known to be effective for adult learning. The five characteristics of the learner-centered teaching (Weimer 2012) approach applied in the CDS Program are:

1. Learner-centered teaching engages students in the hard, messy work of learning. The CDS Program for GCM engages students in the classroom with discussions and hands-on exercises.

2. Learner-centered teaching includes explicit skill instruction. The CDS Program teaches explicit tools and skills related to data science that can be immediately used by the students.
3. Learner-centered teaching encourages students to reflect on what they are learning and how they are learning it. The program includes post-class reflection write-ups at the end of each class. The post-class reflection helps the adult students in the program to summarize what they have learned and how (Wood 1996).
4. Learner-centered teaching motivates students by giving them some control over learning processes. The students in the CDS Program have the independence of specifying the tool to use in the teaching and the data to use as an example in the class. Each student selects a project based on their respective domains and applies the classroom learning to the project.
5. Learner-centered teaching encourages collaboration. The program has been developed around completing prototypes to address data science projects that meet the organization's business needs. In the first two cohorts, the projects were selected independently by students and were carried out individually. However, based on the feedback received and the progress recorded in the first two cohorts of the program, from the third cohort onwards the projects are team-based projects encouraging collaborative learning in the program.

2.4   CDS Program Requisites and Deliverables

The evolution of the CDS program led to a set of pre-requisites and deliverables that were specific to each resident teaching week of the training and which corresponded directly to the stage of eADR activity covered and expected of the CDS participants as indicated in Fig. 2.

End-of-week Deliverables Outline

Week	Pre-requisites	Deliverables
Week 1 - Diagnosis	• Vetted use case ideas with Manager, Process Owner, Data Science CoE team • Optional reading	• Approved use case charter • Team identified • High level project plan • Data collection plan • Thought process map
Week 6 - Design	• Aggregated datasets	• Visualization • Modeling plan • Insights • Updated project plan • Initial Hypothesis • Clean Data
Week 11 - Implementation	• Robust datasets • Thorough understanding of data • Storytelling of observed patterns, hypothesis using visualizations	• Models • Analysis and Model selection • A/B Testing • Summary • Implementation plan

Fig. 2. Pre-requisites and deliverables by eADR stage for CDS Program evolution.

2.5   CDS ADR Project Approach

A critical value to the application of the eADR method to the conduct of DS projects was our discovery of the value of artifact creation and evaluation. As indicated in Fig. 2, the very first CDS training module was education and practice in the conduct of a DS project using the eADR paradigm.

We selected the eADR paradigm to the conduct of DS projects specifically because we needed:

- Design Science Research: A project management approach that emphasized a **guided, emergent, search** through massive data that often only had a tough, sticky, wicked question at its inception.
- Action Research: We knew that the adult learning approach and the expertise needed for many applications of the DS tools would result in the in-situ **intervention** of researchers, experts, and practitioners in the conduct of a DS investigation.
- Artifact Abstraction: We understood that interesting artifacts could be **created** and needed to be **evaluated** at multiple points in a DS project. We had experience where a DS investigation had created and evaluated a very interesting data structure, cleaned and integrated multiple data stores into an innovative data warehouse, developed an innovative approach to visualizing data, designed and evaluated a predictive model, and, in other cases, automated a fully instantiated decision support system to operationally present competitive intelligence from massive data to inform decision-making. We hypothesized that all of these artifacts had the ability to be potentially innovative and of utility to the CDS and the organization when they were created in a DS project.
- CDS Iterative Method: DS demands a methodical and, yet, often agile approach for the investigation of multiple possible alternatives. It appeared improbable to researcher and practitioner alike that a DS project could move from data scrubbing to an instantiated decision support system based upon one or more interesting insights into data alone. Moreover, we recognized that even the generation of an algorithm or a predictive model would likely occur through **iterative** activities of the DS team.

Consequently, we began our approach to performing data science projects with a presentation and discussion of a project management method that would exploit each opportunity above for a guided, emergent search across multiple data sources (structured, unstructured, proprietary, public) where we intervened with practitioners to iteratively create and evaluate artifacts for the identification of competitive intelligence that could inform decision-making in the organization.

Our principle was that the Citizen Data Scientist "co-produces" solutions through collaboration with the client system. The DS project combines *theoretical* knowledge and experience with *practical* knowledge and experience. The *outcome* 'emerges'; where the outcome is some artifact that represents 'a better future.' The citizen data scientist is engaged as a participant observer, is empathetic, seeks to gain understanding of the 'values of the relevant actors,' avoids conjecture, and employs pattern recognition to conceptualize and test various solutions, in situ. We offered an eADR approach as outlined in Mullarkey and Hevner (2019) and described in Fig. 3 involving the stages of Diagnosis, Design, Implementation, and Evolution. We anticipated that the iterative action research approach outlined in Fig. 4 would occur multiple times in each Stage as the CDS team builds and evaluates multiple artifacts that would commonly be created in that stage.

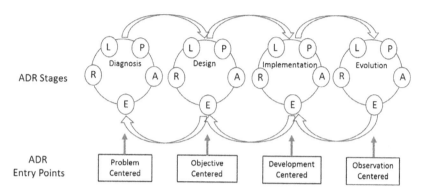

Fig. 3. CDS Project Stages. Illustrates the nature of the interventions at each stage in the eADR method. Adapted from (Mullarkey and Hevner 2019). Note: In the eADR Cycle: P = Problem Formulation/Planning, A = Artifact Creation, E = Evaluation, R = Reflection, and L = Learning.

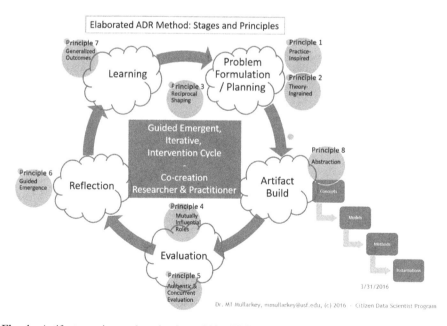

Fig. 4. Artifact creation and evaluation within CDS project stages. Adapted from (Mullarkey and Hevner 2019).

Our practical project management approach was led by citizen data scientist teams using a guided emergent search to ask interesting questions worth exploring through a scientific process. The process itself values artifacts where artifacts can be data sets, RFP guidelines, requirements definitions, linkage tables, cluster analyses, map BOMs, data visualizations, decision trees, recommender algorithms, scripts, queries, dashboards, reports, sentiment analyses, correlation matrices, new decision support systems, new recommender systems, new information systems, and completely new technologies.

2.6   CDS ADR Project Assessment

We collected data on the approach the CDS teams used to build and evaluate innovative IT artifacts as they moved through their CDS projects from Diagnosing to Design to Implementation and ultimately Evolution of their DS artifacts. This evaluation focused on the nature of the contributions and types of impacts to the organization being made by the CDS teams as they pursue their projects.

Important measures of organizational impact from this informal learning approach are the quantity and qualities of the artifacts built and evaluated by the teams in each DS iterative cycle and by DS project stage. Across the first two CDS cohorts, the artifacts built and evaluated included: Data sets, RFP guidelines, requirements definitions, linkage table, cluster analyses, map BOMs, visualizations of data, decision trees, recommender algorithms, scripts, queries, dashboards, reports, sentiment analyses, and correlation matrices. Over time, we identified a macro-nature to the artifacts that tended to be built and evaluated by eADR stage as indicated in Fig. 5.

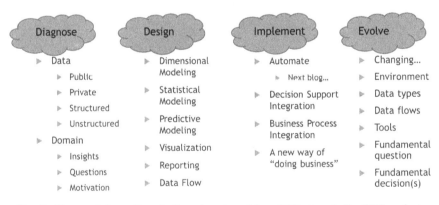

Fig. 5. Nature of the artifacts built and evaluated by eADR stage in the CDS project.

These artifacts are all important to the eventual design and implementation of new decision support systems, new recommender systems, new information systems, business process integration, and new technologies. In every case, one or more artifacts are built and evaluated for every iteration within each DS Stage. Table 2 presents a summary of artifact creation results across the first two cohorts. The columns relate to the activity stages of the eADR process described below. Upon completion of the second cohort's training – roughly 48 weeks after the start of the very first cohort – a total of 107 artifacts had been built and evaluated by the thirteen trained CDS teams.

Table 2. CDS cohort 1 & 2 artifact evaluation by CDS project stage.

Use case	Diagnose	Design	Build	Implement	Backwards	Artifacts created & evaluated
1	2	1	0	0	1	4
2	5	2	1	0	0	10
3	2	2	2	0	2	8
4	6	4	2	0	0	10
5	8	1	0	0	1	8
6	2	2	1	0	0	4
7	6	2	0	0	1	7
8	5	1	1	0	4	8
9	22	10	3	0	10	25
10	2	1	0	0	1	4
11	2	2	0	0	1	8
12	3	1	1	0	0	6
13	20	3	1	0	7	5
Total	83	32	12	0	28	107
Mean	6.38	2.46	.92	0	2.15	8.23

Table 2 suggests that of the first 107 artifacts created and evaluated by the first 13 trained CDS teams, that 83 were developed in the Diagnosis stage of the DS project, 32 in the Design stage, and 12 in the Build stage. In one sense, there is no surprise that early in the project lifecycle more of the artifacts occur during the Diagnosing stage of the DS project. Our observation was that these artifacts were also diagnosing in nature in that the CDS project teams were gaining understanding of all of the data available and creating very exploratory artifacts for structured, unstructured, public, and private data. The artifacts thus created included tables, data dictionaries, cleaned data pools, initial data visualization, and various data transformations (e.g. voice to text).

Teams also distinguished between building components of a completely implemented system (Build) and the full system implementation (Implement). Both of these are actually Implementation stage in the eADR proposed by Mullarkey and Hevner (2019). Thus, it was a revelation but not surprising upon reflection that no complete system had been fully implemented within the first year of the projects' initiation – particularly since these were the first DS projects ever conducted by these CDS teams.

A key reflection of the organization leadership was that the artifacts built and evaluated at each stage and prior to any full implementation of a system were in and of themselves extremely valuable. Each was valued as proof of project progress and many were valued as returns on the investment made by the leadership in the projects and the training. In several cases, for example, the DS project teams created new, innovative aggregations of public and private data (e.g. supply chain vendor data pools) that were useful to the business in and of themselves for decision-making or analysis and in many cases useful to other project teams in progress.

Additionally, we observed that nine of the teams reported moving 'backward' from Design to Diagnosing or from Build to Design thereby confirming the eADR principle of iterative, cyclical movement between stages in the method.

3 Discussion and Contributions

Our work with a Fortune 100 client in situ led to the recognition that the dearth of degree-qualified data scientists in the market and at their company challenged their ability and capacity for the conduct of scientific investigation of interesting large data. Moreover, where those expert data scientists do exist and can be hired by the firm, they are frequently skilled in only one area of DS – they might be skilled in data structures and manipulation, statistics and analytics, predictive and confirmatory modeling, or data visualization. And, such DS experts hired into a firm frequently lack fundamental understanding of the domain in ways that make them effective at asking the best DS questions and interpreting the DS results.

Together, the firm's practitioners and our researchers identified the key reasons to develop citizen data scientists – domain experts within the organization – for the conduct of DS projects. Those reasons included:

- the fact that access to interesting data was much more available across the enterprise,
- the DS tools (SQL, NoSQL, statistical, programming, visualization, etc.) possess user interfaces that make them accessible to less technical 'citizens' within the firm,
- processing power is much more available on the desktop and across the enterprise needed to analyze and manipulate massive data, and,
- the domain experts possessed the requisite technical capacity to learn the tools and were much better positioned to identify key areas of inquiry that would most likely lead to interesting insights.
- The domain experts had the ability to interpret the results in ways that might lead to competitive advantages and support better decision making in the firm.

We recognized that these citizen data scientists (CDS) needed a scientific, methodical approach to conducting any DS project. A bunch of tools was not enough. And, we recognized that the DS project was a search activity where the key insights and solutions that improved decision making within the firm would emerge as the investigation of the interesting data occurred over time with multiple tools. Thus, we chose to introduce the action research ingrained approach to DSR – the elaborated ADR (Mullarkey and Hevner 2019) – and found evidence that CDSs were able to move from Diagnosing to Design to Implementation of automated systems for the repeatable synthesis of interesting data into insights that aided daily, weekly, and monthly decision-making.

We found that the eADR grounded DS project management approach actually provided a significant benefit in its focus on the abstraction and evaluation of artifacts during fast, flexible iterative investigation efforts. Each evaluated artifact afforded the

CDS project teams an innovative look at the question(s) being asked and offered a measure of success that could be shared with the firm's leadership as the DS project progressed. These artifacts also offered a shared learning opportunity when made available to a DS community so that other DS inquiries could take advantage of prior work across the DS network.

We found that the guided emergent search approach was uniquely appropriate for DS projects where even the problem might be poorly understood but where interesting questions could be formed to investigate massive data. Moreover, the approach benefited from an informal, adult learning integration of the training in project management and DS tools with the immediate application to a real DS project opportunity. The firm valued the immediate impact across a variety of business units and the evidence of artifacts created.

We also made the observation that our approach to the CDS program fundamentally "flipped" the typical relationship of training to organizational change. Normally we see methodologies implemented though some sort of administrative/organizational mechanism (e.g., organizational structure, adoption of a development model, retaining an external consultant to guide the process). In this case, however, the implementation of eADR is an integral element of an educational program. Effectively, education becomes the mechanism through which organizational change is achieved, as opposed to being an activity that normally precedes the change. Similar observations can be made about the impact of the Toyota Production System (focused on the lean transformation of the organization to eliminate waste) and GE's Six Sigma Program (focused on the transformation of the organization through the elimination of variation).

The CDS Program as designed and implemented has the potential to transform the organization that "revels in the variation" to find hidden insights and patterns that generate competitive intelligence that improves the decision making. This has important potential implications, since it suggests developing an educational program that simultaneously implements an organizational process change may be a way to address changes needed to address wicked problems.

Moreover, in a Lean-Six Sigma inculcated organization, the CDS approach (method, tools, mindset) offers the enterprise a complementary means of organizational transformation that builds upon (and does not destroy) the existing expertise, project management, and outcomes of these precedent continuous improvement methods.

Our key contributions include:

- The concept of a citizen data scientist as a full-fledged participant in and driver of effective data science projects in organizations.
- The design and definition of a data science project management method that emphasizes iterative artifact creation and evaluation to explore multiple possible alternatives in the search for hidden insights in massive data.
- Evidence that a DS PM approach can convert hidden insights into instantiated decision support systems that can exploit the new found intelligence into competitive advantage.
- The content of a design science research curriculum intended to train domain experts to be citizen data scientists.

- The potential value of eADR as a methodical, guided emergent search approach in addressing data science investigations.
- The degree to which the CDS curriculum itself is an example of eADR and serves as a mechanism for implementing eADR approaches across the organization.
- The value that the building and evaluation of artifacts, abstracted iteratively as the data science project evolves, provides to the CDS project team and to the organization.
- And, the opportunity eADR might possess when applied to iteratively learning from and evolving (1) the CDS course content, (2) the actual CDS project definition and management, (3) the repository of abstracted, tested and evaluated DS artifacts, and, (4) the enterprise-wide calculation and recognition of the value of the competitive intelligence generated by the CDS projects when performed by trained CDS individuals and teams over time.

The partner company believes that the CDS program not only solves the problem of filling the gaps in trained personnel, but, in fact, leads to a transformation in mindset and practice around the investigation of massive data that revels in the variation and finds hidden insights that offer competitive advantages.

4   Limitations and Future Research Directions

This research is benefited by the longitudinal nature of the study across our cohorts as we demonstrated a scientific method grounded in eADR approaches to the conduct of CDS projects in a manufacturing organization. A limitation is that the method has not been studied in other organizations to evaluate and/or adapt the application of the eADR method, the tools, and/or the abstraction of artifacts.

An opportunity that this presents is the dissemination of the CDS program to additional companies. Across multiple companies we should be able to evaluate the informal STEM learning approach taken, the eADR project management effectiveness, the iterative evaluation and cataloguing of artifacts, the building and effectiveness of resultant instantiated decision support systems, and the transformation of the enterprise governance of data science investigations.

A second opportunity for future research direction is a Research in Service to Practice project that will evaluate the ongoing informal education collaboration between researchers and the existing firm. The proposed research would involve a multiple method protocol centered on developing case studies relating to the past and current participants in the CDS program, paying particular attention to the data science artifacts developed during and subsequent to the program. Using eADR methods, the findings will both broaden our understanding of informal learning collaborations between academic institutions and industry and guide ongoing iterative improvements to the CDS program itself.

A third opportunity is to use a practice-based approach to defining exemplars of the types of artifacts built and evaluated at each stage in the DS project and the specific tools and techniques used to build and evaluate those artifacts at each stage. Some patterns have already begun to emerge that suggest that the nature of the artifacts change as the projects mature over time toward fully instantiated systems. And, there appears to be a corollary evolution in the specific tools and techniques used at each stage in the DS project that can be further investigated.

The CDS program is in its nascence and should evolve to optimize the CDS method, tools, techniques, and mindset (guided, emergent, artifact search) that can aid organizational transformation around the investigation of massive data to generate competitive advantage.

References

Gregor, S., Hevner, A.: Positioning and presenting design science research for maximum impact. Manage. Inf. Syst. Q. **37**(2), 337–355 (2013)

Hevner, A., March, S., Park, J., Ram, S.: Design science research in information systems. Manage. Inf. Syst. Q. **28**(1), 75–105 (2004)

Kolb, D.A.: Learning Style Inventory, Revised Edition. McBer & Company, Boston, MA (1985)

Lohr, S.: Where STEM jobs are (and where they aren't). New York Times, 1 November 2017. https://www.nytimes.com/2017/11/01/education/edlife/stem-jobs-industry-careers.html

Markow, W., Braganza, S., Taska, B., Miller, S., Hughes, D.: The Quant Crunch: how demand for data science skills is disrupting the job market. Burning Glass Technologies, pp. 1–25 (2017)

Moore S.: Gartner says more than 40 percent of data science tasks will be automated by 2020, 16 January 2017. https://www.gartner.com/newsroom/id/3570917

Mullarkey, M.T., Hevner, A.R.: Entering action design research. In: Donnellan, B., Helfert, M., Kenneally, J., VanderMeer, D., Rothenberger, M., Winter, R. (eds.) DESRIST 2015. LNCS, vol. 9073, pp. 121–134. Springer, Cham (2015). https://doi.org/10.1007/978-3-319-18714-3_8

Mullarkey, M.T., Hevner, A.R.: An elaborated action design research process model. Eur. J. Inf. Syst. **28**(1), 6–20 (2019)

Sein, M., Henfridsson, O., Purao, S., Rossi, M., Lindgren, R.: Action design research. MIS Q. **35**(1), 37–56 (2011)

Weimer, M.: Learner-centered teaching and transformative learning. In: Taylor, E.W. (ed.) The Handbook of Transformative Learning: Theory, Research, and Practice, pp. 439–454. Jossey Bass, San Francisco (2012)

Wood, D.M.: Learning from experience through reflection. Org. Dyn. **24**(3), 3648 (1996)

A Novel Hybrid Optical Character Recognition Approach for Digitizing Text in Forms

Roland Graef[1]($\boxtimes$) and Mazen M. N. Morsy[2]

[1] University of Ulm, Ulm, Germany
roland.graef@uni-ulm.de
[2] German University in Cairo, Cairo, Egypt
mazen.morsy@student.guc.edu.eg

Abstract. The huge amount of document-based processes has considerably contributed to the need of automated systems which are able to appropriately digitize text in documents concerning forms. For example, the text in scanned administrative forms is not accessible without an adequate conversion from pixels to editable text. Against this background, many organizations tap the potential of Optical Character Recognition (OCR) as it is capable of supporting the digitization of text in documents. However, there is still a lack of integrated OCR approaches, considering both handwritten and machine printed texts, which are both of major importance in the context of digitizing text in forms. To address this problem, we propose a new hybrid OCR approach recognizing handwritten and machine printed text based on neural networks in an integrated perspective. We demonstrate the practical applicability of our approach using publicly available forms on which the approach could be successfully applied. Finally, we evaluate our novel hybrid approach in comparison to existing state-of-the-art approaches.

Keywords: Forms · Optical Character Recognition ·
Long Short-Term Memory Networks

1 Introduction

In today's fast-paced digitized world, almost half of the work activities across all sectors of the global economy show potential for automation [1]. In practice, many organizations already aim to tap the potential of automated processes by intensifying invests in digitization [2]. For instance, the major German insurer Allianz Deutschland AG offers customers the opportunity to submit required documents (e.g. invoices, cost estimates or prescriptions) as images taken via smartphone camera [3]. To guarantee the further processing in this context, the textual information contained in images of documents has to be digitized in terms of converting the pixels comprising text into editable text format. As a consequence, a huge amount of document-based processes is still present [4–7]. In particular forms (e.g. administrative or data entry forms) account for a major part of document-based processes [5]. According to the data book of the internal revenue service, for instance, almost 90 million paper filled tax returns and supplemental forms have been submitted by US citizens in the year 2017 [8].

© Springer Nature Switzerland AG 2019
B. Tulu et al. (Eds.): DESRIST 2019, LNCS 11491, pp. 206–220, 2019.
https://doi.org/10.1007/978-3-030-19504-5_14

Consequently, organizations face the challenge to manage the huge amount of forms in an efficient way and foster the development of a fast and easy digitization process for further automated processing in order to reduce costs and employees' time expenditure.

To address these challenges and tap the potential of document-based process automation, OCR systems can be used to digitize textual information in scanned documents in an automated manner [4, 5, 9–11]. Indeed, OCR systems have already been successfully applied in many real-world scenarios, creating value by automating processes [6, 9, 12]. In fact, OCR technology can lead up to a 60% reduction of document-processing costs [12]. The basic idea of OCR systems is to stepwise localize and recognize text in scanned documents [5, 10, 13]. The concept behind is that pixels comprising text are converted into editable text format, referred to as text recognition. Considering documents in terms of filled-in forms, they vary in layout structure, style and size, impeding the localization and therefore also the recognition of the textual information. Nevertheless, a typical form can be characterized by two parts containing the desired textual information [5]. On the one hand, a pre-printed machine text properly guiding the user. On the other hand, textual information filled in by the user in terms of handwritten or machine printed text. As a consequence, both handwritten and machine printed text have to be taken into account to successfully automate the digitization process of forms. Actually, literature already provides well-founded approaches for the recognition of handwritten [14–22] and machine printed text [10, 11, 13, 23–26], respectively. However, there is still a lack of integrated approaches considering both types of textual information. Therefore, in the context of digitizing the huge amount of forms, merging these two research streams is essential. Nevertheless, trying to cope with this problem constitutes a challenging task as both types of textual information have to be localized, distinguished and recognized in each form. To address this research gap, we propose a new hybrid OCR approach recognizing handwritten and machine printed text in an integrated perspective to adequately digitize forms.

Since our integrated approach is able to distinguish and to recognize both types of textual information contained in the same form, it offers the following two major benefits for an advanced process automation: First, a manual pre-selection of documents is obsolete, since each document containing either handwritten or machine printed text can be appropriately digitized. Second, as the machine printed and the handwritten text are often adjacent and related text regions, determining the type of text allows to associate the handwritten with the machine printed text independent from the underlying layout structure. The latter is in particular substantial if organizations receive forms with unknown layout from third-party organizations. For instance, various insurers (e.g. Allianz Deutschland AG) receive forms from financial service providers (e.g. MLP [27]) who rely on their own template comprising pre-printed machine text as well as handwritten text filled-in by a customer during a consultation appointment. Hence, the layout and content of these forms are not known beforehand to the insurers.

Following the six activities of Peffers et al. [28] to conduct design science research, the remainder of this paper is structured as follows: After discussing the relevance of the problem and its motivation within this introduction (activity 1: *"problem identification and motivation"*), we provide an overview of the related work and identify the research gap (activity 2: *"define the objectives for a solution"*). In Sect. 3, we propose our artifact as a hybrid optical character recognition approach localizing, classifying and recognizing handwritten as well as machine printed text (activity 3: "*design and development*"). In Sect. 4, we demonstrate the practical applicability of the artifact (activity 4: "*demonstration*") by using publicly available forms [29] and evaluate our novel hybrid approach (activity 5: "*evaluation*") in comparison to existing OCR approaches. Finally, we conclude with a summary of the findings, a discussion of limitations and an outlook on future research (activity 6: "*communication*").

2   Related Work and Research Gap

Research already provides approaches for digitizing text in different kinds of documents as for example invoices, postal envelopes, or bank checks [6, 7, 30, 31]. In this context, the digitization process with respect to OCR can be described as the stepwise process of localizing, classifying and recognizing text in documents [5, 10, 13]. Thereby, multiple research streams focus independently from each other on the different steps of OCR. While some researchers concentrate on localizing text in documents through document layout analysis algorithms [32–34], others investigate the distinction between handwritten and machine printed text [35–38]. Further research streams have developed approaches for either handwritten [14–22, 39, 40] or machine printed text recognition [10, 11, 13, 23–26]. In the context of digitizing text in forms, all of the mentioned research streams in OCR seem promising, since forms exist in different layout types and often comprise handwritten as well as machine printed text.

A recent survey [32] examines a wide range of algorithms published over the last ten years for analyzing the layout of documents. By doing so, Eskenazi et al. [32] group these algorithms into three clusters. While the first two clusters contain algorithms constrained to specific layout types, only the third cluster contains approaches for localizing text independent of the layout structure. On a related note, Smith [34] for example developed an established Hybrid Page Layout Analysis algorithm as part of the Tesseract OCR approach. Therefore, Smith [34] relies on Connected Component Analysis by joining all pixels belonging to text within a document to the corresponding text regions. Further, not coherent text regions are separated from each other by determining the boundaries of text regions based on their alignment. Since the mentioned approach [34] is designed to focus on localizing text in documents independent of the layout structure, it seems also appropriate to adequately localize text in forms.

In order to digitize text in forms, especially the distinction between handwritten and machine printed text is decisive so that a feasible recognition can be ensured for each type of textual information [38]. In this respect, research has considered the classification of these two types of text by extracting different features from text regions [35–38]. Literature can particularly be classified by the type of features extracted [36]. While some authors extract statistical features (e.g., standard deviation of pixel intensities) [35], others base their features on geometric properties (e.g., pixel intensity) [38]. Further authors extract gradient based features describing, for example, the change in pixel intensity [37]. By doing so, the shape of a text is characterized which seems a promising means to distinguish between handwritten and machine printed text in forms.

In the context of either handwritten or machine printed text recognition, research already provides approaches for converting each type of text independently into an editable format. Both research areas yield so-called segmentation based [10, 11, 13, 18, 19, 23–25, 41, 42] and segmentation free approaches [14–17, 20–22, 39, 40]. Segmentation refers to the process of dividing each word into the characters it contains [10]. On this account, literature has developed segmentation based approaches to segment the frequently overlapping characters in handwritten text [18, 19]. Salvi et al. [18], for instance, propose a respective graph model to determine an adequate segmentation. To do so, a wide set of possible segmentation boundaries is used as vertices, which are connected by weighted edges, representing the probability of recognizing a character between two possible segmentation boundaries. By this means, the average longest path reveals the best segmentation deduced from the graph model.

Other research focuses on the recognition of handwritten text detached from segmentation [14–17, 20–22, 39, 40]. Along these lines, Hidden Markov Models have been one of the first segmentation free approaches [20, 39]. Hidden Markov Models describe a generative model, which can be trained either on whole words or on individual characters. However, literature suggests using discriminative models, since these approaches generally seem to outperform Hidden Markov Models [15]. Hence, current state-of-the-art approaches apply discriminative models in terms of Long Short-Term Memory Networks (LSTMs) for text recognition [14–17, 21, 40, 43]. LSTMs constitute a specific type of Recurrent Neural Networks as neurons in the network are modeled by a recurrent connection. Thus, LSTMs are capable of learning long term dependencies as, for instance, contextual information contained in text [15]. As LSTMs require an input of sequential data, for example the sequential vertical pixel slices of an image, they are able to segment and recognize text at the same time. Graves et al. [15], for example, use bidirectional LSTMs which process an image from left to right as well as from right to left to fully grasp the contextual dependencies contained in the text.

While handwritten text varies, for instance in height, width, strokes or writing style of each individual letter, machine printed text is more consistent regarding its letters as well as the space amongst them [16]. Against this background, research started to address the recognition of machine printed text by segmentation based approaches [10, 11, 13, 26]. In this regard, Xue [13] for instance uses the classical Template Matching approach to associate each segmented character to the most similar character within a set of selected templates. However, in the case of an insufficient segmentation (e.g. due to distorted text) segmentation based approaches can no longer ensure an appropriate recognition. Thus, further research provides segmentation free approaches for recognizing machine printed text [23–26, 41, 42]. In this line of research, approaches resemble those proposed for handwritten text recognition. While some authors apply Hidden Markov Models [23, 24], others rely on machine learning algorithms to recognize and segment machine printed text simultaneously [25, 41, 42]. Indeed, the idea of using LSTMs has been transferred for recognizing machine printed text, showing a strong potential to outperform existing approaches [25].

To sum up, LSTMs seem a very promising means to cope with the current challenges in the context of digitizing text in forms. Since forms in our context comprise handwritten as well as machine printed text in different positions, the approaches from page layout analysis, text classification, as well as handwritten and machine printed text recognition are all relevant to adequately localize, classify and recognize the textual information within a form. However, first promising approaches dealing with both types of text are not able to appropriately address our problem [6, 7, 30, 31]. These approaches have been developed for recognizing text in bank checks [6, 7, 31] or in postal letters [30]. Although these approaches use heuristics to distinguish handwritten and machine printed text, they only classify the whole document image either as machine printed or handwritten. Thus, images containing both types of information at the same time are not focused. In this regard, these authors do not take an integrated perspective from a methodical point of view.

Indeed, to the best of our knowledge, so far none of the recent studies in text recognition has considered localizing and distinguishing between textual information in conjunction with recognizing both handwritten and machine printed text at the same time while taking an integrated perspective by not only classifying forms as hand-written or machine printed but rather combining research streams by regarding both, handwritten and machine printed text in the same form. To address this gap, we aim at developing, a novel hybrid text recognition approach, combining LSTMs with each other in a well-founded way.

3   Hybrid Approach for Digitizing Text in Forms

3.1   Basic Idea and Overview of the Hybrid Approach

The aim of this paper is to develop an OCR approach for localizing, distinguishing and recognizing handwritten as well as machine printed text, representing the underlying types of information contained in forms. Independent of a form's underlying structure, our approach is well-suited to convert text in forms into editable text format in an automated manner. Our approach comprises three steps (cf. Fig. 1).

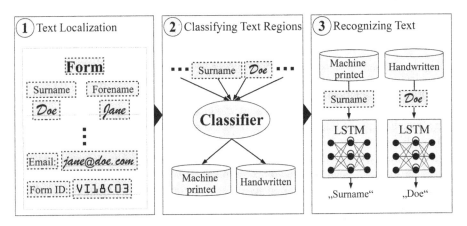

Fig. 1. Hybrid OCR approach for digitizing text in forms.

In the first step, a form is analyzed regarding the position of both handwritten as well as machine printed text to be recognized. To do so, we rely on approaches from page layout analysis using Connected Component Analysis for localizing text regions in forms [34, 44, 45]. The second step builds upon the localized text regions from the first step. In order to ensure a sound recognition we distinguish both, handwritten and machine printed text comprised by the text regions, referring to established approaches in the same context [37] as well as in the related area of visual object recognition [46]. The third step of our approach uses the classified text regions to recognize the contained text in a form. Inspired by state-of-the-art approaches using LSTMs for text recognition [15–17, 21, 40, 43] we state two LSTMs, one for the recognition of each type of text. As LSTMs are able to incorporate contextual information of the data while learning, they reveal convincing results for text recognition. Finally, we end up recognizing both types of textual information contained in forms, converting each text region from image format into editable text. In the following subsections, we present our hybrid three-step approach for digitizing text in forms in detail.

3.2   First Step: Text Localization

The aim of the first step is to localize text regions in a form, regardless of whether it comprises handwritten or machine printed text. To approach this issue, we deduce the horizontal and vertical positions of rectangular regions, enclosing the desired textual information. On a related note, literature in page layout analysis has often applied Connected Component Analysis with convincing results [33, 34, 44, 45]. Consequently, we use this method on forms in order to localize the desired text regions. In accordance with most studies, we assume a bi-level representation for each pixel (binarized forms) as given, which is not restrictive due to the existence of approaches for binarizing forms.

Connected Component Analysis can be considered as the process of joining all neighboring pixels in a form with the same pixel value, resulting in so-called connected components. More precisely, a connected component is defined as the maximum set of pixels such that each pixel owns the same pixel value while at the same time a path of neighboring pixels is contained between any two pixels of the set. Here, a neighboring pixel constitutes an adjacent pixel in vertical or horizontal direction while it is optional to further regard diagonally adjacent pixels as neighbors. As a result, Connected Component Analysis yields to the localization of all connected components within a form as, for instance, a single letter. Further on, to obtain the whole text regions of interest within a form, the connected components for each text region in the form have to be joined separately. In order to do so, we first propose a heuristic filtering using features of connected components (e.g. width, height or pixel density [34, 44]) to remove those connected components only comprising noise. Besides, a kind of separator is required to keep a set of connected components belonging to the same text region apart from the others. Accordingly, we define a separator as an area of any height and width containing only pixels belonging to the background of the form and bounding a text region in horizontal direction. By this means, all connected components can be joined from separator to separator, resulting in the overall text regions comprising the handwritten and machine printed text in forms. An appropriate way to determine the separators in forms is applying text line detection algorithms as for example, tab-stop detection or white space analysis [34, 44]. To sum up, the first step localizes each handwritten as well as machine printed text region contained in a form based on Connected Component Analysis and separators. The localized text regions enable a sound classification in the following step.

3.3 Second Step: Classifying Text Regions

The aim of the second step is to classify the text regions so that an appropriate recognition for each type of text is enabled. Hence, we declare a classifier (e.g. an Artificial Neural Network [47]) which is trained on a set of handwritten and machine printed text regions. In keeping with this, features have to be extracted from the text regions for training as well as for prediction. According to literature, the extraction of so-called Histograms of Oriented Gradients (HOG) descriptors states a well-established feature extraction approach for describing the shape of objects within images [13, 46]. Moreover, the HOG descriptors provide convincing results for distinguishing between handwritten and machine printed text while being independent of the text's language [37]. At the same time, these feature descriptors can be extracted from any type of image format (e.g. binarized forms). For these reasons, HOG descriptors provide an appropriate means to distinguish between handwritten and machine printed text in forms.

More precisely, HOG descriptors characterize the shape of a text region within a form by the changes in local pixel intensities. In order to establish the HOG descriptors, first, the local horizontal and vertical gradients for each pixel of a text region are determined, which describe the changes in pixel intensities in the respective direction. Both gradients are derived based on sliding windows, measuring for each pixel the differences between its neighboring pixel values.

As a result, the horizontal and vertical gradients for each pixel constitute the overall local gradients. Accordingly, the length and orientation of the overall gradients describe the intensity and the direction of changes in local pixel intensities. Further on, to obtain the HOG descriptors, histograms over the magnitude of the overall local gradients regarding the orientation are derived. Therefore, a text region is divided into a fixed number of rectangular subregions, while for each subregion the corresponding histogram of overall gradients is determined. To do so, a fixed number of equally sized bins is set to accumulate those gradients' magnitudes which have the same orientations within the specific range of a bin. Finally and to gain the HOG descriptors, the discrete values of all subregion histograms are concatenated to form the corresponding feature vector of a text region used to train and predict with the classifier. To sum up, the second step uses a classifier based on HOG descriptors in order to distinguish between handwritten and machine printed text regions localized by the first step. Thus, a reasonable recognition of both types of text is enabled in the next step.

3.4 Third Step: Recognizing Text

The aim of the third step is to recognize the text enclosed by the text regions. In handwriting recognition literature, current state-of-the-art approaches rely on LSTMs leading to convincing results [15–17, 21, 40, 43]. Moreover, literature has also proven LSTMs to be successful in recognizing machine printed text [25]. Obviously, machine printed text is even more consistent regarding its form and size than handwritten text, allowing LSTMs to recognize machine printed text in a sound way. Accordingly, we state two LSTMs, one for the recognition of handwritten and the other for the recognition of machine printed text.

LSTMs represent a specific kind of Recurrent Neural Networks, since neurons in the network own a recurrent connection. By this means, LSTMs learn and interpret the contextual information in text regions, as each character in natural language is dependent on the characters surrounding it. In order to do so, LSTMs keep an internal memory in their neurons, combining knowledge of previously processed pixels with the pixels they are currently processing. Since the internal memory is capable of storing information over an extraordinary long period, even long-term dependencies among pixels or characters are established [15]. Along these lines, the architecture of LSTMs is in particular characterized by three so-called gates, namely the input gate, the output gate and the forget gate. These gates constitute the cornerstones of LSTMs as they control the storage and access of information to the internal memory within each recurrently connected neuron. In detail, the input gate operates over the incoming information by deciding to which extent this information is taken into account for enriching the internal memory. Thereby, incoming information constitutes both, the pixels currently processed and the information gained from previously processed pixels delivered by the recurrent connection. Similarly, the output gate controls the extent to which information is passed over to the next iteration of the neuron via the recurrent connection. Besides, also the final output of the neuron is influenced by the output gate. Further, the forget gate can be considered as a reset function, managing the amount of information kept in the internal memory of the neuron. In terms of text recognition, this architecture allows LSTMs to encode text by stepwise processing a text region, for example by its successive vertical slices of pixels. However, a stepwise processing of a text region in one specific direction only allows LSTMs to consider previously processed pixels for recognizing characters. Hence, recognition is enhanced if also the information following the current input is regarded. For instance, the recognition of a character is improved if both the previous and the following character are known by the network. For this reason, we rely on LSTMs traversing a text region from left to right as well as from right to left at the same time, referred to as Bidirectional LSTMs.

We model the output of both, the LSTMs for handwritten and machine printed text recognition using the Connectionist Temporal Classification approach [40], which is widely applied in conjunction with Bidirectional LSTMs by state-of-the-art approaches in text recognition [15–17, 21, 25, 43]. Connectionist Temporal Classification allows LSTMs to appropriately separate text regions while simultaneously recognizing characters. As a result, LSTMs can be trained with text regions comprising a whole word instead of training character by character. In order to do so, the Connectionist Temporal Classification provides a probability distribution over all characters of the specified vocabulary in each step during the stepwise processing of a text region by LSTMs. With the aim of maximizing the joint probability over all steps, a character is selected as output in each step. Since one step relates to only a small part of a character within a text region, choosing the optimal character regarding the overall probability in each step yields an output containing the desired characters multiple times (e.g. "JJaaann-neeee"). Thus, all subsequent outputs of the same character can be joined. To further enable the recognition of words including the same character multiple times in succession (e.g. "William"), an additional blank label (denoted "_") is added to the specified vocabulary. Consequently, the blank label is chosen as an output ahead of each to be recognized character, in particular between character doublets (e.g. "_Ww_ii_ll_lll_ iiii_aaa_mmm"). Similarly, all subsequent outputs of the same character between blank labels can be merged, leading to the final output for the recognition of text enclosed by a text region.

To sum up, the third step uses two Bidirectional LSTMs, one for each type of textual information classified in the second step. To do so, the Bidirectional LSTMs process a text region stepwise from left to right and right to left at the same time. While processing a text region, recognition and segmentation of characters are conducted simultaneously by means of the Connection Temporal Classification approach, which appropriately models the output of the Bidirectional LSTMS. Finally, the three-step-approach yields in the recognition of the whole handwritten and machine printed text contained within a form. Therefore, organizations are provided with an automated approach in order to convert text within forms into editable text.

4   Demonstration and Evaluation of Our Approach

4.1   Dataset of Representative Forms

In order to demonstrate the practical applicability and evaluate the effectiveness of our approach, we used a set of 3,369 binarized images of filled-in forms provided by the publicly available NIST Special 19 Database [29]. This database offers researchers the opportunity to assess the results of OCR approaches. Each form in our dataset comprises about 215 text regions containing 128 of machine printed English text regions for guidance of the user. Moreover, each form contains about 87 handwritten English text regions in terms of a date, a zip code, a city name as well as various numbers and words filled in by 3,600 writers. Since both types of textual information are present in each form, the typical characteristics of forms (cf. Sect. 1) are met. Hence, the dataset provides an appropriate setting to apply our novel hybrid approach in order to digitize text in forms in an automated way.

4.2   Demonstration

In the following, we demonstrate the applicability of our approach. To do so, we first apply pre-processing in terms of skew correction for each form. The purpose of skew correction is to realign obliquely scanned forms, since an appropriate text localization and recognition is dependent on the alignment of a form [6, 10, 48]. As our set of forms is already provided in binarized form no further pre-processing is required.

Following the first step of our approach, we used Connected Component Analysis in order to localize text regions within the forms by employing the Tesseract library [49]. By doing so, all coherent pixels comprising handwritten and machine printed text are joined. Further, tab-stops are used as separators to keep different text regions apart from each other. Tap-stops represent the vertically aligned edges of text lines and have proven useful in separating text regions [34].

For the second step, training data is required to distinguish between handwritten and machine printed text via a classifier. In keeping with this, we collected 3,500 handwritten text regions as well as further 3,500 machine printed text regions from 500 forms and manually labeled each regarding its class of text. On this basis, we were able to extract the HOG descriptors by dividing each text region into 256 evenly sized rectangular subregions while choosing eight bins for calculating the histograms. By doing so, we are in line with recent research [37]. Further on, we decided to use an Artificial Neural Network [47] as classifier due to its great potential to grasp the general idea behind complex tasks [50]. To train the network we split the set of HOG descriptors into 90% training and 10% validation data. Thus, overfitting can be reduced by training the network until the loss on the validation data stops to decrease. To do so, we used a one-layer architecture with Softmax as activation function and optimized the learning rate resulting in a value of 0.001.

In order to perform the third step, further training data is required for an appropriate text recognition. However, existing datasets for handwritten text recognition could not meet our requirements regarding English as the underlying language and a balanced distribution of words in text regions. To enhance the performance of LSTMs a balanced training dataset of different words is necessary to ensure a consistent and correct text recognition. For these reasons, we collected 7,000 handwritten text regions from the same 500 forms used in the second step and manually labeled them with respect to the text they contain. By this means, we were able to train one-layer bidirectional LSTMs by applying Connectionist Temporal Classification (due to a limited amount of training data we treated numbers and letters separately). Again using the same proportion of training and validation data, we optimized the performance as well as the learning rate which yielded in a value of 0.0001. For recognizing machine printed text, we used a bidirectional LSTM network, pre-trained on over 400,000 machine printed text regions based on Connectionist Temporal Classification [49]. In sum, each LSTM recognizes the corresponding localized and classified handwritten or machine printed text region within a form. Hence, costs and efforts for document-based processes in organizations can be reduced by digitizing text in forms in an automated manner.

4.3   Evaluation

In order to evaluate our approach, we manually checked the results obtained by each of the steps. More precisely, we randomly selected 50 forms not included in the training or validation of any step for the purpose of evaluation. On this basis, we inspected the results for over 10,000 text regions in order to ensure a rigorous evaluation. We computed for each step well-established evaluation metrics (cf. "Step 1–3" in Table 1) while carrying errors forward if at least one part of a text region has been localized. In addition, we compared the text recognition results of our hybrid approach with competing artifacts from OCR literature (cf. "Comparison" Table 1).

Table 1. Evaluation results for each of the three steps and comparison with competing artifacts.

Step 1: Text Localization			
Merge	*Split*	*Miss*	*False Detection*
0.43%	3.96%	2.03%	0.33%

Step 2: Classifying Text Regions			
	Precision	*Recall*	*F1-Score*
Machine Printed	87.68%	87.29%	87.42%
Handwritten	80.04%	80.34%	80.04%

Step 3: Recognizing Text – Character Accuracy		
Handwritten	*Machine Printed*	*Total*
77.98%	91.28%	86.05%

Comparison: Hybrid Approach to Competing Artifacts – Overall Character Accuracy		
LSTMs – suitable for Handwritten Text	*Abbyy Finereader – suitable for Machine Printed Text*	*Hybrid Approach*
48.47%	66.33%	82.69%

To evaluate the first step, we calculated the commonly applied metrics in page layout analysis [32, 33] namely *Merge*, *False Detection*, *Miss* and *Split* (cf. "Step 1" in Table 1). Our results reveal that 0.43% of the localized regions erroneously overlap more than one text region (cf. "Merge" in Table 1) while 3.96% of actual text regions are localized as multiple text regions (cf. "Split" in Table 1). Although both of these errors impede text recognition, splits affected the recognition less, as they mainly divided text regions in horizontal direction. In contrast, merges lead to localized regions containing additional parts of words above or underneath the actual region. Hence, the low share of merges turns out beneficial in favor of a higher share of splits. Further on, 2.03% of text regions could not be localized (cf. "Miss" in Table 1). Obviously, this type of error inevitably impaired the results for text recognition. At last, only 0.33% of localized regions were mistaken as a text region (cf. "False Detection" in Table 1). In our case, false detections comprise single pixels induced by a careless scanning process. Since these single pixels mostly lead to no recognition at all, the text recognition step is scarcely affected by false detections. In comparison to the results of other authors using the same metrics, our results indicate a high quality for localizing text regions [33].

For evaluating the second step, we refer to the well-known measures *Precision*, *Recall* and *F1-Score*, which are widely used to assess the results of classification tasks (cf. "Step 2" in Table 1). By calculating these measures, false detections and misses could not be taken into account whereas merges and splits affected the results (note: merges can only be considered if they contain the same type of textual information). As the share of handwritten (machine printed) text regions accounts for 40.47% (59.53%), classifying text regions randomly would approximately reflect this share for the precision. In contrast, the random baseline for the recall yields 50.00% for choosing indifferently between the two available classes. Our results indicate that 80.04% (87.68%) of text regions classified as handwritten (machine printed) text have been correctly assigned to this class (cf. "Precision" in Table 1). Similarly, 80.34% (87.29%)

of text regions actually belonging to the class of handwritten (machine printed) text have been classified correctly (cf. "Recall" in Table 1). Although our results outperform some of the studies in literature [36], there also exist authors who achieved higher rates for distinguishing these two types of text [35]. However, a fair comparison with these authors is not given, as they manually prepared their text regions for evaluation whereas our results rely on the localized text regions from the first step.

In order to evaluate the third step, we decided to use the well-founded *character accuracy* measure, which has often been applied in terms of handwritten and machine printed text recognition [15, 17, 25] (cf. "Step 3" in Table 1). The character accuracy is based on the number of character insertions, substitutions and deletions required to convert the recognized text into the true text. By determining the character accuracy, we included merges and splits as well as misclassified text regions, which have been processed by the incorrect LSTM. Nevertheless, our approach reached a character accuracy of 77.98% (91.28%) for recognizing handwritten (machine printed) text. Considering the comparatively low amount of training data, the results suggest a high potential in our self-trained LSTMs in recognizing handwritten text. In addition, this also implies that a higher precision and recall rate in the second step could considerably contribute to improve the character accuracy. Furthermore, our results reveal that misclassified text regions can be still recognized to a certain extent. In total, 86.05% of the text contained in the forms has been correctly recognized (cf. "Total" in Table 1). Studies inspecting text recognition with different machine learning algorithms measure accuracy in terms of correctly classified characters or words [13, 14]. For instance, Xue [13] reaches an accuracy of 83.3% using Support Vector Machines to recognize handwritten digits by classifying each digit in one of the ten classes 0–9. However, classifying an image of a digit in one of ten classes is obviously less complex than our task. In contrast, Balci et al. [14] apply Convolutional Neural Networks to classify handwritten words and thereby recognize 31% of words completely correct. To ensure a fair comparability, we calculated analogously to Balci et al. [14] that our approach recognized 49.63% (85.88%) of handwritten (machine printed) text regions completely correct. From this point of view, our results reveal a promising text recognition accuracy.

Since the well-known OCR approach Abbyy Finereader [51] as well as LSTMs trained on handwritten text constitute often used state-of-the-art approaches [17, 21], we refer to these approaches as baselines for comparison (cf. "Comparison" in Table 1). In order to compare the approaches with each other, we determined the character accuracy for the forms, but in this case included not localized text regions in the results. Accordingly, our hybrid approach reached an overall character accuracy of 82.69%. In contrast, the Abbyy Finereader approach reached a value of 66.33% for the overall character accuracy. While the Abbyy Finereader approach was well-suited to recognize machine printed text, it was mostly unable to recognize handwritten text. At last, LSTMs trained on handwritten text regions performed worst by recognizing 48.47% of all characters in the forms. Although the accuracy reached by the implementation of our approach seems not sufficient to fully automate the digitization process of forms, even organizations suffering from a limited amount of training data can apply our approach in a semi-automated way where employees verify the text recognition results. Consequently, not only employees' time expenditure and thus, costs can be reduced, but also further training data can be collected to fully automate the digitization process.

5   Conclusion, Limitations and Future Research

Nowadays, organizations face the challenge of automating the huge amount of document-based processes, particularly for forms. Since forms comprise handwritten as well as machine printed text, research provides promising approaches for digitizing both types of textual information independently. Nevertheless, until now literature does not provide sufficient approaches combining handwritten and machine printed text recognition. Hence, we contribute to research and practice by proposing a novel hybrid OCR approach combining handwritten and machine printed text recognition in an integrated perspective to automate processes by appropriately digitizing forms. Our hybrid approach localizes text regions contained in a form, classifies each as either handwritten or machine printed text and recognizes the text by means of the corresponding LSTM network. As a result, the whole text within a form is converted to editable format in an automated manner. We demonstrated and evaluated our approach using a dataset of representative publicly available forms. The results of the evaluation reveal that our hybrid approach provides higher accuracy in recognizing handwritten and machine printed text compared to other state-of-the-art OCR approaches.

Nevertheless, our work also has some limitations which may constitute the starting point for future research. In this paper we focused on text recognition from an overall perspective. Future research could further enhance the results of each step, for example, by combining multiple classifiers in the second step. Furthermore, we only considered one dataset, for which we applied and evaluated our approach. Thus, we encourage future research to evaluate our three-step approach on further datasets. Going a step further, the question arises how our approach could be applied to digitize forms independent of forms' layout structure. As a promising starting point, it seems reasonable to associate handwritten with machine printed text regions by considering the content in and the distance between both types of text regions. Summing up, we believe that our study is an important step towards the combination of handwritten and machine printed text recognition. We hope our work will stimulate research in this exciting area.

References

1. Manyika, J., Chui, M., Miremadi, M., et al.: A future that works: automation, employment, and productivity. McKinsey Global Institute (2017)
2. Geissbauer, R., Khurana, A., Arora, J.: Industry 4.0: Building the Digital Industrial Enterprise. PwC (2016)
3. Allianz Deutschland AG. https://www.allianz.de/gesundheit/private-krankenversicherung/rechnung-einreichen/#app. Accessed 30 Jan 2019
4. Weintraub, A., Le Clair, C.: The Forrester Wave™. Multichannel Capture, Q3 2012. Forrester Research, Inc. (2012)
5. Rehman, A., Saba, T.: Neural networks for document image preprocessing: state of the art. Artif. Intell. Rev. **42**(2), 253–273 (2014)
6. Ahmad, I., Mahmoud, S.A.: Arabic bank check processing. State of the art. J. Comput. Sci. Technol. **28**(2), 285–299 (2013)
7. Palacios, R., Gupta, A.: A system for processing handwritten bank checks automatically. Image Vis. Comput. **26**(10), 1297–1313 (2008)

8. Department of the Treasury Internal Revenue Service: Internal Revenue Service Data Book. https://www.irs.gov/pub/irs-soi/17databk.pdf. Accessed 14 Jan 2019
9. McKinsey & Company: Bots, algorithms, and the future of the finance function. https://mck.co/2LcvwaM. Accessed 30 Jan 2019
10. Chaudhuri, A., Mandaviya, K., Badelia, P., Ghosh, S.K.: Optical Character Recognition Systems for Different Languages with Soft Computing. SFSC, vol. 352. Springer, Cham (2017). https://doi.org/10.1007/978-3-319-50252-6
11. Singh, A., Desai, S.: Optical character recognition using template matching and back propagation algorithm. In: 3rd ICICT, pp. 1–6. IEEE (2016)
12. Dohrmann, T., Pinshaw, G.: The Road to Improved Compliance – A McKinsey Benchmarking Study of Tax Administrations. McKinsey & Company, Washington, D.C. (2009)
13. Xue, Y.: Optical Character Recognition. Department of Biomedical Engineering, University of Michigan (2014)
14. Balci, B., Saadati, D., Shiferaw, D.: Handwritten Text Recognition Using Deep Learning. CS231n: Convolutional Neural Networks for Visual Recognition, Stanford University, Course Project Report (2017)
15. Graves, A., Liwicki, M., Fernández, S., et al.: A novel connectionist system for unconstrained handwriting recognition. IEEE Trans. Pattern Anal. Mach. Intell. 31(5), 855–868 (2009)
16. Su, B., Zhang, X., Lu, S., et al.: Segmented handwritten text recognition with recurrent neural network classifiers. In: 13th ICDAR, Tunis, Tunisia, pp. 386–390. IEEE (2015)
17. Shkarupa, Y., Mencis, R., Sabatelli, M.: Offline handwriting recognition using LSTM recurrent neural networks. In: 28th BNAIC, pp. 88–95. Springer (2016)
18. Salvi, D., Zhou, J., Waggoner, J., et al.: Handwritten text segmentation using average longest path algorithm. In: WACV, pp. 505–512. IEEE (2013)
19. Lee, S.-W., Kim, S.-Y.: Integrated segmentation and recognition of handwritten numerals with cascade neural network. IEEE Trans. Syst. Man Cybern. Part C (Appl. Rev.) 29(2), 285–290 (1999)
20. El-Yacoubi, A., Gilloux, M., Sabourin, R., et al.: An HMM-based approach for off-line unconstrained handwritten word modeling and recognition. IEEE Trans. Pattern Anal. Mach. Intell. 21(8), 752–760 (1999)
21. Chakraborty, B., Mukherjee, P.S., Bhattacharya, U.: Bangla online handwriting recognition using recurrent neural network architecture. In: 10th ICVGIP. ACM (2016)
22. Kaltenmeier, A., Caesar, T., Gloger, J.M., et al.: Sophisticated topology of hidden Markov models for cursive script recognition. In: 2nd ICDAR, pp. 139–142. IEEE (1993)
23. Al-Muhtaseb, H.A., Mahmoud, S.A., Qahwaji, R.S.: Recognition of off-line printed Arabic text using Hidden Markov Models. Sig. Process. 88(12), 2902–2912 (2008)
24. Din, I.U., Siddiqi, I., Khalid, S., et al.: Segmentation-free optical character recognition for printed Urdu text. Eur. Assoc. Sig. Process. J. Image Video Process. 2017(62), 1–18 (2017)
25. Breuel, T.M., Ul-Hasan, A., Al-Azawi, M.A., et al.: High-performance OCR for printed English and Fraktur using LSTM networks. In: 12th ICDAR, pp. 683–687. IEEE (2013)
26. Naz, S., Hayat, K., Razzak, M.I., et al.: The optical character recognition of Urdu-like cursive scripts. Pattern Recogn. 47(3), 1229–1248 (2014)
27. MLP Finanzberatung SE. https://mlp.de/lebenssituationen/beruf/berufsunfaehigkeitsschutz-risikoanfrage-bei-zweifeln/. Accessed 30 Jan 2019
28. Peffers, K., Tuunanen, T., Rothenberger, M.A., et al.: A design science research methodology for information systems research. JMIS 24(3), 45–77 (2007)
29. Grother, P., Hanaoka, K.: NIST special database 19 handprinted forms and characters 2nd Edition. National Institute of Standards and Technology, Technical report (2016)

30. Srihari, S.N.: Recognition of handwritten and machine-printed text for postal address interpretation. Pattern Recogn. Lett. **14**(4), 291–302 (1993)
31. Gorski, N., Anisimov, V., Augustin, E., et al.: Industrial bank check processing. The A2iA CheckReaderTM. IJDAR **3**(4), 196–206 (2001)
32. Eskenazi, S., Gomez-Krämer, P., Ogier, J.-M.: A comprehensive survey of mostly textual document segmentation algorithms since 2008. Pattern Recogn. **64**, 1–14 (2017)
33. Clausner, C., Antonacopoulos, A., Pletschacher, S.: ICDAR2017 competition on recognition of documents with complex layouts. In: 14th ICDAR, pp. 1404–1410. IEEE (2017)
34. Smith, R.W.: Hybrid page layout analysis via tab-stop detection. In: 10th ICDAR, pp. 241–245. IEEE (2009)
35. Malakar, S., Das, R.K., Sarkar, R., et al.: Handwritten and printed word identification using gray-scale feature vector and decision tree classifier. Procedia Technol. **10**, 831–839 (2013)
36. Srivastva, R., Raj, A., Patnaik, T., et al.: A survey on techniques of separation of machine printed text and handwritten text. IJEAT **2**(3), 552–555 (2013)
37. Saidani, A., Kacem, A., Belaid, A.: Arabic/Latin and machine-printed/handwritten word discrimination using HOG-based shape descriptor. ELCVIA **14**(2), 1–23 (2015)
38. Zagoris, K., Pratikakis, I., Antonacopoulos, A., et al.: Distinction between handwritten and machine-printed text based on the bag of visual words model. Pattern Recogn. **47**(3), 1051–1062 (2014)
39. Marti, U., Bunke, H.: Text line segmentation and word recognition in a system for general writer independent handwriting recognition. In: 6th ICDAR, pp. 159–163. IEEE (2001)
40. Graves, A., Fernández, S., Gomez, F., et al.: Connectionist temporal classification. Labelling unsegmented sequence data with recurrent neural networks. In: 23rd ICML, pp. 369–376. ACM (2006)
41. Jacobs, C., Simard, P.Y., Viola, P., et al.: Text recognition of low-resolution document images. In: 8th ICDAR, pp. 695–699. IEEE Computer Society (2005)
42. Amin, A.: Recognition of printed Arabic text based on global features and decision tree learning techniques. Pattern Recogn. **33**(8), 1309–1323 (2000)
43. Puigcerver, J.: Are multidimensional recurrent layers really necessary for handwritten text recognition? In: 14th ICDAR, pp. 67–72. IEEE (2017)
44. Tran, T.A., Na, I.-S., Kim, S.-H.: Hybrid page segmentation using multilevel homogeneity structure. In: 9th IMCOM, pp. 78:1–78:6. ACM (2015)
45. He, L., Ren, X., Gao, Q., et al.: The connected-component labeling problem. A review of state-of-the-art algorithms. Pattern Recogn. **70**, 25–43 (2017)
46. Dalal, N., Triggs, B.: Histograms of oriented gradients for human detection. In: 2005 CVPR, pp. 886–893. IEEE Computer Society (2005)
47. Park, D.C., El-Sharkawi, M.A., Marks, R.J., et al.: Electric load forecasting using an artificial neural network. IEEE Trans. Power Syst. **6**(2), 442–449 (1991)
48. Bloomberg, D.S., Kopec, G.E., Dasari, L.: Measuring document image skew and orientation. In: Document Recognition II, vol. 2422, pp. 302–317 (1995)
49. The Tesseract open source OCR engine. https://github.com/tesseract-ocr/tesseract. Accessed 30 Jan 2019
50. Bengio, Y., LeCun, Y., et al.: Scaling learning algorithms towards AI. In: Large-Scale Kernel Machines, vol. 34, no. 5, pp. 1–41 (2007)
51. Abby FinerReader. https://www.abbyy.com/de-de/finereader/. Accessed 30 Jan 2019

Anomaly-Based Duplicate Detection: A Probabilistic Approach

Andreas Obermeier[✉]

University of Ulm, 89069 Ulm, Germany
andreas.obermeier@uni-ulm.de

Abstract. The importance of identifying records in databases that refer to the same real-world entity ("duplicate detection") has been recognized in both research and practice. However, existing supervised approaches for duplicate detection need training data with labeled instances of duplicates and non-duplicates, which is often costly and time-consuming to generate. On the contrary, unsupervised approaches can forego such training data but may suffer from limiting assumptions (e.g., monotonicity) and providing less reliable results. To address the issue of generating high-quality results using easy to acquire duplicate-free training data only, we propose a probabilistic approach for anomaly-based duplicate detection. Duplicates exhibit specific characteristics which differ significantly from the characteristics of non-duplicates and therefore represent anomalies. Based on the grade of anomaly compared to duplicate-free training data, our approach assigns the probability of being a duplicate to each analyzed pair of records while avoiding limiting assumptions (of existing approaches). We demonstrate the practical applicability and effectiveness of our approach in a real-world setting by analyzing customer master data of a German insurer. The evaluation shows that the results provided by the approach are reliable and useful for decision support and can outperform even fully supervised state-of-the-art approaches for duplicate detection.

Keywords: Duplicate detection · Unsupervised classification · Data quality

1 Introduction

Pairs of records in a database that represent one and the same real-world entity, typically called duplicates, are one of the most prevalent and critical reasons for poor data quality [1–3]. A large variety of problems arises from duplicates, for instance, misjudgments of customers [4], incorrect strategic and operational decisions [2], and additional operative expenses [5]. Therefore, it is of crucial importance to reliably identify duplicates, which is the primary goal of approaches for duplicate detection. For instance, a subsequent merge into a single ("golden") record can be performed to alleviate the data quality problems after identifying the duplicates.

Traditionally the proposed approaches for duplicate detection rely on rulesets or supervised learning techniques [6] which need training data to classify the pairs of records into duplicates and non-duplicates reliably. The first have to be handcrafted for every domain and typically involve manually set thresholds. The latter require training

© Springer Nature Switzerland AG 2019
B. Tulu et al. (Eds.): DESRIST 2019, LNCS 11491, pp. 221–236, 2019.
https://doi.org/10.1007/978-3-030-19504-5_15

data from both classes (i.e., duplicates and non-duplicates), which is often not readily available in real-world situations but has to be generated. This (manual) generation of training data is typically costly and time-consuming [7]. Thereby, it is especially difficult to obtain enough cases of duplicates, whereas non-duplicates are typically easy to obtain [8]. To alleviate this drawback, several approaches using unsupervised learning have been proposed [7–12]. However, these approaches often involve limiting assumptions (e.g., monotonicity) and cannot quite keep up with supervised approaches in terms of classification performance (cf. Sect. 2).

To address these challenges, we propose an approach for duplicate detection exploiting the fact, that duplicates exhibit typical characteristics which significantly differ from those of non-duplicates [3]. For instance, failures during (repeated) data capturing which provoke misreported values (e.g., typos) result in duplicates which tend to have very similar or even equal values for all attributes. An example of such a duplicate is given by the records 3 and 4 in Table 1. Besides, real-world events such as marriage or relocation can result in duplicates which have substantially different values for some of the attributes [3]. For example, the records 1 and 2 in Table 1 represent a duplicate caused by relocation with significantly differing values for the attribute street and equal values for all other attributes. As such patterns are typically not observed in a duplicate-free dataset in a large number, they can be considered as anomalies. Our approach makes use of this fact, and we argue that the principles and the knowledge base of probability theory are adequate and valuable, providing well-founded methods to describe and analyze whether pairs of records may be seen as an anomaly and a duplicate, respectively. More precisely, we aim to derive a probability of whether a specific pair of records is a duplicate based on the grade of anomaly of the pair of records compared to a training dataset of sample non-duplicates. Thus, the presented anomaly-based probabilistic approach for detecting duplicates provides a way to detect duplicates using duplicate-free training data only, which – to the best of our knowledge – has not been addressed by existing approaches yet (cf. Sect. 2).

Table 1. Illustration of four records in a customer dataset as examples for duplicates

ID	First name	Last name	Street	Date of birth
1	Jane	Doe	North Street 1	12.06.1983
2	Jane	Doe	South Road 3	12.06.1983
3	John	Smith	Bella Road 14	06.12.1976
4	Jon	Smith	Bela Road 14	06.12.1976

Following a design-oriented approach [13], the remainder of the paper is structured as follows: In Sect. 2, we discuss related work and clarify the research gap. In Sect. 3, we develop our anomaly-based probabilistic approach for duplicate detection and propose possible ways to instantiate it using duplicate-free training data. Section 4 contains a demonstration and evaluation of the practical applicability and effectiveness of the approach using real-world customer master data of a German insurer. Finally, we conclude, reflect on limitations and provide an outlook on future research.

2   Related Work

Literature provides a variety of well-known approaches for duplicate detection [14–16]. The two major strategies for duplicate detection are probability-based vs. deterministic duplicate detection [17]. To address the fact, that without a real-world test it cannot be said with certainty whether a pair of record represents a duplicate [3], a probability-based approach is preferable. Also, commonly used deterministic approaches often rely on complex handcrafted rulesets [18] and typically do not outperform probability-based approaches [17]. Thus, in the following, we focus on probability-based approaches. Thereby, we first discuss the common basis of supervised and unsupervised approaches (i.e., the Fellegi-Sunter framework). Then, we depict supervised approaches and finally describe unsupervised approaches.

The classical framework for probability-based duplicate detection was presented by Fellegi and Sunter [19]. It serves as a foundation for various probability-based supervised and unsupervised approaches [20–23]. Works based on the framework of Fellegi and Sunter share the main concept of grasping syntactical agreements and similarities as a distinctive characteristic of duplicates. They model the probability of a given pair of records to be a duplicate based on similarities of the respective records' attribute values. To quantify the similarities, a comparison vector, typically comprising one similarity measure per attribute is introduced. These comparisons might lead to binary outcomes (e.g., "value of attribute x agrees") or continuous outcomes, often between zero and one (e.g., "Jaro-similarity of the values of attribute x"). The main objective in the Fellegi-Sunter framework is to classify each pair of records into one of three mutually exclusive subsets based on the comparison vector: the set of duplicates, the set of non-duplicates and the set of pairs requiring manual review.

However, existing supervised approaches based on the Fellegi-Sunter framework are characterized by three major limitations. First, the classification incorporates decision rules based on independence or monotonicity assumptions. The independence assumption states, that agreements or disagreements of attribute values of a pair of records occur independently. The monotonicity assumption states that higher similarities of attribute values lead to a higher probability of being a duplicate and vice versa. These assumptions, which are discussed in more detail in [3], may lead to misclassifications as independence and monotonicity assumptions are typically violated in practical applications [6, 20, 22]. Second, the classification relies on syntactical similarities without considering real-world events such as relocation or marriage as possible causes of duplicates. However, in the case of a real-world event such as relocation or marriage, one or more similarities (e.g., for address-related attributes in the case of a relocation) might be low even though the pair of records indeed represents a duplicate. An example for the real-world event relocation is given by the first two records in Table 1: even though the values for the attribute street are very dissimilar, the pair of records represents a duplicate caused by relocation. Thus, not considering these real-world events can lead to false negatives as the semantics behind possible disagreements for some attribute values are not grasped [3]. This may lead to false negatives, as duplicates caused by real-world events are possibly misclassified as non-duplicates. Third, the supervised approaches based on the Fellegi-Sunter framework rely on training data including labeled pairs of records from both classes, duplicates and non-duplicates. However, in practice, the generation of such a training dataset is costly and time-consuming, especially the identification of a sufficient number of duplicates [7, 8]. To address the first two limitations, Heinrich et al. [3] presented a probability-based approach for duplicate detection which does not suffer from independence or monotonicity assumptions and accounts for real-world events causing duplicates. However, the presented approach is supervised and relies on costly to generate training data, which contains labeled instances from both classes.

Unsupervised approaches for duplicate detection try to alleviate the need of training data [7–12]. These approaches yielded promising results without the need for training data but also exhibit some limitations. First, many of the proposed approaches indeed avoid any independence assumptions but replace them with a monotonicity assumption [7, 8, 11]. However, this assumption is violated in many practical applications and thus may lead to inadequate results [3, 6]. Second, the unsupervised approaches often base their decision upon a (weighted) sum of the attribute-wise similarities of the pairs of records [9, 10, 12]. As the decision is made up upon a sum of similarities, those approaches cannot decide whether the lower value of the sum can be explained by a real-world event (e.g., low similarity for address-related attributes in the case of a relocation). Therefore, they are prone to false negatives in the case of such real-world events causing duplicates.

To conclude, existing approaches for probability-based duplicate detection have several limitations. They often are based on limiting independence or monotonicity assumptions. Additionally, real-world events causing duplicates are typically neglected. Finally, supervised approaches need costly to generate training data from both classes (i.e., duplicates and non-duplicates), whereas unsupervised approaches generally cannot quite keep up with supervised approaches in terms of classification performance. To address this research gap, we propose an anomaly-based probabilistic approach for duplicate detection in the following.

3   A Novel Approach for Duplicate Detection

In this section, we develop a novel approach for anomaly-based probabilistic duplicate detection. First, we outline the general setting and the basic idea. Then, we discuss the design of our approach in three steps. Finally, we outline possible ways to instantiate the approach.

3.1   General Setting and Basic Idea

We consider a dataset with records representing entities by means of attributes (e.g., a relation in a database). The set of records is denoted by $T = \{t_1, \ldots, t_n\}$ and the set of attributes by $\{a_1, \ldots, a_m\}$. In the example given in Table 1, for instance, the attribute value of first name for t_1 is Jane. The set $T \times T$ contains all pairs (t_i, t_j) of records. Pairs of records in $C := \{(t_i, t_j) \in T \times T | i \neq j\}$ may possibly be a duplicate (e.g., if both records t_1 and t_2 represent the same real-world entity). Based on their interrelations, duplicate detection aims to decide whether they are a duplicate or not.

The main idea of our approach is to estimate the probability of being a duplicate for a given pair of records based on its grade of anomaly compared to duplicate-free training data. To give an example, in duplicate-free data pairs of records which have equal values in all attributes are typically very rare. Hence, if we observe many of such pairs in a dataset to be analyzed, their estimated duplicate probability would be rather high. To formalize this idea, we introduce a feature vector comprising information on the interrelation of the pair of records in numerical values (e.g., attribute-wise similarities). Then, the density at the point of the feature vector of the pair of records in question is assessed in the dataset to be analyzed. By comparing this value with the expectation for the density at this point in duplicate-free data, we aim to uncover possible anomalies. More precisely, pairs of records with an associated density higher than expected for duplicate-free data are further analyzed. For these pairs of records, we derive an estimation for the probability of being a duplicate. This estimation is based on the distribution of the density in the duplicate-free training data and avoids any monotonicity or independence assumptions. Thereby, the approach concentrates on regions of the dataset to be analyzed where more pairs of records lie than expected when assuming duplicate-free data. Thus, our approach is based on easy to acquire duplicate-free training data only, while still yielding at reliable results comparable to fully supervised approaches. Moreover, the clear interpretation of the results of our approach as probabilities allows the integration into a decision calculus (e.g., based on decision theory) to support decision-making in a well-founded manner.

3.2   Design of an Anomaly-Based Approach for Duplicate Detection

We propose an approach designed in three steps. First, we ground our approach on a probability space. Second, we formalize the interrelation of a pair of records in terms of a feature vector. Third, we estimate the probability that a pair of records is a duplicate based on the grade of anomaly compared to duplicate-free training data.

Ad (Step 1): We model the duplicate status of a pair of records as an outcome in the probability space $(\Omega, 2^{\Omega}, P)$. We particularly refer to the outcomes D (representing a duplicate) and $\overline{D}$ (representing a non-duplicate). This definition ensures that the outcomes are mutually exclusive and collectively exhaustive (i.e., $\overline{D} \cap D = \varnothing$, $\overline{D} \cup D = \Omega$). For our approach, we focus on the values $P(D)$, representing the probability that a considered pair of records is a duplicate. These probabilities depend on the pair of records (t_i, t_j) as characteristic patterns of interrelations may possibly point to a duplicate. To give an example, matching values for all attributes may indicate a duplicate. Typically, such characteristic patterns are rare in duplicate-free data. To account for these characteristic patterns, we aim to evaluate the conditional probabilities $P(D|(t_i, t_j))$ for all pairs of records to be analyzed.

Ad (Step 2): Conditioning on the pair of records (t_i, t_j) needs to be formalized to enable an application. To do so, information on the interrelation of the pair of records can be expressed by numerical values (e.g., attribute-wise similarities). For concise representation, these values are combined in a vector, which is called feature vector in the following. For example, the feature vector may comprise one or more similarity measures per attribute. To allow for maximum flexibility regarding the interrelations, no kind of independence, monotonicity or other specific interrelation between the components of our feature vector is assumed. More precisely, the feature vector is formed by mapping (t_i, t_j) onto a f-dimensional vector $\zeta_{i,j} := C \to \mathbb{R}^f, f \in \mathbb{N}$, so that it holds $P(D|(t_i, t_j)) = P(D|\zeta_{i,j})$ for outcome D.

Ad (Step 3): To estimate the probability of being a duplicate for a given pair of records (t_i, t_j) with an associated feature vector $\zeta_{i,j}$, we compare the value of the density $\varrho_{i,j}$ at the point of $\zeta_{i,j}$ in the dataset to be analyzed with the density one might expect in data which contains no duplicates. Thereby, the density $\varrho_{i,j}$ refers to the value of the probability density function associated with the distribution of all feature vectors ζ contained in the dataset to be analyzed at the point of $\zeta_{i,j}$. This (scalar) value can be interpreted as the relative likelihood of observing a pair of records with feature vector $\zeta_{i,j}$ in the dataset to be analyzed. If the density at the point of $\zeta_{i,j}$ in the dataset to be analyzed is higher than the density expected for duplicate-free data at the same point, the unexpectedly high density at that point might represent an anomaly. To determine the expected value for the density $\hat{\varrho}_{i,j}$ at $\zeta_{i,j}$ in data without duplicates, we analyze the probability distribution function $\hat{p}(\hat{\varrho}_{i,j})$ in duplicate-free training data (with the circumflex indicating the measurement in the training data). To obtain this distribution, a sampling-process can be performed. Thereby, N random samples of the size of the dataset to be analyzed are drawn from the training dataset. For each sample, the density at $\zeta_{i,j}$ is calculated. Based on this information, the probability distribution function $\hat{p}(\hat{\varrho}_{i,j})$ of the density $\hat{\varrho}_{i,j}$ and the associated expected value $\widehat{E}(\hat{\varrho}_{i,j})$ can be derived. A high number of samples N increases run time but yields more exact estimations.

Based on the mutually exclusive and collectively exhaustive outcomes D and $\overline{D}$, the density $\varrho_{i,j}$ at $\zeta_{i,j}$ in the dataset to be analyzed can be split into two summands: one part caused by duplicates $\varrho_{i,j}^D$ and one part caused by non-duplicates $\varrho_{i,j}^{\overline{D}}$:

$$\varrho_{i,j} = \varrho_{i,j}^D + \varrho_{i,j}^{\overline{D}} \tag{1}$$

Our goal is to estimate the probability $P(D|\zeta_{i,j})$ of being a duplicate for a pair of records with feature vector $\zeta_{i,j}$. Evidently, if $\varrho_{i,j}^D$ is known, this task would be trivial: the probability is then given by the ratio of the density $\varrho_{i,j}^D$ caused by duplicates and the overall density $\varrho_{i,j}$. To give an example, if half of the density at $\zeta_{i,j}$ is caused duplicates the probability of being a duplicate for a pair of records with the feature vector $\zeta_{i,j}$ is 50%. However, the value of $\varrho_{i,j}^D$ is not known, as the true duplicate statuses are not known. To estimate its value, its expected value $E(\varrho_{i,j}^D)$ can be assessed. Then, the probability $P(D|\zeta_{i,j})$ can be estimated by the share of this estimation $E(\varrho_{i,j}^D)$ with respect to the overall density $\varrho_{i,j}$ at this point in the dataset to be analyzed:

$$P(D|\zeta_{i,j}) = \frac{E(\varrho_{i,j}^D)}{\varrho_{i,j}} \tag{2}$$

To evaluate $E\left(\varrho_{i,j}^D\right)$ we apply the definition of the expected value if the density in the dataset to be analyzed at $\zeta_{i,j}$ is higher than expected in duplicate-free data. Thereby, we use the standard definition of the expected value (i.e., $E(x) = \int_{-\infty}^{\infty} x \cdot p(x) dx$ for the random variable x). Otherwise, $E\left(\varrho_{i,j}^D\right)$ is set to zero as no unexpectedly high density representing an anomaly is observed:

$$E\left(\varrho_{i,j}^D\right) = \begin{cases} 0 & \text{for } \varrho_{i,j} \leq \widehat{E}\left(\hat{\varrho}_{i,j}\right) \\ \int_0^{\varrho_{i,j}} \varrho_{i,j}^D \cdot p\left(\varrho_{i,j}^D\right) d\varrho_{i,j}^D & \text{for } \varrho_{i,j} > \widehat{E}\left(\hat{\varrho}_{i,j}\right) \end{cases} \tag{3}$$

Note, that $\varrho_{i,j}^D$ must be greater or equal to zero because of its definition as density and it must be smaller than $\varrho_{i,j}$ because of Eq. (1). Thus, $p\left(\varrho_{i,j}^D\right)$ becomes zero for values smaller than zero or greater than $\varrho_{i,j}$, which explains the boundaries of the integral in Eq. (3). In the following, we concentrate on pairs of records with an associated density higher than the expected density in duplicate-free data, possibly representing a duplicate (i.e., $\varrho_{i,j} > \widehat{E}(\hat{\varrho}_{i,j})$). As we only use non-duplicates for training, we cannot directly assess the distribution of the density of duplicates $p\left(\varrho_{i,j}^D\right)$. Thus, $p\left(\varrho_{i,j}^D\right)$ must be rewritten. Reflecting upon Eq. (1) it is obvious that a density $\varrho_{i,j}^D$ caused by duplicates corresponds to a density of $\varrho_{i,j} - \varrho_{i,j}^D$ caused by non-duplicates. Therefore, the distribution of $\varrho_{i,j}^D$ can be estimated by the distribution of $\varrho_{i,j} - \varrho_{i,j}^D$ in duplicate-free data:

$$p\left(\varrho_{i,j}^D\right) = \hat{p}\left(\varrho_{i,j} - \varrho_{i,j}^D\right) \tag{4}$$

By combining Eqs. (3) and (4) we obtain:

$$E\left(\varrho_{i,j}^D\right) = \int_0^{\varrho_{i,j}} \hat{p}\left(\varrho_{i,j} - \varrho_{i,j}^D\right) \cdot \varrho_{i,j}^D \, d\varrho_{i,j}^D \quad \text{for } \varrho_{i,j} > \widehat{E}\left(\hat{\varrho}_{i,j}\right) \tag{5}$$

Note, that the integral in Eq. (5) can be evaluated easily, as the distribution $\hat{p}\left(\varrho_{i,j} - \varrho_{i,j}^D\right)$ is known from the sampling procedure performed on the duplicate-free training data and the density $\varrho_{i,j}$ at $\zeta_{i,j}$ can be derived from the dataset to be analyzed. Finally, combined with Eq. (2) the estimated probability of being a duplicate for a pair of records with feature vector $\zeta_{i,j}$ depends only on two inputs (i.e., the distribution $\hat{p}\left(\varrho_{i,j} - \varrho_{i,j}^D\right)$ estimated using the duplicate-free training data and the density $\varrho_{i,j}$ derived from the dataset to be analyzed) and is given by:

$$P\left(D|\zeta_{i,j}\right) = \frac{\int_0^{\varrho_{i,j}} \hat{p}\left(\varrho_{i,j} - \varrho_{i,j}^D\right) \cdot \varrho_{i,j}^D \, d\varrho_{i,j}^D}{\varrho_{i,j}} \tag{6}$$

3.3   Possible Ways to Instantiate the Approach

To instantiate our approach, we especially need a dataset of sample non-duplicates. One way to obtain such data is to clean up a representative dataset manually. For example, if a customer dataset is to be assessed, a random sample of pairs of customer records (t_i, t_j) can be drawn and cleansed by hand. For domain experts, such a manual cleansing is usually straightforward to carry out with a high degree of reliability (i.e., expert estimations will not substantially change over time or between experts). However, such a cleansing procedure might be time-consuming and expensive. Therefore, another possible source for training data is company-owned (historical) data. This data may, for example, stem from previous data quality projects. This represents an opportunity to reuse the results of analyses (e.g., already cleansed data) conducted in the past. For example, a dataset, which was cleansed once, can be held duplicate-free by applying our approach. Finally, a promising option to obtain a duplicate-free dataset is to analyze publicly available data and publications (e.g., from federal statistical offices).

The duplicate-free data obtained in one of the described ways can be used to estimate the distribution $\hat{p}\left(\varrho_{i,j} - \varrho_{i,j}^D\right)$ based on duplicate-free data. We propose two methods[1] for this estimation: (i) an interval-based approach and (ii) kernel density estimation. Additionally, the density $\varrho_{i,j}$ in the dataset to be analyzed can also be assessed using these methods. Thus, both inputs of Eq. (6) can be derived.

Ad (i): The interval-based approach aims at estimating the densities appearing in Eq. (6) in a frequentist approximation. To do so, H sets of intervals $I_{h,l} \subset \mathbb{R}, 1 \leq l \leq f$ and $1 \leq h \leq H$ (with $H \in \mathbb{N}$) are defined. Each set contains f intervals (one interval for each dimension of the feature vector ζ). Then, for each set of intervals a multidimensional interval $I_h \subset \mathbb{R}^f$ with $I_h = I_{h,1} \times I_{h,2} \times \ldots \times I_{h,f}$ is constructed. The number of intervals H and their structure influence performance and require particular attention. For ease of notation, we use absolute frequencies in the following. The density $\varrho_{i,j}$ at $\zeta_{i,j}$ in the dataset to be analyzed is represented by the absolute frequency ϱ_h of pairs of records with feature vectors contained in interval I_h (i.e., $\zeta_{i,j} \in I_h$). The discrete probability distribution $\widehat{P}(\hat{\varrho}_h = k)$ (for $k \in \mathbb{N}$) based on the training data represents the probability distribution $\hat{p}(\hat{\varrho}_{i,j})$ for duplicate-free data. As described in Sect. 3.2, a sampling-process can be performed to obtain the probability distribution. Therefore, N random samples of the size of the dataset to be analyzed are drawn from the training dataset. For each sample, the absolute frequencies in the defined intervals are calculated (denoted by $\hat{\varrho}_{h,n}$ with $1 \leq n \leq N$). Then the discrete probability distribution for the frequency of pairs of records in each interval in duplicate-free data is given by:

$$\widehat{P}(\hat{\varrho}_h = k) \approx \frac{1}{N} \sum_{n=1}^{N} \mathbb{I}_{\{\hat{\varrho}_{h,n} = k\}} \tag{7}$$

---

[1] Mathematical pseudocode for both methods of instantiation is available at: https://github.com/aoberm/Anomaly-Based-Duplicate-Detection.

Given this distribution derived from the duplicate-free training data and the frequency ϱ_h measured in the dataset to be analyzed and based on Eq. (6) it holds:

$$P(D|\zeta_{i,j}) = \frac{\sum_{\varrho_h^D=0}^{\varrho_h} \widehat{P}(\hat{\varrho}_h = \varrho_h - \varrho_h^D) \cdot \varrho_h^D}{\varrho_h} \quad \text{for } \zeta_{i,j} \in I_h \text{ and } \varrho_h > \widehat{E}(\hat{\varrho}_h) \quad (8)$$

Ad (ii): However, in some scenarios, it might be difficult to determine an appropriate set of intervals to apply the interval-based approach. Therefore, one may aim at using non-parametric density estimation methods like kernel density estimation [24]. In our setting, kernel density estimation can be used to estimate the value of the density $\varrho_{i,j}$ in the dataset to be analyzed. Also, after performing the sampling procedure on the training data, the density $\hat{\varrho}_{i,j}$ can be estimated in each sample using kernel density estimation. Finally, the distribution of these densities $\hat{p}(\hat{\varrho}_{i,j})$ over all samples can be estimated in the same way. Generally, any density function $p(x)$ of a random variable x can be estimated using a kernel density estimator $y(x)$. Based on a sample x_i (with $i = 1,\ldots,n$) drawn from x, the distribution of x is estimated by summing up and normalizing kernel functions K (typically Gaussians) placed over the values of x_i:

$$y(x) = \frac{1}{n}\sum_{i=1}^n K(x - x_i) \approx p(x) \quad (9)$$

4 Demonstration and Evaluation

In this section, we evaluate (E1) the practical applicability and (E2) the effectiveness of our approach for duplicate detection. First, we discuss the reasons for selecting the case of an insurer and describe the analyzed customer dataset. Then, we show how the approach could be instantiated for this case. Finally, we present the results of its application and compare them to those of two state-of-the-art approaches.

4.1 Case Selection and Dataset

To evaluate (E1) and (E2), the approach was applied to a customer dataset of a major German provider of life insurances. Duplicates are a significant source of data quality problems in the insurer's customer master data. However, this data is of particular importance for the insurer (e.g., for customer relationship management). Hence, the insurer aimed to identify respective duplicates to address this data quality problem.

To apply and evaluate our approach with regard to detecting duplicates, the insurer provided us with a subset of its customer record data containing four master data attributes. Each record in this subset has a value for both the attribute first name and the attribute last name. In addition, for each customer street and house number are stored in the attribute street. Finally, the attribute date of birth is stored in a standard date format. These attributes are typical for customer master data and were used to apply and evaluate our approach. More precisely, 90,040 pairs of records were analyzed.

Before applying the approach, an instantiation is necessary. In our case, we had access to golden matches (i.e., the duplicate status was known for all pairs of records in the dataset) from a previous project that aimed at identifying duplicates in the dataset. In this project, we access to a data expert of the insurer and thus to further confidential data (e.g., the customers' bank accounts). This allowed a careful search for duplicates and ensured an accurate identification of duplicates. All pairs of records were labeled accordingly as duplicates vs. non-duplicates. In total, 1,891 pairs of records (i.e., 2.1% of the analyzed 90,040 pairs of records) were duplicates. Moreover, 476 of these 1,891 duplicates were created by one of the real-world events marriage, relocation or a combination of both. This high percentage (i.e., 25.2% of the duplicates) underlines the fact that an approach for duplicate detection should be able to handle real-world events causing duplicates. The known duplicate status for all pairs of records allowed a rigorous evaluation of our approach. To do so, our approach was implemented using Python, and a 10-fold cross-validation was applied to account for possible variations caused by the random selection of training data. In each fold, the duplicate-free training data was constructed based on 90% of the dataset by dropping all contained duplicates. Then the probabilities of being a duplicate where estimated for the remaining 10% of the dataset in each fold by applying our approach.

4.2   Instantiation of Our Approach for Duplicate Detection

To instantiate our approach, we let the feature vector comprise four string-based similarities based on the attribute values of each pair of records. Being a frequent and established choice for attributes representing names [25], Jaro-Winkler similarity [26] was selected for the attributes first name, last name, and street. The Jaro-Winkler similarity of two strings accounts for the number of matching characters as well as the minimum number of character transpositions required to transform one string into the other, putting more weight on the first characters. To weight all digits equally, Levenshtein similarity [27] was used for the attribute date of birth. The Levenshtein similarity accounts for the minimum number of edits (i.e., deletions, insertions and substitutions) required to transform one string into the other.

To instantiate the approach using the interval method, we identified 54 disjoint multidimensional intervals. The probability distribution $\widehat{P}(\hat{\varrho}_h = k)$ was calculated for each interval in a sampling-process (with $N = 1,000$) based on the training data as described in Sect. 3.3. In the following, the instantiation of our approach based on the interval method is referred to as "intervals". For the instantiation of our approach based on the kernel density estimation method, in the following referred to as "KDE", we used a common implementation presented by [28] and the same evaluation method (i.e., a 10-fold cross-validation) and sampling-process (with $N = 1,000$) as for the interval method.

4.3   Application and Results

As each pair of records was in the dataset to be analyzed for one of the cross-validation's folds, our approach yielded estimations for the probabilities of being a duplicate for all 90,040 pairs of records. The approach assigned a very low duplicate probability to the vast majority of pairs of records, regardless of the chosen instantiation. More precisely, the interval method assigned a probability below 10% to 84.8% of the pairs of records and the KDE method to 89.3%. Only a few pairs of records were assigned with a high probability over 60% (i.e., 2.2% for the interval method and 2.1% for the KDE method), which closely resembles the actual ratio of duplicates in the dataset (i.e., 2.1%). Such a distribution of estimated duplicate probabilities is favorable, as it builds the basis for a clear and comprehensible classification. To conclude, the approach could be applied which proves its practical applicability (E1) and provided useful results (cf. also (E2) below). After initial instantiation, it could be applied repeatedly, automated and without determination of additional parameters or distributions. This supports both efficiency and practical applicability (E1).

Our approach aims to determine duplicate probabilities for pairs of records which can also be used to classify into duplicates and non-duplicates. Therefore, to evaluate the effectiveness of our approach (E2), we first analyze the quality of the provided probability estimations (E2.1). Then, the effectiveness regarding classification (E2.2) is assessed.

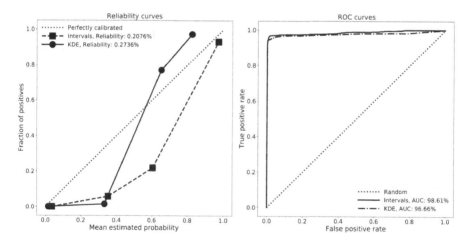

Fig. 1. Reliability and receiver operating characteristic curves for the two instantiations

To enable well-founded decisions based on the estimated duplicate probabilities, it must be ensured that the estimated probabilities correspond to the actually observed relative frequencies (E2.1), which can be assessed in terms of reliability [29–32]. In our context reliability expresses that the mean of the estimated duplicate probabilities in a (probability-)interval should closely resemble the relative frequency of duplicates in that (probability-)interval. Reliability can be evaluated using the reliability curve [33]. To calculate the points of this curve, the data is arranged to bins according to the estimated duplicate probability. Then, the mean of the estimated duplicate probability ("mean estimated probability"), as well as the actual relative frequency of duplicates ("fraction of positives"), is calculated and plotted for each bin. For a perfectly reliable estimation, the reliability curve lies on the diagonal. Reliability can also be quantitatively assessed in terms of the reliability score, which is defined as the mean squared deviation from the diagonal weighted by the number of cases in each bin [34]. Therefore, the smaller the value of the reliability score, the smaller the discrepancy between the estimated probabilities and the actually observed relative frequencies. The left section of Fig. 1 shows the reliability curves of the two instantiations of our approach. To obtain enough pairs of records in each bin, the number of bins was set to four. Low reliability scores (i.e., 0.21% for the interval method and 0.27% for the KDE method) show that our approach assigns reliable probabilities (E2.1). Some discrepancies occur for mediocre probabilities. However, they have no significant impact on the overall reliabilities as most of the pairs of records lie in the first or the last bin, where the probability estimates are accurate. More precisely, 99,2% (interval method) resp. 96,6% (KDE method) of the pairs of records lie in the first or the last bin.

Based on the estimated probabilities, duplicates can be distinguished from non-duplicates. Thus, to evaluate this aspect, we determined the discrimination of the estimated duplicate probabilities. The discrimination was assessed in terms of the area under curve (AUC) under the receiver operating characteristic (ROC) curve [35]. The ROC curve is drawn by plotting the true positive rate of a classification based on the estimated duplicate probabilities against the false positive rate when the classification threshold is varied. The ROC curves are given in the right section of Fig. 1. For each instantiation, the ROC curve is very close to the curve of perfect discrimination. With an area under the ROC curve of 98.61%, the probabilities based on the interval method show slightly better discrimination in our application than the probabilities based on the KDE method (96.66%). Overall, these results support that the probabilities provided by our approach can discriminate between duplicates and non-duplicates.

To further analyze the ability to discriminate between duplicates and non-duplicates (E2.2), the pairs of records exhibiting a duplicate probability above 50% were classified as duplicates and vice versa. Thus, each pair of records was classified into its most probable class. We compare the effectiveness of the classification based on our approach to the well-known state-of-the-art approaches "ECM" and "SVM" implemented in the Python Record Linkage Toolkit (PRLTK) [36]. Thereby, ECM is an unsupervised expectation-maximization approach based on the Fellegi-Sunter framework and SVM a supervised approach using support vector machines with linear kernels. For these two competing artifacts, a configuration of the similarity measures for each attribute was necessary. Thereby, the same similarity measures as in the instantiations of our approach were chosen for reasons of comparability.

Table 2. Performance measures for classification into duplicates and non-duplicates.

	Accuracy	Precision	Recall	F1	TP	FP	TN	FN
Intervals	**99.60%**	87.64%	**94.13%**	**90.77%**	1,780	251	87,898	111
KDE	99.53%	85.51%	93.65%	89.40%	1,771	300	87,849	120
ECM (PRLTK)	80.46%	6.68%	64.04%	12.10%	1,211	16,914	71,235	680
SVM (PRLTK)	99.18%	**95.42%**	63.93%	76.57%	1,209	58	88,091	682

Like for our approach, a 10-fold cross-validation was performed for the (supervised) state-of-the-art approach SVM. As the second compared state-of-the-art approach ECM does not need any training data, the respective results are shown for one single pass. To assess the quality of the classification into duplicates and non-duplicates, the performance measures accuracy, precision, recall and F-measure (F1) are provided in Table 2. Thereby, the best value for each performance measure achieved by one of the methods is marked in bold. Additionally, the exact numbers of true positives (TP), false positives (FP), true negatives (TN), and false negatives (FN) are also disclosed in Table 2. On the given dataset, our approach provides very promising results. Indeed, regardless of the method chosen for instantiation, the classification is very effective (E2.2). For instance, if the interval method is used, the classification based on our approach is able to identify 94.13% of the duplicates contained in the dataset (recall). Without giving customized intervals and using the KDE method, our approach is still able to identify 93.65% of the duplicates. In this application, our approach also exhibits maximum precision (i.e., the highest proportion of pairs of records classified as duplicates which actually are duplicates) when instantiated with the interval method, with a value of 87.64%. Overall, using this instantiation leads to a very high accuracy as 99.60% of the pairs of records are correctly classified. Moreover, the maximal value of 90.77% for the F-measure is achieved by this instantiation.

While the (unsupervised) ECM approach suffered from a very low precision of only 6.68%, resulting in an unsatisfactory F-measure of 12.10%, our approach was able to outperform even the fully supervised SVM approach. While the SVM approach was somewhat restrictive with judging pairs of records to be a duplicate, the few pairs of records identified as duplicates by this approach were almost all correctly classified, resulting in a high precision of 95.42%. However, the SVM approach mainly just identified the rather obvious duplicates, leading to this high precision but a critically low recall. More precisely, the SVM approach was only able to identify 63.93% of the duplicates as indicated by the recall. Further analysis revealed, that the SVM approach only identified 23 of the 476 duplicates, which were created by one of the real-world events marriage, relocation or a combination of both. Reasons for this fact have already been discussed in Sect. 2: Indeed, real-world events causing duplicates can lead to false negatives in approaches who grasp similarities in all attributes as a distinctive feature of duplicates. Overall, based on the given dataset our approach seems better suited to identify duplicates, even when compared to the supervised SVM approach regardless of the chosen instantiation method.

5   Conclusion, Limitations and Future Work

Duplicates are a major source of data quality problems in (customer) databases. Therefore, the detection of duplicates is important in both research and practice. In this paper, we present an anomaly-based probabilistic approach for this task. It aims at determining the probability for a pair of records to be a duplicate using sample non-duplicates for training only. Existing approaches are hampered by the need for expensive to generate training data or limiting assumptions (i.e., independence and monotonicity) or their low sensitivity towards duplicates created by real-world events. A formal definition of the approach was given in three steps, and two possibilities for its instantiation are provided. Moreover, the practical applicability and the effectiveness of the approach are evaluated based on real-world customer master data from a German insurer. The approach needs no expensive to generate training data but uses only sample non-duplicates for probability estimations. Additionally, it avoids limiting assumptions (e.g., independence or monotonicity). Moreover, in contrast to existing approaches, our approach can handle both, duplicates created by real-world events such as relocation or marriage and duplicates created by failures during data capturing (e.g., multi-captures and/or typos). Due to the interpretation of the results of our approach as probabilities, the integration into a decision calculus (e.g., expected value calculus) can be done easily and in a well-founded manner. The evaluation shows that the provided probabilities are reliable. Furthermore, when performing a classification into duplicates and non-duplicates, the presented approach showed promising results and outperformed an unsupervised and even a fully supervised competing artifact.

Nevertheless, our work also has limitations which may constitute the starting point for future research. In this paper, the approach was applied to a real-world customer dataset in the insurance-domain. Future research could evaluate it on further datasets containing master data. Furthermore, the dataset included a low percentage of duplicates, which is typical for real-world datasets. However, in datasets with a high percentage of duplicates, some anomalies representing duplicates might be obscured by other (more frequent) anomalies in the first run of our approach. Therefore, the (if necessary repeated) application of our approach on further (synthetical) data comprising a high number of duplicates could also provide interesting insights. Further evaluations could also explore different possibilities to instantiate our approach or the possibility of transferable results across datasets from the same or even different domains.

References

1. Fan, W.: Data quality. From theory to practice. ACM SIGMOD Rec. **44**(3), 7–18 (2015). https://doi.org/10.1145/2854006.2854008
2. Helmis, S., Hollmann, R.: Webbased Dataintegration. Approaches to Measure and Maintain the Quality of Information in Heterogeneous Databases Using a Fully Web-Based Tool. Springer, Heidelberg (2009)
3. Heinrich, B., Klier, M., Obermeier, A.A., Schiller, A.: Event-driven duplicate detection: a probability-based approach. In: Proceedings of the 26th ECIS (2018)
4. Bleiholder, J., Schmid, J.: Dataintegration and deduplication. In: Daten- und Informationsqualität, pp. 121–140. Springer, Heidelberg (2015)
5. Draisbach, U.: Partitioning for Efficient Duplicate Detection in Relational Data. Springer, Heidelberg (2012)
6. Christen, P.: Automatic record linkage using seeded nearest neighbour and support vector machine classification. In: Proceedings of the 14th ACM SIGKDD, pp. 151–159 (2008)
7. Christen, P.: A two-step classification approach to unsupervised record linkage. In: Proceedings of the 6th AusDM, pp. 111–119 (2007)

8. Lehti, P., Fankhauser, P.: Unsupervised duplicate detection using sample non-duplicates. In: Spaccapietra, S. (ed.) Journal on Data Semantics VII. LNCS, vol. 4244, pp. 136–164. Springer, Heidelberg (2006). https://doi.org/10.1007/11890591_5
9. Elfeky, M.G., Verykios, V.S., Elmagarmid, A.K.: TAILOR: a record linkage toolbox. In: Proceedings of the 18th ICDE, pp. 17–28 (2002)
10. Gu, L., Baxter, R.: Decision models for record linkage. In: Williams, G.J., Simoff, S.J. (eds.) Data Mining. LNCS (LNAI), vol. 3755, pp. 146–160. Springer, Heidelberg (2006). https://doi.org/10.1007/11677437_12
11. Ravikumar, P., Cohen, W.W.: A hierarchical graphical model for record linkage. In: Proceedings of the 20th UAI, pp. 454–461 (2004)
12. Jurek, A., Deepak, P.: It pays to be certain: unsupervised record linkage via ambiguity minimization. In: Phung, D., Tseng, V.S., Webb, G.I., Ho, B., Ganji, M., Rashidi, L. (eds.) PAKDD 2018. LNCS (LNAI), vol. 10939, pp. 177–190. Springer, Cham (2018). https://doi.org/10.1007/978-3-319-93040-4_15
13. Peffers, K., Tuunanen, T., Rothenberger, M.A., Chatterjee, S.: A design science research methodology for information systems research. JMIS 24(3), 45–77 (2007)
14. Christen, P.: Data Matching: Concepts and Techniques for Record Linkage, Entity Resolution, and Duplicate Detection. Springer, Heidelberg (2012). https://doi.org/10.1007/978-3-642-31164-2
15. Elmagarmid, A.K., Ipeirotis, P.G., Verykios, V.S.: Duplicate record detection. A survey. IEEE Trans. Knowl. Data Eng. 19(1), 1–16 (2007)
16. Winkler, W.E.: Overview of record linkage and current research directions. U.S. Bureau of the Census (2006)
17. Tromp, M., Ravelli, A.C., Bonsel, G.J., Hasman, A., Reitsma, J.B.: Results from simulated data sets. Probabilistic record linkage outperforms deterministic record linkage. J. Clin. Epidemiol. 64(5), 565–572 (2011)
18. Hettiarachchi, G.P., Hettiarachchi, N.N., Hettiarachchi, D.S., Ebisuya, A.: Next generation data classification and linkage. Role of probabilistic models and artificial intelligence. In: Proceedings of the 4th IEEE GHTC, pp. 569–576 (2014)
19. Fellegi, I.P., Sunter, A.B.: A theory for record linkage. J. Am. Stat. Assoc. 64(328), 1183–1210 (1969)
20. Belin, T.R., Rubin, D.B.: A method for calibrating false-match rates in record linkage. J. Am. Stat. Assoc. 90(430), 694–707 (1995)
21. Steorts, R.C., Hall, R., Fienberg, S.E.: A Bayesian approach to graphical record linkage and deduplication. J. Am. Stat. Assoc. 111(516), 1660–1672 (2016)
22. Thibaudeau, Y.: The discrimination power of dependency structures in record linkage. U.S. Bureau of the Census (1992)
23. Winkler, W.E.: Improved decision rules in the Fellegi-Sunter model of record linkage. In: Proceedings of Survey Research Methods Section, pp. 274–279. American Statistical Association (1993)
24. Scott, D.W.: Multivariate Density Estimation. Theory, Practice, and Visualization. Wiley, Hoboken (2015)
25. Cohen, W., Ravikumar, P., Fienberg, S.: A comparison of string metrics for matching names and records. In: KDD Workshop on Data Cleaning, pp. 73–78 (2003)
26. Winkler, W.E.: String comparator metrics and enhanced decision rules in the Fellegi-Sunter model of record linkage. U.S. Bureau of the Census (1990)
27. Levenshtein, V.I.: Binary codes capable of correcting deletions, insertions, and reversals. Sov. Phys. Dokl. 10(8), 707–710 (1966)
28. Seabold, S., Perktold, J.: Statsmodels. Econometric and statistical modeling with python. In: Proceedings of the 9th Python in Science Conference, pp. 57–61 (2010)

29. Hoerl, A.E., Fallin, H.K.: Reliability of subjective evaluations in a high incentive situation. J. Roy. Stat. Soc. Ser. A (General) **137**(2), 227–230 (1974)
30. Murphy, A.H., Winkler, R.L.: Reliability of subjective probability forecasts of precipitation and temperature. Appl. Stat. **26**(1), 41–47 (1977)
31. Murphy, A.H., Winkler, R.L.: A general framework for forecast verification. Mon. Weather Rev. **115**(7), 1330–1338 (1987)
32. Sanders, F.: On subjective probability forecasting. J. Appl. Meteorol. **2**(2), 191–201 (1963)
33. Bröcker, J., Smith, L.A.: Increasing the reliability of reliability diagrams. Weather Forecast. **22**(3), 651–661 (2007)
34. Murphy, A.H.: A new vector partition of the probability score. J. Appl. Meteorol. **12**(4), 595–600 (1973)
35. Hanley, J.A., McNeil, B.J.: The meaning and use of the area under a receiver operating characteristic (ROC) curve. Radiology **143**(1), 29–36 (1982)
36. de Bruin, J.: Python Record Linkage Toolkit. https://github.com/J535D165/recordlinkage. Accessed 4 Jan 2019

Design Science Research Applications in Emerging Topics

Design Science Research for the Humanities – The Case of Prosopography

Jacky Akoka[1,2], Isabelle Comyn-Wattiau[3(✉)], Cédric du Mouza[1], and Nicolas Prat[3]

[1] CEDRIC-CNAM, Paris, France
jacky.akoka@lecnam.net, dumouza@cnam.fr
[2] TEM-Business School, Paris, France
[3] ESSEC Business School, Cergy, France
{wattiau,prat}@essec.edu

Abstract. The humanities focus on understanding human beings and cultures. They include such disciplines as history, literature, and the arts. Digital humanities, defined as the application of IT to research and teaching in the humanities, is well established as a field in its own right. More particularly, research in the humanities is in demand of innovative and useful IT artifacts. This makes it a relevant application area for design science research (DSR). This also raises specific challenges to DSR researchers, due to the specific stakeholders and knowledge domains that come into play in the digital humanities. This paper focuses on prosopography, a branch of digital humanities that represents and interprets historical data, sourced from texts describing historical person's life. Starting from typical issues addressed by prosopographical researchers, we identify relevant IT artifacts to address these issues, making DSR relevant for prosopographical research. We adapt and instantiate Hevner's DSR framework to the specific case of prosopography, as a first step towards defining a DSR framework for the humanities more generally. Based on this adapted and instantiated DSR framework, we propose two artifacts: requirements and a methodology for prosopography. We demonstrate the methodology on a prosopography scenario.

Keywords: Prosopography · Design science research · Requirements · Methodology · Digital humanities

1 Introduction

The humanities focus on understanding and defining human beings and cultures. They include such disciplines as history, anthropology, literature, art history, ethics, philosophy, and jurisprudence [1]. The relevance of IT for the humanities is epitomized by the term "digital humanities", "broadly defined to encompass the common ground between information technology and problems in humanities research and teaching" [2]. Traditionally, the terms "humanity computing" or "computing in the humanities" were used. The change of terms reflects a profound change [3]: while "humanities computing" implied that IT in the humanities was relegated to technical support, "digital humanities" is a field in its own right, requiring tight collaboration between IT

© Springer Nature Switzerland AG 2019
B. Tulu et al. (Eds.): DESRIST 2019, LNCS 11491, pp. 239–253, 2019.
https://doi.org/10.1007/978-3-030-19504-5_16

and humanities researchers. In this paper, while defining digital humanities as the applications of IT to research and teaching in the humanities, we focus on research.

Research in the humanities is in demand of innovative and useful IT artifacts. This makes research in the humanities a relevant application area for DSR. This also raises specific challenges to DSR researchers, due to the specific stakeholders and knowledge domains that come into play in the digital humanities. For example, DSR projects in the humanities build artifacts aimed at researchers in the humanities, as opposed to professionals in companies.

The research presented in this paper results from a collaboration between DSR researchers and historians, in the context of a joint project pertaining to prosopography. Prosopography is a domain of digital humanities, analyzing information on sets of individuals in the context of historical societies by means of a collective study of their lives [4]. This project is therefore a case in point to illustrate the relevance of DSR for digital humanities, and the need to adapt DSR for the humanities.

Over the past few decades, many historians have collected and analyzed data describing the individual lives of historical persons using prosopographical approaches. Prosopography is a branch of historical research targeting common characteristics of large groups of individuals that appear in historical sources, generally poorly documented. It aims at representing and interpreting historical data, sourced from texts describing historical persons' life. Despite progress in prosopographical research, there is still room for improvement in the following aspects: (1) Analysis of historical data depends heavily on the reliability and the quality of the source material (demographic, economic, administrative, religious, family archives, etc.). (2) Interpreting historical data suffers from the relative scarcity of source material. (3) Representing the time and uncertainty dimensions related to people, locations, events, and source material is crucial and remains an open issue. (4) Prosopography deals with information that is often incomplete, imprecise, and contradictory. Therefore, there is a need to develop data models accommodating all types of uncertainty including the one characterizing the dating phenomena. (5) Finally, the definition and the choice of a prosopographical methodology remains an open problem. In this study, we focus on formalizing a methodology whose purpose is to help prosopographical researchers. Our objective is to take advantage of DSR to provide researchers in prosopography with a set of requirements and the methodology supporting their needs. These artifacts can help them deal with the problems they encounter, especially those mentioned above.

This paper is organized as follows: Sect. 2 illustrates the relevance of DSR for prosopography. It presents typical IT artifacts that are relevant to prosopography, and identifies the research gaps by pointing out artifacts that have not been developed yet or are at an early development stage. In Sect. 3, we adapt and instantiate Hevner's DSR framework [5, 6] for prosopography, as a first step towards defining a DSR framework for the humanities more generally. In Sect. 4, we present a set of requirements characterizing prosopographical projects. A methodology is proposed in Sect. 5 fulfilling these requirements. The methodology is demonstrated in Sect. 6, using an illustrative scenario based on the Studium Parisiense prosopographical database. Finally, the conclusion and future work are discussed in Sect. 7.

2   Design Science Research and Prosopography

DSR has been the subject of growing attention within the IS community and has become a distinctive research paradigm. With its focus on the creation of artifacts to solve real-life problems, DSR consists in building and evaluating artifacts [5, 7]. Many different authors have defined the notion of DSR artifact. March and Smith proposed an artifact typology composed of four categories: constructs, models, methods, or instantiations [7]. Winter has added a fifth category called theory [8]. Samuel-Ojo et al. have considered a fifth category called better design theories [9]. Offermann et al. have proposed a typology of artifacts based on a literature review of all DESRIST publications and a special MISQ issue on design science [10]. In this paper, we use the typology of Sangupamba Mwilu et al. [11] which details the artifact types of [7] as follows: construct (language, meta-model, concept), model (system design, ontology, taxonomy, framework, architecture, requirement), method (methodology, guideline, algorithm, method fragment, metric), and instantiation (implemented system, example). In Table 1, we illustrate some relevant artifacts for prosopographical research, thereby illustrating the relevance of DSR for prosopography. The artifact types are shown in italics.

Table 1. Some relevant artifacts for prosopographical research.

Issue	Relevant artifacts
Schematically represent statements about persons in historical sources	Factoid (*concept*), prosopographical database (*implemented system*)
Extract named entities to automatically find persons, places, and facts in historical sources	Named entity resolution (*ontology*, *algorithm*)
Represent time	*Ontology*
Manage uncertainty	Query *language* taking uncertainty into account, *ontology* representing uncertainty, algebra of fuzzy sets (*language*)
Choose among historical sources	*Metrics* assessing the quality of sources
Study historical social networks	Social network analysis (*algorithm*)
Infer historical knowledge from sources	Machine learning (*algorithm*)
Support the whole prosopographical research process	*Methodology*, *guidelines*, associated *ontologies* and conceptual models (*system design*)

In our view, any prosopographical project can benefit from Hevner's framework. Indeed, most prosopographic projects verify most of its features. A limited number of projects use the factoid model to represent prosopographical data [12]. A notable example is Prosopography of Anglo-Saxon England (PASE), based on a factoid model, composed of assertions made by the project team that a source "S" at location "L" states something ("F") about person "P" [13]. Another example of a project based on the factoid model is the Roman Republic project [14]. Besides, constructs such as the concepts of event, time, and uncertainty are used by many prosopographical projects, such as PASE, Studium Parisiense, Prosopography of the Byzantine Empire, China Biographical Database Project, The Making of Charlemagne's Europe, and Paradox of Medieval Scotland [15].

Event, time, and uncertainty are central to any prosopographical project. In the event-based approach [16], a person can play different roles. Events are linked to other events, persons, places, time periods, and documents. Time can be the source of vagueness and/or uncertainty. Allen proposes a time model based on time intervals [17]. The time model in AROM-ST [18] offers several time types including instant, interval, multiInstant, and multiInterval types. Uncertainty is defined as "a general concept that reflects our lack of sureness about something or someone" [19]. In the URREF ontology [20], uncertainty encompasses a variety of aspects including ambiguity, incompleteness, vagueness, randomness, and inconsistency. These uncertainties may be supported by different uncertainty models or theories, such as probability theory, possibility theory, fuzzy sets, etc.

Most existing digital prosopography projects use relational databases. However, no prosopographical project uses conceptual modeling to derive the associated logical model, such as the relational one. Let us mention a recent paper proposing a generic conceptual model for prosopographical databases [21]. In addition, an important artifact is missing in most prosopographical projects: a structured methodology encompassing the whole prosopographical research process. In our view, this methodology must be derived from an exhaustive set of requirements. For a prosopographical project to be considered a DSR project, these two aspects (a set of requirements and a methodology) must be provided. This is precisely the purpose of this article.

3 Positioning DSR for Prosopography in Hevner's DSR Framework

In this paper, we are concerned with the development and the evaluation of prosopographical projects. Our aim is to produce two artifacts (a set of requirements and a methodology) that are useful to historians.

Figure 1 provides an overview of [5] framework for information systems research instantiated with the main elements of prosopographical context. The framework makes explicit two modes (develop/build and justify/evaluate) and links these to business needs (relevance) and applicable knowledge (rigour). In order to position DSR for prosopography in Hevner's framework, we map the elements characterizing prosopographical projects in the framework.

Hevner et al. argue that the business need is "assessed within the context of organizational strategies, structures, culture and existing business processes". In our case, historians are the people involved in prosopographical projects using database technologies. The business needs are expressed by the means of requirements.

According to Hevner et al., "the knowledge base provides the raw materials from and through which IS research is accomplished". In our case, foundations and methodologies refer to both IS and prosopography domains. Prosopographical projects use models (conceptual and quality models), methodologies like database design,

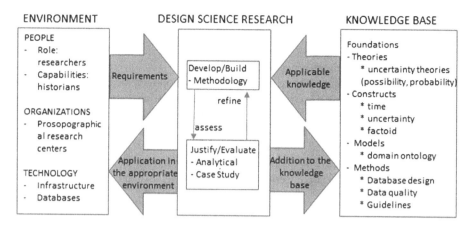

Fig. 1. Adaptation and instantiation of Hevner's DSR framework for prosopographical projects

ontologies such as CIDOC-CRM, theories (possibility theory, probability theory, or fuzzy set theory for uncertainty management), data analysis and data quality metrics. All these elements constitute the applicable knowledge.

Requirements ("business needs" in [5]) are inputs to the relevance cycle [6]. Thus, they play a key role in Hevner's DSR framework. To measure the extent to which DSR in prosopographical research differs from typical DSR (where requirements are business needs expressed by practitioners), the "four worlds" of requirements engineering [22] are illuminating. These four worlds are the subject world (application domain), the usage world (organizational context), the system world (IT artifact, in DSR vocabulary), and the development world (corresponding to the world of DSR researchers). According to Jarke and Pohl, the four worlds differ in their stakeholders, areas of expertise, and languages, among other things [22].

Focusing on the usage world and the subject world, we see fundamental differences between typical DSR and DSR in prosopography:

- In typical DSR, the usage world consists in business users (practitioners) in an organizational context. Their requirements correspond to business needs. In DSR for prosopographical research, historians constitute the usage world. Thus, DSR researchers build and evaluate artifacts for other researchers whose organizations are research laboratories or universities. This raises many issues. For example, what does usefulness mean in this case? It is not "practical" usefulness as in typical DSR. Is action research still applicable to artifact building and evaluation in this context and if so, how should it be adapted?
- In typical DSR, the subject world is a functional and/or a business activity area (for example, marketing in the domain of consumer packaged goods). In DSR for prosopography, the domain is history, which has its specific theories and, more generally, knowledge bases. These knowledge bases are far from the traditional knowledge bases of DSR researchers, whose culture typically combines the disciplines of engineering and management.

Thus, DSR for prosopography is radically different from typical DSR, both as regards the environment (e.g., stakeholders), and the knowledge bases. This implies a fundamental change in the DSR framework, and we contend that this is also true of DSR in the humanities more generally.

DSR must produce and evaluate novel artifacts. Prosopographical research seeks to achieve this by developing a methodology supporting historians' research activities. In order to ensure the methodology is useful to prosopographical researchers, we perform an evaluation using an illustrative scenario based on the prosopographical database Studium Parisiense [23].

In this section, we have shown that Hevner's framework is appropriate for our purpose. The two artifacts are described in the following sections.

4   Requirements for Prosopographical Projects

Baskerville et al. discuss the nature of the relation between requirements and designed artifacts reflecting about the fit/misfit between a set of requirements and one or more designed solutions [24]. Patas et al. elaborated some reflections about the relation between requirements and components [25].

By capitalizing on the work of Baekgaard [26], we consider that prosopographic requirements represent a design artifact of DSR. A state of the art on requirements in DSR is presented by Braun et al. [27]. Hevner considers that the relevance cycle initiates design science research with an application context that provides the requirements for the research [6].

Requirements engineering consists mainly in eliciting, analyzing business needs, and translating them into specifications [28]. Thus, we have parsed the seminal paper entitled *A Short Manual to the Art of Prosopography* [29] and interpreted its content in terms of IS requirements. The resulting specification is expressed using natural language. Table 2 lists the main requirements that characterize a prosopographical project and, in italics, a partial citation of the corresponding paragraph found in [29].

Historical sources used by historians are characterized by partial data on people, places and events. Therefore, R3 allows us to deal with this problem. In addition, prosopography research uses sources from different countries and exploited by researchers using different languages. In order to deal with this peculiarity of proso-pographical projects, we introduce R4. The presence of R5 is explained by the fact that several decision points are based on the expertise of historians. Thus, the tasks relating to the identification of sources, to their qualification, to the definition of needs as well as to obtaining good arbitrations belong to the expertise of the researchers in prosopog-raphy. In addition, existing ontologies do not consider relative evaluation. Traceability in prosopography is the capability to trace historical events. It is interpreted as the ability to verify historical persons' lives, their location by means of recorded identification. Given the fact that traceability is a fundamental characteristic of prosopography, R6 is needed. R8 can be justified by the fact that historians are not just using sources to create a narrative, but they are also analyzing them. They tend to compare a source to other sources: looking at a variety of sources to find out whether they converge or diverge on a topic and detecting inaccuracies. R10 is a data quality issue. The idea of prosopography

Table 2. Main requirements of prosopographical research projects.

R1: Design a database describing the target population including a step devoted to defining the requirements in terms of geographic, chronological and thematic scope (*By 'prosopography' we mean the database and the listing of all persons from a specific milieu defined chronologically and geographically established preparatory to a processing of the prosopographical material from various historical angles*)

R2: Write queries to the database in order to interpret, summarize and present the results (*It is meant to answer questions that transcend the simple clear-cut answers in the questionnaire... Prosopography is more than constructing and building a databank from which answers to research questions flow forth automatically*)

R3: Manage missing data (*dealing with missing data and its repercussions*)

R4: Manage multilingualism specificities (*More and more prosopographical research is being conducted by international research teams*)

R5: Integrate the domain knowledge which allows to prefer one source to another (*Not all sources are equally suitable for prosopographical inquiries... An honorary inscription with a full career list is more valuable than a votive inscription*)

R6: Manage traceability requirements, i.e. sourcing all the information (*The application of strict historical criticism to each scrap of source material is essential. To do so requires knowing the prime source from which the data originate. One must always strive to be able to evaluate with what purpose the source provides these data... it is necessary to link every fact to a source or reference*)

R7: Manage contradictory information (*When two sources contradict each other, we can at least choose one or the other interpretation on rational grounds*)

R8: Manage inaccurate information (*which fact is derived from a primary source and which is derived from secondary literature*)

R9: Questionnaire handling: Handle the questionnaire in a flexible way, i.e. open questions, free text or open list of answer choices (*in most cases the realities of research teach us that the questionnaire has to be handled in a flexible way... Depending on the historical period ... and the nature and size of the prosopographical population, the questionnaire will contain 'open' or multiple-choice questions*)

R10: Manage the data entry process: the latter should include a pilot phase that prowls the questionnaire so that it can then better define multiple-choice answers (*Especially at the start of a new research project it is preferable to gather as much information as possible without directly standardizing the structure of the answers*)

R11: Manage fields with multiple values (*naming, if necessary, the variants... in some cases it is advisable to standardize the name*)

R12: Manage dates with imprecisions: dates can be defined by intervals possibly "fuzzy" *terminus post quem* (limit after which) and *terminus ante quem* (limit before which) (*life dates (birth, marriage, etc.)... often these are termini post or ante quem*)

R13: Manage the data entry process. The latter may require a large collection phase, followed by a phase of duplication or reconciliation when the quality of the sources does not allow from the outset to distinguish homonymous individuals for example or to bring together synonymous elements (*It is important to work pragmatically while filling in the database and to further structure the mass of data, allowing us to keep asking new research questions and to combine different sorts of information*)

R14: Manage the levels of information. Two levels of information may be considered (raw data and interpretation) (*presenting both the prosopographical database (and possible synoptic tables) and the interpretations*)s is, nevertheless, to move from unstructured information available in sources that are, at best, texts in natural language (sometimes signs on stones or objects in archaeological excavations) to structured information in a database, more easily used for analysis, hence the challenge of data quality. R11 is of great importance since there exist many fields with multiple values, for example proper names that are a subject in itself (onomastics). It is for this reason that there is a stage of the prosopographical method which is onomastics, at the end of which we must have a standardization of a name or an identifier for people. R14 points out two levels of information. The first one corresponds to the raw information extracted from the source. The second one is related to a more interpreted information resulting from a judgment by a historian.

Transforming the requirements into a relevant useful implemented system requires a DSR methodology dedicated to prosopographical projects. We present such a methodology in the next section.

5 A Methodology for Prosopographical Research

A methodology supporting historians is of substantial importance in prosopographical research, helping them to structure their research process. Let us remind that a prosopographical project aims at selecting a target group of people that share desired characteristics for solving the research question at hand. Such projects require implemented systems such as databases to facilitate the analysis of the target group of people. Thus a methodology supporting the prosopographical research process combines tasks dedicated to historians as well as tasks undertaken by DSR researchers. As shown in Fig. 2, the methodology consists of sixteen steps, extending the approach proposed by De Ridder-Symoens [30].

The proposed methodology is a tight interweaving of tasks performed by historians and by DSR researchers. In steps 1, 2, 3, 6, 13, 14, 15, and 16, historians are main actors. Steps 4, 5, 10, 11, and 12 are the purview of information system specialists. Finally, steps 7, 8, and 9 need a tight collaboration between specialists from the two domains, or researchers with combined expertise in both fields. For space reasons, we only describe below the main features of these tasks:

- Step 1 (Research questions) aims at determining the general research objective, defining the research questions, and formulating general working hypotheses. It might be necessary to formulate explanatory and/or predictive models. It comes down to defining in advance the desired results.
- Step 2 (Scope definition) aims at defining the target population (i.e. the group of persons to be studied) and the geographic, demographic, chronological, and thematic boundaries. It encompasses formulating specific working hypotheses and specific historical questions concerning the target group. Sometimes the thematic boundaries are complex and must be refined iteratively. As an example, identifying mathematicians in a medieval university when mathematics is not a discipline requires the elicitation of other information.
- Step 3 (Sources identification and qualification) consists in identifying the sources likely to facilitate the answer to the research questions. The historian reads and

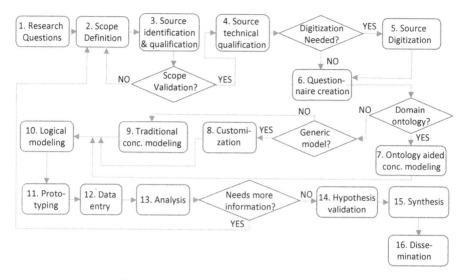

Fig. 2. Main steps of the proposed methodology

analyzes source material and the general historical and theoretical literature. A special effort should be devoted to the issue of uncertainty and the reputation of these sources.

- Step 4 (Source technical qualification) determines whether some relevant sources must be digitized. The IS researcher evaluates the quality of information in the sources. She also estimates the proportion of quantitative data.
- Step 5 (Digitization) consists in transforming historical sources into digital format. It is required when some relevant sources were not yet digitized. Many digitization techniques are available [31] and are out of the scope of this paper.
- Step 6 (Questionnaire creation) develops prosopographical notices for each person in the group under study. The problems related to the ambiguity of certain data contained in these notices are to be considered.
- Steps 7, 8 and 9 are dedicated to conceptual modeling. Depending on the proso-pographical project, we propose three alternative ways to conduct this conceptual modeling. If a domain ontology is available, Step 7 is performed based on this ontology such as recommended in [32]. Otherwise, a generic conceptual model may be customized as proposed in [21]. If the latter is not appropriate, a traditional (without the help of ontologies) conceptual modeling is conducted.
- Step 10 (Logical modeling) takes into account on the one hand the queries and, on the other hand, the technical qualification of the sources, to opt for a relational database (DB) (data very structured, controllable volumes, queries well managed by SQL), a document DB (very voluminous text data, wish to query in full text), a graph DB (queries mainly focused on the links between individuals, the course of individuals, etc.), a graph-document DB (mix of the two previous cases), etc.

- Step 12 (Data entry) can take several forms, including manual data entry, migration from existing systems, automatic acquisition after digitization. The more integrity constraints are present, the more data quality may be improved.
- Step 13 (Analysis) performs statistical analysis, in particular using statistical techniques, data analysis, and Artificial Intelligence (AI) techniques.
- Step 14 (Hypothesis validation) allows historians to validate or infirm their hypotheses and, depending on data, define explanatory and/or predictive models.
- Step 15 (Synthesis) synthesizes the results by combining and interpreting the data and sketches a wide historical context.
- Step 16 (Dissemination) makes results available for all historians.

In terms of IS research, the main tasks involve artifact building. Moreover, Steps 1, 13 and 14 may encompass the preparation, development and validation of explanatory models. This methodology is the result of an enrichment of the principles proposed in [30] which correspond to Steps 1, 2, 3, 6, 13, 14, 15, and 16. We added the routine design steps as described by engineers who work for historians (Steps 5, 10, 11, and 12). Finally, we completed the methodology with steps enriching the approach with new DSR artifacts. Step 4 is a prerequisite for evaluating data quality, data volume, categorizing data types (numeric data, images, text, etc.), thus anticipating quality issues. Steps 7, 8 and 9 are alternative ways to perform conceptual modeling in this context borrowing from the literature. We submitted a first version of the methodology to historians. They partially validated it. We identified the need for better separating the tasks depending on who is in charge. As an example, Steps 3 and 4 result from splitting one step in our first version. We also added the two alternatives *Scope Validation* and *Needs more information* in order to better stick to their practice. They also suggested to add iterations at each step. But, for clarity reasons, we did not add all these iterations in the figure. Finally, they were very interested in such a representation of their scientific process. They were also convinced that they need uncertainty management, conceptual modeling, and, more generally, they were very interested in the efforts that could improve the genericity of IT artifacts developed for supporting prosopographical research. This allows us to validate the usefulness of the methodology. This usefulness may be largely improved by providing each step with guidelines.

The next section demonstrates the methodology, based on an illustrative scenario defined with historians in the context of the joint project mentioned in the introduction.

6   Demonstration of the Methodology

Five possible DSR genres have been described by Peffers et al. [33], namely Information Systems Theory, Design-Oriented Research Methodology, Explanatory Design Theory, Action Design Research, and Design Science Research Methodology (DSRM). The latter focuses on applicable artifact development. The authors view the process as a flexible one and less concerned with design rigor. According to these authors, DSRM does not require that the design should be based on formal theory. Finally, in this genre, artifact evaluation does not necessitate a formal process embedded in the design effort. We argue that the methodology described above fits into this genre. Capitalizing on

Peffers' genres, we perform a demonstration based on an illustrative scenario, which is a simple method, but one of the three most common evaluation techniques [34]. In terms of the taxonomy of evaluation methods of Prat et al. [34], the evaluation method used here is characterized as follows: *criterion* = efficacy; *evaluation technique* = illustrative scenario; *form of evaluation* = analysis or logical reasoning; *secondary participants* = researchers (historians in the present case); *level of evaluation* = real example or examples (a real research question and real data), *relativeness of evaluation* = absolute.

The illustrative scenario is related to the Studium Parisiense project. This project aims at creating an online biographical-bibliographic database describing members of Paris' schools and university since the appearance of the cathedral school at the end of the XIth century until the end of the Middle Ages (around 1500). The project currently totals more than 16,000 records, of which almost 9,000 are already digitized using an XML format. Each individual is described by a structured sheet that gives all the known biographical information (origin, university curriculum, ecclesiastical career, place of residence, writings—more than 10% of the individuals are authors). Historians complain that their current database does not allow them sophisticated queries and are aware of new possibilities offered by more recent technologies. Thus, they accepted to unfold with us the steps of our methodology. They proposed many research questions. For space reasons, we only provide some of them below:

- *How many students are enrolled in the whole Paris University? Globally, between the clergy and laypeople, according to the origins, between the arts and medicine, etc.? These are complex queries since Paris University did not have a register. Unlike other universities in Europe, students only registered with a master.*
- *How are students' courses organized? What are the practices regarding the successions of disciplines? The rules for obtaining all grades and the official duration of courses are known but what is the difference between these rules and practice?*
- *I am interested in Italian students who have spent time at the University of Paris, to measure the impact of this stay on their career.*
- *How did certain fields of knowledge develop at this period? As an example, mathematics was not a discipline, but I would like to extract all the individuals showing interest in topics like arithmetic, algebra, etc.*

The historians had already performed source identification and qualification as part of an earlier project creating the XML database. We performed the technical qualification of sources and decided that the first prototype would be built by limiting ourselves to the migration of the XML database. However, this migration will not only transfer the data from the old system to the new one. It will also dedicate some effort in structuring more information and encoding uncertainty such that automatic querying may take it into account. Our technical qualification of data contained in the current database allowed us to note that when historians entered information in the database, they introduced one or more question marks. The current questionnaire thus must be adapted in order to make it easier to take into account the level of confidence in data. To the best of our knowledge, there is no ontology depicting specifically their research domain. Thus they plan to use the generic model and the customization process proposed by Akoka et al. [21]. Given the nature of the data and the research questions present and anticipable, after presenting the interest of the different logical models, the graph database is preferred. They do not need to store documents. Many of their questions require only simple statistics. However, we also suggested them to look for pattern identification in students' paths. The graph database will also allow the visualization of social networks of students (Step 15). This illustrative scenario allows us to demonstrate the utility of our approach. Historians have indicated the interest of the approach in structuring their approach and appreciating the possibilities of improvement thanks to a better appropriation of data modeling tools and the representation of uncertain information.

In this paragraph, we describe briefly how our methodology meets the list of requirements identified in Sect. 4. Table 3 maps the requirements to the steps of the methodology. Let us notice that requirements R4, R5, R6, R7, R8, and R12 are all covered by the conceptual modeling steps in the sense that we propose to model uncertainty at this level, thus encompassing accuracy, completeness, and all data quality criteria.

Table 3. Mapping between requirements and steps of the methodology

Requirement	Step
R1: Database needed	11 (Prototyping)
R2: Complex queries	13 (Analysis)
R3: Manage missing data	4 (Source technical qualification)
R4: Multilingualism	7 or 8 or 9 (Conceptual modeling)
R5: Domain knowledge	7 or 8 or 9 (Conceptual modeling)
R6: Traceability	7 or 8 or 9 (Conceptual modeling)
R7: Manage contradictions	7 or 8 or 9 (Conceptual modeling)
R8: Manage inaccuracies	7 or 8 or 9 (Conceptual modeling)
R9: Questionnaire handling	6 (Questionnaire creation)
R10: Data entry process	12 (Data entry)
R11: Multivalue fields	10 (Logical modeling)
R12: Manage dates	7 or 8 or 9 (Conceptual modeling)
R13: Data entry process	12 (Data entry)
R14: Multi-level information	15 (Synthesis)

7   Conclusion and Further Research

Digital humanities encompass a wide range of research, such as digitizing ancient manuscripts, building spatio-temporal visualizations, analyzing large collections of data, practicing innovative pedagogy based on digital resources, etc. In this paper, we contributed to research in the digital humanities by addressing the prosopographical approach used by historians studying ancient social networks. Here, we distinguish between design research, which "is aimed at creating solutions to specific classes of relevant problems by using a rigorous construction and evaluation process", and design science, which "reflects the design research process and aims at creating standards for its rigor" [8]. We contributed to design science by adapting Hevner's DSR framework to prosopography. Our paper is also part of design research in that we propose two original artifacts: (1) a set of requirements describing the context of historians who use prosopography as a research method, (2) a methodology that both sequences and combines the tasks of historians and DSR researchers at a fine-grained level. A first evaluation of the methodology is proposed in the paper.

Future research will take different paths: (1) evaluating the methodology by applying it to a real case study, (2) developing guidelines to enrich each step of the method, (3) identifying missing artifacts for prosopographical researchers, and (4) extend the framework to other digital humanities research approaches.

Acknowledgements. This research has been partly funded by a national French grant (ANR Daphne 17-CE28-0013-01).

References

1. Humanities Council of Washington, DC. Defining the humanities – A work in progress (2001). http://www.wdchumanities.org/docs/defininghumanities.pdf
2. Alliance of Digital Humanities Organizations. Digital Humanities 2009 – Call for papers (2009). https://mith.umd.edu/dh09/index.html%3Fpage_id=54.html
3. Berry, D.M.: Introduction: understanding the digital humanities. In: Berry, D.M. (ed.) Understanding Digital Humanities, pp. 1–20. Palgrave Macmillan, London (2012). https://doi.org/10.1057/9780230371934_1
4. Stone, L.: Prosopography. Daedalus **100**(1), 46–79 (1970)
5. Hevner, A.R., March, S.T., Park, J., Ram, S.: Design science in information systems research. MIS Q. **28**(1), 75–105 (2004)
6. Hevner, A.R.: A three cycle view of design science research. Scand. J. Inf. Syst. **19**(2), 4 (2007)
7. March, S.T., Smith, G.F.: Design and natural science research on information technology. Decis. Support Syst. **15**(4), 251–266 (1995)
8. Winter, R.: Design science research in Europe. Eur. J. Inf. Syst. **17**(5), 470–475 (2008)
9. Samuel-Ojo, O., et al.: Meta-analysis of design science research within the IS community: trends, patterns, and outcomes. In: Winter, R., Zhao, J.L., Aier, S. (eds.) DESRIST 2010. Lecture Notes in Computer Science, vol. 6105, pp. 124–138. Springer, Heidelberg (2010). https://doi.org/10.1007/978-3-642-13335-0_9
10. Offermann, P., Blom, S., Schönherr, M., Bub, U.: Artifact types in information systems design science – a literature review. In: Winter, R., Zhao, J.L., Aier, S. (eds.) DESRIST 2010. LNCS, vol. 6105, pp. 77–92. Springer, Heidelberg (2010). https://doi.org/10.1007/978-3-642-13335-0_6
11. Sangupamba Mwilu, O., Comyn-Wattiau, I., Prat, N.: Design science research contribution to business intelligence in the cloud – a systematic literature review. Future Gener. Comput. Syst. **63**, 108–122 (2016)
12. Pasin, M., Bradley, J.: Factoid-based prosopography and computer ontologies: towards an integrated approach. Digit. Sch. Humanit. **30**(1), 86–97 (2013)
13. Bradley, J., Short, H.: Texts into databases: the evolving field of new-style prosopography. Lit. Linguist. Comput. **20**(Suppl.), 3–24 (2005)

14. Figueira, L., Vieira, M.: Modelling a Prosopography for the Roman Republic (2017). https://dh2017.adho.org/abstracts/091/091.pdf
15. Bradley, J., Pasin, M.: Annotation and ontology in most humanities research: accommodating a more informal interpretation context. In: NeDiMaH Ontology Workshop (2012)
16. Westermann, U., Jain, R.: Toward a common event model for multimedia applications. IEEE Multimedia **14**(1), 19–29 (2007)
17. Allen, J.F.: Maintaining knowledge about temporal intervals. Commun. ACM **26**(11), 832–843 (1983)
18. Moisuc, B., Miron, A., Villanova-Olivier, M., Gensel, J.: Spatiotemporal knowledge representation in AROM-ST. In: Innovative Software Development in GIS, pp. 91–119 (2012)
19. National Research Council (US): Risk Analysis and Uncertainty in Flood Reduction Studies. National Academies Press, Washington, D.C. (2000)
20. Costa, P.C.G., Laskey, K.B., Blasch, E., Jousselme, A.L.: Towards unbiased evaluation of uncertainty reasoning: the URREF ontology. In: International Conference on Information Fusion (2012)
21. Akoka, J., Comyn-Wattiau, I., Lamassé, S., Du Mouza, C.: Modeling historical social networks databases. In: Proceedings of the 52nd HICCS Conference (2019)
22. Jarke, M., Pohl, K.: Establishing visions in context: toward a model of requirements processes. In: Proceedings of the 14th International Conference on Information Systems (ICIS), AIS (1993)
23. Genet, J.P., Idabal, H., Kouamé, T., Lamassé, S., Priol, C., Tournieroux, A.: General introduction to the stadium project. Mediev. Prosopogr. **31**, 156–172 (2016)
24. Baskerville, R., Pries-Heje, J., Venable, J.: Soft design science methodology. In: Proceedings of the 4th DESRIST Conference. ACM, p. 9 (2009)
25. Patas, J., Milicevic, D., Goeken, M.: Enhancing design science through empirical knowledge: framework and application. In: Jain, H., Sinha, A.P., Vitharana, P. (eds.) DESRIST 2011. LNCS, vol. 6629, pp. 32–46. Springer, Heidelberg (2011). https://doi.org/10.1007/978-3-642-20633-7_3
26. Baekgaard, L.: Conceptual model of artifacts for design science research. In: Twenty-First Americas Conference on Information Systems, Puerto Rico (2015)
27. Braun, R., Benedict, M., Wendler, H., Esswein, W.: Proposal for Requirements Driven Design Science Research. In: Donnellan, B., Helfert, M., Kenneally, J., VanderMeer, D., Rothenberger, M., Winter, R. (eds.) DESRIST 2015. LNCS, vol. 9073, pp. 135–151. Springer, Cham (2015). https://doi.org/10.1007/978-3-319-18714-3_9
28. Sommerville, I.: Software Engineering. International Computer Science Series. Addison Wesley, Boston (2004)
29. Verboven, K., Carlier, M., Dumolyn, J.: A short manual to the art of prosopography. In: Keats-Rohan, K.S.B. (ed.) Prosopography Approaches and Applications. A Handbook, pp. 35–69. Unit for Prosopographical Research (Linacre College), Oxford (2007)
30. De Ridder-Symoens, H.: Prosopografie en middeleeuwse geschiedenis: een onmogelijke mogelijkheid?. Handelingen der Maatschappij voor Geschiedenis en Oudheidkunde te Gent, **45**(1) (1991)
31. Barbero, B.R., Ureta, E.S.: Comparative study of different digitization techniques and their accuracy. Comput.-Aided Des. **43**(2), 188–206 (2011)
32. Sugumaran, V., Storey, V.C.: The role of domain ontologies in database design: an ontology management and conceptual modeling environment. ACM Trans. Database Syst. **31**(3), 1064–1094 (2006)

33. Peffers, K., Tuunanen, T., Niehaves, B.: Design science research genres: introduction to the special issue on exemplars and criteria for applicable design science research. Eur. J. Inf. Syst. **27**(2), 129–139 (2018)
34. Prat, N., Comyn-Wattiau, I., Akoka, J.: A taxonomy of evaluation methods for information systems artifacts. J. Manag. Inf. Syst. **32**(3), 229–267 (2015)

Mapping Data Associations in Enterprise Systems

Tamara Babaian$^{(\boxtimes)}$, Wendy Lucas, and Alina Chircu

Bentley University, Waltham, MA 02452, USA
{tbabaian,wlucas,achircu}@bentley.edu

Abstract. The use of visualizations to access and process enterprise data has been proposed as a boost to the usability of enterprise systems. Yet, novel user interfaces do not always yield the expected gains in performance. To realize the potential benefits from using a visual approach, it is important to examine the effectiveness of visualizations in a specific task context and to follow an itera- tive, evaluation-driven process for identifying and addressing shortcomings in their design and execution. In this paper, we present the results of a study examining the effectiveness of a visual interface called Association Map (AM) for exploring ternary associations of data versus a typical tabular interface from a popular enterprise system. This latest version of AM evolved from earlier versions that underwent similar evaluations and we discuss the design choices that were important for achieving user performance gains in accuracy and time- on-task compared to earlier versions and to table-based interfaces. Findings presented here help build the case for incorporating task-driven visual interfaces into traditional table-based representations used in enterprise systems to improve both the user experience and task-related outcomes. Furthermore, they provide insights for investigating the theoretical foundations behind what makes a visual interface work.

Keywords: Human-computer interaction · Interactive visual interfaces · Information systems · Enterprise systems · Visualization techniques · Association Map

1 Introduction

Interactive visualizations are instrumental in a variety of domains, ranging from medical training to climate science to news reporting. They have yet to gain a foothold, however, in the more mundane systems in ubiquitous use for managing daily work processes. Years of observatory and empirical research on hurdles faced by users of enterprise systems have highlighted the need for more intuitive interfaces [4, 18].

Our research is motivated by the goal of advancing the state of enterprise software by incorporating visual interfaces that improve the experience and outcomes for users of enterprise systems. While studies have shown that such users would benefit from and would like access to these kinds of interfaces [13, 15, 24], their use in process-oriented systems remains limited. Most workplace systems still employ table- and form-based interfaces for decision making and other tasks requiring data analysis and manipulation.

© Springer Nature Switzerland AG 2019
B. Tulu et al. (Eds.): DESRIST 2019, LNCS 11491, pp. 254–268, 2019.
https://doi.org/10.1007/978-3-030-19504-5_17

At the same time, studies of enterprise system users have shown that both novices and experienced users prefer interfaces with useful visualizations, expressing their opinion that visual approaches help them cope with complexity [1, 15].

Interactive visualizations are employed more and more prominently in business reporting, story-telling and journalism, but their use as interfaces to data-intensive tasks in workplace applications is less common. Embedding off-the-shelf visual approaches in workplace information systems does not always work, since workplace tasks often require fine-tuning of the general approach to meet specific task context and needs [24].

The research presented here follows the design research approach [12, 20, 32] to create an interactive visual interface, called an Association Map (AM), for representing associations between three entity types (see Figs. 1, 2 and 3). The relevance of the work to practice arises from the fact that ternary relationships, such as those represented by AM commonly occur in enterprise decision making contexts. Examples include doctors treating patients for specific conditions, or businesses providing services to different clients. These relationships are typically presented in a tabular format, with each association recorded in a set of rows of associated items, as can be seen in Fig. 4. The figure presents a snapshot of the Oracle Reports – an enterprise system interface displaying an association of materials, vendors supplying them, and plants using the materials. As in most other major enterprise systems, the tabular interface employs selection and sorting features, like those of Excel, to access and manipulate the data. Despite the popularity of spreadsheets, relying on Excel for enterprise analysis and reporting tasks is considered to be detrimental to the accuracy and immediacy of that analysis. Instead, employees are encouraged to perform all tasks within the enterprise system to avoid errors and ensure completeness [7]. Use of visualizations within enterprise systems has been proposed as a way to boost usability and prevent the users' circumventing the system via workarounds [16]. The AM2.0 interface exemplifies this approach.

We have conducted a design study with multiple iterations of a design-evaluation cycle, using laboratory experiments for a rigorous evaluation of the usefulness and suitability of the design artifact, the Association Map, to enterprise system tasks. Laboratory evaluations were followed by a thorough, theoretically and empirically motivated analysis, leading to redesign and extensions of the interface reported in prior publications. In this paper we make the following contributions:

- We report on a comparison study of AM2.0 – the latest version of the AM interface – with a typical table-based representation from Oracle SQL Developer. The experimental evaluation shows statistically significant comparisons in favor of AM2.0 for measurements of time, correctness, and user satisfaction.
- Studies of earlier versions of AM [1, 2] found they compared favorably to their tabular counterparts in terms of task completion time, user preferences, and perceived mental effort; correctness comparisons, however, were not definitive. Here we report the improvements made in AM2.0, which incorporated user suggestions and lessons learned from those earlier evaluations.

These findings help build the case for incorporating visual interfaces into workplace information systems; furthermore, the evolution of the AM interface and its comparison with table-based interfaces provides a case for investigating the theoretical foundations behind what makes a visual interface work.

2 Related Work

Despite the explosion in visualization research, studies that place interactive visualizations in the context of workplace systems and specific tasks are relatively rare.

Chang et al. developed a visual interface for fraud detection in financial transactions [6]. The Strings-and-Beads visualization and the search-by-example technique, which they developed in the process, demonstrate that developing and deploying tools for real-world settings leads to development of novel approaches, representations and algorithms, motivated by the demands of one application, yet having wide applicability beyond that particular application.

Dilla and Raschke [8] present an overview and analysis of the visual tools for accounting fraud detection developed so far. They also analyze the requirements on the visual interfaces for fraud detection and propose research questions investigating the efficacy of visual interlaces based on the properties of the task, its cognitive demands, and characteristics of the decision maker, such as level of expertise and cognitive style. They use cognitive fit theory [28] to perform their analysis.

Sedlmair et al. developed MostVis - a visual interface for searching and browsing a hierarchical catalog used by engineers of an automotive company [23, 24]. In user studies the tool compared favorably to the existing text-based tools on tasks requiring browsing, cross-checking, grouping and analysis of data, when used by both novice and expert users. In the process of iterative development of MostVis, researchers adapted the generic visualization and added features, motivated by the engineers' work practices, to support search, grouping, list-view of the results, history tracking, exporting and printing. These interaction features added to the visualization in MostViz are also appropriate for AM, as using data in an engineering or business context usually does not end with simply reviewing it to find an answer to a question.

Recognizing the need for theoretical foundations of the interdisciplinary field of interactive visualizations, researchers are working on combining theories of perception and cognition, interaction design and usability methods to define and understand the phenomena behind visualization effectiveness (e.g. [21, 22, 26]). A lot of attention is directed at empirical studies evaluating the efficacy of specific kinds of visualization for specific tasks, as in comparisons of visualizations of hierarchical structures (e.g. [3, 14, 25]), or tables versus graphs (e.g. [5, 9, 28]), yet the results are not always in agreement [8, 31]. Other studies look at individual differences of users affecting their performance with visual approaches [27, 30].

3 AM2.0

AM2.0, like its predecessors, described briefly in Sect. 5.1, presents association data between three entities using a node-link diagram based on Heer et al. [11], with nodes representing entity instances and links representing associations between entities.

Two types of entity instances are shown on the left and right sides of the perimeter of a circle, with a third type appearing along the vertical diameter (see Figs. 1, 2 and 3). The interactive features of the visualization enable the selection of entity instances, resulting in the highlighting of binary and/or ternary associations involving those instances. The search interface appearing above the mapping visualization contains fields in which the user can specify selection values for each of the three entities. These fields are populated automatically when a selection is made in the visualization via a mouse click. For example, when a Vendor instance is selected, as in Fig. 1, the Vendor field in the search interface is populated with that vendor's identifier. Furthermore, the visualization:

- highlights and enlarges the selected vendor node on the left side, along with its label,
- highlights and thickens the lines connecting that vendor to material instances in the center and those materials to plant instances on the right, and
- highlights and enlarges the nodes and labels associated with the connected materials and plants.

When a middle entity is selected, as in Fig. 2, links to nodes to the left and to the right use different colors, indicating that the two highlighted relationships (material-supplied-by-vendor and materials-used-in-plant) are binary. Contrast this to Fig. 3, where a plant and a vendor have been specified in the search. Now the highlighted relationship is a ternary one between Vendor, Material and Plant entities, connecting the vendor to all materials it supplies to the selected plant (likewise, Fig. 1 highlighted links represent a ternary relationship).

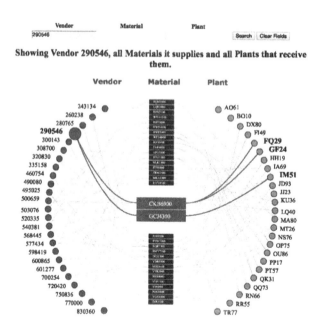

Fig. 1. A screenshot of AM2.0 resulting from the selection of a Vendor node (on the left)

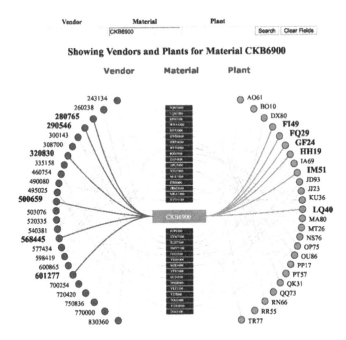

Fig. 2. A Material node is selected (in the middle column), revealing its associations with Vendors and Plants (on left and right sides, respectfully).

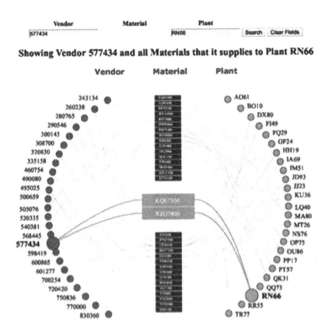

Fig. 3. Results of searching on a Vendor and Plant, revealing all materials supplied by that vendor to that plant.

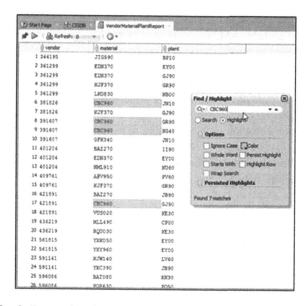

Fig. 4. Oracle Reports interface showing results of search for a particular material.

4 Experimental Evaluation

We conducted a laboratory study comparing how AM2.0 and a table-based interface from Oracle SQL Developer Reports (Fig. 4) assist users in various tasks involving analysis of ternary associations.

Previous studies with earlier versions of AM versus grid-based interfaces from an SAP enterprise system [1, 2] found the AM interfaces were preferred by the majority of study participants, but the results pertaining to the average number of correctly answered questions were mixed, with one study showing slightly higher accuracy with a tabular interface. The primary intent of the experimental evaluation presented here was to determine if updates made to the AM interface would realize the goal of improving both user accuracy (i.e., number of correct answers) and efficiency (i.e., time on task) vs. performance with a tabular interface. We also wanted to see if these gains would be present for questions of varying difficulty.

4.1 Procedure

The experiment used a randomized crossover repeated measures design. Forty-one graduate students at a business university were randomly split into two groups and interacted with both interfaces, AM2.0 and Oracle Reports, in random order to eliminate order effects. All participants were students in a graduate data management course and were awarded extra credit towards their grade. They had all used Oracle SQL developer before but not the specific interface used in the experiment. The majority had less than six months of experience with Oracle, with three having between seven months and two years.

Participants first completed a short demographic questionnaire, followed by the Oracle component and the AM2.0 component in randomized order. For each component, participants viewed a video tutorial, completed a practice round with the interface, and then performed the required tasks, which consisted of answering nineteen questions of varying difficulty. The simplest questions required examining associations of a single item, e.g. *'List all plants that receive materials from Vendor 436219'* or *'How many different plants receive materials from Vendor 678495?'* More difficult questions involved examining, combining or comparing associations of two or more items, e.g. *'Which materials does Vendor 591141 supply to Plant OT60?'* or *'From the materials used in plant LV60 list those that are not used by any other plant.'* To ensure equivalent complexity between the AM and Oracle components while avoiding the learning effect, the tasks in both components were based on data that were labeled differently but had the same number of items in each entity and isomorphic association structures.

After completing the tasks with the two interfaces, participants answered questions eliciting their feedback on the learnability, complexity, enjoyment and usefulness of each interface on a seven-point Likert scale. Lastly, participants answered questions concerning their perceptions, preferences, and suggested improvements.

4.2   Results

4.2.1   Time on Task

Table 1 presents descriptive statistics for the total time spent in answering 19 questions using each of the two interfaces.

Table 1. Descriptive statistics for total time (in seconds) spent on 19 tasks with AM2.0 vs. Oracle for all subjects (N = 41).

	AM2.0	Oracle
Minimum	562.8 s	824.1 s
Maximum	1774.1 s	4036.2 s
Mean	1071.2 s	1567.9 s
Std. Deviation	268.2 s	585.4 s

To test for differences between the interfaces in the time spent answering each question, we performed a two-factor (interface and question) repeated measures ANOVA analysis using the GLM Repeated Measures procedure in IBM SPSS Statistics 25 and the rules recommended by Field [10]. The main effects for the interface and question type were significant and in favor of AM; however, the interaction effects were not significant. The difference in average time per question between the two interfaces was statistically significant ($p < 0.001$), with the average time spent per question using AM2.0 (95% confidence interval 51.9 s–60.8 s) being lower than the time spent using Oracle (95% confidence interval 72.8 s–92.2 s). Furthermore, the time differences among the 19 questions were significant ($p < 0.001$), confirming our experimental design in which we employed questions of varying difficulty, requiring different solving strategies and therefore leading to different completion times.

Figure 5 shows the estimated marginal means of the time spent per question using AM2.0 vs. Oracle, as well as the corresponding 95% confidence intervals based on the previously described statistical analysis.

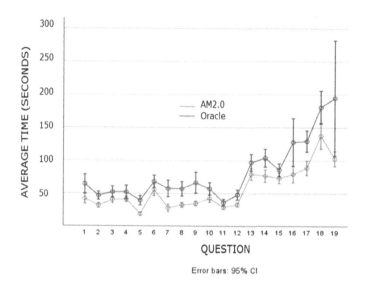

Fig. 5. Estimated marginal means of time spent per question (in seconds) with AM2.0 vs Oracle.

4.2.2   Accuracy of Responses

Descriptive statistics for the accuracy of the participants' responses, measured by the number of correct, incomplete and wrong responses to the 19 task questions, are shown in Table 2.

Table 2. Accuracy descriptive statistics for 19 questions with AM2.0 vs. Oracle for all participants (N = 41).

Accuracy count	AM2.0		Oracle	
	Mean (%)	SD	Mean (%)	SD
Correct	17.95 (94%)	1.38	16.54 (87%)	2.17
Incomplete	0.61 (3%)	0.95	1.07 (6%)	1.56
Wrong	0.39 (2%)	0.89	1.29 (7%)	1.25

To test for accuracy differences between the two interfaces, we performed one-way (interface) repeated measures ANOVA analyses for count data (total number of correct, incomplete and wrong answers, respectively, for the 19 questions) using the GEE Repeated Measures procedure with a Poisson distribution in IBM SPSS Statistics 25. The results indicated that there were significant differences in favor of AM2.0 for the number of correct ($p < 0.001$), incomplete ($p < 0.01$) and wrong ($p < 0.01$) answers.

The estimated marginal means for the number of correct answers were 17.95 for AM2.0 (95% confidence interval 17.54–18.37) and 16.54 for Oracle (95% confidence interval 15.89–17.21), indicating a relatively small but significant accuracy advantage of AM2.0 versus Oracle.

Figure 6 shows the total number of participants (out of forty-one) with correct answers on each question. For fifteen of the questions, participants achieved greater accuracy with the AM interface than with Oracle, while accuracy was the same on two questions and higher with Oracle for two questions (number 15 and 18) that were among the more difficult ones. The last seven questions required more complex solution strategies and also yielded greater average time-on-task measures, as can be seen from Fig. 5.

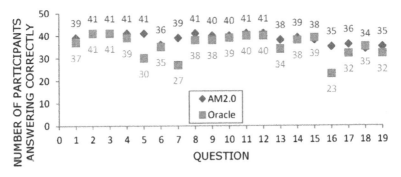

Fig. 6. Total number of participants (out of 41) with correct answers for each question using AM2.0 vs Oracle. The top number for each question corresponds to AM2.0 and the bottom to Oracle

4.2.3 Subjective Ratings

Users' satisfaction with a visualization bears a strong effect on their willingness to adopt it for use in their work. Study participants were surveyed immediately after their use of each interface on a variety of themes: the usefulness of the tutorial and practice rounds; the learnability and complexity of the interface; the usefulness of features like sorting and searching; and their perceptions from working with each interface. To summarize, assessments of the tutorial and practice rounds were highly favorable for both interfaces.

Table 3. Subjective ratings on a seven or eight point Likert-style scale averaged across all participants. The word interface in each statement was replaced with *AM* or *Oracle SQL Developer Reports,* as appropriate.

Abbreviation	Statement	AM mean	ORA mean	AM mean-ORA mean	P-value
Easy to learn	The interface was easy to learn (Disagree Strongly (1) - Agree-Strongly (7))	6.88	6.02	0.85	p < 0.001
Complex	The interface was complex (Disagree Strongly (1) - Agree-Strongly (7))	1.85	3.68	−1.83	
Crowded	The interface was crowded (Disagree Strongly (1) - Agree-Strongly (7))	2.54	4.24	−1.71	
Interactive	The interface was interactive (Disagree Strongly (1) - Agree-Strongly (7))	6.07	3.61	2.46	
Too much info	The interface displayed too much information (Disagree Strongly (1) - Agree-Strongly (7))	2.66	4.17	−1.51	
Sorting useful	The sorting feature was useful to me in answering the questions. (I was not aware of this feature (1), Disagree Strongly (2) - Agree-Strongly (8))	5.56	7.41	−1.85	
Searching useful	The searching feature was useful to me in answering the questions. (I was not aware of this feature (1), Disagree Strongly (2) - Agree-Strongly (8))	7.78	6.12	1.66	
Exciting	Using the interface for these tasks was (Unexciting (1) – Exciting (7))	6.10	3.88	2.22	
Dull/Neat	Using the interface for these tasks was (Dull (1) - Neat (7))	6.17	3.78	2.39	
Not fun/Fun	Using the interface for these tasks was (Not fun (1) – Fun (7))	6.02	3.24	2.78	
Unappealing/Appealing	Using the interface for these tasks was (Unappealing (1) – Appealing (7))	6.15	3.56	2.59	
Boring/Interesting	Using the interface for these tasks was (Boring (1) – Interesting (7))	5.98	3.20	2.78	

While participants found both interfaces easy to learn, they rated AM more favorably on all other qualities, with the greatest differences in means on interactivity and user experience-related qualities of degrees of excitement, neatness, fun, appeal, and interest. Thirty-nine of the participants chose AM2.0 as the interface they would intend to use, with the remaining two being undecided. All questions and responses are available upon request. All questions and averaged answers (on a seven or eight point Likert scale) are detailed in Table 3.

4.2.4   Open Response Summary

When comparing AM2.0 with Oracle Reports, participants often emphasized clarity of presentation of the former interface contributing to their understanding of the relationships between the three entities. Users mentioned that the necessity of scrolling the Oracle Report table in order to locate all associations relevant to the task caused confusion and a sense that they are likely to make a mistake.

Users frequently mentioned the usefulness and appeal of AM2.0's interactivity, and mentioned that they were able to perform the tasks faster with AM compared to the Oracle interface. Many users mentioned the AM interface being fun, interesting and exciting. Users characterized the Oracle interface as being "difficult to see", dull and inefficient.

To the question of which interface they intend to use, out of forty one, all but two users, who selected Undecided as their answer, chose the Association Map. One of the undecided users did not provide any explanation, the other wrote that "While with the Association Map you could see more clearly the connections between the items, the SQL report was more straight forward [sic]."

5   Discussion

In this section we outline the evolution of the AM interface, detailed in [1, 2], starting with the earliest AM interface and highlighting the features, which, we believe, were critical for the performance improvement achieved by the latest version. We outline the most consequential design choices and lessons learnt from this multi-stage project.

5.1   Differences from Previous Versions

The AM2.0 interface presented in this paper has evolved from earlier versions through redesign and extensions driven by user testing and comparative evaluations with tabular, grid-based interfaces. Participants in those studies were asked for their feedback regarding the usability and usefulness of the interface. Furthermore, errors participants made in using the earlier versions of AM were analyzed to come up with improvements and extensions. The initial interface visualized only small data sets (see Fig. 7). A subsequent version, AM-L, could handle larger data sets via panning of nodes and labels (see Fig. 8). Table 4 summarizes the differences between the design of AM2.0 and AM-L.

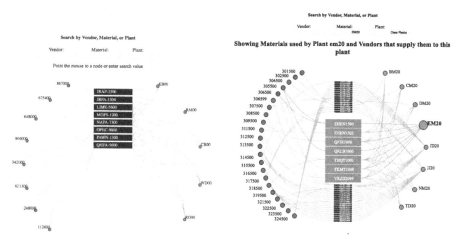

Fig. 7. The earliest version of AM interface   **Fig. 8.** AM-L with panning and zooming

Table 4. Summary of features in AM2.0 vs. AM-L

Static Presentational differences

- Improved positioning of circles for more accurate labeling: circles are positioned in equi-vertical distance, instead of equi-arc distance. (Users of an earlier version had reported difficulties associating the correct label with a linked circle and mistakenly listed a neighboring circle's identifier.)
- Added a *Vendor – Material – Plant* header above the mapping to address confusion concerning its components.
- Clarified statement label under the search interface, describing the result set.

Presentational differences in interaction

- Added transformations of all text labels in the result set using boldface and larger font, instead of just transforming the label for the selected item.
- Highlighted search field content with a yellow background color. (Pilot study participants reported that not noticing the population of the value(s) in the field led to misinterpretation of the result set.)
- Added the population of a search field with an item's identifier value in response to the user clicking on that item. (This maintains consistency between two selection mechanisms: search and clicking.)

Non-presentational changes in interaction

- Improved mechanism for copy/pasting label values into an external document.
- Added a Search button.

Other

- Added transformation of the circular node by enlarging it in response to the user hovering the mouse over it.
- Added transformations of the text labels associated with the hovered item using boldface and larger font.

5.2   Design Lessons Learnt

Following the evaluation of AM2.0 presented here, we have further analyzed and compared AM-L, AM2.0 and tabular interfaces using a theoretically-grounded framework of visualization Leverage Points [19], which describes how various characteristics of a visualization facilitate perceptual and analytical processes involved in performing a task. Here we offer the following insights regarding the design of the visual features and interaction components derived through this analysis. We reserve the full description of the analysis for another paper due to space limitations.

1. The performance advantages of using AM interfaces over the tabular ones are influenced by the choice of the visual representation based on a node-link diagram as a natural and common model for conceptualizing and visualizing relationships. The success of this visual representation for the types of tasks used in the study is evidenced by users' comments about the visualization helping them understand the tasks, and by the time-on-task and accuracy metrics.
2. Presenting all of the data on one screen, with selection and detailed review enabled by zooming and panning, is an important factor influencing user performance and satisfaction with the AM interfaces. Table-based interfaces, in turn, require scrolling over pages of information, which causes user self-reported distraction from the focus on the relationship of items.
3. A likely performance advantage of using AM interface compared to tables lies in the AM's interaction model: while selecting an item in a table only highlights the item itself, in AM, every interaction/selection of an item(s) immediately highlights all of its links to the related items. Such dynamic visual grouping of the related items helps users quickly visualize the associations.
4. The improvement in answer accuracy measures in AM2.0 compared to AM-L is likely due to a greatly enhanced methods of highlighting the selected items and improved labeling of items (see Presentational differences in interaction and Static Presentational differences items in Table 4).

6   Conclusions and Future Work

The results of the laboratory study presented here show promise for the AM interface as a means for improving user efficiency and accuracy over the tabular interface typically encountered in process-driven enterprise systems. The visual interface was preferred by the participants in our study, yielding statistically significant performance gains in both accuracy and time-on-task measures for AM2.0 versus the tabular interface. The critical next step is to test this approach and collect feedback from actual enterprise system users in the workplace.

Although developing an artifact that improves user performance is, by itself, a useful result, it is no less important to understand the reasons *why* one interface is superior to another. In the field of interactive data visualization this kind of understanding is an open research question, with the visualization design and evaluation being, largely, an ad hoc activity, guided by a few known theoretically or empirically motivated guidelines, but with no explicit use of a foundational theory [17, 29]. In this work, we presented lessons learnt from the evolution of the AM interface and the key factors behind its empirically confirmed advantages over the tabular interfaces. This is especially interesting in light of a long history of research regarding effectiveness of graphs over tables [5, 9, 28]. We will devote a future paper to a full exposition of the Leverage Point [19] analysis of the visual and interactive characteristics of the AM interface, grounded in theory of human cognition.

References

1. Babaian, T., Lucas, W., Chircu, A.M., Power, N.: Interactive visualizations for workplace tasks. In: Hammoudi, S., Maciaszek, L.A., Missikoff, M.M., Camp, O., Cordeiro, J. (eds.) ICEIS 2016. LNBIP, vol. 291, pp. 389–413. Springer, Cham (2017). https://doi.org/10.1007/978-3-319-62386-3_18
2. Babaian, T., Lucas, W., Chircu, A., Power, N.: Extending an association map to handle large data sets. In: Yamamoto, S. (ed.) HIMI 2017. LNCS, vol. 10273, pp. 3–21. Springer, Cham (2017). https://doi.org/10.1007/978-3-319-58521-5_1
3. Barlow, T., Neville, P.: A comparison of 2-D visualizations of hierarchies. In: INFOVIS, p. 131. IEEE (2001)
4. Calisir, F., Calisir, F.: The relation of interface usability characteristics, perceived usefulness, and perceived ease of use to end-user satisfaction with enterprise resource planning (ERP) systems. Comput. Hum. Behav. 20, 505–515 (2004)
5. Cardinaels, E.: The interplay between cost accounting knowledge and presentation formats in cost-based decision-making. Acc. Organ. Soc. 33, 582–602 (2008)
6. Chang, R., et al.: Scalable and interactive visual analysis of financial wire transactions for fraud detection. Inf. Vis. 7, 63–76 (2008)
7. Deakins, J.: Unveiling the ERP Pain-O-Meter. https://www.cio.com/article/3253963/enterprise-resource-planning/unveiling-the-erp-pain-o-meter.html
8. Dilla, W.N., Raschke, R.L.: Data visualization for fraud detection: practice implications and a call for future research. Int. J. Acc. Inf. Syst. 16, 1–22 (2015)
9. Elting, L.S., Martin, C.G., Cantor, S.B., Rubenstein, E.B.: Influence of data display formats on physician investigators' decisions to stop clinical trials: prospective trial with repeated measures. BMJ 318, 1527–1531 (1999)
10. Field, A.: Discovering Statistics Using IBM SPSS Statistics. SAGE, Thousand Oaks (2013)
11. Heer, J., Bostock, M., Ogievetsky, V.: A tour through the visualization zoo. Commun. ACM 53, 59 (2010)
12. Hevner, A., March, S., Park, J., Ram, S.: Design science in information systems research. MIS Q. 28, 75–105 (2004)
13. Kettelhut, V.V., Vanschooneveld, T.C., McClay, J.C., Mercer, D.F., Fruhling, A., Meza, J.L.: Empirical study on the impact of a tactical biosurveillance information visualization on users' situational awareness. Mil. Med. 182, 322–329 (2017)
14. Kobsa, A.: User experiments with tree visualization systems. In: Proceedings of the IEEE Symposium on Information Visualization, pp. 9–16. IEEE Computer Society (2004)
15. Lambeck, C., Fohrholz, C., Leyh, C., Müller, R.: (Re-) Evaluating user interface aspects in ERP systems - an empirical user study. In: Proceedings of the 47th Hawaiian International Conference on System Sciences. IEEE Computer Society (2014)

16. McKendrick, J.: Enterprise software slows down digital transformation, survey suggests. https://www.zdnet.com/article/enterprise-software-is-the-biggest-roadblock-to-digital-transformation/
17. Munzner, T.: Visualization Analysis and Design. A K Peters/CRC Press, Boca Raton (2014)
18. Parks, N.E.: Testing & quantifying ERP usability. In: Proceedings of the 1st Annual Conference on Research in Information Technology, pp. 31–36. ACM (2012)
19. Patterson, R.E., et al.: A human cognition framework for information visualization. Comput. Graph. **42**, 42–58 (2014)
20. Peffers, K., Tuunanen, T., Rothenberger, M.A., Chatterjee, S.: A design science research methodology for information systems research. J. Manag. Inf. Syst. **24**, 45–77 (2007)
21. Pike, W.A., Stasko, J., Chang, R., O'Connell, T.A.: The science of interaction. Inf. Vis. **8**, 263–274 (2009)
22. Saket, B., Endert, A., Stasko, J.: Beyond usability and performance: a review of user experience-focused evaluations in visualization. In: Proceedings of the Sixth Workshop on Beyond Time and Errors on Novel Evaluation Methods for Visualization, pp. 133–142. ACM (2016)
23. Sedlmair, M., Isenberg, P., Baur, D., Butz, A.: Information visualization evaluation in large companies: challenges, experiences and recommendations. Inf. Vis. **10**, 248–266 (2011)
24. Sedlmair, M., Bernhold, C., Herrscher, D., Boring, S., Butz, A.: MostVis: an interactive visualization supporting automotive engineers in MOST catalog exploration. In: Proceedings of the International Conference on Information Visualisation, pp. 173–182 (2009)
25. Stasko, J., Catrambone, R., Guzdial, M., Mcdonald, K.: An evaluation of space-filling information visualizations for depicting hierarchical structures. Int. J. Hum.-Comput. Stud. **53**, 663–694 (2000)
26. Tarrell, A., Fruhling, A., Borgo, R., Forsell, C., Grinstein, G., Scholtz, J.: Toward visualization-specific heuristic evaluation. In: Proceedings of the Fifth Workshop on Beyond Time and Errors: Novel Evaluation Methods for Visualization, pp. 110–117. ACM (2014)
27. Toker, D., Conati, C., Steichen, B., Carenini, G.: Individual user characteristics and information visualization: connecting the dots through eye tracking. In: Proceedings of the SIGCHI Conference on Human Factors in Computing Systems, pp. 295–304. ACM (2013)
28. Vessey, I.: Cognitive fit: a theory-based analysis of the graphs versus tables literature*. Decis. Sci. **22**, 219–240 (1991)
29. Ware, C.: Information Visualization: Perception for Design, 3rd edn. Morgan Kaufmann, Waltham (2012)
30. Ziemkiewicz, C., Crouser, R.J., Yauilla, A.R., Su, S.L., Ribarsky, W., Chang, R.: How locus of control influences compatibility with visualization style. In: 2011 IEEE Conference on Visual Analytics Science and Technology (VAST), pp. 81–90. IEEE (2011)
31. Ziemkiewicz, C., Kosara, R.: The shaping of information by visual metaphors. IEEE Trans. Vis. Comput. Graph. **14**, 1269–1276 (2008)
32. Zimmerman, J., Forlizz, J., Evenson, S.: Research through design as a method for interaction design research in HCI. In: Proceedings of the SIGCHI Conference on Human Factors in Computing Systems, pp. 493–502. New York, NY (2007)

Why Should I Trust a Blockchain Platform? Designing for Trust in the Digital Car Dossier

Liudmila Zavolokina(✉), Noah Zani, and Gerhard Schwabe

University of Zurich, Binzmuehlestrasse 14, 8050 Zurich, Switzerland
{zavolokina, schwabe}@ifi.uzh.ch, noah.zani@outlook.com

Abstract. Trust is a crucial component for successful transactions regardless of whether they are executed in physical or virtual spaces. Blockchain technology is often discussed in the context of trust and referred to as a trust-free, trustless, or trustworthy technology. However, the question of how the trustworthiness of blockchain platforms should be demonstrated and proven to end users still remains open. While there may be some genuine trust in the blockchain technology itself, on an application level trust in an IT artifact needs to be established. In this study, we examine how trust-supporting design elements may be implemented to foster an end user's trust in a blockchain platform. We follow the design science paradigm and suggest a practically useful set of design elements that can help designers of blockchain platforms to build more trustworthy systems.

Keywords: Blockchain · Trust · Trustworthiness · Understandability

1 Introduction

Trust is a crucial component for successful transactions regardless of whether they are executed in physical or virtual spaces (e.g., online marketplaces) [1]. Blockchain technology is often discussed in the context of trust (which is claimed to be its main benefit [2]) and referred to as a trust-free, trustless (meaning that it eliminates need for trust between transacting parties), or trustworthy (meaning that it can be trusted because of its design) technology [3–6]. In recent years, it has attracted much attention from academics and practitioners. More and more blockchain implementations have emerged spanning different areas – from widely-spread cryptocurrencies [2] to rarer blockchain-based land registries [7] – to solve various real-world problems in which the presence of trust plays a crucial role.

Trust brought by blockchain technology is achieved by the transparent and immutable procedure of creating and storing transactions in a ledger [8]. However, the question of how the trustworthiness of blockchain platforms should be demonstrated and proven to end users still remains open [8]. While there are a growing number of research articles that address the technical design of blockchain systems (focusing on system architecture) or the fit of the technology in specific cases, there are only a few that focus on the user's perspective [9], which is essential when establishing the promised trust.

© Springer Nature Switzerland AG 2019
B. Tulu et al. (Eds.): DESRIST 2019, LNCS 11491, pp. 269–283, 2019.
https://doi.org/10.1007/978-3-030-19504-5_18

Certain factors hinder the end user's formation of trust in blockchain-based platforms, and therewith mitigate the benefits the technology may offer and hold back its acceptance and usage [10–13]. Amongst others, these factors include lack of experience with the technology and lack of understanding of how blockchain systems function, privacy concerns and liability issues [8, 10, 11]. In contrast to existing platforms where a user trusts one service provider, blockchain systems require trust in the whole community of users (in case of public blockchains) or in several service providers simultaneously (in case of consortium blockchains). Furthermore, there is no 'one-size-fits-all' blockchain technology: different design decisions [14] influence implementation of blockchain-based platforms and their final outcomes (e.g., usefulness for end users and ability to solve the addressed problems). This variety of possible 'configurations' calls for more careful investigation of design alternatives and their appropriateness. To leverage the benefits the technology offers and to foster its acceptance, these challenges must be overcome. While there may be some genuine trust in the blockchain technology itself, on an application level trust in an IT artifact needs to be established. To do this, trust-supporting design elements (TSDEs) can be implemented. These TSDEs represent single features or groups of features that positively influence the trust of an end user in an IT artifact [15].

In this study, we take an exploratory approach and, using the example of a specific blockchain platform called "car dossier" (which we describe later in a corresponding section), examine how trust-supporting design elements may be implemented to foster an end user's trust in a blockchain platform [13, 16]. Thus, we state the following research question:

RQ. What trust-supporting design elements foster trust of an end user in a blockchain platform?

More specifically, we focus on the problem of the end user's lack of understanding of a blockchain platform (for example, about its purpose, functionality, etc.), which hinders the formation of trust [8, 10]. The study follows the design science paradigm and aims to suggest a practically useful set of design elements that can help designers of blockchain platforms to build more trustworthy systems. It is important to note that: (1) the research is initiated as a result of a problem which was observed in practice and in recent studies briefly covered by the literature; (2) the research is carried out as part of a larger blockchain design project, where researchers are involved in design activities, specification of requirements, and actual implementation of the system; and (3) the research does not aim to find completely new TSDEs, but to integrate pre-existing knowledge in the context of blockchain platforms and observe if such knowledge is useful to address the problem of the end users' lack of understanding.

The remainder of the paper is structured as follows: In the next section, we investigate the existing body of knowledge about trust in blockchain platforms with the focus on a user's perspective. Then, in the *Car Dossier* section, we present the project and the blockchain platform that is our target for trust support. In the *Design* section we describe the process used in this research, and the proposed TSDEs for the blockchain platform. This section is followed by *Evaluation*, where we present the results of feedback from end-users, we collected. Finally, we discuss the results of this study and draw conclusions.

2   Related Work

2.1   Trust in IT Artifacts

Despite its importance, it is not easy to conceptualize trust, and there is no commonly accepted definition of it. One possible definition that reflects converging understanding is that trust refers to two components: (1) "positive expectations regarding the other party in a risky situation" [17], and (2) willingness to be vulnerable [18]. Other definitions mention the presence of uncertainty and risk, under which trust occurs. Trust plays an important role in different contexts: interpersonal relationships, organizational behaviors, conflict management, and business transactions [19–23]. By its nature, trust is inter-personal. However, the concept of trust has been expanded to IT artifacts and in recent years has been gaining importance in IS and HCI research. Scholars explore trust in IT artifacts (e.g., how it is established, how it changes over time, what factors influence it, what design implications we may derive to build up trust in systems, etc.) as it is of crucial importance for the acceptance and adoption of IS [24]. An IT artifact can play two roles in trust relationships: (1) the role of mediator between two humans, a trustor and a trustee, or (2) the role of a trustee, if the IT artifact is trusted in by the end user [25]. In this study, we explore the latter in order to come up with design ideas to establish the end user's initial trust in a blockchain platform by making it easier to understand. However, we acknowledge the importance of further research into how blockchain platforms change the way we trust other humans and institutions.

In the role of trustee, an IT artifact should directly build trust. Antecedents of trust, explored in IS and HCI literature, can be used to inform trust-supporting design elements in information systems [25]. Understandability of how an information system works, transparency over how the output of a system was achieved, information accuracy, reliability of a system as well as explicit communication about system's activities are important antecedents of trust in an IT system [26, 27] to resolve issues associated with lack of knowledge, experience or understanding of a used system. These antecedents of trust lead us in our design of TSDEs in order to support trust formation in a blockchain platform.

Trust literature suggests that technology can transmit signals of trustworthiness as effectively as humans do [28]. Signals can help the trustor form expectations of trustee's behavior. They play an especially important role in first-time or one-time interactions, in which the trustor does not have any previous experience of the trustee or may have made inaccurate assumptions about them [28]. However, the presence of trust signals in the design of a system is not, in itself, enough to result in high levels of its perceived trustworthiness: their reliability and cost structure must be taken into account [28]. Good signals are considered to be easy and cheap to provide for trustworthy players and difficult and costly for untrustworthy ones [28]. Traditionally, trust signals in e-commerce and website design include reviews from previous customers, trust seals, references, and many more, widely known from the marketing literature. In our study, we use the concept of signaling trustworthiness to design the TSDEs for our blockchain platform.

2.2   Trust in Blockchain Technology

The discussion around the concept of trust in the context of blockchain technology has begun in design science research, HCI, and information systems in the past couple of years [6]. As the main benefit of the technology is claimed to be trust [2], there is a need to understand if and how trust relationships differ from existing concepts, and how this difference changes the design of systems. However, as the trust literature suggests [25], it is important to differentiate between trust mediated by technology (for example, transferring bitcoins from one individual to another without relying on a bank) and trust in the capabilities of the technology to fulfil its purpose (for example, trust of a bitcoin owner in the bitcoin network). The latter is a prerequisite for blockchain technology usage and adoption [2], and should be in place to enable trust between transacting parties mediated by technology [29]. Thus, in our study, we focus on how trust in blockchain technology may be established.

Earlier studies suggest that blockchain may be a solution when establishing trust in cases where data integrity is an issue in records management, given that proper security architecture and infrastructure management should be in place [3, 8, 30]. However, the establishment of trust by blockchain technology is affected by certain limitations. For example, there is no guarantee that the stored data is reliable [30], and there should be additional mechanisms for data quality management [31]. In general, blockchain, as an infrastructure alone, does not suffice to instill trust in an end user: this should be established at an application level [32]. For this, certain design features, like assessment of stored information or visibility of parties that provide this information, should be in place and adjusted to the certain business needs of an implemented platform [32].

Furthermore, trust in blockchain is hindered by lack of technical understanding and experience [6, 10]. These factors, combined with the complexity of the technology and the potential for monetary losses due to them, cause feelings of insecurity and uncertainty among users, which then lead to difficulties in building up trust in the technology [10]. Some studies consider this factor to be the most significant barrier to the adoption of blockchain technology [33]. Though it is probably too early to properly conduct research into the adoption of the technology and its applications due to their immaturity and experimental character, we nevertheless acknowledge the existing need for additional trust support in blockchain platforms. However, examination of the existing trust in blockchain technology [34] suggests that it is not a new kind of trust that is being created (or changed fundamentally), but rather a shift from trust in one market player to others in the blockchain ecosystems. Thus, trust in the technology should be understood in known terms and established by traditional mechanisms [34]. In order to give the user a better understanding of the technology, an explanation should be given. It is not necessary to describe the technology in detail, but rather to explain the basic concepts and to help the user understand how the high-level functionality works. To achieve this, video tutorials or simple illustrations are often helpful. In website design, information components about a company and/or a product embedded in the site serve as external signals, helping to build trust [35]. These information components may also include information regarding how privacy and security measures are implemented as signals of the trustworthiness and benevolence of the service provider [35]. It is crucial that this type of information is properly and promptly communicated. In our research, we explore what traditional signaling mechanisms, such as information components, may be implemented in a blockchain platform to enhance its trustworthiness.

3 Car Dossier

This study is part of a larger action design research project [36], called the Car Dossier project. The project runs in Switzerland and is designed by a consortium of companies from the car-related ecosystem: an insurance company, a car dealer and importer, a car sharing company, a road traffic authority, a software company, and two universities. Together, these companies are implementing a so-called car dossier that encompasses a car's history over its entire life cycle, from the moment of production to the moment of disposal. The primary goal of the car dossier project is to reduce information asymmetries in the used-car market, and to digitalize and improve the processes, minimize redundancies, and establish a trusted ecosystem for car-related data management between all the players involved into the life cycle of a car [5, 31, 32, 37][1]. Though the project has a number of facets which are crucial considerations for the design of the platform (like platform governance, business model, privacy), we focus on its application level and the perspective of its end users: car buyers, willing to consult the car dossier to assess the quality of a used car they intend to buy. This simple scenario gives an idea of a setting in which the car dossier platform is used by a car buyer: *Max, a 45-year-old plumber from Zurich, intends to buy a used car. He searches on an online portal UsedCarsPortal.ch for a 5-year-old VW Golf, which is offered by Nancy. Max contacts Nancy to check whether the information about the condition of the car corresponds to what is published online. Nancy mentions that there is a blockchain-based car dossier available for the car, which may convince Max that the information she has provided is genuine. Max is interested in viewing the car dossier, however, he is not sure whether he can trust it either: he has not heard about blockchain before.* To leverage the value of the capabilities and benefits the technology may bring to Max, there should be additional clarification of what makes the platform trustworthy and why Max can rely on it. This serves as a starting point for the design of the current study. The upcoming chapter explains how the TSDEs were designed to support the end users' understanding of the car dossier, establishing trust and helping Nancy and Max to complete the deal confidently and efficiently.

4 Design

4.1 Methods

The development of TSDEs follows the design science paradigm [38–41]. Design science research is aimed at finding new solutions for both known and unknown problems [42]. Solutions produced by design science research should be applicable to

---

[1] Due to space limitations, we omit the discussion about why blockchain was a feasible solution that the participants opted for. We encourage the reader to consult the referenced articles.

resolve classes of problems and thus be generalizable [36]. While the design science cannot, on its own, provide sufficient evidence to support developed hypotheses, its activities often help to formulate the hypotheses and initially filter out those which are not worthy of further development [43]. No specific order is imposed when moving between the world of specific problems and solutions, and the world of general problems and solutions [43, 44]. Design science researchers may start with the creation of a specific solution for a specific problem and then generalize it, or work the other way round by starting from a generic problem, creating a generic solution and then applying it to a specific problem to demonstrate its value [36, 43, 44]. In this study, we took an exploratory approach, used a mixed strategy and combined techniques from design thinking [45] and design science research. This research originates from a specific problem that we observed in the car dossier, is abstracted to the problem of users' resistance to use the platform due to lack of understanding of blockchain platforms. As is typical for DSR projects, the development takes place in multiple design-evaluate iterations [46].

The first step involved a broad search for pre-existing solutions to problems of a lack of understandability and trustworthiness in website and system design, which included literature research and exploration of existing practices. An extensive list of possible ideas for TSDEs was generated. No specific criteria or restrictions regarding the feasibility of the components were set. The result was a list of 25 TSDEs, which was then further refined in subsequent steps. To reduce the wide variety of TSDEs to a smaller set of feasible TSDEs, a short survey[2] was created. In total, 22 respondents aged between 20 and 49 (12 female, 10 male) participated in the survey. The intention of the survey was to identify TSDEs perceived as important and relevant, and to exclude those that were perceived as inappropriate or unhelpful. To make the survey more comprehensive, we grouped the 25 TSDEs into four categories. The selected categories were *user interface, soft factors, labels,* and *information*. The participants were asked to rank the TSDEs in the preferred order of importance or relevance. Based on the feedback from participants of the survey, for a more realistic setting, it was decided that the TSDEs should be consistently embedded in the car dossier integrated in an online used-car sales website. This provided familiarity with the situation (by eliminating possible distractions caused by completely new software) for future evaluation participants. The prototypes of the TSDEs were created with a wireframe tool: Balsamiq[3]. The created prototypes were then evaluated in another short survey. The aim of the second survey (completed by the same participants) was to further test the components found to be most important or relevant in the first step by enhancing them with visual information, enabling the participants to see the prototyped TSDEs. These were then refined in terms of their feasibility and design in a workshop with the car dossier project team (the workshop took place in July 2018, with 16 project members). After this process, the final most relevant TSDEs were chosen to be implemented. Finally, the implementation of the TSDEs was evaluated by nine participants aged between 20 and 50 (5 female, 4 male).

---

[2] The surveys referred to in this paper can be provided upon request.

[3] https://balsamiq.com/.

4.2   Design and Implementation of TSDEs

As mentioned before, we started from a specific problem observed in the blockchain project. We found confirmation of this problem in the recent IS literature [10, 33]. The generic solution is informed by three antecedents of trust [25]: understandability, reliability, and information accuracy. They lead us in the design of our specific solution, where we illustrate specific TSDEs, developed for the car dossier. This process is illustrated in Fig. 1. Table 1 then shows how the designed TSDEs are matched to the mentioned antecedents of trust. TSDEs in the user interface category (such as "Embedding the information in a known system", "As much information as possible at a glance" or "Keeping the design as lean possible") were not implemented as separate TSDEs but were followed as guidelines for the prototyping. As a starting point, a sketched website for an online used-car sales platform was created, into which the individual TSDEs were embedded. The TSDEs selected after the first survey are described in Table 2 in the order they were presented in the survey.

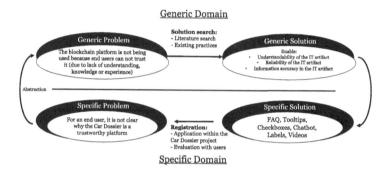

Fig. 1. Generic and specific domains in the design

Table 1. TSDEs matched to proposed generic requirements

Generic requirements		Antecedents of trust [25]	TSDEs					
			FAQ	Toolt ips	Check- boxes	Chat bot	Labels	Videos
	Enable:	Understandability of the IT artifact	✓	✓		✓		✓
		Reliability of the IT artifact					✓	
		Information accuracy in the IT artifact			✓			

5   Evaluation

In this section we present the results of the evaluation of the designed TSDEs from three iterations: results of the second survey, the workshop, and the interviews when the actual implementation was completed. The ranking of the TSDEs from the survey is

Table 2. Prototypes of the TSDE

TSDE1. FAQ

FAQ is a mechanism mainly used in e-commerce to provide information about a service or a product in a way that is easy to understand (by answering frequently asked questions), thus helping to resolve issues in understanding [48]. FAQ can be accessed via an embedded link. It encompasses frequently asked and relevant questions regarding the car dossier and answers to them. It includes the following categories of questions: general (e.g., what the car dossier is, who its users are); financial (e.g., how the car dossier is financed, how much the car dossier costs); data and privacy (e.g., what data is collected, how it is processed, how data privacy is achieved); and technical (e.g., what the technology behind the car dossier is, what functionalities the car dossier offers).

TSDE2. Tooltips

Tooltips is a way to extend user knowledge with additional information in case they need it [49]. The tooltips make it possible to show predefined content when the user moves their cursor over a certain element of the website. In the example shown, a short explanation is displayed when the user navigates their cursor to the words "Car Dossier".

TSDE3. Checkboxes

Checkboxes (also called checkmarks) are a simple way to reflect a positive or a negative quality, which goes along with ratings in e-commerce [28]. They help the end user to better understand if a product (in our case data) is of good or bad quality. The checkboxes make it possible to show which data came directly from the car dossier when the end user views the information through a third-party sales platform and not on the car dossier platform itself. When viewed on a third-party platform, the end user sees checkboxes next to the 'verified' data together with a note or legend. If the end user were to view the data directly on the car dossier platform, the checkboxes would be obsolete because all data would have a check mark.

Vehicle Data

Price: 25'000 $
Condition: Used
Mileage: 60'158 ⊘
Power: 110 PS ⊘
Consumption: 4.9 litre/100km ⊘
Fuel type: ⬛⬛⬛⬛⬛ ⊘
Color: ⬛⬛⬛⬛⬛ ⬛⬛⬛
Gearing type: ⬛⬛⬛⬛ ⊘

The data have been **verified** ⊘
by the **Car Dossier**.

TSDE4. Chatbot

A chatbot can help by answering questions a user might have in real time. Though it provides the very same information as the FAQ does (in our design), it simulates a conversation with a person which is appealing for a user in terms of trust under the condition that the chatbot reacts as naturally as a human does [50]. A question can be written and submitted in the text field. Based on this, the chatbot can then check the question against a database with predefined content and provide a corresponding answer. In the example, the chatbot uses the same questions that are used in TSDE1 FAQ.

TSDE5 – TSDE7. Labels (governmental / university / certification)	
Labels are powerful trust signals [51] because they can show that an organization supports the development of the application, or ensure validity of the provided data. Thus, trust in this particular organization (if it is a reputable and trustworthy one) is transferred into the application. The first possibility is a governmental label such as the label of a federal office, that supports the project. As part of this possibility, another conceivable option would be the label of one or several regional road traffic authorities that are involved in the project or can verify data. If trust in government is high, it would make end users confident that the data in the car dossier is genuine and that it can be trusted. The second possibility would be a label from a university. Research activities that underlie the development and bring transparency over it may enhance the trustworthiness of the whole platform. The third possibility sets a quality seal or a test report from an independent third party that specifically examines and audits blockchain platforms. To the authors' knowledge, no such body exists in Switzerland at the time of this work, however, there are several companies that have begun auditing blockchain platforms. With the increasing popularity and spread of such platforms, this is classified as a possibility for the future.	

TSDE8 and TSDE9. Videos (instructional / comic)	
Literature suggests that visual information in general, and short videos specifically, are more beneficial in trust building on websites [52]. The last two TSDEs show two different types of video, which are intended to increase trustworthiness in the car dossier by allowing the end user to visualize information about it. The first illustration represents a more traditional instructional video with an instructor explaining certain facts (e.g., how blockchain technology works or what the functionalities of the car dossier are). The second one is an example of an animated comic video that is intended to present facts as simply as possible, using graphics and drawings to represent a possible scenario (problem and solution) in which the car dossier may be useful.	

shown in the Table 3. The most relevant TSDE in terms of providing more understandability and trustworthiness was FAQ (TSDE1). Among the labels, the governmental label (TSDE5) (that the Road Traffic Authority approves or supports the platform) was considered much more important than a certification label (TSDE7) (e.g., that the platform was audited) and moderately more important than the label from a university (TSDE6). Comparing the comic video (TSDE9) and the instructional video

(TSDE8), the comic video was widely welcomed by the participants. At that point, we didn't ask the participants to explain why, but this iteration helped us to identify the most welcomed TSDEs, that were later discussed in a workshop with the project team.

Table 3. Ranked TSDEs and their categories

TSDE Name	Category	Rank
TSDE1. FAQ	Information	1
TSDE5. Governmental label	Labels	2
TSDE9. Comic video	Information	3
TSDE4. Chatbot	Information	4
TSDE6. University label	Labels	5
TSDE2. Tooltips	Information	6
TSDE3. Checkboxes	User interface	7
TSDE7. Certification label	Labels	8
TSDE8. Instructional video	Information	9

In the workshop, checkboxes in particular were considered several times as useful, "*are a good eye-catcher*" (P6)[4] and thus arouse interest. In addition, tooltips have been considered several times as useful, not only to show information on the car dossier itself, but to explain more specific information in selected contents. If some data is shown in an aggregated form (e.g., the current mileage state and not each mileage record event), tooltips can be useful to explain how the data was aggregated where checkboxes are not appropriate. However, tooltips were considered overwhelming for end users when integrated in an online used-car sales platform and would rather make more sense in the car dossier platform itself. As a result, the final implementation did not include labels. Labels for the car dossier were also intensively discussed. On the one hand, they were classified as interesting for end users and can attract the attention of the user if they recognize a certain reliable organization. Labels can also make valuable contributions to the security of the platform ("*for the security part we need a check or a label*" (P4)) and for data protection. On the other hand, important hurdles and limitations in the implementation of labels were mentioned, which led to them being excluded them from the final implementation. "*University of Zurich as a label will certainly not work. For legal reasons*" (P1). Labels from other project partners are also unlikely to be realized. The problem with this would be that the organization issuing the labels would have to somehow guarantee/check the data and the platform and assume liability. However, it would be possible to "*use the car dossier itself as a label (...) and showing what percentage of data is car dossier verified*" (P1). The feedback regarding FAQ was relatively uncontroversial and the basic statements about them were as positive as those in the results of the surveys, "*FAQs are pretty well accepted*" (P6) or "*for me, FAQs are still the variant where I get the best answers*" (P10). The situation was different with the chatbot, which on the one hand was

---

[4] The quotes here and further in the text are taken from the workshop (P) and interviews (T).

identified as high potential and worth trying out, but on the other hand opinions like "*I do not know what I can actually do with chatbots*" (P10) were expressed. With the videos, the general consensus was clear that it's worth trying, but only in the form of animation/comic videos. A statement, made by one of the participants about traditional instructional videos, made it clear that they should no longer be used for such purposes. Finally, all TSDEs except for tooltips (TSDE2), labels (TSDE5-7) and instructional video (TSDE8) were implemented.

During the evaluation of the TSDEs' implementation, each participant was provided with a scenario that they were asked to role play. Each person was a customer who wanted to buy a used car because they had changed their job and needed to commute to work. They had already selected a car on an online platform. They saw that a car dossier existed for the car and that some of the displayed data originated from it. Now that they were aware of it, they wanted to find out more. In order to establish whether the TSDEs helped to improve understandability and perceived trustworthiness of the system, each participant was asked to use the platform and answer two of several questions (about the team, functionalities of the car dossier, its business model, and how their personal data was handled). The order of TSDEs to be tested and the choice of questions to be answered per TSDE were different for each participant to diminish the learning effects. To capture a deeper understanding of the feelings the users experience, semi-structured interviews were conducted immediately after the test.

The interviews revealed certain tendencies regarding the popularity and readiness for use of the individual TSDEs. In seven out of nine interviews, the **FAQ (TSDE1)** was mentioned in response to the question "*Which component would you most likely use to search for more information?*". The FAQ was favored by the majority of participants, largely due to the fact that it is a widely recognized feature on websites. Participants welcomed the information in the FAQ: "*thinking that various questions have been covered in the FAQ (...) increases my confidence*" (T9). As a potential for improvement here, participants suggested communicating transparently what the interests of the individual stakeholders (an insurance company, a car sharing company, etc.) in the project are. The **comic video (TSDE9)** also generally performed well. However, some participants wished to have more content in the video. The video provided basic information in a short time, which "*could give a good overview*" (T4) and makes it easier to arouse the interest of end users: "*Video stands out from the others*" (T3). However, few participants explicitly asked for more content to be made available in the video. However, it was recognized that it is important to ensure the video is not too long: the right length was considered to be around 90 s. The reaction to the **chatbot (TSDE4)** was mixed, from a single vote as first choice to some very negative attitudes. None of the participants regularly used chatbots. Six of the nine interviewees had never used a chatbot before. The mentioned experiences are neutral or negative: "*you ask in five different ways and you get the same answer every time*" (T7). However, there were positive comments about how "*to ask exactly what you need and actually get a short answer*" (T2) and some participants even preferred it to a conventional FAQ. This was especially noticeable among participants with little or no technical affinity, who were unfamiliar with chatbots. The **checkboxes (TSDE3)** were rated exclusively neutral or positive, with the neutral votes stating that the checkboxes in themselves offer little added value. Checkboxes alone cannot bring much value for trust and require additional explanation of their purpose. The positive opinions, however, often implicitly required an initial trust in the car dossier.

6 Discussion and Conclusions

Our study demonstrates a possible set of TSDEs for blockchain platforms. Having conducted this study, we can make several observations. Firstly, we would like to confirm the problems identified by the literature (lack of understanding, knowledge and experience with the blockchain technology, which lead to lower levels of trust) that may be observed not only in studies of public blockchains (e.g., bitcoin, described in [6]), but also for those blockchain platforms where parties are known (permissioned blockchains developed by a consortium), like in the case of the car dossier. Still, to a user who has less affinity with technology and is less trend-conscious, the trustworthiness of a platform should be communicated in a straightforward way to instill trust. In particular, support to develop understandability is a crucial antecedent of trust in the case of blockchain platforms [25]. To do that, existing mechanisms (like FAQ and videos) that users are already familiar with are very helpful [34]. In order to develop understandability of a platform, information about its purpose and functionality should be provided. In the case of blockchain platforms, where data quality is an issue [31], information about data providers and their incentives to be a part of the system and to provide data can be especially relevant. Additionally, we noticed that a user-centered approach is helpful in designing such TSDEs. For example, in the FAQ, most of the questions are those that users would generate themselves. The comic video was much more popular as it introduced a simple problem which any user would be familiar with (the purchase of a used car) and the solution the car dossier brings. This way, the user could relate to the situation much better and thus understand the purpose of the car dossier. In contrast, the chatbot produced an opposite effect. Most of the users were not familiar with its purpose and functionality, leading to negative experiences.

Secondly, we argue that to make blockchain platforms more trustworthy, reliability (another antecedent of trust) should be addressed [30]. To do that, we designed several labels which verified that the data in the car dossier was genuine and showed users that the project was supported by one of several institutions. Though end users welcomed such labels, like the governmental or university labels, there are legal limitations in their implementation. Furthermore, they might be more or less useful for trust support depending on the level of trust in these institutions. Therefore, trust in a blockchain platform may increase or decrease by transfer of trust from institutions to platform. In countries where there is no trust in government, usage of a governmental label will not increase the level of trust and might, in fact, be a negative influence. As mentioned before, trust in blockchain platforms differs in the sense that the role of platform provider changes. Instead of having one trusted party, there might be many (like a blockchain consortium in the case of the car dossier) with different levels of trust. This shift should be certainly studied further. Additionally, we see a potential for blockchain platforms, which are perfectly suited for authentication purposes [7], to issue trust labels by themselves and, by doing so, create a new business model.

Thirdly, we aimed to provide information accuracy (the last antecedent of trust we addressed). Though we have seen a positive reaction to the designed TSDE checkboxes, their use is limited to platforms that integrate data from a blockchain platform, like the used-car sales platform in our case, with the integrated data from the car dossier. Though visually appealing, checkboxes in the car dossier itself would not make much sense. Furthermore, an initial level of trust in the car dossier is still needed to ensure confidence in these checkboxes, as reported by participants of our study. Thus, we encourage researchers to continue design studies on trust for blockchain platforms.

This research has following limitations: we acknowledge that the number of participants in both surveys and the interview does not allow for generalizable conclusions about which TSDEs are the most effective in building trust. Furthermore, in our case, the integration of the car dossier in a used-car sales platform was necessary to make the situation more familiar to the users. However, it is important to study what effect TSDEs have when use of the car dossier is isolated from the used-car sales platform. Additionally, it is worthwhile to search and develop further TSDEs for blockchain platforms that are not covered in this study. These may be TSDEs which proved to be powerful in other contexts, or completely new ones. Concerning future research, we see potential in developing studies that examine user perception of blockchain platforms, their trustworthiness, and acceptance of these platforms.

Acknowledgement. This research has been funded by the Innosuisse under the project name "Blockchain Car Dossier". We thank the project partners for their feedback and involvement.

References

1. Son, J.-Y., Tu, L., Benbasat, I.: A descriptive content analysis of trust-building measures in B2B electronic marketplaces. Commun. AIS **18**, 6 (2006)
2. Fleischmann, M., Ivens, B.: Exploring the role of trust in blockchain adoption: an inductive approach. In: Proceedings of the 52nd HICSS (2019)
3. Seebacher, S., Schüritz, R.: Blockchain technology as an enabler of service systems: a structured literature review. In: Za, S., Drăgoicea, M., Cavallari, M. (eds.) IESS 2017. Lecture Notes in Business Information Processing, vol. 279, pp. 12–23. Springer, Cham (2017). https://doi.org/10.1007/978-3-319-56925-3_2
4. Beck, R., Stenum Czepluch, J., Lollike, N., Malone, S.: Blockchain–the gateway to trust-free cryptographic transactions. In: ECIS (2016)
5. Notheisen, B., Cholewa, J.B., Shanmugam, A.P.: Trading real-world assets on blockchain. Bus. Inf. Syst. Eng. **59**, 425–440 (2017)
6. Sadhya, V., Sadhya, H., Hirschheim, R., Watson, E.: Exploring technology trust in bitcoin: the blockchain exemplar (2018)
7. Miscione, G., Ziolkowski, R., Zavolokina, L., Schwabe, G.: Tribal governance: The business of blockchain authentication. In: HICSS (2018)
8. Elsden, C., Manohar, A., Briggs, J., Harding, M., Speed, C., Vines, J.: Making sense of blockchain applications: a typology for HCI. In: Proceedings of the 2018 CHI (2018)

9. Ostern, N., Cabinakova, J.: Pre-prototype testing: empirical insights on the expected usefulness of decentralized identity management systems. Presented at the Proceedings of the 52nd Hawaii International Conference on System Sciences, 8 January (2019)
10. Ostern, N.: Do you trust a trust-free transaction? Toward a trust framework model for blockchain technology. Presented at the ICIS (2018)
11. Schlegel, M., Zavolokina, L., Schwabe, G.: Blockchain technologies from the consumers' perspective: what is there and why should who care? In: HICSS (2018)
12. Koens, T., Poll, E.: The drivers behind blockchain adoption: the rationality of irrational choices. In: Mencagli, G., et al. (eds.) Euro-Par 2018. LNCS, vol. 11339, pp. 535–546. Springer, Cham (2019). https://doi.org/10.1007/978-3-030-10549-5_42
13. Söllner, M., Hoffmann, A., Hoffmann, H., Leimeister, J.M.: How to use behavioral research insights on trust for HCI system design. In: CHI 2012. ACM (2012)
14. Morabito, V.: Business Innovation Through Blockchain. Springer, Cham (2017)
15. Leimeister, J.M., Ebner, W., Krcmar, H.: Design, implementation, and evaluation of trust-supporting components in virtual communities for patients. J. Manage. Inf. Syst. **21**(4), 101–131 (2005)
16. Lee, J.D., See, K.A.: Trust in automation: designing for appropriate reliance (2004)
17. Faems, D., Janssens, M., Madhok, A., Looy, B.V.: Toward an integrative perspective on alliance governance: connecting contract design, trust dynamics, and contract application. Acad. Manag. J. **51**, 1053–1078 (2008)
18. Mayer, R.C., Davis, J.H., Schoorman, F.D.: An integrative model of organizational trust. Acad. Manag. Rev. **20**, 709–734 (1995)
19. Dirks, K.T., Ferrin, D.L.: The role of trust in organizational settings. Organ. Sci. **12**, 450–467 (2001)
20. Lewis, W., Agarwal, R., Sambamurthy, V.: Sources of influence on beliefs about information technology use: an empirical study of knowledge workers. MIS Q., 657–678 (2003)
21. Williamson, O.E.: Markets and Hierarchies. New York 2630 (1975)
22. Williamson, O.E.: Calculativeness, trust, and economic organization. J. Law Econ. **36**, 453–486 (1993)
23. Zaheer, A., McEvily, B., Perrone, V.: Does trust matter? Exploring the effects of interorganizational and interpersonal trust on performance. Organ. Sci. **9**, 141–159 (1998)
24. Söllner, M., Hoffmann, A., Leimeister, J.M.: Why different trust relationships matter for information systems users. Eur. J. Inf. Syst. **25**, 274–287 (2016)
25. Söllner, M., Hoffmann, A., Hoffmann, H., Wacker, A., Leimeister, J.M.: Understanding the formation of trust in IT artifacts. Presented at the ICIS (2012)
26. Hoffmann, A., Hoffmann, H., Söllner, M.: Fostering initial trust in applications–developing and evaluating requirement patterns for application websites. In: 21st European Conference on Information Systems (ECIS) (2013)
27. Hoffmann, A., Söllner, M., Hoffmann, H., Leimeister, J.M.: Towards trust-based software requirement patterns. In: Requirements Patterns (RePa). IEEE (2012)
28. Riegelsberger, J., Sasse, M.A., McCarthy, J.D.: The mechanics of trust: a framework for research and design. Int. J. Hum.-Comput. Stud. **62**, 381–422 (2005)
29. Loebbecke, C., Lueneborg, L., Niederle, D.: Blockchain technology impacting the role of trust in transactions: reflections in the case of trading diamonds. In: ECIS (2018)
30. Lemieux, V.L.: Trusting records: is Blockchain technology the answer? Rec. Manag. J. **26**, 110–139 (2016)
31. Zavolokina, L., Spychiger, F., Tessone, C., Schwabe, G.: Incentivizing data quality in blockchains for inter-organizational networks – learning from the digital car dossier. Presented at the ICIS (2018)

32. Zavolokina, L., Miscione, G., Schwabe, G.: Buyers of lemons: addressing buyers' needs in the market for lemons with blockchain technology. In: 52nd HICSS, p. 10 (2018)
33. Sadhya, V., Sadhya, H.: Barriers to adoption of blockchain technology (2018)
34. Auinger, A., Riedl, R.: Blockchain and trust: refuting some widely-held misconceptions. Presented at the ICIS (2018)
35. Öksüz, A., Walter, N., Pfeiffer, T., Becker, J.: Designing trust in websites-an evaluation of leading infrastructure as a service providers' websites. In: PACIS, p. 357 (2014)
36. Sein, M.K., Henfridsson, O., Purao, S., Rossi, M., Lindgren, R.: Action design research. MIS Q. **35**, 37–56 (2011)
37. Bauer, I., Zavolokina, L., Leisibach, F., Schwabe, G.: Exploring blockchain value creation: the case of the car ecosystem. In: Proceedings of the 52th HICSS, p. 10 (2018)
38. Von Alan, R.H., March, S.T., Park, J., Ram, S.: Design science in information systems research. MIS Q. **28**(1), 75–105 (2004)
39. Peffers, K., et al.: A design science research methodology for information systems research. J. Manage. Inf. Syst. **24**(3), 45–77 (2007)
40. Baskerville, R., Pries-Heje, J., Venable, J.: Soft design science methodology. In: 4th International Conference on Design Science Research in Information Systems and Technology (2009)
41. Nunamaker, J.F., Briggs, R.O., Derrick, D.C., Schwabe, G.: The last research mile: achieving both rigor and relevance in information systems research. J. Manag. Inf. Syst. **32**, 10–47 (2015)
42. Anderson, J., Donnellan, B., Hevner, A.: Exploring the relationship between design science research and innovation: a case study of innovation at Chevron. In: Helfert, M., Donnellan, B. (eds.) EDSS 2011. CCIS, vol. 286, pp. 116–131. Springer, Heidelberg (2012). https://doi.org/10.1007/978-3-642-33681-2_10
43. Bider, I., Johannesson, P., Perjons, E., Johansson, L.: Design science in action: developing a framework for introducing IT systems into operational practice (2012)
44. Lee, J.S., Pries-Heje, J., Baskerville, R.: Theorizing in design science research. In: Jain, H., Sinha, A.P., Vitharana, P. (eds.) DESRIST 2011. LNCS, vol. 6629, pp. 1–16. Springer, Heidelberg (2011). https://doi.org/10.1007/978-3-642-20633-7_1
45. Brown, T., Wyatt, J.: Design thinking for social innovation. Dev. Outreach **12**, 29–43 (2010)
46. Hevner, A.R.: A three cycle view of design science research. Scand. J. Inf. Syst. **19**, 4 (2007)
47. Collier, J.E., Bienstock, C.C.: How do customers judge quality in an e-tailer? MIT Sloan Manag. Rev. **48**, 35 (2006)
48. Vinkovits, M., Zimmermann, A.: Defining a trust framework design process. In: Furnell, S., Lambrinoudakis, C., Lopez, J. (eds.) TrustBus 2013. LNCS, vol. 8058, pp. 37–47. Springer, Heidelberg (2013). https://doi.org/10.1007/978-3-642-40343-9_4
49. Jenkins, M.-C., Churchill, R., Cox, S., Smith, D.: Analysis of user interaction with service oriented chatbot systems. In: Jacko, J.A. (ed.) HCI 2007. LNCS, vol. 4552, pp. 76–83. Springer, Heidelberg (2007). https://doi.org/10.1007/978-3-540-73110-8_9
50. Grabner-Kraeuter, S.: The role of consumers' trust in online-shopping. J. Bus. Ethics **39**, 43–50 (2002)
51. Chen, L., Pu, P.: Trust building in recommender agents. In: Proceedings of the Workshop on Web Personalization, Recommender Systems and Intelligent User Interfaces at the 2nd International Conference on E-Business and Telecommunication Networks. Citeseer (2005)

Adaptive Workflow Design Based on Blockchain

Daniel Narh Treku$^{(\boxtimes)}$ ⓘ and Jun Sun ⓘ

Information Systems Department, VCOBE,
University of Texas Rio Grande Valley, Edinburg, TX 78539, USA
{daniel.treku01,jun.sun}@utrgv.edu

Abstract. Increasingly, organizational processes have become more complex. There is a need for the design of workflows to focus on how organizations adapt to emergent processes while balancing the need for decentralization and centralization goal. The advancement in new technologies especially blockchain provides organizations with the opportunity to achieve the goal. Using blockchain technology (i.e. smart contract and blocks of specified consensus for deferred action), we leverage the theory of deferred action and a coordination framework to conceptually design a workflow management system that addresses organizational emergence (e-WfMS). Our artifact helps managers to predict and store the impact of deferred actions. We evaluated the effectiveness of our system against a complex adaptive system for utility assessment.

Keywords: Workflow · Emergent organization · Coordination · Blockchain · Smart contract

1 Introduction

Recurrently, large multi-unit organizations face the need for effective design of work processes that leverage contemporary technological advancements, such as blockchain technologies, to achieve efficiency goals. Relatedly, these multi-unit organizations are faced with the need to balance demands for centralized technology systems while improving the flexibility in usage at localized levels in maximizing cost and service efficiencies, and process effectiveness [1].

Consequently, organizations design and leverage automated yet adaptable workflow management systems (WfMS) to achieve these aims. Effective workflow processes ensure that an organization continues to control aspects of the work process that need direct decisions and allow for discretion in the processes that require creativity and indirect decisions. Key issues for specifying and modeling workflows "relate to task definition, task coordination and correctness of execution requirements" [2, p. 3]. Workflow models or systems thus represent embedded systems of the organizing logic of the organization. Hence, their design is critical to the strategic goals of the organization. In this study, the concept of workflows is referred to as a composite set of tasks comprised of coordinated computer-based and human activities [3]. A workflow model is defined as an illustrative schema or a formal computer representation of work procedures that controls the sequence of performed tasks.

© Springer Nature Switzerland AG 2019
B. Tulu et al. (Eds.): DESRIST 2019, LNCS 11491, pp. 284–299, 2019.
https://doi.org/10.1007/978-3-030-19504-5_19

A "new logic of organizing" embraces organizations as an emergent phenomenon and affords "managerial rationale for designing and evolving specific organizational arrangements in response to an enterprise's environmental and strategic imperatives" [4, p. 107]. Within the context of this logic of organizing, this study argues that, since organizational processes have become more integrative and complex, there is the need to design workflow models that incorporate organizational emergent process that are often blurred and irreducible. Emergence requires adaptation, resulting in 'complex adaptive systems' [32]. The study, therefore, seeks to design workflows principled on this new organizing logic through the development and use of theoretically driven effective and adaptive workflow systems that address emergent dispositions of contemporary multi-unit organization. The nature of blockchain technology allows for decentralization with its distributed ledger but also automation of activities to satisfy centralization goals. We discuss its tenets and its role in designing emergent organizational WfMS (e-WfMS) in later sections.

In practice, several WfMSs in use purport to offer the needed adaptivity and flexibility while meeting centralized goals via automation. Prior studies have advanced the need for the adaptive workflow to address issues with rigid automated workflows. However, these studies are grounded on proprietary conceptualized frameworks and largely lack formal theoretical support necessary to explain complex phenomena [5]. Such formal theories are the kernel theories required to advance design-related explanatory and prescriptive theory [6, 7]. Our e-WfMS design approach for a multi-unit an organization leverages the theory of deferred action (TDA) that provides a framework for addressing adaptivity and emergence in organizational work systems and processes. Based on TDA, we design a model that views workflow systems as deferred models of reality where a purposive workflow design structure is imposed on reality (current real systems) but actors are allowed to shape the design in the context of real situations in anticipation of achieving a future state [8]. In this study, we focus on adoption of an in-house (localized) smart contract, a blockchain technology, in ensuring adherence to legal dictates of the business environment and the specification of details of deferred action after consensus is reached between approving agents after negotiations in the coordination. A coded block of deferred action enables system actions that address mandatory emergent demands (such as automatic creation of future roles, processes and triggers with effective timestamps and triggers).

The specificity of our design – how it departs from prior studies – is three folds. First, the information system addressed in this study is more specific – the design of a WfMS for a multi-unit organization. Secondly, our agent-based modeling is theoretically backed. Thirdly, we leverage blockchain technologies with regards to smart contracts with storage of consensus built in the coordination processes as deferred actions. The last, which is the major premise of our study, relates to the underlying assertion of Patel et al.'s [9] work that emergence cannot be predicted. Whiles we agree to this generality of emergence conception, it is practically the attempt to address this "wicked problem" [6] that calls for intuitive design approach. By this, the study does not claim to predict emergence exclusively, but the approach used allows for attempted prediction based on a theoretically-backed coding process that captures emergence in the short term and long term for organizational managers to make informed decisions. Our research objective thus seeks to address this problem by not only dealing with contingency factors but explaining how an e-WfMS can be effectively designed. An e-WfMS that addresses organizational emergence as a concept of coordination logic for building simulated predictions of short-term and long-term emergence. We model this as vector error correction (VEC) model of co-integrated parameters. Succinctly the research question we seek to answer is *how short-term coordination efforts affect long-term coordination efforts in informing the design of emergent multi-unit organization emergence for WfMS?*

The rest of the paper is organized as follows. The next section discusses workflows and associated management issues. Generally, the design methodology follows [10] work. We explore organizational design literature and organizational adaptation to provide the organizational principles required for our design as well as the main kernel theory used. Based on the theory of deferred action, we combine the underlying assumptions from the proffered justificatory knowledge to extract explanatory and theoretical design constructs necessary for the conceptual design and construction of our artifact. Based on the design principles, we posit two propositions necessarily to address the relevance of our conceptual design. Further, evaluation approach and discussion sections are provided. Next, we discuss implications to theory and practice. We conclude by identifying limitations to our study and areas for future research.

2   Research Background

2.1   Adaptive Workflow Systems

Alter [11] argues that the core of the information systems field should not necessarily be "IT artifact" but "IT-enabled work systems." WfMSs embody work systems that support business processes by coordinating activities within the business processes [12]. These assertions underscore the relevance of IT-mediated workflow studies. Workflows can be referred to as a composite set of tasks comprised of coordinated computer-based and human activities [3], and a workflow model is an illustrative schema or a formal computer representation of work procedures that controls the sequence of performed tasks. Largely the need for control has informed specifications of workflows schema where the structure is rigid and characteristic of with several pitfalls such inability of users to make discretionary error identification for timely fixes.

Current technological advancements and the need for greater flexibility, organizational creativity and learning in system development implies that workflows systems must be adaptive to improve productivity [13]. Several studies have advanced the need for the adaptive workflow to address issues with rigid automated workflows. However, these studies are grounded on proprietary conceptualized frameworks and largely lack formal theoretical support necessary to explain complex phenomena [5]. Such formal theories are the kernel theories required to advance design-related explanatory and prescriptive theory [6, 7]. The prevailing workflow systems in practice exemplify this disposition. These systems either provide smart user interfaces or flexible definitions of BPMN (business process model and notations) and DMN (decision models and notation) specifications with the view of aiding adaptivity. Mostly these are virtualization tools with less analytical capabilities buttressing the lack of theoretical backing in their design [14].

In their argument for the need for a new organizing logic in contemporary organizational design, Sambamurthy and Zmud [4] argued that even effective organizational systems are inadequate to shape appropriate insights for current business practices. They argue that the epitome of this new logic is a design that deals effectively with the emerging processes. Thus, the workflow system must do more than just having adaptive tendencies. The capability to organize IT-related activities that address this logic is seen the integrating structures available. The problem is pronounced when these integrating structures generate emergent processes that require further new adaptive processes. Although numerous adaptive systems have been fashioned to allow requisite integrating structures, lack of theoretical grounding and the rigidity imposed on the business process representation and enactment limits these systems [15]. What is needed in workflow modeling, aside the incorporation of an emergent process, is a "theoretical framework for the representation, analysis, and manipulation of workflow systems" [12, p. 9]. This study aims at deriving a set of design principles for adaptive workflow processes that are based on formal kernel theory and addresses the emergent demands of current organizational designs. The design approach, therefore, leverages the theory of deferred action that provides a framework for addressing adaptive and emergence concepts in the design of information systems [8]. The next sub-section discusses the role of blockchain as an emerging technology that emerging multi-unit organization could leverage in managing their workflows.

2.2   Blockchain Technology

Businesses have several examples of networks of individuals and organizations that collaborate to create value and wealth through the exchange of assets – information resources, goods and services – along these networks [16]. In multi-unit organizations, the coordination of activities and the consensus that is built around these coordinated activities are vital in the growth of the organization. Adaptive systems, however, due to the flexibility and adaptivity of WfMSs, actors' (agents') motives in negotiations and decision-making may be disparate and their activities may be clandestine. In high discretionary business environments before business processes are institutionalized, these may thwart automation (or centralization) goals. Thus, there is a need for integrity and auditability in the adaptation of work processes. It is also important that this integrity of the system be agreed upon by relevant agents in the processes.

Blockchain technology provides the basis for a dynamic shared ledger that can efficiently and effectively expedite transactional activities among parties in the business networks [16]. Blockchain technology is a distributed ledger [17] which serves as an integrable and immutable datastore that can aid alignment of business processes and actors' activities and business goals [18] while removing transaction costs associated with intermediaries. Traditionally, blockchain was regarded as the technology behind cryptocurrencies (e.g. bitcoin) [19] which deals with the double spend problem in finance but now seen as a real alternative in many application areas [20] such as supply chain [21], internet of things (IoT), security and privacy [22], as well as WfMSs [18]. We focus on the innovative role of blockchain in the design of e-WfMSs for multi-unit emergent organizations. By leveraging the shared-ledger system, blockchain technology solves the pitfalls of transaction governance. Essentially blockchain encompasses four areas of design which are relevant to the e-WfMS design principles. These are: decentralization (work is done at different nodes without a need for the third party to build trust), data integrity and security (immutability in data stored), transparency and auditability (transparency in transaction and audits acceptable by all actors), and automation (balancing centralization goals with network involvement. For instance, use of smart contracts where ideals of the contracts are stored after consensus and requisite actions are triggered by the system) [18]. Blockchain implementation can either be public or private. For public, anyone can add to the chain whiles private chains call for approval by designated actors. We focus on permission blockchain technology (private implementation) because the study focuses on a design that addresses a phenomenon in business or private organizations. Specifically, the study illustrates the use of "smart contract" (a blockchain technology) using the a permissioned hyperledger platform enabled by IBM technologies. "A smart contract is a set of software-driven rules that encapsulate the terms agreed to by the parties involved" [17]. The specification of the contract details in the smart contracts will enable automated executions termed trans-actions without the need for human intervention or intermediaries. For a critical review of blockchain literature, see Kokina et al. [17].

3   Kernel Theories

The theory of deferred action (TDA) provides us with design dimensions for designing complex adaptive systems. Its strength is in the prediction that some aspects of orga-nization work emerge and the recognition that organizational agents will respond to emergence as deferred action [8, 9]. It addresses the focal issue of designing emergent process-aware adaptive workflows required in current design organizations that affords a process perspective of the organizing logic of digitally innovative systems. Secondly, it provides the theoretical backing needed to produce artifacts from design-relevant explanatory and prescriptive theory. The core assumption of TDA is organization, organizational data, information and knowledge as well as stable systems are all emergent temporally [23]. Thus, in designing a workflow system, although the system may be designed as stable in its current state, it would be thought of as a deferred information system. This is Patel's [8] deferred model of reality (model ontology) dimension of TDA that reflects emergence and enables appropriate responses by actors as deferred actions while pursuing predetermined goals (current adaptive specifications).

Emergence requires present, contextual, and situational aspects and historicity to be factored into the design [9]. In our context, emergence is defined as the patterns that arise through interactions of multi-unit agents, the inter-unit interactions with WfMS and the multi-unit responses to factors that affect coordinated processes (either con-tingent or based on the past events). Patel et al. [9], based on TDA, used agent-based simulation to assess how agents behave in emergent organizations in the present context of planned action (the real or more observable dimension the theory). As much as TDA improved our understanding for designing emergent organizations, their work provides avenues for advancing knowledge in the design of emergent organization via workflow systems by redefining the information ontology of the emergent organization as a set of coordination activities that involves agents of multi-units of the organization.

This redefinition is in line with the criticality of identity (agents and their roles) and coordination advanced for embracing the new organizing logic [4]. Figure 1 delineates the focus of our study and affords the use of specific kernel theories to identify agents, their roles and behavior as well as the factors that inform their actions. Consequently, the study employs Williams and Karahanna's [1] framework of coordinating processes in multi-unit organizations.

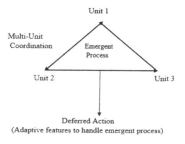

Fig. 1. Coordination in a multi-unit organization

4   Design Principles on Coordination Logic

At the heart of organizational emergent processes is the view of coordination activities as a temporally unfolding process of interrelated actions [1]. This view underlines the study's conception of the new organizing logic, espoused earlier and reechoes the TDA's circumspection of temporality notion in designing emergence into systems. To this end, we focus succinctly on two coordination mechanisms critical in designing emergent workflow systems. These are generative mechanisms of consensus-making and a unit-aligning mechanism [1]. According to William and Karahanna [1], each coordinating effort is made up of structural and inner contextual design principles. The structural principle specifies features for "operating mode" (objective, output, and accountability of coordination efforts) and "composition" (i.e., the arrangement of actors and the effectiveness of leadership and influence of managerial rationale). The inner contextual principle embraces the coordinating climate (i.e., the influence of trust and the nature of communication between organizational actors) and engagement logic (i.e., the influence of relevance, action orientation and potential organizational impact of anticipated coordination events).

Additionally, outer contexts of economic, industry/sector, legal and technological which affects the internal coordination processes are specified as design principles. This study leverages smart contracts in ensuring adherence to these outer contextual dictates of the business environment and the specification of deferred action after consensus is reached among approving agents after coordination and negotiation processes. A block of deferred action enables system actions that address mandatory emergent demands (such as automatic creation of future roles and processes based on already coded effective dates). Effective actions become adaptive actions, and because a block is a shared-ledger, activities can be assessed by all actors associated with the process including new actors enabled by the system.

5 Design Process

Design science creates and evaluates IT artifacts intended to solve identified organizational problems [24]. Our design approach follows the methodology of Peffers et al. [10]. Having motivated our research objectives, we identified the kernel theories and justificatory knowledge bases required to sufficiently address the research question. Next, we generated design principles that would enable explicit specification of the artifact in solving the identified problem. The discussion below describes the use of the iterative components of Peffers et al.'s [10] design research methodology.

5.1 Exploratory and Confirmatory Focus Group Discussion

An exploratory focus group meeting was carried out to explore these underlying assumptions of coordination for the design of emergent systems involving a three-unit organizational process—this exercise aimed at refining assumptions that followed heuristic processes of problem restructuring and artifact satisficing [25]. The coordination mechanisms were discussed, and the tentative design features and schemas for the artifact were modified after prior modeling efforts. The research question in the exploratory focus group discussion concentrated on how these coordinating mechanisms would be specified as design features for addressing emergent processes. *Based on the design principles, a confirmatory focus group discussion was used to assess the conceptual artifact design [26]. Feedback was used to further improve the design as shown in Fig. 2.*

5.2 Applying Design Principles

To address future impact of outer context and the other coordination elements, the study used agent-based modeling where event or happenings are specified in the binary form of '0' and '1' based on short and long-term time goals. For instance, for an organization that recognizes the need to adopt smart contracts (blockchain technology) as part of its long-term future processes, the specification of this long-term future event is '1'. If the use of this specific aspect of the blockchain is already in place or about to be introduced, then the event is coded 0 representing short to implementation. In our context, long-term events are those of which the execution extends beyond one year (the next fiscal cycle) whereas short-term events reflect decision-making goals to be addressed within a year.

In another example, when the organization perceives that its processes may be impacted by new political and legal rules that may lead to a new emergent process in the long-term (generally more than a year), a binary '1' is specified by the system administrator based on consensus. The issue of the temporality of emergence phenomenon is addressed by allowing for changes in agent-based modeling as organizations perception of the impact of future events changes. The coordination design principles are assigned values that identify each coordination activity and the respective agents or actors. The valuation is based on the criticality of the coordinated efforts and the actors involved. The value generated is the value of the short and long-term factors for the time series. The data frequency would be daily, and the information would be

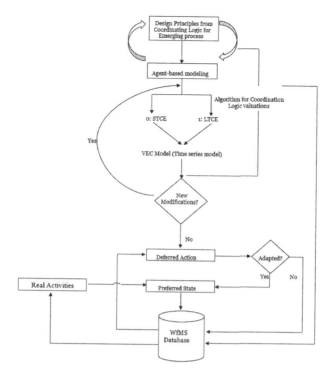

Fig. 2. Conceptual design of e-WfMS artifact

stored automatically in the workflow database. The study, therefore, proposes another artifact – an algorithm – designed for the calculation of these time series values based on defined rules and elements of the coordinated activities.

The description above allows the use of coordinating logic design principles for the agent modeling and the capture of deferred actions as though contextual factors of the coordination conception had already taken effect. For instance, in our main artifactual model, the study leverages the use of 'smart contracts' of blockchain technology as a new and representative emerging organizational design logic and an example for outer contextual factors. All the coordination principles among a three-tier multi-unit organization were specified in the algorithms for coding (programming environment). Based on the discussion we posit the following propositions:

Proposition 1: Short-term coordination activities will affect long-term coordination activities such that a change in the short-term consideration will impact positively impact long-term emergent efforts.

Proposition 2: The design artifact when used to analyze scenarios of coordinated activities with emergence undertones will yield significant positive results. That is, the design of WfMS that incorporates design perspectives is likely to be better positioned (more agile) compared with a system without our design perspectives.

5.3   Evaluation Approach

Our evaluation methods incorporate both experimental and analytical approaches and to some extent an observational approach [24]. The experimental procedure is the simulation processes contained in the agent-based modeling. The simulated outcomes are used as time series data for modeling the prediction of emergence. Specifically, we use the vector error correction model (i.e., cointegration vector autoregression model). This model addresses cointegration impacts and momentum effects of interacting variables (short and long-term emergence) by differencing the factors to the first-order to achieve stationarity and forecasting ability. The estimation model is then included in the coding process for our WfMS that caters for the emergent multi-unit organization. The use of case studies for evaluation is more pseudo-observational rather than observational – we use real cases to observe the behavior of our artifact, but these cases are applied as narratives rather than experiential. Finally, the advantages of this system compared to other systems would then be discussed.

The simulation approach follows, chronologically, the processes of user selection, routine and atypical composite task selection, scenario design, the design of attributes of scenario, recording data, coding textual data from the focus group, quantitative analysis of coded data and real-world testing. Thus, this simulation approach aids artifact utility evaluation via a confirmatory focus group. It would also aid to assess whether all coordinated activities necessary for the future anticipated event can be captured by the prototyped system and applied when needed. Additionally, two real business processes from prior case studies by Williams and Karahanna [1] were used as scenarios in a confirmatory focus group discussion for the evaluation. These are adapted and represents the two generative coordination mechanisms at the heart of emergent processes. The last step of the simulation approach may not be elaborate for this study and would be realized at the modified prototypal stage of the artifact in the simulation process.

6   Conceptual Artifact Evaluation

6.1   Case Study Analysis

The organizational case to implement our conception of WfMS is adopted from William and Karahanna [1] study. The adopted case describes an IT Advisory Committee (ITAC) coordinating efforts at an organization. For a full narration of the case, see William and Karahanna [1, p. 939]. For illustrative purposes, this study focuses on how actors (agents), their roles and integrating activities generate events that inform emergence. There were 19 actors involved in the coordinating activities. We coded these actors ordinally, according to their rankings. The rank of an actor has ramifications on consensus making. Consider Table 1 for illustrative purposes.

Table 1. Agents and their ranks that define roles (Adopted from ITAC case)

Actor/Agent	Level of influence
Chief Information Officer	1
ITAC Chair and major Division IT Director	1
Public Service Sub-Committee Chair	1
Advanced Computing Sub-Committee Chair	1
Former ITAC Chair and Division IT Director	2
Division IT Director	2
Advanced Computing Sub-Committee Chair	3
IT Managerial Committee Rep	3
Central IT Budget Director	1

6.2 Algorithm for Coordination Logic Calculation (ACLC) – Algorithm 1

Each day data would be recorded based on ongoing activities and the actors involved and the consensus made. The algorithm would be iterative as events changes in a day. At the end of the business day, it records the value in the ACLC column. The smaller the calculated value the most critical the event is. After negotiation and decision making, the tentative time of implementation is set via consensus. If no consensus is reached, the situation deemed disparate but may change by the day. Each unique event is automatically assigned a primary ID. A cumulative adjustment to ACLC (CA-ACLC) would be calculated if an event changes in the days ahead and it is most likely the calculated value would be high also indicating less important activity.

Table 2 gives the parameters for ACLS calculation: fundamental ACLC formula = [(importance of event) × (sum of actors' level of influence (rank)) × (consensus level)]. So, for a moderate priority and high consensus event that requiring short term action and involving an actor ranked, one (1) and two actors ranked three (3), the calculation for STCE, coded 0, would be 2 × 1 × (1 + 3 + 3) yielding a value of 14 which is adjusted cumulatively. The inverse values of these measures are used in the time series plot to estimate impacts of emerging events.

Table 2. Parameters and value assignment for ACLC calculation

Importance of event			Level of influence	Consensus level		
Priority	Moderate	Least	Rank of exchanging actors involved in an event	High	Low	Disparate
1	2	3	1, 2, 3….	1	2	3

6.3 Vector Error Correction (VEC) Estimation of Simulated Data

Vector error correction model enables forecast of the cointegrating dynamics of the regressors (LTCE and STCE). The model can easily transition into a vector autoregression (VAR) model to explain other dynamics of the regressors even when they are not cointegrated, hence our use of VEC. To test proposition one, the VEC model is used to plot a time series (Day against CA-ACLC) to examine the relationship between short term consensus and long-term consensus impacts. This is critical for would aid decision making as it informs the organization on what activity has the greatest impact on ongoing organizational activities. With such analytical input on emerging phenomenon, an organization would be able to estimate the time points which present bubbles or bursts for critical organizational decision making and resource allocation needs.

In Table 3, for brevity, we aggregated the consensus level and importance of event as ranked values. In practice, these represent the weighted summations of various logics that underlie unit-aligning mechanism and consensus-making mechanisms in organizational activities. The inverse of the adjusted ACLC values is used to plot the time series graph so that the greater value shows higher premium effect.

Table 3. Generating simulation data for VEC time series plot

Days	Short-term (STCE, within 3 months)	STCE ACLC	STCE CA-ACLC	Long-term (LTCE, after 3 months)	LTCE CA-ACLC	Cumulative adjustment (CA) of ACLC
1	0 (TS1)	14	14	1		
2	...	...	15.6	....	...	...
⋮						

For cointegration of LTCE and STCE to exist, consider the following linear combination of two coordination effort types: $STCE_t + \beta LTCE_t = d_t$

Equilibrium in long-run emergence exists if for a given constant β, the difference, d_t is stationary. This means short run deviations away from the long-run equilibrium, $STCE_t = -\beta LTCE$ are observed when $d_t \neq 0$. Having stationarity means the short run deviations are only temporal, and if long-run equilibrium exists; $STCE_t$ and $LTCE_t$ are said to be cointegrated with vector $[1, \beta]$. The two coordination types are integrated of the order one $I(1)$, and d_t is integrated of the order zero $I(0)$. We tested for stationarity using GLS augmented Dickey-Fuller unit root tests [27, 28] in STATA 14. We then estimate the following:

$$\Delta STCE_t = a_s + \alpha_S(STCE_{t-1} + \beta LTCE_{t-1})$$
$$+ \sum_{j}^{k} a_{ss}(j)\Delta STCE_{t-j} + \sum_{j=1}^{k} a_{sL}\Delta LTCE_{t-j} + \varepsilon_{st}$$
$$\Delta LTCE_t = a_H + \alpha_H(STCE_{t-1} + \beta LTCE_{t-1})$$
$$+ \sum_{j}^{k} a_{LS}(j)\Delta STCE_{t-j} + \sum_{J=1}^{k} a_{LL}\Delta LTCE_{t-j} + \varepsilon_{Ht}$$

Where α_S and α_L speed of adjustments which explains how much of current decisions affect long-term decision. A convergence can also be estimated to explain at what point both decisions produce the same effect or value. If no cointegrating relationship exists between the two coordination efforts, both long-run and short-run speed of adjustments equal zero for the null hypotheses. The alternative is our proposition one.

6.4   Pseudo Code for Storing Actionable Consensus – Algorithm 2

The pseudo code to facilitate implementation of conceptual design is depicted above. For integrity and adherence to consensus decisions, a hyperledger blockchain records the actors and the actionable consensus decisions in a smart contract. This decision can only be modified after consensus by the same parties at their nodes of the blockchain. The results from the time series indicate the unique activities having the greater impact. This impact is empirically factored into the operationalization of algorithm two. Next is the assessment of organizational actors on whether they would accept system adaptation based on impact factor-related decisions. When decision is deemed better and accepted, the action is block-chained via the use of in-house multi-unit smart contract. Specific decision metrics and triggers are coded in the smart contract to facilitate realization of deferred action.

The program development is influenced by the conceptual flow shown in Fig. 2 and the discussions above. Time series estimations are interpreted and presented at each node (actors on the blockchain network) to allow for negotiation, consensus and decision making. As noted earlier, the decision mix characterizes the smart contract document for that specific coordination event on the network and in the organization at large. Modification to this contract begins from time zero. Decision reached is time stamped and parties involved are recorded. Parties by the written code can modify decision outcomes later. Future endeavors to this study should entail continual and extensive evaluation of computation cost and running time of the algorithms to optimize implementation and maximize system efficiency.

```
Modification = 0//decision 0 is a no modification dummy decision based on time series output
STCE_CA-ACLC = 0
LTCE_CA-ACLC = 0
smartContract = 1

for modification = 0 to n: //agents peruse output from time series for specific cumulative STCE and LTCE's
    if decision = 1: // implies agents or actors on the network have agreed that decision outcome from
    //time series is better than previous decision
            update STCE and LCTE cumulative adjustment values, CA-ACLC
            return STCE_CA-ACLC
            return LTCE_CA-ACLC

    elif decision = 0: //implies no new decision and consensus reached
            return (store) modification = 0 on database as deferred action
            // with timestamp. Smart contract details (e.g. hiring, resource allocation, onboarding, cost
            //cutting, meeting legal requirements, etc.) are specified.
            n = 0
            store as deferred action i

    else modification = modification + 1    //this implies new modifications, for loop continues

pass

if deferred action i is triggered or acted upon

    //implies action has been adapted into organizational workflow processes and blockchain in-house
    //smart contract terminates on the specific business process negotiations. Each approved and executed
    //transaction per the smart contract is stored as transaction ids on the shared or distributed
    //hyperledger block and available to all parties.

    smartContract = smartContract + 1 //record is stored by contract number + timestamp in WfMS database

else WfMS runs in current/preferred state until later adaptation events.
```

7 Discussion

We discuss the utilization of business case with respect to the link with the smart contract utilization in the conceptual design artifact and in line with our propositions. In a future prototypical assessment, proposition two can be evaluated using Patel et al.'s [9] complex adaptive system as a benchmark system to assess the effectiveness of our design artifact. Nonetheless the use of confirmatory focus group discussion helped to address key stakeholder concerns.

We utilized IBM's permissioned hyperledger fabric and hyperledger composer component (a proprietary blockchain platform for the illustration) on Blockchain Platform 2.0 to illustrate the use of smart contracts in capturing consensus. In implementing the use of smart contract, two components are key. The blockchain code and the blockchain network. The blockchain code (program script) governed transactions (i.e. the details smart contracts among the agents). This lines of coding or contractual terms are installed on the hyperledger platform as contract (s). In real organizations with coordinating teams on business events, multi-units could be several and agents each unit may have no or more than one actor participating in the business event. Our blockchain network was executed each unit or actor having a unique IP address and ID. Requisite actors are added by invitation and approval of existing parties. Communication among approving actors were enabled by the network channels. The discussion is what facilitates the complete execution of algorithm two (2) and depicts the key role of blockchain technology in this research. In the business environment, several smart contracts entailing multiple decision points can be executed depending on the business events at play in the organization. It is within this context that the impact of proposition one is addressed. The reason being that the chain of activities and consequent extent of utilization is underpinned by the agent-based modeling and the interpretations of the estimations from the VEC model. Based on the decision outcomes in a business case, the conceptual model as well as the generative algorithm used in designing the prototype system can be modified offers and this modification has implications for the contract details and deferred actions.

Having assessed systems from HP, IBM and other research prototypes, Adams et al. [29] outlined six key functionality criteria for commercial adaptive workflow system conceptualization and implementation. These are; flexibility and use, adaptation via reflection, dynamic evolution of work practices, locality of change and comprehensibility of process models and the elevation of exceptions to "first-class citizens". A critical review of this literature shows that our conceptualization affords these six functionality criteria.

8 Implications for Theory and Practice

This design study contributes to the theory of designed action by exploring how emergence could be designed. We also advance Patel et al.'s [9] study with the use of theory to model agents and their coordinated activities. Our approach encompasses contingency factors, the roles of the agents (included in the algorithm for calculation) and the past histories of organizational activities. It shows how stakeholders can be used to design e-WfMS and provide recommendations for organizational managers. The nature of ACLC algorithm which encompasses individual level as well as group level parameters points to the macro-micro-macro multilevel theorization of organizational coordinating efforts that define future organizational emergence [1]. Thus, managers making decision based on the VEC forecasting model can have a better assurance of the impact at different levels in the organization.

9 Conclusion

The study derives design principles from the theory of deferred action and the coordination framework to model an e-WfMS artifact. Such an emergent system allows for the use of smart contracts in recording consensus from the coordinating activities that organizational agents engage in for the realization of key strategic goals of an emergent organization.

The study is limited by the omission of granular representations of workflow schema in the conceptual design. Granularity in the representation is not the focus of this study but future studies can explore our design of organizational emergence with such granularity to allow for clearer implementation. Narenda's [30] insightful study on flexible workflow and multi-agent interactions provides a critical bridge for such granularity in the e-WfMS design approach. The level of analysis is in this study is inter-unit. The study can be extended by examining different unit of analysis. The study can be used to design intra-unit or group emergent processes in the organization in which the impact of external units could be treated as an environmental or contextual factor. Finally in contexts such health care sector where coordination activities are central to the quality of care [31] and decision outcomes could be fatal, conceptualization of emergent workflow system would be vital in optimizing quality outcomes.

References

1. Williams, C.K., Karahanna, E.: Causal explanation in the coordinating process: a critical realist case of federated IT governance structures. MIS Q. **37**, 933–964 (2013)
2. Basu, A., Kumar, A.: Research commentary: workflow management issues in e-business. Inf. Syst. Res. **13**, 1–14 (2002). https://doi.org/10.1287/isre.13.1.1.94
3. Lei, Y., Singh, M.P.: A comparison of workflow metamodels. In: ER-97 Workshop on Behavioral Modeling and Design Transformations: Issues and Opportunities in Conceptual Modeling, Los Angeles (1997)
4. Sambamurthy, V., Zmud, R.W.: Research commentary: the organizing logic of an enterprise's IT activities in digital era—a prognosis of practice and call for research. Inf. Syst. Res. **11**, 105–114 (2000)
5. Joosten, S., Brinkkemper, S.: Fundamental concepts for workflow automation in practice. In: Proceedings of the International Conference on Information Systems (ICIS 1995). AIS, Amsterdam (1995)
6. Hevner, A.R., Chatterjee, S.: Design Research in Information Systems: Theory and Practice. Springer, New York (2010). https://doi.org/10.1007/978-1-4419-5653-8

7. Kuechler, W., Vaishnavi, V.: A framework for theory development in design science research: multiple perspectives. J. Assoc. Inf. Syst. **13**, 395–423 (2012)
8. Patel, N.V.: Theory of deferred action. Organization and Systems Design, pp. 83–107. Palgrave Macmillan, London (2006)
9. Patel, N.V., Eldabi, T., Khan, T.M.: Theory of deferred action: agent-based simulation model for designing complex adaptive systems. Organ. Syst. Des. **23**, 521–537 (2010). https://doi.org/10.1057/9780230625419_4
10. Peffers, K., Tuunanen, T., Rothenberger, M.A., Chatterjee, S.: A design science research methodology for information systems research. J. Manag. Inf. Syst. **24**, 45–77 (2007)
11. Alter, S.: Same words, different meanings: are basic IS/IT concepts our self-imposed tower of babel? Commun. AIS. **3**, 1–89 (2000)
12. Reijers, H., Vanderfeesten, I., van der Aalst, W.M.P.: The effectiveness of workflow management systems: a longitudinal study. Int. J. Inf. Manag. **36**, 126–141 (2016)
13. Cooper, R.B.: Information technology development creativity: a case study of attempted radical change. MIS Q. **24**, 245–276 (2000)
14. Basu, A., Blanning, R.W.: A formal approach to workflow analysis. Inf. Syst. Res. **11**, 17–36 (2000)
15. van der Aalst, W.M.P., Berens, P.J.S.: Beyond workflow management: product-driven case handling. In: International ACM SIGGROUP Conference on Supporting Group Work (GROUP 2001), pp. 42–51, New York (2001)
16. IBM: Blockchain Essentials. https://courses.cognitiveclass.ai/courses/course-v1: developerWorks+BC0101EN+v1/info
17. Kokina, J., Mancha, R., Pachamanova, D.: Blockchain: emergent industry adoption and implications for accounting. J. Emerg. Technol. Account. **14**, 91–100 (2017). https://doi.org/ 10.2308/jeta-51911
18. Fridgen, G., Radszuwill, S., Urbach, N., Utz, L.: Cross-organizational workflow management using blockchain technology - towards applicability, auditability, and automation. Presented at the Hawaii International Conference on System Sciences (2018)
19. Beck, R., Muller-Bloch, C.: Blockchain as radical innovation: a framework for engaging with distributed ledgers as incumbent organization. Presented at the 50th Hawaii International Conference on System Sciences, Waikoloa, Hawaii (2017)
20. Nofer, M., Gomber, P., Hinz, O., Schiereck, D.: Blockchain. Bus. Inf. Syst. Eng. **59**, 183–187 (2017)
21. Korpela, K., Hallikas, J., Dahlberg, T.: Digital supply chain transformation toward blockchain integration. In: 50th Hawaii International Conference on System Sciences, Waikoloa, Hawaii (2017)
22. Dorri, A., Kanhere, S.S., Jurdak, R., Gauravaram, P.: Blockchain for IOT security and privacy: the case study of a smart home. In: 2017 IEEE International Conference on Pervasive Computing and Communications Workshops, Kona, Big Island, Hawaii (2017)
23. Dwivedi, Y.K., Wade, M.R., Schneberger, S.L.: Information Systems Theory: Explaining and Predicting Our Digital Society. Springer, New York (2012). https://doi.org/10.1007/978-1-4419-6108-2
24. Hevner, A.R., March, S.T., Park, J., Ram, S.: Design science in information systems research. MIS Q. **28**, 75–105 (2004). https://doi.org/10.2307/25148625
25. Gregory, R.W., Muntermann, J.: Research note—heuristic theorizing: proactively generating design theories. Inf. Syst. Res. **25**, 639–653 (2014)
26. Tremblay, M.C., Hevner, A.R., Berndt, D.J.: Focus group for artifact refinement and evaluation in design research. Des. Res. Inf. Syst. **26**, 599–618 (2010). https://doi.org/10. 1007/978-1-4419-5653-8_10

27. Pesaran, M.H.: A simple panel unit root test in the presence of cross-section dependence. J. Appl. Econom. **22**, 265–312 (2007)
28. Dickey, D., Fuller, W.A.: Distribution of the estimators for autoregressive time series with a unit root. J. Am. Stat. Assoc. **74**, 427–431 (1979)
29. Adams, M., Edmond, D.: The Application of Activity Theory to Dynamic Workflow Adaptation Issues, p. 17 (2003)
30. Narendra, N.C.: Design considerations for incorporating flexible workflow and multi-agent interactions in agent societies. J. Assoc. Inf. Syst. **3**, 77–113 (2002). https://doi.org/10.17705/1jais.00024
31. Romanow, D., Rai, A., Keil, M.: CPOE-Enabled coordination: appropriation for deep structure use and impacts on patient outcomes. MIS Q. **42**, 189–212 (2018). https://doi.org/10.25300/MISQ/2018/13275
32. Alaa, G.: Derivation of factors facilitating organizational emergence based on complex adaptive systems and social autopoiesis theories. Emerg. Complex. Organ. **11**(1), 1–19 (2009)

Design Principles for E-Learning that Support Integration Work: A Case of Action Design Research

Amir Haj-Bolouri[✉]

School of Economics, Business, and IT, University West, Trollhättan, Sweden
`amir.haj-bolouri@hv.se`

Abstract. Design principles are prescriptive knowledge that offers theory-based guidelines for Design Science Research in Information Systems. This paper introduces and proposes a set of design principles for e-learning that support integration work. The design principles are proposed based on two cycles of Action Design Research. The cycles were conducted in the organizational setting of stakeholders and end-users known as integration workers, which are responsible for supporting the integration process of newly arrived immigrants of society. Overall, the contributions of this paper are (1) e-learning technologies that support integration work, (2) prescriptive knowledge in form of design principles for designing e-learning technologies that support integration work, and (3) an explicit case of Action Design Research that demonstrates the process of shaping and re-shaping design principles through two different cycles.

Keywords: Design principles · Action Design Research ·
Design Science Research · Information Systems · Integration work · E-Learning

1 Introduction

E-learning is a well-established idea of promoting Information Technologies (IT) for open, distance and flexible forms of learning and teaching. Universities have adopted this idea to support and enhance learning and teaching in the settings of higher education (e.g. universities) [1]. For example, e-learning technologies such as *Learning Management Systems* (LMS) have been designed and marketed to educational institutions to support teaching and learning [2]; scholars have built academic communities for diffusing relevant body of knowledge about e-learning [3, 4]; and last but not least, professional IS-designers and developers have developed innovative IT for successful use of e-learning in higher education [5]. It has thus been the convergence of the technological and pedagogical developments that has driven e-learning innovation and its collaborative potential to create and sustain a community of learners [6].

However, prior studies [7–9] indicate how the need of designing and implementing e-learning technologies, has reached settings that are not situated in higher education. Rather, such settings are situated in organizations that emphasize practices that support the integration process of newly arrived immigrants (hereafter referred to as *newcomers*). Such practices are generally referred to as *integration work* [10].

© Springer Nature Switzerland AG 2019
B. Tulu et al. (Eds.): DESRIST 2019, LNCS 11491, pp. 300–316, 2019.
https://doi.org/10.1007/978-3-030-19504-5_20

Integration work consists of practices that transcend the traditional setting of universities and asserts the process of informing and teaching newcomers how the very foundation of a society is constituted with respect to aspects such as a society's laws, regulations, values, etc. [10]. Examples of integration work include, online civic engagement of newcomers [8]; civic identities that support civic experiences of newcomers [9]; and civic orientation programs that inform newcomers what it means to live in their host society [7]. Consequently, the need of using e-learning technologies that have the capacity to support integration work, and the people who work with it (hereafter referred to as *integration workers*), is not currently mapped with any theory-based guidance for how to design such technologies [10].

1.1 Problem Statement and Research Aim

Knowledge on how to design traditional e-learning technologies in general, has been explicated into formulations of prescriptive knowledge such as for example design theories [e.g. 12, 13], which are inspired by Design Science Research (DSR) in the field of Information Systems (IS) [14, 15]. Such knowledge proposes IS-researchers and practitioners, guidelines on how to design e-learning technologies that are intended to support teachers at higher education. Consequently, alternatives for e-learning technologies have been suggested to offer a better fit for the requirements of tertiary e-learning and the broader settings within which it operates [16]. However, those technologies have explicitly been addressing the settings of higher education alone and not settings that support integration work or any other practice that emphasizes a teaching and learning discourse outside higher education. Arguably, this creates a general problem for IS-researchers and practitioners that are in urge of designing sufficient e-learning technologies for settings outside of higher education.

As an attempt to address this problem, the research aim of this paper is to produce and propose prescriptive knowledge in form of design principles, which offer IS-researchers and practitioners, theory-based guidance for designing e-learning technologies that support integration work. The purpose of achieving this aim is two-folded and fits the essential philosophy of DSR, which is, (1) to build efficient and sufficient IT-artifacts that address or solve real world problems and to produce research outcomes that accumulate the academic body of knowledge within the field of IS [14, 16–18]. Therefore, in order to accomplish this aim, and to produce a contribution that is relevant for both practice and the academic community of IS, two cycles of Action Design Research (ADR) [11] were performed in an organization that works with integration work and the outcomes of this will be reported throughout this paper.

The rest of the paper is structured as follow. First, a section of related research on two central topics (e-learning, design principles) of this paper will be provided. After that, information about ADR as the chosen research method is presented. Thereafter, the two subsequent ADR-cycles, together with how each activity was executed, are depicted, and finally, the paper ends with a set of concluding remarks.

2 Related Research

This section exhibits related research on e-learning with focus on how e-learning literature expresses the need of e-learning technologies that can be used in settings that performs teaching and learning outside higher education. Subsequently, this section depicts knowledge about prescriptive knowledge in DSR, with a particular emphasis on design principles.

2.1 Research on E-Learning

Research on e-learning [19–23] stresses an importance of transcending traditional e-learning technologies, in order to offer alternatives that are more adaptable, personalized, and easily available for a broader audience (e.g. teachers, learners) situated in other domain of works than solely the setting of higher education. Researchers [23] argue that old traditional e-learning technologies (e.g. LMS) suffer from isolated flaws (e.g. non-flexibility, non-personalized), making it less sufficient for the modern landscape of workplaces to adopt and use. Additionally, the modern landscape of workplaces (outside the setting of higher education) is highly affected by heterogeneity among an organization's practitioners with respect to their background, education, culture, expertise, and professional roles, making it difficult for organizations to efficiently and sufficiently implement and use stiffly framed e-learning technologies [24–26].

As a response to such issues, e-learning scholars advocate for e-learning and technologies that are adaptable and flexible toward different practices and organizational settings. For example, scholars such as [26] argue for a set of e-learning features that support different kind of target groups (e.g. teachers, learners) with respect to aspects such as: support of both individual reflection and collaborative knowledge building or epistemic practices; integration of theoretical knowledge with participants' practical experience; face-to-face dialogues; a progressive problem-solution orientation; support for the explication of implicit knowledge. Others [27, 28] who have studied the implementation and use of e-learning in organizations outside the settings of higher education, argue that too framed e-learning technologies make it difficult for non-academic organizations to adopt and use such successfully, because traditional e-learning was first and foremost designed and developed for universities. Furthermore, scholars such as [29, 30] argue that there is a general need for theoretical e-learning contributions that incorporate the aspect of heterogeneity with respect to elements such as: different norms and values among teaching and learning communities; flexible learning styles that match learning content; learning content that is adapted towards different learner-profiles; support of multimodality and large variation of IT-literacy among participants.

However, in order to address and realize such visions that incorporate variety and adaptability toward non-formal settings of teaching and learning, the question of how to design e-learning technologies that support such visions, arises. In turn, such question is framed within the realms of producing subsequent prescriptive knowledge that informs the design process. Hence, more knowledge about this in general, is needed.

2.2   Research on Design Principles

DSR in IS [13, 14, 16–18, 31–33] positions design principles as a highly accepted form of DSR-contributions [30–33]. Design principles are generally characterized as prescriptive knowledge [33] that capture knowledge about the design of specific artifact solutions (e.g. e-learning technologies) that belong to a general class of artifacts [32]. However, early works of Walls et al. [14] proposed Information Systems Design Theories (ISDT's) as a body of prescriptive knowledge that provide IS-researchers and practitioners guidelines for informing the design process. Guidelines and principles are thus conceptually interrelated, as one can for instance see in a paper by Markus et al. [31], where they argue that principles can exist in the shape of a set principles that offer guidance to the process of technology development. Additionally, Gregor and Jones [15] identify two distinct types of principles: (1) principles of form and function; (2) principles of implementation. Following these lines of reasoning, contemporary literature within the domain of DSR [34–39] estimate design principles as prescriptive knowledge that suggests action and formulates desired goals at various levels, ranging from being estimated as nascent DSR-outcomes [40] to fully matured DSR-outcomes [41]. Nevertheless, seminal methodologies within the domain of DSR, such as the ADR-method [11], propose design principles as a sufficient outcome of iterative activities of design, evaluation, reflection, and learning.

3   Research Approach

In order to govern this research, Sein et al.'s [11] ADR-method was chosen as the appropriate research method. Subsequently, the ADR-method provides a sufficient framework (shown in Fig. 1) for conducting research that emphasizes stages of building, intervening, and evaluating artifacts in organizational settings.

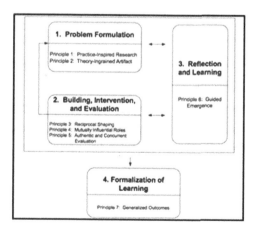

Fig. 1.   Action Design Research framework [11]

The ADR-method promotes a participatory philosophy that facilitate researchers to collaborate and work together with practitioners, stakeholders, and end-users of an organization, in an ADR-team. The collaboration of an ADR-team takes place in the organizational setting of practitioners, stakeholders, and end-users, iteratively. Additionally, the iterative nature of ADR incorporates the shaping and re-shaping of design principles as formalized learning outcomes of each cycle. In turn, Iterative cycles of ADR enables sufficient building, intervention, and evaluation of prototype versions, which evolve through each cycle and constitute the final artifact version. Consequently, the design process of an artifact is informed by theories that explain and predict, or theories that inform prescriptive knowledge such as design theories [14, 15]. Furthermore, according to Sein et al. [11], the artifact emerges through the interaction between design and use, meaning that the artifact shall reflect organizational implications due to technological intervention. The artifact is thus considered as a bundle of technologies that operate within the frame of an organization's social enterprise (e.g. culture, norms).

3.1 Empirical Setting

The empirical setting of this research was set in an organization that works with integration work (the organization is kept anonymous due to the reviewing process of this paper). In summary, the organization is a municipal entity responsible for organizing and performing a civic orientation program that support newcomers' integration process in society. Essentially, the program helps newcomers learn explicit knowledge about society such as laws, regulations, democracy, norms, values, and other practically oriented issues that help them cope with their host society. The newcomers are extremely heterogeneous with respect to their background, culture, beliefs, education, and worldviews in general, making it a challenging task for the integration workers to organize and perform the civic orientation program. Consequently, the integration workers have different roles and areas of responsibilities (depicted in Table 1) for organizing and preforming the civic orientation program.

Table 1. Integration workers of the civic orientation program

Integration worker	Professional role
Tutors	Are responsible for organizing and teaching 60 h of civic orientation for a particular group of newcomers. The group of newcomers vary due to their origin and native language. In turn, tutors perform their sessions through the newcomers' native language. The sessions are performed in classroom-settings, but are now in need of a blended learning approach that provides the sessions through support of e-learning (e.g. distance learning) as well as through face-to-face teachings in classroom-settings

(*continued*)

Table 1. (*continued*)

Integration worker	Professional role
Content producers	Are responsible for producing civic orientation content that is shaped and provided in different formats for different users. Tutors use the content as supporting slides subsequent teaching sessions, whereas newcomers are provided with a book. Content producers are, due to the need of expanding civic orientation content, in need of collaborative technologies that help them create, update, share, and distribute content digitally
Coordinators	Are responsible for coordinating various sessions of civic orientation. Coordinators coordinate scheduling for the tutors but they do not work directly with newcomers, as the tutors do

The integration workers were included as stakeholders and end-users of the ADR-team, whereas the newcomers were not involved in subsequent cycles of ADR due to lack of availability and interest.

3.2 Research Methods

A set of qualitative research methods (depicted in Table 2) were chosen to populate the stages of each ADR-cycle with data collection activities. The qualitative nature of the methods was preferred and chosen due to the explorative nature of ADR, where a researcher (together with the rest of the ADR-team) enters the research context to identify a specific problem that is relevant for the organization and its practitioners. This resonates well with Sein et al.'s [11] approach to instantiate and deploy early designs of the artifact into the organization, in order to address immediate practical problems and key-learnings of design, intervention, and evaluation.

Table 2. Selected set of research methods

Research method	Description
In-depth interviews	Were used to build an initial awareness of the integration workers' practice and daily work, with respect to crucial challenges of organizing and performing their tasks. Additionally, the interviews were conducted to explore the integration workers' conceptions and expectations of organizing and performing civic orientation through support of e-learning technologies. The interviews followed an interview guide proposed by [42]. The interviews were documented through field-notes and sound-recording
Participatory workshops	Were used to foster the idea of participatory design and learning and to establish an early reciprocal space for collaboration and knowledge sharing. The workshops were documented through field-notes and sound-recording

Both type of methods (workshops and interviews) were used in both of the ADR-cycles. Additionally, the collected data was analyzed through a process of transcribing and open coding, which was performed continuously throughout the two ADR-cycles.

4 Action Design Research Cycles

The ADR-cycles were (shown in Fig. 2) initiated in December 2013 and ended in November 2016. Since then, additional work has been undertaken to reflect, abstract, and extract knowledge into various forms of contributions. Past activities of each cycle have been reported through research papers that comprise findings of each cycle [7, 43–45, 48] (references are kept anonymous for the reviewing process of this paper). The proposed design principles of this research are thus considered as formalized outcomes of cycle two that incorporate the evolvement of outcomes from both cycles. Each cycle will be explicated as follow in subsequent sub-sections.

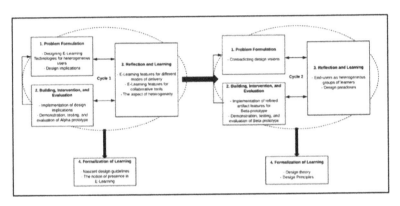

Fig. 2. Two cycles of Action Design Research

4.1 The First Action Design Research Cycle

The first ADR cycle initiated in late December 2013 and ended in mid January 2015. During the first stage of **Problem Formulation**, the ADR-team was established, consisting of one researcher, two assisting scholars, four coordinators, four tutors, two content producers, and one manager. Initially, eleven set of in-depth interviews and two participatory workshops were conducted together with the integration workers of the ADR-team. The interviews were held by the researcher, one and one with each integration worker, whereas the workshops were organized and conducted collectively with the whole ADR-team. The interviews revealed a strong sense of heterogeneity among the integration workers, with respect to their background, culture, beliefs, education, professional roles, areas of responsibilities, IT-literacy, as well as conceptions and expectations of the case outcomes. Throughout the interviews, each and every integration worker shared his/her worldview (e.g. beliefs, expectations, attitudes) concerning their past-experiences of using e-learning. Some of the integration workers were very familiar with e-learning as a concept, whereas others did not have any experience of either using or working with e-learning in general. For instance, when asked what their experiences of using online collaborative tools (e.g. Google Drive) are, and how they have used them previously, they answered:

"I have not used such technologies before... but if it is like using MS Word on the computer, then it shouldn't be any problem at all..." (Tutor 1)

"This is rather new to me... to use and collaborate instantly with my colleagues online... I have never thought about it before... but I think it's sounds like a good idea..." (Coordinator 1)

"Yes I have used Google Technologies before and it is similar to what you are saying I guess... so it should not be a problem at all..." (Content Producer 1)

Another question that emerged during the interviews, concerned the strategy of organizing and performing civic orientation content (e.g. slides, book, video) through support of e-learning. For instance, when asked about the availability of civic orientation content online, the respondents shared a rather unison view:

"Well... in my opinion... all content must be openly accessed for the public, so we can share essential information about society to everyone online..." (Tutor 2)

"The plan is to provide all of our content and sessions open for everyone who needs or wants to participate, online as well as in the classroom..." (Manager)

"I don't see why we should restrict our program.... Hmmm... I believe that we should keep it open for everyone who wants to join and participate..." (Coordinator 2)

As a complement to the interviews, the two participatory workshops were organized and conducted to elaborate ideas and requirements for a conceptual design of the alpha-prototype (first version of the e-learning artifact). Here, inspired by the PD-literature [46, 47], the integration workers were encouraged to actively share their ideas openly, by first writing them on post-its, putting them on the wall, and then individually presenting, motivating, and sharing their ideas. In summary, the workshops produced a set of design implications for the alpha-prototype, whereas the interviews illuminated the end-users of the artifact as heterogeneous groups of end-users. Here, strictly speaking, both the integration workers as well as newcomers (who participate in the civic orientation program), are end-users – integration workers use the artifact to organize and perform civic orientation, whereas the newcomers use the artifact to learn civic orientation.

The second stage of **Building, Intervention, and Evaluation** initiated through design activities that concerned the form and content of the prototype. Here, design implications were used to synthesize a set of early and testable design features. The features were instantiated into the alpha-prototype and demonstrated and tested through two workshops. Inspired by e-learning literature [20–24], a set of design features for online collaboration were built into the prototype to demonstrate how civic orientation content can be produced, maintained, shared, and published easily. During the first workshop, the integration workers tested and evaluated the features' usability by mapping them with their areas of responsibilities (e.g. producing content, using content for teaching). Based on input and feedback from the first workshop, the second workshop incorporated and demonstrated a set of advanced learning modules (intended to be used by newcomers). Here, the integration workers inquired the interface and content of the modules, by interacting and evaluating their responsiveness and sufficiency. The modules were designed with minimalistic symbols, colors, and content, in order to evaluate and re-design incrementally, without having to reduce or add more design elements than necessary. Furthermore, during the second workshop, the concept of 'embedded learning objects' [6] emerged and was chosen as a term for addressing the online content. The workshop ended with a roundtable discussion about future design issues, which lead to a decision about designing further features for online collaboration and different modes of delivering civic orientation content.

The third stage of **Reflection and Learning** identified and addressed the main challenges of designing e-learning technologies, which support the civic orientation program, as challenges mainly coupled with the problematic aspect of heterogeneity – e.g. different pedagogies to teach, different approaches toward distributing and sharing content. From the perspective of integration workers, they are in need of technologies that support their different areas of responsibilities and professional roles, as well as incorporating their heterogeneous identities with respect to their cultural discrepancies, age differences, language barriers, IT-illiteracy, education and knowledge base, etc. An essential reflection was thus that it is crucial to consider the differences among the integration workers as a facet rather than hindrance, because they are all competent professionals that participate in a shared community of practice for supporting newcomers' process of integration. From the perspective of newcomers however, it is more complicated, because they are even more heterogeneous – e.g. being highly scholars, to analphabets. An essential reflection was thus that it is important to provide sessions of civic orientation (as well as civic orientation content) through various modes of delivery, ranging from advanced learning modules, to basic modules that incorporate text, to images in various languages that support the heterogeneity of newcomers, to face-to-face interaction in a classroom.

Deriving from the reflections and key-learnings from the third ADR-stage, the final stage of **Formalization of Learning** concerned theorizing a set of nascent design guidelines for designing information systems and technologies for heterogeneous groups of end-users (shown in Table 3). The design guidelines were formulated with the ultimate goal of supporting heterogeneity and to provide an open digital learning experience of civic orientation.

Table 3. Nascent design guidelines for designing information systems and technologies for heterogeneous groups of end-users

Guideline	Explanation and rationale	Implications
1. Flexible modes of content delivery	Features that are flexible and adaptable toward delivery of learning content for various target groups of end-users (integration workers and newcomers)	Can help providing adaptability toward different profiles of end-users and thus personalize content toward a specific group of participants
2. Non-redundant distribution of content	Enable a common set of technologies for collaboration, production, and distribution	Can help asynchronous and synchronous content production and distribution

(continued)

Table 3. (*continued*)

Guideline	Explanation and rationale	Implications
3. Large variation in IT-literacy	Provide intuitively easy content-in-use for heterogeneous participants (e.g. newcomers), as well as incorporating heterogeneous practitioners (e.g. integration workers) task efficient technologies	Insights of heterogeneity, with respect to IT-literacy, can help understanding the challenges of which different end-users face when using different parts of one and a same system
4. Multimodal and multilingual features	Support of teaching and learning content through multimodal features (e.g. images, sounds, videos) in a wide range of foreign languages	Can help bridging various learning requirements (due to heterogeneity among the participants) with a less standardized profiling of participants (e.g. participants that are not solely students at universities)
5. Advanced forms of learning	Distribute various forms of extensive learning content such as advanced learning modules and embedded learning objects	Can help understanding heterogeneity among participants as an enabler and necessity for adaptable forms of feature complexity, which ranges for novice to advanced participants

An additional learning outcome concerned the problematic aspect of *presence* in e-learning in general, where different elements of presence (e.g. social presence, cognitive presence) (described by [6]) needs to be taken into consideration in order to support a successful e-learning experience. However, due to the pedagogical circumstances of the civic orientation program – in terms of experiencing learning and developing knowledge about society through dialogues (dynamic interaction) and reading book (static interaction) – integration workers need to learn how to mix different approaches in order to provide their teachings through various modes of delivery, including distance learning through video conferencing, pre-recorded lectures, and blended learning that combines the digital and the physical room (e.g. classroom). In turn, newcomers will, through the advanced learning modules, have the opportunity to learn additional subjects that are not covered through the ordinary lectures. These issues made it difficult to rely on how prior e-learning literature (e.g. [6]) conceptualize and understand presence from the perspective of traditional teaching and learning (situated in higher education). Therefore, a conceptualization of presence was made in order to transcend the discussions about presence in traditional e-learning contexts (universities), to offer an alternative notion of presence that captures the complexity of heterogeneity among practitioners and participants of e-learning outside the traditional setting, emphasizing the presence of being-in-the-world [45].

4.2 The Second Action Design Research Cycle

The second ADR cycle initiated in the end of January 2015 and ended in November 2016. During the first stage of **Problem Formulation**, key-learning outcomes from the first cycle were incorporated to move towards the design of features that embrace an open-ended e-learning artifact. However, after conducting a new set of interviews with the integration workers, a transition in their opinions about providing civic orientation through an open-ended system, became evident. For instance, when asked whether or not they were satisfied with the progression of incorporating an open-ended philosophy in the alpha-prototype, the respondents answered:

"We cannot offer everything for free because there are other municipalities that will have to use our material and technologies... I think that everyone would benefit from having a high quality system that is only available for relevant individuals and not the entire public..." (Manager)

"I don't feel comfortable with providing my teaching material openly to everyone... I want to customize and enable the material to only a handful of individuals that have the right to participate in my sessions..." (Tutor 1)

"It will become difficult to produce content that is sufficient for the public... I think we should have a restrictive system that is only open to participants and us who work with the program..." (Content Producer 1)

Answers from the interviews (such as the ones illustrated above) implied that the integration workers have shifted their view and now want a system that is restricted and not open for the public to use. As an implication, this was addressed as contradicting design visions among the integration workers' ideas about how the future system (ensemble artifact) shall be governed toward its end-users.

During the second stage of **Building, Intervention, and Evaluation**, new features were designed for user authentication, video conferencing, instantiating course sites through a template of design of form and content, and administrative features for content production and distribution. Additionally, a formal schema and architecture were elaborated and defined for the final beta prototype (shown in Figs. 3 and 4).

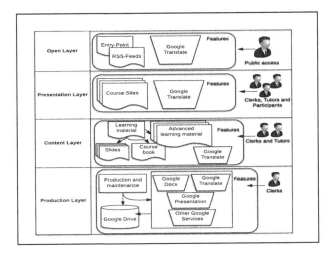

Fig. 3. Formal schema of final beta prototype version

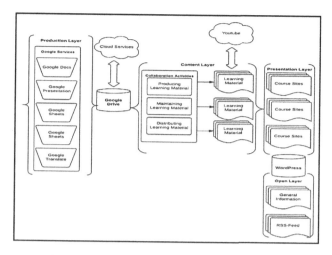

Fig. 4. Architecture of final beta prototype version

The formal schema in Fig. 3 depicts the different layers of the final beta prototype version of the artifact, with respect to features, technologies, and user rights (OBS: 'clerks' is a group name for coordinators and content producers), whereas Fig. 4 exhibits the technical architecture of the final beta prototype (for more detailed description about both, please address [43]). Furthermore, the technologies and features of the final beta prototype (shown in Figs. 3 and 4) were tested and evaluated through a final participatory workshop. After the workshop was conducted, the integration workers were satisfied with the results of the final prototype. However, through usability tests and observations, it became evident that the integration workers preferred to use one and the same features differently. For instance, all of the tutors (four tutors) had different approaches towards understanding how to publish online content for their respective course sites. One of the tutors, responsible for a group of newcomers, did not appreciate the combination of text and images on his/her course site. Rather, he/she wanted only to use the course site as a repository for video lectures. Whereas, another tutor wanted to publish links and embed animations that illustrated social phenomena such as what democracy means and how one can exhibit one's own personal rights in society. These differences created a tension between the integration workers, but was understood as a necessity for providing e-learning features that are adaptable and flexible. Consequently, they were, by the researcher of the ADR-team, understood as *wicked problems* [49] because there were (at that point of time) no definitive or obvious way of addressing the problem, nor did the ADR-team have any specific ways of solving the problem.

Thus, during the third stage of **Reflection and Learning** (which was conducted continuously throughout the whole second cycle), the wicked problems became identified as an issue to address through further prescriptive knowledge. Consequently, during this third stage, the wicked problems (shown in Table 4) became addressed as logical contradictions concerning design visions and decisions, which emerge due to the involvement of integration workers in iterative stages of ADR. In addition, the wicked problems were addressed as a class of problems.

Table 4. Identified wicked problems

Wicked problem	Explanation
WP1. Designing for transparency and restriction	Design visions of an open-ended features that enable external transparency, shifted to designing for restriction. This happened due to a sense-making process through early test and evaluation of prototype versions
WP2. Designing for standardization and customization	Design features that support standardized as well as non-standardized (customized) content, create demands on appropriate pedagogies that support the heterogeneity of newcomers – standardized content may be to general and not feasible for all newcomers, whereas a customized solution can personalize the content
WP3. Designing for physical and digital presence	Design features that enable participants and tutors to comport fruitfully through support of various modes of presence (physical, digital)

Another reflected learning outcome was that the end-users of the artifact are considered as *heterogeneous groups of learners* - both in the meaning of learning how to use sufficient technologies for organizing and conducting the civic orientation program (integration workers as end-users), but also, how to use the technologies for learning civic orientation (newcomers as end-users).

These two reflected learning outcomes were, in the final stage of **Formalizing Learning Outcomes**, formalized and incorporated into a refined set of design principles (shown in Table 5), and a design theory (which is described in a separate research paper [48]).

Table 5. Proposed design principles

Principle	Explanation and rationale	Implications
1. Facilitate boundary crossing	Literature on E-Learning [6, 19, 20, 26] and communities of practice [50] informed the design of artifact features that enable practitioners with different roles to cross boundaries and to develop a sensible understanding about similarities and differences as an asset for community and knowledge development	Can help addressing the first paradox, by enable boundary crossing between the different layers of the ensemble artifact (as proposed in Fig. 1) and thus incorporate both external transparency as well as restriction. Additionally, asynchronous/synchronous interaction enable practitioners to share knowledge regardless of time and space

(continued)

Table 5. (*continued*)

Principle	Explanation and rationale	Implications
2. Enable a reciprocal space for collaboration	A physical and/or digital space that enables practitioners to collaborate with each other on the basis of practice inspired challenges, which opens up for a perspective taking and making	Can help understanding the second design paradox through sufficiency of balancing different beliefs, values, and expectations in a shared space for interaction and collaboration between practitioners as well as participants
3. Provide a dual use of content as a boundary object	Heterogeneous groups of end-users have different needs and purposes of using one and the same artifact. As a boundary object [50], the artifact connects and provide different target groups (integration workers, newcomers) with sufficient features and content	Can help clarifying the use of teaching and learning content as a boundary object for competence and knowledge development among two very different groups of end-users (practitioners and participants)
4. Adapt toward heterogeneous modes of presence	Heterogeneity among practitioners and participants, manifests and gets comported through different modes of presence (social, teaching, learning) [6] and needs to be incorporated carefully through adaptable features of teaching and learning. Adaptable and flexible e-learning features need thus to be operationalized in order to encourage the teaching and learning experience sufficiently, for both group of learners (integration workers and newcomers)	Can help understanding the third paradox by facilitate a teaching and learning experience that takes the practitioners' and participants heterogeneous cultures, beliefs, norms, values, and knowledge base in general, into consideration. Supporting technologies and pedagogies shall thus be equipped with adaptability toward the heterogeneous modes of presence of which practitioners and newcomers comport themselves through

Ultimately, the proposed design principles (shown in Table 5) shall help DSR-researchers and IS-practitioners in the following ways, (1) for DSR-researchers, the principles identify implications that are subject to empirical validation, as well as being prescriptive knowledge that incorporate an understanding of wicked problems concerning e-learning that support integration work; (2) for IS-practitioners (e.g. IS-designers) the principles offer theory-based guidance about how to design e-learning technologies that support integration work; (3) for the IS-researchers that study e-learning as a phenomenon, the principles serve as an alternative medium for understanding the use of e-learning outside the settings higher education.

5 Concluding Remarks

This research has unpacked the process of (1) producing e-learning technologies for the support of integration work, (2) producing design principles for e-learning that support integration work, iteratively. The design principles have been proposed as an essential outcome of two ADR-cycles. Consequently, the proposed design principles address the problematic issue of heterogeneity among teachers and learners. The significance of this research provides a contribution towards the DSR-community through the use of the ADR-method, as well as illuminating an explicit process that inform the shaping and re-shaping design principles. Furthermore, the outcomes of this research contributes to the IS-literature with a focus on e-learning, by demonstrating a case of designing e-learning technologies that are sufficiently usable for contexts outside the setting of higher education. The limitations of this research however, are two-folded: (1) due to page limitations, greater amount of analyzed data could not be illustrated to show the process of shaping and re-shaping of design principles (both nascent and final version); (2) the proposed design principles were extracted from one case only. However, through sufficient and efficient DSR in IS, other IS-researchers can now adopt, test, or elaborate the proposed set of design principles for further relevant discussions and research.

References

1. DeFreitas, S., Oliver, M.: Does e-learning policy drive change in higher education? A case study relating models of organizational change to e-learning implementation. J. High. Educ. Policy Manage. **27**(1), 81–95 (2005)
2. Luck, L., Jones, D., McConachie, J., Danaher, P.A.: Challenging enterprises and subcultures: interrogating 'best practice' in Central Queensland University's course management systems, best practice in university learning and teaching: learning from our challenges. Theme Issue Stud. Learn. Eval. Innov. Dev. **1**(2), 19–31 (2004)
3. Lee-Post, A.: E-learning success model: an information systems perspective. Electron. J. eLearning **7**(1), 61–70 (2009)
4. Garrison, D.R., Cleveland-Innes, M., Fung, T.S.: Exploring causal relationships among teaching, cognitive and social presence: student perceptions of the community of inquiry framework. Internet High. Educ. **13**(1), 31–36 (2010)
5. Siritongthaworn, S., Krairit, D., Dimmitt, N.J., Paul, H.: The study of e-learning technology implementation: a preliminary investigation of universities in Thailand. Educ. Inf. Technol. **11**(2), 137–160 (2006)
6. Garrison, D.R.: E-Learning in the 21st Century: A Framework for Research and Practice. Taylor and Francis, London (2011)
7. Anonymized due to being the author of this paper and due to the reviewing process
8. Raynes-Goldie, K., Walker, L.: Our space: online civic engagement tools for youth. In: Bennett, W.L. (ed.) Civic Life Online: Learning How Digital Media Can Engage Youth, pp. 161–188. MIT Press, Cambridge (2008)
9. Bers, M.U.: Civic identities, online technologies: from designing civics curriculum to supporting civic experiences. Tufts University (2008)

10. Westerlind, M.: Knowing at work: a study of professional knowledge in integration work directed to newly arrived immigrants. Doctoral Dissertation, University West (2016)
11. Sein, M.K., Henfridsson, O., Purao, S., Rossi, M., Lindgren, R.: Action design research. MIS Q. **35**(1), 35–56 (2011)
12. Jones, D.: An information systems design theory for e-learning. The Australian National University (2011)
13. Jones, D., Gregor, S.: The formulation of an information systems design theory for e-learning. In: First International Conference on Design Science Research in Information Systems and Technology, pp. 356–373 (2006)
14. Walls, J., Widmeyer, G.R., El Sawy, O.A.: Building an information system design theory for vigilant EIS. Inf. Syst. Res. **3**(1), 36–59 (1992)
15. Gregor, S., Jones, D.: The anatomy of a design theory. J. Assoc. Inf. Syst. **8**(5), 312–335 (2007)
16. Jones, D., Gregor, S., Lynch, T.: An information systems design theory for Web-based education. In: IASTED International Symposium on Web-based Education (2003)
17. Venable, J.: The role of theory and theorizing in design science research. In: Proceedings of DESRIST (2006)
18. Vaishnavi, V., Kuechler, W.: Design Science Research Methods and Patterns. Innovating Information and Communication Technology. Auerbach, New York (2007)
19. Tynjälä, P.: Perspectives into learning at the workplace. Educ. Res. Rev. **3**(2), 130–154 (2008)
20. Wang, M.: Integrating organizational, social, and individual perspectives in Web 2.0-based workplace e-learning. Inf. Syst. Front. **13**(2), 191–205 (2011)
21. Park, J.H., Wentling, T.: Factors associated with transfer of training in workplace e-learning. J. Workplace Learn. **19**(5), 311–329 (2007)
22. Wang, M., Vogel, D., Ran, W.: Creating a performance-oriented e-learning environment: a design science approach. Inf. Manag. **48**(7), 260–269 (2011)
23. Cheng, B., Wang, M., Mørch, A.I., Chen, N.S., Spector, J.M.: Research on e-learning in the workplace 2000–2012: a bibliometric analysis of the literature. Educ. Res. Rev. **11**, 56–72 (2014)
24. Ellis, P.F., Kuznia, K.D.: Corporate e-learning impact on employees. Glob. J. Bus. Res. **8**(4), 1 (2014)
25. Rana, H., Lal, M.: E-learning: issues and challenges. Int. J. Comput. Appl. **97**(5) (2014)
26. Tynjälä, P., Häkkinen, P.: E-learning at work: theoretical underpinnings and pedagogical challenges. J. Workplace Learn. **17**(5/6), 318–336 (2005)
27. Cheng, B., Wang, M., Moormann, J., Olaniran, B.A., Chen, N.S.: The effects of organizational learning environment factors on e-learning acceptance. Comput. Educ. **58**(3), 885–899 (2012)
28. Admiraal, W., Lockhorst, D.: E-learning in small and medium-sized enterprises across Europe: attitudes towards technology, learning and training. Int. Small Bus. J. **27**(6), 743–767 (2009)
29. Kolas, L., Staupe, A.: A personalized e-learning interface. In: EUROCON: The International Conference on "Computer as a Tool", pp. 2670–2675. IEEE (2007)
30. Becker, K., Newton, C., Sawang, S.: A learner perspective on barriers to e-learning. Aust. J. Adult Learn. **53**(2), 211 (2013)
31. Markus, M.L., Majchrzak, A., Gasser, L.: A design theory for systems that support emergent knowledge processes. MIS Q. **26**(3), 179–212 (2002)
32. Lindgren, R., Henfridsson, O., Schultze, U.: Design principles for competence management systems: a synthesis for an action research study. MIS Q. **28**(3), 435–472 (2004)

33. Seidel, S., Chandra Kruse, L., Szekely, N., Gau, M., and Stieger, D.: Design principles for sensemaking support systems in environmental sustainability transformations. Eur. J. Inf. Syst. (2017)

34. Germonprez, M., Kendall, J.E., Mathiassen, L., Young, B., Warner, B.: A theory of responsive design: a field study of corporate engagement with open source communities. Inf. Syst. Res. 28(1), 64–83 (2016)

35. Yang, L., Su, G., Yuan, H.: Design principles of integrated information platform for emergency responses. Inf. Syst. Res. 23(3), 761–786 (2012)

36. Babaian, T., Xu, J., Lucas, W.: ERP prototype with built-in task and process support. Eur. J. Inf. Syst. (2017)

37. Chandra Kruse, L., Seidel, S., Purao, S.: Making *use* of design principles. In: Parsons, J., Tuunanen, T., Venable, J., Donnellan, B., Helfert, M., Kenneally, J. (eds.) DESRIST 2016. LNCS, vol. 9661, pp. 37–51. Springer, Cham (2016). https://doi.org/10.1007/978-3-319-39294-3_3

38. Gregor, S., Imran, A., Turner, T.: A 'sweet spot' change strategy for a least developed country: leveraging e-government in Bangladesh. Eur. J. Inf. Syst. 23(6), 655–671 (2014)

39. Meth, H., Mueller, B., Maedche, A.: Designing a requirement mining system. J. Assoc. Inf. Syst. 16(9), 799–837 (2015)

40. Heinrich, P., Schwabe, G.: Communicating nascent design theories on innovative information systems through multi-grounded design principles. In: Tremblay, M.C., VanderMeer, D., Rothenberger, M., Gupta, A., Yoon, V. (eds.) DESRIST 2014. LNCS, vol. 8463, pp. 148–163. Springer, Cham (2014). https://doi.org/10.1007/978-3-319-06701-8_10

41. Gregor, S., Hevner, A.: Positioning and presenting design science research for maximum impact. MIS Q. 37(2), 337–355 (2013)

42. Boyce, C., Neale, P.: Conducting in-depth interview: a guide for designing and conducting in-depth interviews for evaluation input (2006)

43. Haj-Bolouri, A., Bernhardsson, L., Bernhardsson, P.: CollaborGeneous: A Framework of Collaborative IT-Tools for Heterogeneous Groups of Learners. New Horizons in Design Science: Broadening the Research Agenda (2015)

44. Haj-Bolouri, A., Kruse Chandra, L., Iivari, J., Flensburg, P.: How Habermas' philosophy can inspire the design of information systems: the case of designing an open learning platform for social integration. Selected Papers of the IRIS, Issue Nr 7. 2 (2016)

45. Haj-Bolouri, A., Flensburg, P.: Conceptualizing the essence of presence in distance education through digital dasein. Int. J. E-Learn. 16(2), 149–173 (2017)

46. Kensing, F.: Methods and Practices in Participatory Design. IT University Press, Copenhagen (2003)

47. Schuler, D., Namioka, A.: Participatory Design: Principles and Practices. Erlbaum, Mahwah (1993)

48. Haj-Bolouri, A., Bernhardsson, L., Bernhardsson, P., Svensson, L.: An information systems design theory for adaptable e-learning. In: 49th Hawaii International Conference on System Sciences (HICSS), pp. 4414–4423 (2016)

49. Rittel, H.J.W., Webber, M.W.: Dilemmas in a general theory of planning. Policy Sci. 4(2), 155–169 (1973)

50. Wenger, E.: Communities of Practice: Learning, Meaning, and Identity. Cambridge University Press, Cambridge (2010)

Author Index

Printed in the United States
By Bookmasters